WOMEN AND DEVELOPMENT

Articles, Books and Research Papers
Indexed in the
Joint World Bank-International Monetary Fund Library,
Washington, D.C.

G.K. Hall & Co., Boston, Massachusetts
1987

Copyright © 1987 Joint World Bank-International Monetary Fund Library.
ISBN 0-8161-0464-6

Introduction

The role of women in economic development has been historically significant, although frequently neither well understood nor documented. Recently, greater recognition has been given to women's importance in the modern development process. This recognition has been accompanied by an increase in the treatment of this subject in the literature, particularly in the last decade.

As part of its effort to assure that the crucial role of women in bringing about the success of development projects was recognized, the World Bank established the office of Adviser on Women in Development in 1977. To help support the activities of this office, a collection of documentation in this area was begun in earnest. Many of the citations in this bibliography come from that collection, while others come from the catalog of the Joint World Bank–International Monetary Fund Library, and from the Joint Library's online bibliographical index.

This bibliography is indexed by author, title, and subject, and arranged in one alphabet. The materials included in this bibliography represent the result of serious and systematic collection efforts in this area during the period 1977 to 1986. This bibliography is, therefore, indicative of existing collections, and does not claim to present an exhaustive description of the literature on the subject. To facilitate the goal of sharing this collected bibliography, the Joint Bank-Fund Library graciously agreed to release these materials. Since the entries in this bibliography were merged from different source files that followed different approaches to the literature, some inconsistencies in the use of subject headings will be noticeable. It is hoped that any inconvenience caused by these occasional variations will be offset by the advantage of having access to this unique resource.

An earlier version of this bibliography was distributed at the World Conference on the United Nations Decade for Women, Nairobi, Kenya, in 1985.

1975-1985: decennie de la femme. LE MONDE (PARIS) July 14/15, 1985, Special supplement, p. I, III-IX.

Aba riots or Igbo 'women's war'? Ideology, stratification, and the invisibility of women. By: Van Allen, Judith. In: Women in Africa: studies in social and economic change. Edited by Nancy J. Hafkin and Edna G. Bay. (Stanford, Stanford University Press, 1976), pp. 59-85.

ABDEL KADER, SOHA

Abdel Kader, Soha. Research on the status of women, development and population trends in the Arab states: an annotated bibliography. In: Bibliographic guide to studies on the status of women: development and population trends. (New York, Bowker, UNIPUB; Paris, Unesco, 1983), pp. 67-81.

ABDULLAH, LASHIDAH

Abdullah, Lashidah. Subordination right across the board. FAR EASTERN ECONOMIC REVIEW (HONGKONG) January 5, 1984, 123:31-32. Discusses the status of women in Malaysia.

ABDULLAH, NORAINI

Abdullah, Noraini. Equality of Malay women -- real but restricted. FAR EASTERN ECONOMIC REVIEW (HONGKONG) April 10, 1986, 132:38-39.

Ability in pre-schoolers, earnings and home-environment. By: Grawe, Roger. Series: World Bank Staff Working Papers, No. 322. (Washington, DC, World Bank, 1979), 92 pp.

Aboriginal woman: male and female anthropological perspectives. By: Rohrlich-Leavitt, Ruby and Sykes, Barbara. In: Toward an anthropology of women. Edited by Rayna R. Reiter. (New York, Monthly Review Press, 1975), pp. 110-26.

ABU, KATHARINE

Oppong, Christine and Abu, Katharine. Changing maternal role of Ghanaian women: impacts of education, migration and employment. INTERNATIONAL LABOUR OFFICE. WORLD EMPLOYMENT PROGRAMME RESEARCH. POPULATION AND LABOUR POLICIES PROGRAMME. WORKING PAPER (GENEVA) February 1984, No. 143:1-184.

ACCAD, EVELYNE

Accad, Evelyne. Theme of sexual oppression in the North African novel. In: Women in the Muslim world. Edited by Lois Beck and Nikki Keddie. (Cambridge, MA, Harvard University Press, 1978), pp. 617-28.

ACHARYA, MEENA

Acharya, Meena and Bennett, Lynn. Women and the subsistence sector: economic participation and household decision making in Nepal. Series: World Bank Staff Working Papers, No. 526. (Washington, DC, World Bank, 1983), 140 pp.

ACHARYA, MEENA [ET AL.]

Acharya, Meena [et al.]. Status of women in Nepal: Vol. 1, Background report. (Kathmandu, Centre for Economic Development and Administration, 1979), 4 pts in 1 vol. CONTENT: Pt. 1, Acharya, Meena, Statistical profile of Napalese women: a critical review. - Pt. 2, Bennett, Lynn, Tradition and change in the legal status of Napalese women. - Pt. 3, Pradhan, Bina, Institutions concerning women in Nepal. - Pt. 4, Shrestha, Indira, Annotated bibliography of women in Nepal.

ACOCK, ALAN C.

Acock, Alan C. and Deseran, Forrest A. Off-farm employment by women and marital instability. RURAL SOCIOLOGY (PROVO, UTAH) Fall 1986, 51:314-27. The impact of farm women's paid work experience on the quality and stability of their marriages is examined in the context of two competing frameworks - status competition and status enhancement.

Action oriented assessment of rural's women's participation in development. By: United Nations Development Programme. Series: Evaluation Study (United Nations Development Programme), No. 3. (New York, United Nations Development Programme, 1980), 226 pp.

Activite economique des femmes du Tiers monde et perspectives de baisse de leur fecondite. By: Samman, Mouna Liliane. TIERS-MONDE (PARIS) April/June 1983, 24:367-76.

ACUNA, ISABEL CHACON

Acuna, Isabel Chacon. Research experience with rural women. In: Latin American women: the meek speak out. Edited by June H. Turner. (Silver Spring, MD, International Educational Development, 1980), pp. 29-38. Discusses women in Costa Rica.

Adaptation of Polynesian female migrants in New Zealand. By: Graves, Nancy B.. In: Women in the cities of Asia: migration and urban adaptation. Edited by James T. Fawcett, Siew-Ean Khoo and Peter C. Smith. (Boulder, CO, Westview Press, 1984), pp. 365-93.

Address to the Board of Governors of the World Bank and International Finance Corporation. By: Conable, Barber B.. (Washington, World Bank, September 30, 1986), 11 pp.

Advancement of rural women: the emerging networks. By: Ahmad, Zubeida. CERES, FAO REVIEW ON AGRICULTURE AND DEVELOPMENT (ROME) March/April 1986, 19:31-35.

Advantages of functional education and credit facilities for Javanese rural women. By: Bangern, Masliana. In: The endless day: some case material on Asian rural women. Edited by T. Scarlett Epstein and Rosemary A. Watts. Series: Women in development, Vol. 3. (Oxford, England, New York, Pergamon Press, 1981), pp. 128-54.

AFGHANISTAN

Tavakolian, Bahram. Women and socioeconomic change among Sheikhanzai nomads of western Afghanistan. MIDDLE EAST JOURNAL (WASHINGTON) Summer 1984, 38:433-53. Based on observations made in 1976-1977.

AFRICA

African women: the unequal partners. NEW AFRICAN (LONDON) May 1981, p. 16-20.

African women step out. NEW AFRICAN (LONDON) November 1985, No. 218:7-13. Features a few of the hundreds of successful women that are making a new impact on Africa today in politics, professions, business and art.

Agarwal, Bina. Women and technological change in agriculture: Asian and African experience. INSTITUTE OF ECONOMIC GROWTH. [PAPERS] (DELHI) July 1984, No. E/103/84:1-55.

Allison, Caroline. Women, land, labour and survival: getting some basic facts straight. IDS BULLETIN, INSTITUTE OF DEVELOPMENT STUDIES AT THE UNIVERSITY OF SUSSEX (BRIGHTON) July 1985, 16:24-30. This article concentrates on the questions of land access; household compositions; and the survival strategies women rely on in periods of imminent or perceived crisis.

AFRICA

Anyaoku, Emeka. Women; changing attitudes: a cooperative effort. AFRICA REPORT (NEW YORK) March/April 1985, 30:p. 21. The author suggests that while African governments have acknowledged the importance of strengthening women's contributions to their national economies, effective change can only come about through cooperative efforts which take into account African cultural and traditional values.

Basse, Marie-Therese. Women, food and nutrition in Africa: perspective from Senegal. FOOD AND NUTRITION (ROME) 1984, 10, No. 1:65-79. Also includes: Economic change and the outlook for nutrition, prepared by the Food and Agriculture Organization of the United Nations.

Bifani, Patricia. How Kenyan peasants, pastoralists and peri-urban women see water problems. WATERLINES (LONDON) January 1986, 4:16-19.

Carr, Marilyn. Technology and rural women in Africa. INTERNATIONAL LABOUR OFFICE. WORLD EMPLOYMENT PROGRAMME RESEARCH. TECHNOLOGY AND EMPLOYMENT PROGRAMME. WORKING PAPERS (GENEVA) July 1980, No. 61:1-45.

Cole, Bernadette. Where to get a loan. WEST AFRICA (LONDON) November 10, 1986, No. 3610:p. 2362. Reports on Women's World Banking (WWB), an independent financial organisation set up to advance and promote entrepreneurship among women within their local economies.

Cole, Bernadette. UN women's decade; preparing the way. WEST AFRICA (LONDON) October 29, 1984, No. 3506:2165-66. Reports from Tanzania on the African regional preparatory meeting which will constitute the 'African position' at the UN End of Women's Decade Conference.

Date-Bah, Eugenia and Stevens, Yvette. Rural women in Africa and technological change: some issues. LABOUR AND SOCIETY (GENEVA) April/June 1981, 6:149-62.

Davies, Wendy. Slow progress on women's health. NEW AFRICAN (LONDON) August 1985, No. 215:p. 42.

Dey, Jennie. Women in African rice farming systems. FOOD AND AGRICULTURE ORGANIZATION OF THE UNITED NATIONS. INTERNATIONAL RICE COMMISSION NEWSLETTER (ROME) December 1983, 32:1-4.

AFRICA

Diaroumeye, Fatoumata Agnes. Le role compare de la femme dans les milieux ruraux et urbains en Afrique. MONDES EN DEVELOPPEMENT (PARIS) 1982, No. 40:481-82.

Due, Jean M. and Summary, Rebecca. Constraints to women and development in Africa. JOURNAL OF MODERN AFRICAN STUDIES (OXFORD) March 1982, 20:155-66.

End of the UN decade: what advances for African women? AFRICA REPORT (NEW YORK) March/April 1985, 30, Special issue p. 4-82..

Experience of the Association of African Women for Research and Development (AAWORD); a workshop report prepared for the high-level meeting on the review of technical cooperation among developing countries. DEVELOPMENT DIALOGUE (UPPSALA) 1982, No. 1/2:101-113. Reviews the existing studies on African women and highlights some of their important consequences. The origin and early history of AAWORD is outlined and an account is given of its objectives, policies and programmes.

Fleming, Victoria. Women and development. WEST AFRICA (LONDON) December 7, 1981, No. 3358:2921-22. Discusses the progress and the pitfalls halfway through the International Decade for Women.

Goncet, Odette. Technologies appropriees pour les femmes africaines. MONDES EN DEVELOPPEMENT (PARIS) 1985, 13, No. 49:193-99.

Guyer, Jane I.. Women's work in the food economy of the cocoa belt: a comparison. BOSTON UNIVERSITY. AFRICAN STUDIES CENTER. WORKING PAPERS (BOSTON) 1978, No. 7:1-35.

Hamid, Rizu. Why women are wasted. NEW AFRICAN (LONDON) July 1983, No. 190:48. Describes some of the objectives and activities of the Commonwealth Women and Development Unit set up in the Commonwealth Secretariat in 1980.

Harrison, Charles. Plight of Africa's women. TIMES (LONDON) August 1, 1985, p. 4. Suggests that female workers' lack of status can be blamed for much of the famine crisis.

AFRICA

Holford, Nicky. Easing the burden of women in a developing society: a host of good intentions. NEW AFRICAN (LONDON) December 1981, p. 39-40. Discusses the new UN Convention for the prevention of discrimination against women, which was adopted in September, and suggests that the measure should influence customs and practices all over Africa.

Hottinger, Arnold. Women in Islam. SWISS REVIEW OF WORLD AFFAIRS (ZURICH) October 1980, 30:8-14.

Jouffrey, Roger. La paysanne africaine au travail. AFRIQUE CONTEMPORAINE, DOCUMENTS D'AFRIQUE NOIRE ET DE MADAGASCAR (PARIS) April/June 1983, 22:23-29.

Ki-Zerbo, Jacqueline. Women and the energy crisis in the Sahel. UNASYLVA (ROME) 1981, 33, No. 133:5-10.

Konie, Gwendoline. Women in southern Africa; gaining political power. AFRICA REPORT (NEW YORK) March/April 1983, 28:11-14.

Koopman Henn, Jeanne. Feeding the cities and feeding the peasants: what role for Africa's women farmers? WORLD DEVELOPMENT (OXFORD) December 1983, 11:1043-55.

Kratz, Achim. La conference mondiale des femmes et la femme africaine. MOIS EN AFRIQUE (PARIS) April/May 1986, 21:160-66.

Marshall, Susan E.. Politics and female status in North Africa: a reconsideration of development theory. ECONOMIC DEVELOPMENT AND CULTURAL CHANGE (CHICAGO) April 1984, 32:499-524. Assesses the applicability of two major theoretical perspectives for explaining national differences in female status among the five North African Muslim states of Morocco, Algeria, Tunisia, Libya, and Egypt, utilizing a composite female modernity index derived from secondary sources. The author also proposes an alternative theoretical framework to explain these divergent national patterns of female participation, highlights the central role of political elites in the late-developing states and suggests an empirical relationship between government policy toward women and female access to the modern sector in North Africa.

AFRICA

Matsepe-Casaburri, Ivy. Women in southern Africa; legacy of exclusion. AFRICA REPORT (NEW YORK) March/April 1983, 28:7-10. Presents a brief overview of the position of women, with a focus on those belonging to disadvantaged groups.

Mbilinyi, Marjorie J.. Participation of women in African economies. UNIVERSITY OF DAR ES SALAAM. ECONOMIC RESEARCH BUREAU. PAPER (DAR-ES-SALAAM) 1971, No. 71.12:1-32.

McCormick, John and Akello, Grace. Africa's population crisis. NEW AFRICAN (LONDON) January 1984, No. 196:21-23. Discusses the causes of Africa's runaway population growth, and asks how womeen could benefit from population control.

Muchena, Olivia. Women in southern Africa; are women integrated into development? AFRICA REPORT (NEW YORK) March/April 1983, 28:4-6.

Perry, Alison. Bearing the burden. WEST AFRICA (LONDON) April 22, 1985, No. 3530:785-86. Looks at the important role women playin the agricultural sector and at the severe handicpas they face, due to their double work-load and a discriminatory system.

Rogombe, Rose Francine. Women; equal partners in Africa's development. AFRICA REPORT (NEW YORK) March/April 1985, 30:17-20.

Safilios-Rothschild, Constantina. Persistence of women's invisibility in agriculture: theoretical and policy lessons from Lesotho and Sierra Leone. POPULATION COUNCIL. CENTER FOR POLICY STUDIES. WORKING PAPERS (NEW YORK) September 1982, No.88:1-31.

Savane, Marie Angelique. El empleo de la mujer, los cambios sociales y la liberacion femenina; el caso de Africa. COMERCIO EXTERIOR (MEXICO, D.F.) August 1980, 30:861-66. Ponencia presentada en la Mesa II, "Recursos humanos y empleo en los paises en desarrollo," del Sexto Congreso Mundial de Economistas.

Savane, Marie Angelique. Le plan d'action de Lagos et les femmes. AFRICA DEVELOPMENT (DAKAR) January/June 1982, 7:142-48. With English summary.

Staudt, Kathleen. Policy strategies at the end of the decade. AFRICA REPORT (NEW YORK) March/April 1985, 30:71-5.

AFRICA

Staudt, Kathleen A.. Women's politics in Africa. STUDIES IN THIRD WORLD SOCIETIES (WILLIAMSBURG) June 1981, No. 16:1-28.

Steady, Filomina Chioma. African women, industrialization and another development; a global perspective. DEVELOPMENT DIALOGUE (UPPSALA) 1982, No. 1/2:51-64.

Steady, Filomina Chioma. Nairobi '85:African women at the end of the decade. AFRICA REPORT (NEW YORK) March/April 1985, 30:4-8. Discusses the World Conference on the United Nations Decade for Women, to be held in Nairobi, Kenya, July 15-26, 1985.

Tadesse, Zenebworke. Bringing research home. DEVELOPMENT (ROME) 1984, No. 4:50-54. Discusses on the question of research on women in Africa.

Wangari, Esther and Koivukari, Mirjami. Women; the plight and the strength. DEVELOPMENT FORUM (NEW YORK) June 1986, p. 8-9. Suggests that evidence is growing that the workload of women is increasing more than ever before and that their general condition is deteriorating.

Wiese, Eva-Maria. Frauen tragen die Last der Entwicklung; Beispiele aus West-Afrika. E & Z, ENTWICKLUNG UND ZUSAMMENARBEIT (BONN) January 1985, 26:8-10.

Wiese, Eva-Maria. Women in rural development. D & C, DEVELOPMENT AND COOPERATION (BONN) March/April 1985, No. 2:14-17. The author suggests that, in spite of some accomplishments during the "Decade for Women", the prevailing situation of rural women indicates for Africa that for the majority of them development has so far only meant an increase of functions associated with their roles, without reaping the benefits of either a proportionately acknowledged status or any justified income benefits.

Willis, David K.. Meet an African farmer ... and her husband. CHRISTIAN SCIENCE MONITOR (BOSTON) July 5, 1985, p. 9-10. Discusses the role of women in producing food and the need for greater focus on rural women.

Women: breaking a path; the end of the Decade for Women. WEST AFRICA (LONDON) July 22, 1985, No. 3543:1495-1500.

Women and politics in twentieth century Africa and Asia. STUDIES IN THIRD WORLD SOCIETIES (WILLIAMSBURG) June 1981, No. 16:1-160.

AFRICA

Women in southern Africa; bibliography. AFRICA REPORT (NEW YORK) March/April 1983, 28:54-55.

Women in the media. WEST AFRICA (LONDON) March 4, 1985, No. 3523:414-15.

African women: identity crisis? Some observations on education and the changing role of women in Sierra Leone and Zaire. By: Rousseau, Ida Faye. In: Women cross-culturally: change and challenge. Edited by Ruby Rohrlich-Leavitt. (The Hague, Mouton, 1975), pp. 41-52.

African women: the unequal partners. NEW AFRICAN (LONDON) May 1981, p. 16-20.

African women and national development. By: Lewis, Shelby. In: Comparative perspectives of Third World women: the impact of race, sex and class. Edited by Beverly Lindsay. (New York, Praeger, 1980), pp. 31-54.

African women, industrialization and another development; a global perspective. By: Steady, Filomina Chioma. DEVELOPMENT DIALOGUE (UPPSALA) 1982, No. 1/2:51-64.

African women step out. NEW AFRICAN (LONDON) November 1985, No. 218:7-13. Features a few of the hundreds of successful women that are making a new impact on Africa today in politics, professions, business and art.

African women; their struggle for economic independence. By: Obbo, Christine. Series: Women in the Third World series. (London, Zed Press, 1981), 166 pp.

Africa's population crisis. By: McCormick, John and Akello, Grace. NEW AFRICAN (LONDON) January 1984, No. 196:21-23. Discusses the causes of Africa's runaway population growth, and asks how womeen could benefit from population control.

AFSHAR, HALEH

Afshar, Haleh. Women, state and ideology in Iran. THIRD WORLD QUARTERLY (LONDON) April 1985, 7:256-78.

After Nairobi: A retrospective of women's development organizations in Latin America. By: Yudelman, Sally W. GRASSROOTS DEVELOPMENT (ROSSLYN, VA.) 1986, 10, No. 1:20-29.

AGARWAL, BINA

Agarwal, Bina. Women and technological change in agriculture: Asian and African experience. INSTITUTE OF ECONOMIC GROWTH. [PAPERS] (DELHI) July 1984, No. E/103/84:1-55.

Agarwal, Bina. Women, poverty and agricultural growth in India. INSTITUTE OF ECONOMIC GROWTH. [PAPERS] (DELHI) June 1985, No. E/112/85:1-101.

AGARWAL, NINA

Agarwal, Nina. Women, poverty and agricultural growth in India. JOURNAL OF PEASANT STUDIES (LONDON) July 1986, 13:165-220.

AGHAJANIAN, AKBAR

Aghajanian, Akbar. Fertility and family economy in the Iranian rural communities. In: Women in the family and the economy: an international comparative survey. Edited by George Kurian and Ratna Ghosh. (Westport, CT, Greenwood Press, 1981), pp. 297-305.

AGRICULTURAL ASSISTANCE

Nath, Kamla. Women and vegetable gardens in the Gambia: Action AID and rural development. BOSTON UNIVERSITY. AFRICAN STUDIES CENTER. WORKING PAPERS (BOSTON) 1985, No. 109:1-13. Examines Action Aid's program for improving the capacity of rural women to produce garden vegetables and to introduce marketing infrastructures.

AGRICULTURAL CREDIT

Barres, Victoria. Deux programmes de credit bien adaptes aux besoins des femmes du Tiers monde. TIERS-MONDE (PARIS) April/June 1985, 26:435-42. Cet article presente deux programmes de credits d'investissement destines a des femmes pauvres du Tiers Monde, l'un en milieu urbain (Madras, Inde) et l'autre en milieu rural (pays yoruba, Nigeria).

AGRICULTURAL DEVELOPMENT

Agarwal, Nina. Women, poverty and agricultural growth in India. JOURNAL OF PEASANT STUDIES (LONDON) July 1986, 13:165-220.

Wilson, Fiona. Women and agricultural change in Latin America: some concepts guiding research. WORLD DEVELOPMENT (OXFORD) September 1985, 13:1017-35.

AGRICULTURAL EXTENSION

Martius von Harder, Gudrun. Le role des services nationaux d'animation rurale et de vulgarisation agricole aupres des femmes. TIERS-MONDE (PARIS) April/June 1985, 26:317-24.

AGRICULTURAL INNOVATIONS

Agarwal, Bina. Women and technological change in agriculture: Asian and African experience. INSTITUTE OF ECONOMIC GROWTH. [PAPERS] (DELHI) July 1984, No. E/103/84:1-55.

Chand, Ramesh and Sidhu, D. S. Impact of agricultural modernization on labour: use pattern in Punjab with special reference to women labour. INDIAN JOURNAL OF AGRICULTURAL ECONOMICS (BOMBAY) July/September 1985, 40:252-59.

Ray, A. K. and Rangarao, I. V. Impact of technological changes on economic status of female labour. INDIAN JOURNAL OF AGRICULTURAL ECONOMICS (BOMBAY) July/September 1985, 40:244-52.

AGRICULTURAL LABORERS

Chand, Ramesh and Sidhu, D. S. Impact of agricultural modernization on labour: use pattern in Punjab with special reference to women labour. INDIAN JOURNAL OF AGRICULTURAL ECONOMICS (BOMBAY) July/September 1985, 40:252-59.

Deere, Carmen Diana. Division of labor by sex in agriculture; a Peruvian case study. ECONOMIC DEVELOPMENT AND CULTURAL CHANGE (CHICAGO) July 1982, 30:795-811.

Dixon, Ruth. Land, labour, and the sex composition of the agricultural labour force: an international comparison. DEVELOPMENT AND CHANGE (THE HAGUE, etc.) July 1983, 14:347-72.

Jouffrey, Roger. La paysanne africaine au travail. AFRIQUE CONTEMPORAINE, DOCUMENTS D'AFRIQUE NOIRE ET DE MADAGASCAR (PARIS) April/June 1983, 22:23-29.

Laufer, Leslie A.. Substitution between male and female labor in rural Indian agricultural production. YALE UNIVERSITY. ECONOMIC GROWTH CENTER. DISCUSSION PAPER (NEW HAVEN, CONN.) April 1985, No 472:1-24.

Schroeder, Robert and Schroeder, Elaine. Women in Nepali agriculture: all work and no power. JOURNAL OF DEVELOPMENT AND ADMINISTRATIVE STUDIES (KATHMANDU) January 1979, 1:178-92.

AGRICULTURAL PRODUCTS

Lewis, Martha. Developing income generating opportunity for rural women. HORIZONS, U.S. AGENCY FOR INTERNATIONAL DEVELOPMENT (WASHINGTON) January 1983, 2:28-31. Describes how bananas, solar-dried and marketed as banana-figs, promise to boost Jamaican farm women's earnings.

AGRICULTURAL RESEARCH

Mascarenhas, Ophelia. Confronting the male bias in research priorities. CERES, FAO REVIEW ON AGRICULTURE AND DEVELOPMENT (ROME) May/June 1985, 18:28-32. Suggests that agricultural research in most formerly colonial countries has two characteristics: the overemphasis of cash crops and the tendency to ignore women in the planning, development, and implementation of such research.

AGRICULTURE

Bergmann, Hellmuth and Schul, Jean-Jacques. Liste de questions sur le role des femmes dans les projets de developpement agricole. TIERS-MONDE (PARIS) October/December 1980, 21:833-44.

Carew, Joy Gleason. Note on women and agricultural technology in the Third World. LABOUR AND SOCIETY (GENEVA) July/September 1981, 6:279-85.

Gupta, R. P. and Tewari, S. K. Factors affecting crop diversification: an empirical analysis. INDIAN JOURNAL OF AGRICULTURAL ECONOMICS (BOMBAY) July/September 1985, 40:304-09.

Laufer, Leslie A.. Substitution between male and female labor in rural Indian agricultural production. YALE UNIVERSITY. ECONOMIC GROWTH CENTER. DISCUSSION PAPER (NEW HAVEN, CONN.) April 1985, No 472:1-24.

Safilios-Rothschild, Constantina. Persistence of women's invisibility in agriculture: theoretical and policy lessons from Lesotho and Sierra Leone. POPULATION COUNCIL. CENTER FOR POLICY STUDIES. WORKING PAPERS (NEW YORK) September 1982, No.88:1-31.

Saini, Amrik S. and Singh, Raj Vir. Impact of diversification on income, employment and credit needs of small farmers in Punjab. INDIAN JOURNAL OF AGRICULTURAL ECONOMICS (BOMBAY) July/September 1985, 40:310-16.

Saradamoni, K.. Women's status in changing agrarian relations; a Kerala experience. ECONOMIC AND POLITICAL WEEKLY (BOMBAY) January 30, 1982, 17:155-62.

AGRICULTURE

Singh, A. S. and Jain, K. K. Diversification of Punjab agriculture: an econometric analysis. INDIAN JOURNAL OF AGRICULTURAL ECONOMICS (BOMBAY) July/September 1985, 40:298-303.

Thorve, P. V. and Galgalikar, V. D. Economics of diversification of farming with dairy enterprise. INDIAN JOURNAL OF AGRICULTURAL ECONOMICS (BOMBAY) July/September 1985, 40:317-23.

AGROFORESTRY

Fortmann, Louise and Rocheleau, Dianne. Women and agroforestry: four myths and three case studies. AGROFORESTRY SYSTEMS (THE HAGUE) 1985, 2, No. 4:253-72. The involvement of women in agroforestry projects and activities is examined in case studies from the Dominican Republic, India and Kenya. Consideration for including women in agroforestry projects are discussed.

AGUIAR, NEUMA

Aguiar, Neuma. La mujer en la fuerza de trabajo en la America Latina: un resumen introductorio. DESARROLLO Y SOCIEDAD (BOGOTA) January 1984, No. 13:57-79. With English summary.

AGUIRRE, BENIGNO E.

Aguirre, Benigno E.. Women in the Cuban bureaucracies 1968-1974. In: Women in the family and the economy: an international comparative survey. Edited by George Kurian and Ratna Ghosh. (Westport, CT, Greenwood Press, 1981), pp. 375-92.

AHMAD, KARUNA

Ahmad, Karuna. Women's life cycle and identity. ECONOMIC AND POLITICAL WEEKLY (BOMBAY) January 2, 1982, 17:15-17. Discusses a seminar on women, organized by the Indian Council of Social Science Research, New Delhi, Centre for Women's Development Studies, New Delhi, Tata Institute of Social Sciences, Bombay, and Ford Foundation, New Delhi.

AHMAD, PERVEEN

Ahmad, Perveen. Unsung heroines: Bangladesh's unrecognized workforce gains a new self-awareness. FAR EASTERN ECONOMIC REVIEW (HONGKONG) January 5, 1984, 123:26-27.

AHMAD, ZUBEIDA

Ahmad, Zubeida. Advancement of rural women: the emerging networks. CERES, FAO REVIEW ON AGRICULTURE AND DEVELOPMENT (ROME) March/April 1986, 19:31-35.

Ahmad, Zubeida and Loufti, Martha. Decently paid employment -- not more drudgery. CERES, FAO REVIEW ON AGRICULTURE AND DEVELOPMENT (ROME) July/August 1983, 16:40-46. The authors conclude that there is an urgent need for improved living and working conditions for many poor rural women.

Ahmad, Zubeida. Plight of rural women: alternatives for action. INTERNATIONAL LABOUR REVIEW (GENEVA) July/August 1980, 119:425-38.

Ahmad, Zubeida. Rural women and their work: dependence and alternatives for change. INTERNATIONAL LABOUR REVIEW (GENEVA) January/February 1984, 123:71-86.

AHMAD, ZUBEIDA M.

Ahmad, Zubeida M.. Women's work and their struggle to organize. DEVELOPMENT (ROME) 1984, No. 4:36-40.

Ahmad, Zubeida M. and Loutfi, Martha F.. International labour office programme on rural women. (Geneva, International Labour Office, 1981), 28 pp.

Ahmadiyya and urbanization: migrant women in Abidjan. By: Yaccob, May. BOSTON UNIVERSITY. AFRICAN STUDIES CENTER. WORKING PAPERS (BOSTON) 1983, No. 75:1-16.

AHMED, IFTIKHAR

Ahmed, Iftikhar. Rural women and technical change: theory, empirical analysis and operational projects. LABOUR AND SOCIETY (GENEVA) September 1985, 10:289-306.

AHMED, RAHNUMA

Ahmed, Rahnuma. Women's movement in Bangladesh and the left's understanding of the woman question. JOURNAL OF SOCIAL STUDIES (DHAKA) October 1985, No. 30:40-56.

AHMED, ZEENAT

Akbar, S. and Ahmed, Zeenat. Pakistan: mor and tor; binary and opposing models of Pukhtun womanhood. In: The endless day: some case material on Asian rural women. Edited by T. Scarlett Epstein and Rosemary A. Watts. Series: Women in development, Vol. 3. (Oxford, England, New York, Pergamon Press, 1981), pp. 31-46.

AHOOJA-PATEL, KRISHNA

Ahooja-Patel, Krishna. Another development with women. DEVELOPMENT DIALOGUE (UPPSALA) 1982, No. 1/2:17-28. After describing how difficult it was for women to voice their views in the development debate as late as the mid-seventies, the author presents an overview of the contribution women have made and are making in agriculture, industry, health and education.

AINSWORTH, MARTHA

Ainsworth, Martha. Family planning programs; the clients' perspective. Series: World Bank Staff Working Papers, No. 676; Population and Development Series, No. 1. (Washington, DC, World Bank, 1985), 86 pp.

AKBAR, S.

Akbar, S. and Ahmed, Zeenat. Pakistan: mor and tor; binary and opposing models of Pukhtun womanhood. In: The endless day: some case material on Asian rural women. Edited by T. Scarlett Epstein and Rosemary A. Watts. Series: Women in development, Vol. 3. (Oxford, England, New York, Pergamon Press, 1981), pp. 31-46.

AKELLO, GRACE

McCormick, John and Akello, Grace. Africa's population crisis. NEW AFRICAN (LONDON) January 1984, No. 196:21-23. Discusses the causes of Africa's runaway population growth, and asks how womeen could benefit from population control.

Akello, Grace. Self twice-removed: Ugandan woman. Series: Change International Reports: Women and Society, No. 8. (London, Change International Reports, 1983?), 19 pp.

AL-SABAH, S. M.

Al-Sabah, S. M.. Development planning in an oil economy and the role of the woman: the case of Kuwait. (London, Eastlords Publishing, 1983), 380 pp.

ALAUDDIN, MOHAMMAD

Alauddin, Mohammad. Maternal mortality in rural Bangladesh: the Tangail district. STUDIES IN FAMILY PLANNING (NEW YORK) January/February 1986, 17:13-21.

ALGERIA

Benallegue, Nora. Algerian women in the struggle for independence and reconstruction. INTERNATIONAL SOCIAL SCIENCE JOURNAL (PARIS) 1983, 35, No. 4:703-17.

Hakiki-Talahite, Fatiha. Paro e inactividad de las mujeres en Argelia: lo visible y lo invisible. DESARROLLO Y SOCIEDAD (BOGOTA) January 1984, No. 13:139-59. With English summary.

Khodja, Souad. Women's work as viewed in present-day Algerian society. INTERNATIONAL LABOUR REVIEW (GENEVA) July/August 1982, 121:481-87.

Marks, Jon. Algeria thinks of itself as a radical society; women declare war on the power of the patriach. GUARDIAN (LONDON) August 10, 1984, p. 15.

Marshall, Susan E. and Stokes, Randall G.. Tradition and the veil: female status in Tunisia and Algeria. JOURNAL OF MODERN AFRICAN STUDIES (OXFORD) December 1981, 19:625-46.

Algeria thinks of itself as a radical society; women declare war on the power of the patriach. By: Marks, Jon. GUARDIAN (LONDON) August 10, 1984, p. 15.

Algerian women in the struggle for independence and reconstruction. By: Benallegue, Nora. INTERNATIONAL SOCIAL SCIENCE JOURNAL (PARIS) 1983, 35, No. 4:703-17.

ALI, AUSAF

Ali, Ausaf. Status of women. ARABIA; THE ISLAMIC WORLD REVIEW (EAST BURNHAM) October 1986, 6:56-57. Views on the place of women in Islam.

ALLAGHI, FARIDA

Allaghi, Farida and Almana, Aisha. Survey of research on women in the Arab Gulf region. In: Social science research on women in the Arab world. (London, Frances Pinter; Paris, Unesco, 1984), pp. 14-40.

ALLISON, CAROLINE

Allison, Caroline. Women, land, labour and survival: getting some basic facts straight. IDS BULLETIN, INSTITUTE OF DEVELOPMENT STUDIES AT THE UNIVERSITY OF SUSSEX (BRIGHTON) July 1985, 16:24-30. This article concentrates on the questions of land access; household compositions; and the survival strategies women rely on in periods of imminent or perceived crisis.

ALMANA, AISHA

Allaghi, Farida and Almana, Aisha. Survey of research on women in the Arab Gulf region. In: Social science research on women in the Arab world. (London, Frances Pinter; Paris, Unesco, 1984), pp. 14-40.

ALVA, CARMEN ARIMANA

Alva, Carmen Arimana. Squatter settlement decision-making: for men only? In: Latin American women: the meek speak out. Edited by June H. Turner. (Silver Spring, MD, International Educational Development, 1980), pp. 14-24. Examines the situation of women in Peru.

Ambiguous consequences of the socialisation and seclusion of Hausa women. By: Callaway, Barbara J.. JOURNAL OF MODERN AFRICAN STUDIES (OXFORD) September 1984, 22:429-50.

AMRATLAL, JYOTI, [ET AL.]

Amratlal, Jyoti, [et al.]. Women's role in Fiji. (Suva, Fiji, South Pacific Social Sciences Association, 1975), 66 pp.

ANANDAJAYASEKERAM, P.

Due, Jean M. and Anandajayasekeram, P.. Women and productivity in two contrasting farming areas of Tanzania. UNIVERSITY OF ILLINOIS. DEPT. OF AGRICULTURAL ECONOMICS. STAFF PAPER. SERIES E (URBANA) July 1982, No. 82 E-228:1-23.

Ancient song, the new melody in Latin America: women and film. By: Wieser, Nora Jacquez. In: Comparative perspectives of Third World women: the impact of race, sex and class. Edited by Beverly Lindsay. (New York, Praeger, 1980), pp. 179-99.

ANDERSON, C. ARNOLD

Bowman, Mary Jean and Anderson, C. Arnold. Participation of women in education in the Third World. COMPARATIVE EDUCATION REVIEW (NEW YORK) June 1980, 24:S13-32.

ANDERSON, JEANINE

Figueroa, Blanca and Anderson, Jeanine. Women in Peru. Series: Change International Reports: Women in Society, No. 5. (London, Change International Reports, 1981), 16 pp.

ANKER, RICHARD

Anker, Richard. Effect on reported levels of female labour force participation in developing countries of questionnaire design, sex of interviewer and sex/proxy status of respondent: description of a methodological field experiment. INTERNATIONAL LABOUR OFFICE. WORLD EMPLOYMENT PROGRAMME RESEARCH. POPULATION AND LABOUR POLICIES PROGRAMME. WORKING PAPER (GENEVA) July 1983, No. 137:1-76. The methods test described is conducting household surveys in India (Uttar Pradesh state) and Egypt, using different types of questionnaires; male and female interviewers; self-respondents (female only) and proxy-respondents (male and female).

Anker, Richard and Hein, Catherine. Employment of women outside agriculture in Third world countries: an overview of occupational statistics. INTERNATIONAL LABOUR OFFICE. WORLD EMPLOYMENT PROGRAMME RESEARCH. POPULATION AND LABOUR POLICIES PROGRAMME. WORKING PAPER (GENEVA) March 1985, No. 147:1-70.

Anker, Richard. Female labour force participation in developing countries: a critique of current definitions and data collection methods. INTERNATIONAL LABOUR REVIEW (GENEVA) November/December 1983, 122:709-23.

Another development with the "other" sex; a postscript on the Women's Forum in Nairobi. By: Wichterich, Christa. D & C, DEVELOPMENT AND COOPERATION (BONN) November/December 1985, No. 6:11-12.

Another development with women. By: Ahooja-Patel, Krishna. DEVELOPMENT DIALOGUE (UPPSALA) 1982, No. 1/2:17-28. After describing how difficult it was for women to voice their views in the development debate as late as the mid-seventies, the author presents an overview of the contribution women have made and are making in agriculture, industry, health and education.

Another development with women: a view from Asia. By: Mazumdar, Vina. DEVELOPMENT DIALOGUE (UPPSALA) 1982, No. 1/2:65-73.

ANTROBUS, PEGGY

Antrobus, Peggy. Reaching beyond university walls. DEVELOPMENT (ROME) 1984, No. 4:45-49. Describes International Development have provided me with the encouragement to write about the work of the Women and Development (WAND) Unit of the Extra-Mural Department of the University of the West Indies (UWI): SID's Grassroots Strategies and Initiatives Programme (GRIS), and its sincere attempt to integrate a serious concern for women in development issues within the overall programme.

ANYAOKU, EMEKA

Anyaoku, Emeka. Women; changing attitudes: a cooperative effort. AFRICA REPORT (NEW YORK) March/April 1985, 30:p. 21. The author suggests that while African governments have acknowledged the importance of strengthening women's contributions to their national economies, effective change can only come about through cooperative efforts which take into account African cultural and traditional values.

APPROPRIATE TECHNOLOGY

Goncet, Odette. Technologies appropriees pour les femmes africaines. MONDES EN DEVELOPPEMENT (PARIS) 1985, 13, No. 49:193-99.

Arab women in the Gulf. By: Ramazani, Nesta. MIDDLE EAST JOURNAL (WASHINGTON) Spring 1985, 39:258-76.

Arbeitsbelastungen von Frauen im Paketdienst. By: Demmer, Hildegard and Kupper, Bettina. WSI-MITTEILUNGEN (DUSSELDORF) August 1986, 39:522-28.

ARCE, JENNY VALCARCEL

Arce, Jenny Valcarcel. Broken wing. In: Latin American women: the meek speak out. Edited by June H. Turner. (Silver Spring, MD, International Educational Development, 1980), pp. 150-61. Discusses women in Peru.

ARCEO-ORTEGA, ANGELINA

Arceo-Ortega, Angelina. Career-housewife in the Philippines. In: Women in the new Asia; the changing social roles of men and women in South and South-east Asia. Edited by Barbara E. Ward ([Paris], Unesco, 1963), pp. 365-73.

ARELLANO, BAMBI EDDY DE

Arellano, Bambi Eddy de. Integrating women into rural cooperatives: pluses and minuses. In: Latin American women: the meek speak out. Edited by June H. Turner. (Silver Spring, MD, International Educational Development, 1980), pp. 114-25. Discusses women in Bolivia.

ARIFFIN, JAMILAH

Ariffin, Jamilah. Migration of women workers in peninsular Malaysia: impact and implications. In: Women in the cities of Asia: migration and urban adaptation. Edited by James T. Fawcett, Siew-Ean Khoo and Peter C. Smith. (Boulder, CO, Westview Press, 1984), pp. 213-26.

ARIZPE, LOURDES

Arizpe, Lourdes. Les femmes paysannes et la crise agraire en Amerique latine. TIERS-MONDE (PARIS) April/June 1985, 26:325-34.

Arizpe, Lourdes. Women and development in Latin America and the Caribbean; lessons from the seventies and hopes for the future. DEVELOPMENT DIGEST (WASHINGTON) 1982, Vol. 1/2:74-84.

ARNOLD, FRED

Arnold, Fred and Piampiti, Suwanlee. Female migration in Thailand. In: Women in the cities of Asia: migration and urban adaptation. Edited by James T. Fawcett, Siew-Ean Khoo and Peter C. Smith. (Boulder, CO, Westview Press, 1984), pp. 143-64.

ASIA

Agarwal, Bina. Women and technological change in agriculture: Asian and African experience. INSTITUTE OF ECONOMIC GROWTH. [PAPERS] (DELHI) July 1984, No. E/103/84:1-55.

Gothoskar, Sujata. Free trade zones: pitting women against women. ECONOMIC AND POLITICAL WEEKLY (BOMBAY) August 23, 1986, 21:1489-92.

Mazumdar, Vina. Another development with women: a view from Asia. DEVELOPMENT DIALOGUE (UPPSALA) 1982, No. 1/2:65-73.

Tomoda, Shizue. Measuring female labour activities in Asian developing countries: a time-allocation approach. INTERNATIONAL LABOUR REVIEW (GENEVA) November/December 1985, 124:661-76.

ASIA

Unsung heroines. FAR EASTERN ECONOMIC REVIEW (HONGKONG) January 5, 1984, 123:26-40. A series of articles by women writers from a cross-section of Asian countries who survey the position of women in their own societies.

Women and politics in twentieth century Africa and Asia. STUDIES IN THIRD WORLD SOCIETIES (WILLIAMSBURG) June 1981, No. 16:1-160.

Aspects of women's political participation in Sudan. By: El-Bakri and Kameir, E. M.. INTERNATIONAL SOCIAL SCIENCE JOURNAL (PARIS) 1983, 35, No. 4:605-23.

ASWAD, BARBARA C.

Aswad, Barbara C.. Women, class and power: examples from the Hatay, Turkey. In: Women in the Muslim world. Edited by Lois Beck and Nikki Keddie. (Cambridge, MA, Harvard University Press, 1978), pp. 473-81.

Attack on the symptoms. By: Bowring, Philip. FAR EASTERN ECONOMIC REVIEW (HONGKONG) October 24, 1985, 130:62-64. Reviews the World Bank / IMF meetings in Seoul and suggests it left many questions unanswered.

Attitudes of Tanzanian husbands toward the employment of their wives. By: Chijumba, Beat J.. AFRICA DEVELOPMENT (DAKAR) April/June 1983, 8:74-85.

Attitudes of women towards certain selected cultural practices in Kerala State, India. By: Kurian, George and John, Miriam. In: Women in the family and the economy: an international comparative survey. Edited by George Kurian and Ratna Ghosh. (Westport, CT, Greenwood Press, 1981), pp. 131-64.

AUSTRALIA

Chapman, Bruce J. Sex and location differences in wages in the Australian public service. AUSTRALIAN ECONOMIC PAPERS (ADELAIDE) December 1985, 24:296-309.

Eyland, E.A. and Mason, C.A.. Determinants of female employment. ECONOMIC RECORD (MELBOURNE) March 1982, 58:11-17.

Lewis, Donald E.. Measurement of the occupational and industrial segregation of women. JOURNAL OF INDUSTRIAL RELATIONS (SYDNEY) September 1982, 24:406-23.

Lewis, Donald E. Sources of changes in the occupational segregation of Australian women. ECONOMIC RECORD (MELBOURNE) December 1985, 61:719-36.

Awareness and action. By: Helmore, Kristin. CHRISTIAN SCIENCE MONITOR (BOSTON) December 23, 1985, p. 14-16. Part 5 of 5-part series entitled: "The neglected resource; women in the developing world." Discusses increasing awareness among women in the less developed countries of their inferior economic status and of the value of collective action.

AZZAM, HENRY T.

Azzam, Henry T.. Participation of Arab women in the labour force: development factors and policies. INTERNATIONAL LABOUR OFFICE. WORLD EMPLOYMENT PROGRAMME RESEARCH. POPULATION AND EMPLOYMENT PROJECT. WORKING PAPERS (GENEVA) 1979, No. 80:1-83.

Azzam, Henry T. and Shaib, Diana. Women left behind: a study of the wives of Lebanese migrant workers in the oil rich countries of the region. INTERNATIONAL LABOUR OFFICE. WORLD EMPLOYMENT PROGRAMME RESEARCH. POPULATION AND LABOUR POLICIES: REGIONAL PROGRAMME FOR THE MIDDLE EAST. WORKING PAPER (BEIRUT) September 1980, No. 3:1-56.

BABB, FLORENCE E.

Babb, Florence E.. Women in the marketplace: petty commerce in Peru. REVIEW OF RADICAL POLITICAL ECONOMICS (NEW YORK) Spring 1984, 16:45-59.

BACH, REBECCA

Bach, Rebecca and Gadalla, Saad. Mothers' influence on daughters' orientations toward education: an Egyptian case study. COMPARATIVE EDUCATION REVIEW (NEW YORK) August 1985, 29:374-84.

BADOE, YABA MANGELA

Badoe, Yaba Mangela. Gambia; rice and dependency. WEST AFRICA (LONDON) October 24, 1983, No. 3454:2484. Discusses the sexual politics of rice production and concludes that women are the prime losers but the cost to national food production is enormous.

BAFFOUN, ALYA

Baffoun, Alya. Research in the social sciences on North African women: problems, trends and needs. In: Social science research on women in the Arab world. (London, Frances Pinter; Paris, Unesco, 1984), pp. 41-58.

BALD, SURESHT R.

　Mukhopadhyay, Carol C. and Bald, Suresht R.. Gender, politics and modernization: the Indian case. STUDIES IN THIRD WORLD SOCIETIES (WILLIAMSBURG) June 1981, No. 16:91-121.

BANAJI, ROHINI

　Gothoskar, Sujata and Banaji, Rohini. Women, work, organisation and struggle. ECONOMIC AND POLITICAL WEEKLY (BOMBAY) March 5, 1983, 18:339-44. Article based on the conclusions of the authors' forthcoming book "My life is one long struggle... women, work, organisation and struggle".

BANDARAGE, ASOKA

　Bandarage, Asoka. Women in development: liberalism, Marxism and Marxist-feminism. DEVELOPMENT AND CHANGE (THE HAGUE, etc.) October 1984, 15:495-515. Discusses liberal feminism and its Marxist critique on economic modernization and Third world women.

BANERJEE, NIRMALA

　Banerjee, Nirmala. Women and poverty; report on a workshop. ECONOMIC AND POLITICAL WEEKLY (BOMBAY) October 1, 1983, 18:1693-98.

BANGERN, MASLIANA

　Bangern, Masliana. Advantages of functional education and credit facilities for Javanese rural women. In: The endless day: some case material on Asian rural women. Edited by T. Scarlett Epstein and Rosemary A. Watts. Series: Women in development, Vol. 3. (Oxford, England, New York, Pergamon Press, 1981), pp. 128-54.

　Bangkok masseuses: origins, status and prospects. By: Phongpaichit, Rasuk. In: Women in the urban and industrial workforce; Southeast and East Asia. Edited by Gavin W. Jones. Series: Development Studies Centre. Monograph, No. 33. (Canberra, Australia, Australian National University, 1984), pp. 251-58. Series edited by Helen Hughes.

BANGLADESH

　Ahmad, Perveen. Unsung heroines: Bangladesh's unrecognized workforce gains a new self-awareness. FAR EASTERN ECONOMIC REVIEW (HONGKONG) January 5, 1984, 123:26-27.

BANGLADESH

　Ahmed, Rahnuma. Women's movement in Bangladesh and the left's understanding of the woman question. JOURNAL OF SOCIAL STUDIES (DHAKA) October 1985, No. 30:40-56.

　Alauddin, Mohammad. Maternal mortality in rural Bangladesh: the Tangail district. STUDIES IN FAMILY PLANNING (NEW YORK) January/February 1986, 17:13-21.

　Chaudhury, Rafiqul Huda. Effect of mother's work on child care, dietary intake, and dietary adequacy of pre-school children. BANGLADESH DEVELOPMENT STUDIES (DACCA) December 1982, 10:33-61.

　Chaudhury, Rafiqul Huda. Female labour force status and fertility behaviour in Bangladesh: search for policy interventions. BANGLADESH DEVELOPMENT STUDIES (DACCA) September 1983, 11:59-102.

　Chen, Lincoln C.. Where have the women gone? Insights from Bangladesh on low sex ratio of India's population. ECONOMIC AND POLITICAL WEEKLY (BOMBAY) March 6, 1982, 17:364-72.

　Chen, Marty. Poverty, gender, and work in Bangladesh. ECONOMIC AND POLITICAL WEEKLY (BOMBAY) February 1, 1986, 21:217-22. Redefines the three broad classes of rural households in terms of women's labour and income and describes the process of impoverishment from the perspective of women.

　Hye, Hasnat Abdul. Mechanisation in agriculture and women in Bangladesh. JOURNAL OF SOCIAL STUDIES (DHAKA) January 1985, No. 27:78-100.

　Jahangir, B. K. Women and property in rural Bangladesh. JOURNAL OF SOCIAL STUDIES (DHAKA) October 1986, No. 34:87-95.

　Khan, Atiqur Rahman and Jahan, Farida Akhter. Maternal mortality in rural Bangladesh: the Jamalpur district. STUDIES IN FAMILY PLANNING (NEW YORK) January/February 1986, 17:7-12.

　Khan, Zarina Rahman. Women's economic role: insights from a village in Bangladesh. JOURNAL OF SOCIAL STUDIES (DHAKA) October 1985, No. 30:13-26.

BANGLADESH

Khandker, Shahidur R. Women's role in household productive activities and fertility in Bangladesh. YALE UNIVERSITY. ECONOMIC GROWTH CENTER. DISCUSSION PAPER (NEW HAVEN, CONN.) July 1985, No. 488:1-35. Seeks to identify the factors that may affect the role of women in the rural areas of a developing country and the possible impact of these factors on fertility.

Bangladesh: a struggle with tradition and poverty. By: Smock, Audrey Chapman. In: Women: roles and status in eight countries. Edited by Janet Zollinger Giele and Audrey Chapman Smock. (New York, John Wiley, 1977), pp. 83-126.

BANK LOANS

Everett, Jana and Savara, Mira. Bank loans to lower class women in Bombay; problems and prospects. ECONOMIC AND POLITICAL WEEKLY (BOMBAY) August 25, 1984, 19:M113-M119. The authors report the results of an exploratory study of bank loans to lower caste women in Bombay. They seek to shed some light on the problems surrounding and the prospects for bank loans as an economic development strategy for poor women.

BANKS AND BANKING

Patel, I. G.. Promotion of credit to women entrepreneurs. RESERVE BANK OF INDIA, BULLETIN (BOMBAY) December 1981, 35:1059-64. Address at the International Workshop of Women's Banking at Bhaikaka Bhavan, Ahmedabad on December 1, 1981.

BARBADOS

Massiah, Joycelin. Establishing a programme of women and development studies in the University of the West Indies. SOCIAL AND ECONOMIC STUDIES (MONA, JAMAICA) March 1986, 35:151-97.

BARDHAN, KALPANA

Bardhan, Kalpana. Women's work, welfare and status; forces of tradition and change in India, pt. 1. ECONOMIC AND POLITICAL WEEKLY (BOMBAY) December 14, 1985, 20:2207-20.

Bardhan, Kalpana. Women's work, welfare and status; forces of tradition and change in India, pt. 2. ECONOMIC AND POLITICAL WEEKLY (BOMBAY) December 21, 1985, 20:2262-69.

BARNES, CAROLYN

Barnes, Carolyn. Differentiation by sex among small-scale farming households in Kenya. RURAL AFRICANA (EAST LANSING) Winter/Spring 1983, No. 15/16:41-63.

BARON, JAMES N

Bielby, William T. and Baron, James N. Sex segregation within occupations. AMERICAN ECONOMIC REVIEW, PAPERS AND PROCEEDINGS (NASHVILLE) May 1986, 76:43-47.

Le barrage des femmes; les femmes mossi du Burkina-Faso. By: Yoon, Soon-Young. TIERS-MONDE (PARIS) April/June 1985, 26:443-49.

BARRES, VICTORIA

Barres, Victoria. Deux programmes de credit bien adaptes aux besoins des femmes du Tiers monde. TIERS-MONDE (PARIS) April/June 1985, 26:435-42. Cet article presente deux programmes de credits d'investissement destines a des femmes pauvres du Tiers Monde, l'un en milieu urbain (Madras, Inde) et l'autre en milieu rural (pays yoruba, Nigeria).

BARROW, NITA

Barrow, Nita. Nairobi '85; the decade NGO forum. AFRICA REPORT (NEW YORK) March/April 1985, 30:9-12.

BARTA, BARNABAS

Barta, Barnabas and Klinger, Andras. Fertility, female employment and policy measures in Hungary. Series: Women, Work and Development, No. 6. (Geneva, International Labour Organisation, 1984), 88 pp. Published with the financial support of the United Nations Fund for Population Activities (UNFPA).

BARTH, GERALD

Hackenberg, Beverly and Barth, Gerald. Growth of the bazaar economy and its significance for women's employment: trends of the 1970's in Davao City, Philippines. In: Women in the urban and industrial workforce; Southeast and East Asia. Edited by Gavin W. Jones. Series: Development Studies Centre. Monograph, No. 33. (Canberra, Australia, Australian National University, 1984), pp. 259-76. Series edited by Helen Hughes.

BASSE, MARIE-THERESE

Basse, Marie-Therese. Women, food and nutrition in Africa: perspective from Senegal. FOOD AND NUTRITION (ROME) 1984, 10, No. 1:65-79. Also includes: Economic change and the outlook for nutrition, prepared by the Food and Agriculture Organization of the United Nations.

BATLIWALA, SRILATHA

Batliwala, Srilatha. Women and cooking energy. ECONOMIC AND POLITICAL WEEKLY (BOMBAY) December 24, 1983, 18:2227-30. Describes how a woman in poverty has low access to cooking fuel, spends the longest time obtaining it, and puts it to use in stoves which are not only fuel-inefficient, but which also subject her to serious or fatal disease.

BAUER, JANET

Bauer, Janet. New models and traditional networks: migrant women in Tehran. In: Women in the cities of Asia: migration and urban adaptation. Edited by James T. Fawcett, Siew-Ean Khoo and Peter C. Smith. (Boulder, CO, Westview Press, 1984), pp. 269-93.

BAYAT-PHILIPP, MANGOL

Bayat-Philipp, Mangol. Women and revolution in Iran, 1905-1911. In: Women in the Muslim world. Edited by Lois Beck and Nikki Keddie. (Cambridge, MA, Harvard University Press, 1978), pp. 295-308.

Bearing the burden. By: Perry, Alison. WEST AFRICA (LONDON) April 22, 1985, No. 3530:785-86. Looks at the important role women playin the agricultural sector and at the severe handicpas they face, due to their double work-load and a discriminatory system.

BEASLEY, JULIA

Beasley, Julia. It's a man's Third world. GUARDIAN (LONDON) November 5, 1984, p. 12. The author indicates that "Across the cultural divide, sexism is the only thing countries have in common."

BEAUJOT, RODERIC

Beaujot, Roderic. Liberation de la femme et marche matrimonial en Tunisie. POPULATION (PARIS) July/October 1986, 41:853-59.

BECK, LOIS

Beck, Lois. Women among Qashqa'i nomadic pastoralists in Iran. In: Women in the Muslim world. Edited by Lois Beck and Nikki Keddie. (Cambridge, MA, Harvard University Press, 1978), pp. 351-73.

BECKER-SCHMIDT, REGINA

Becker-Schmidt, Regina and Knapp, Gudrun-Axeli. Wertewandel und Widerspruche; Erziehungsorientierungen und -probleme von Arbeiterinnen im Vergleich zweier Generationen. WSI-MITTEILUNGEN (DUSSELDORF) August 1986, 39:558-66.

Behind the veil in Arabia: women in Oman. By: Wikan, Unni. (Baltimore, Johns Hopkins University Press, 1982), 314 pp.

BEHRMAN, JERE R.

Behrman, Jere R. and Wolfe, Barbara L.. Labor force participation and earnings determinants for women in the special conditions of developing countries. JOURNAL OF DEVELOPMENT ECONOMICS (AMSTERDAM) May/August 1984, 15:259-88. The authors focus on labor market conditions for women in Nicaragua.

Wolfe, Barbara L. and Behrman, Jere R.. Determinants of child health, mortality, and nutrition in a developing country. UNIVERSITY OF WISCONSIN-MADISON. INSTITUTE FOR RESEARCH ON POVERTY. DISCUSSION PAPERS (MADISON) January 1981, No. 643-80:1-53. The authors use data collected in a cross-sectional multipurpose survey of women of childbearing age in Nicaragua.

Wolfe, Barbara L. and Behrman, Jere R.. Impact of demographic changes on income distribution in a developing country. JOURNAL OF DEVELOPMENT ECONOMICS (AMSTERDAM) December 1982, 11:355-77. The authors use data from a stratified random sample of about 4,000 women aged 15 to 45 in Nicaragua.

Wolfe, Barbara L. and Behrman, Jere R.. Socioeconomic characteristics of women in a developing country and the degree of urbanization. UNIVERSITY OF WISCONSIN-MADISON. INSTITUTE FOR RESEARCH ON POVERTY. DISCUSSION PAPERS (MADISON) September 1980, 655-81:1-53. The study is based on a stratified random sample of over 4,000 women aged 15-45 in Nicaragua.

Being female in a Muslim minority in China. By: Pillsbury, Barbara L. K.. In: Women in the Muslim world. Edited by Lois Beck and Nikki Keddie. (Cambridge, MA, Harvard University Press, 1978), pp. 651-73.

BELARBI, AICHA

Belarbi, Aicha. Research in the social sciences on women in Morocco. In: Social science research on women in the Arab world. (London, Frances Pinter; Paris, Unesco, 1984), pp. 59-75.

BELIZE

Brockmann, C. Thomas. Women and development in northern Belize. JOURNAL OF DEVELOPING AREAS (MACOMB, ILL.) July 1985, 19:501-14.

BELLONCLE, GUY

Belloncle, Guy. Femmes et developpement en Afrique sahelienne: l'experience nigerienne d'animation feminine (1966-1976). Series: Collection Developpement et Civilisations. (Paris, Editions Ouvrieres, 1980), 212 pp.

BEN MILED, EMNA

Ben Miled, Emna. Etude comparative du statut sexuel des femmes dans le monde mediterraneen, berbere et Africain. REVUE TUNISIENNE DE SCIENCES SOCIALES (TUNIS) 1985, 22, No. 82/83:75-110.

BENALLEGUE, NORA

Benallegue, Nora. Algerian women in the struggle for independence and reconstruction. INTERNATIONAL SOCIAL SCIENCE JOURNAL (PARIS) 1983, 35, No. 4:703-17.

BENNETT, LYNN

Acharya, Meena and Bennett, Lynn. Women and the subsistence sector: economic participation and household decision making in Nepal. Series: World Bank Staff Working Papers, No. 526. (Washington, DC, World Bank, 1983), 140 pp.

BERGER, BRIGITTE

Berger, Brigitte and Corriher, Kurt. Underground women of the Third world. WALL STREET JOURNAL (NEW YORK) July 26, 1985, p. 20. Authors state that in addition to their role in production and marketing, women are acquiring vital leadership skills because informal institutions are springing up to accompany informal economies.

BERGER, IRIS

Berger, Iris. Rebels or status-seekers? Women as spirit mediums in East Africa. In: Women in Africa: studies in social and economic change. Edited by Nancy J. Hafkin and Edna G. Bay. (Stanford, Stanford University Press, 1976), pp. 157-81.

BERGMANN, HELLMUTH

Bergmann, Hellmuth and Schul, Jean-Jacques. Liste de questions sur le role des femmes dans les projets de developpement agricole. TIERS-MONDE (PARIS) October/December 1980, 21:833-44.

BERLINER, JOSEPH S.

Berliner, Joseph S.. Education, labor-force participation, and fertility in the USSR. JOURNAL OF COMPARATIVE ECONOMICS (NEW YORK) June 1983, 7:131-57. The effect of education on Soviet fertility and female labor participation is analyzed in terms of the neoclassical theory of the household.

Bibliographic guide to studies on the status of women: development and population trends. (New York, Bowker, UNIPUB; Paris, Unesco, 1983), 292 pp.

Bibliography on Bangladesh women with annotation. By: Islam, Mahmuda. (Dacca, Women for Women Research and Study Group, [1979]), 63 pp.

BIELBY, WILLIAM T.

Bielby, William T. and Baron, James N. Sex segregation within occupations. AMERICAN ECONOMIC REVIEW, PAPERS AND PROCEEDINGS (NASHVILLE) May 1986, 76:43-47.

BIFANI, PATRICIA

Bifani, Patricia. How Kenyan peasants, pastoralists and peri-urban women see water problems. WATERLINES (LONDON) January 1986, 4:16-19.

"Big women" and politics in a Philippine fishing town. By: Szanton, M. Cristina Blanc. STUDIES IN THIRD WORLD SOCIETIES (WILLIAMSBURG) June 1981, No. 16:123-41.

Bildungswege der Frauen in Ungarn: neue Tendenzen in der Ausbildung und Beschaftigung aus soziologischer Sicht. By: Forray, Katalin R. OSTERREICHISCHE OSTHEFTE (VIENNA) 1986, 28, No. 2:107-25.

Birth order and alienation among college women in Lebanon. By: Tomeh, Aida K.. In: Women in the family and the economy: an international comparative survey. Edited by George Kurian and Ratna Ghosh. (Westport, CT, Greenwood Press, 1981), pp. 81-106.

BIRYUKOVA, ALEXANDRA

Biryukova, Alexandra. Role of the Soviet woman in decision-making in trade union committees and in industry. LABOUR AND SOCIETY (GENEVA) September 1985, 10:307-21.

BISILLIAT, JEANNE

Bisilliat, Jeanne. La participation des femmes aux cooperatives mixtes: temps et ideologie. TIERS-MONDE (PARIS) April/June 1985, 26:409-15.

Black woman: liberated or oppressed? By: Puryear, Gwendolyn Randall. In: Comparative perspectives of Third World women: the impact of race, sex and class. Edited by Beverly Lindsay. (New York, Praeger, 1980), pp. 251-75.

BLAIN, DANIELE

Blain, Daniele. Farming system for women: the case of cassava production in Zaire. CERES, FAO REVIEW ON AGRICULTURE AND DEVELOPMENT (ROME) May/June 1985, 18:43-46.

BLAKE, MYRNA

Blake, Myrna. Constraints on the organization of women industrial workers. In: Women in the urban and industrial workforce; Southeast and East Asia. Edited by Gavin W. Jones. Series: Development Studies Centre. Monograph, No. 33. (Canberra, Australia, Australian National University, 1984), pp. 149-62. Series edited by Helen Hughes.

BLAU, DAVID M.

Blau, David M.. Investments in child nutrition and women's allocation of time in developing countries. YALE UNIVERSITY. ECONOMIC GROWTH CENTER. DISCUSSION PAPER (NEW HAVEN, CONN.) March 1981, No. 371:1-41. The purpose of this study is to investigate the determinants of fertility and home investments in the human capital of children in a context in which women have the option of working in the informal sector as well as the formal sector or no market work. The empirical analysis presented in section III uses data from a 1977-78 survey of households in Nicaragua.

BOCK, GISELA

Bock, Gisela and Duden, Barbara. Labor of love -- love as labor on the Genesis of housework in the West. DEVELOPMENT (ROME) 1984, No. 4:6-14.

BODARD SILVER, CATHERINE

Bodard Silver, Catherine. France: contrasts in familial and societal roles. In: Women: roles and status in eight countries. Edited by Janet Zollinger Giele and Audrey Chapman Smock. (New York, John Wiley, 1977), pp. 259-99.

BOLABOLA, CEMA

Bolabola, Cema. Women in villages: femininity, food and freedom. PACIFIC PERSPECTIVE (SUVA) 1983, 11, No. 2:65-7.

BOLIVIA

Hadorn, Verena. Une place au marche de Sopocachi; travail de femmes en Bolivie. ENTWICKLUNG, DEVELOPPEMENT (BERNE) 1985, No. 19:14-16.

BOLLAG, DANIEL

Bollag, Daniel. Breath of feminism in macho Spain. SWISS REVIEW OF WORLD AFFAIRS (ZURICH) July 1982, 32:21-23.

BONDER, GLORIA

Bonder, Gloria. Los estudios de la mujer y la critica epistemologica a los paradigmas de las ciencias humanas. DESARROLLO Y SOCIEDAD (BOGOTA) January 1984, No. 13:25-38. With English summary.

Bonder, Gloria. Study of politics from the standpoint of women. INTERNATIONAL SOCIAL SCIENCE JOURNAL (PARIS) 1983, 35, No. 4:569-83.

BONILLA DE RAMOS, ELSSY

Bonilla de Ramos, Elssy. La madre trabajadora. UNIVERSIDAD DE LOS ANDES. CENTRO DE ESTUDIOS SOBRE DESARROLLO ECONOMICO. DOCUMENTO (BOGOTA) September 1981, No. 66:1-139.

Bonilla de Ramos, Elssy. La madre trabajadora: una contradiccion. DESARROLLO Y SOCIEDAD (BOGOTA) September 1982, No. 9:67-84.

Bonilla de Ramos, Elssy. La mujer y su imagen en los medios. UNIVERSIDAD DE LOS ANDES. CENTRO DE ESTUDIOS SOBRE DESARROLLO ECONOMICO. DOCUMENTO (BOGOTA) Arpil 1981, No. 64:1-183.

BOSE, SWADESH R.

Bose, Swadesh R.. Some aspects of unskilled labor markets for civil construction in India: observations based on field investigation. Series: World Bank Staff Working Papers, No. 223. (Washington, DC, World Bank, 1975), 47 pp.

BOSERUP, ESTER

Boserup, Ester. Women's role in economic development. (New York, St. Martin's Press, [1970]), 283 pp.

BOTSWANA

Brown, Barbara B.. Impact of male labour migration on women in Botswana. AFRICAN AFFAIRS (LONDON) July 1983, 82:367-88.

Brown, Barbara B.. Women, migrant labor and social change in Botswana. BOSTON UNIVERSITY. AFRICAN STUDIES CENTER. WORKING PAPERS (BOSTON) 1980, No. 41:1-21.

Kossoudji, Sherrie and Mueller, Eva. Economic and demographic status of female-headed households in rural Botswana. ECONOMIC DEVELOPMENT AND CULTURAL CHANGE (CHICAGO) July 1983, 31:831-59.

Novicki, Margaret A.. G. K. T. Chiepe, Minister of Foreign Affairs, Botswana. AFRICA REPORT (NEW YORK) March/April 1985, 30:14-16. An interview with Dr. G. K. T. Chiepe, Botswans's first woman university graduate and first female cabinet minister who discusses the advances of women over the UN Decade and the significance of women's contributions to the economic development of her country.

BOUA, CHANTHOU

Boua, Chanthou. Women in today's Cambodia. NEW LEFT REVIEW (LONDON) January/February 1982, No. 131:45-61.

BOWMAN, MARY JEAN

Bowman, Mary Jean and Anderson, C. Arnold. Participation of women in education in the Third World. COMPARATIVE EDUCATION REVIEW (NEW YORK) June 1980, 24:S13-32.

BOWRING, PHILIP

Bowring, Philip. Attack on the symptoms. FAR EASTERN ECONOMIC REVIEW (HONGKONG) October 24, 1985, 130:62-64. Reviews the World Bank / IMF meetings in Seoul and suggests it left many questions unanswered.

BOYLE, BONNIE

Boyle, Bonnie. Where women come last a beehive is liberation. WASHINGTON POST (WASHINGTON) December 11, 1983, p. C1-C2.

BRAIN, JAMES L.

Brain, James L.. Less than second-class: women in rural settlement schemes in Tanzania. In: Women in Africa: studies in social and economic change. Edited by Nancy J. Hafkin and Edna G. Bay. (Stanford, Stanford University Press, 1976), pp. 265-82.

BRAMBILLA, FRANCESCO

Brambilla, Francesco. Women and development. GIORNALE DEGLI ECONOMISTI E ANNALI DI ECONOMIA (MILAN) September/December 1979, 38, N.S.:619-67. With English summary.

BRANA-SHUTE, ROSEMARY

Brana-Shute, Rosemary. Working class Afro-Surinamese women and national politics: traditions and changes in an independent state. STUDIES IN THIRD WORLD SOCIETIES (WILLIAMSBURG) March 1981, No. 15:33-56.

BRANDTZAEG, BRITA

Brandtzaeg, Brita. Role and status of women in post-harvest food conservation. FOOD AND NUTRITION BULLETIN (TOKYO) January 1982, 4:33-40.

BRAZIL

de Brito, Angela Neves-Xavier. Brazilian women in exile; the quest for an identity. LATIN AMERICAN PERSPECTIVES (BEVERLY HILLS) Spring 1986, 13:58-80.

Humphrey, John. Growth of female employment in Brazilian manufacturing industry in the 1970s. JOURNAL OF DEVELOPMENT STUDIES (LONDON) July 1984, 20:224-47.

Institute for Cultural Action (IDAC). Discovering self-reliance in Paraty. DEVELOPMENT (ROME) 1984, No. 4:41-44. Describes a project of women's education for self-reliance in Paraty, a rural village in Brazil.

Miller, Linda. Patrons, politics, and schools; an arena for Brazilian women. STUDIES IN THIRD WORLD SOCIETIES (WILLIAMSBURG) March 1981, No. 15:67-89.

BRAZIL

Scott, Alison MacEwen. Women and industrialisation: examining the "female marginalisation" thesis. JOURNAL OF DEVELOPMENT STUDIES (LONDON) July 1986, 22:649-80. The article argues for attention to be paid to the micro-level processes which give rise to women's marginalisation.

Brazilian women in exile; the quest for an identity. By: de Brito, Angela Neves-Xavier. LATIN AMERICAN PERSPECTIVES (BEVERLY HILLS) Spring 1986, 13:58-80.

Breaking down barriers and getting in step. By: Chang, MyongSue. FAR EASTERN ECONOMIC REVIEW (HONGKONG) January 5, 1984, 123:39-40. Describes how Korean women have steadily improved their status over the past several decades.

Breath of feminism in macho Spain. By: Bollag, Daniel. SWISS REVIEW OF WORLD AFFAIRS (ZURICH) July 1982, 32:21-23.

Breezes of social change sweep slowly through Senegal. By: Helmore, Kristin. CHRISTIAN SCIENCE MONITOR (BOSTON) March 31, 1986, p. 23. Second in a series entitled: "Voices from the Third world." An interview with Marie-Angelique Savane, president of the Association of African Women for Research and Development.

BRENNER, JOHANNA

Brenner, Johanna and Ramas, Maria. Rethinking women's oppression. NEW LEFT REVIEW (LONDON) March/April 1984, No. 144:33-71. The authors discuss some of the issues raised in Michele Barrett's Women's oppression today.

BRICENO, MARIA ESPERANZA

Briceno, Maria Esperanza. Some sow, others reap. In: Latin American women: the meek speak out. Edited by June H. Turner. (Silver Spring, MD, International Educational Development, 1980), pp. 137-46. The author discusses women in Colombia.

Bringing research home. By: Tadesse, Zenebworke. DEVELOPMENT (ROME) 1984, No. 4:50-54. Discusses on the question of research on women in Africa.

BROCKMANN, C. THOMAS

Brockmann, C. Thomas. Women and development in northern Belize. JOURNAL OF DEVELOPING AREAS (MACOMB, ILL.) July 1985, 19:501-14.

Broken wing. By: Arce, Jenny Valcarcel. In: Latin American women: the meek speak out. Edited by June H. Turner. (Silver Spring, MD, International Educational Development, 1980), pp. 150-61. Discusses women in Peru.

BRONSTEIN, AUDREY

Bronstein, Audrey. Triple struggle; Latin American peasant women. (London, WOW Campaigns, 1982), 268 pp. Contains interviews with women in Ecuador, Bolivia, Peru, El Salvador and Guatemala.

BROOKS, GEORGE E., JR.

Brooks, George E., Jr.. Signares of Saint-Louis and Goree: women entrepreneurs in eighteenth-century Senegal. In: Women in Africa: studies in social and economic change. Edited by Nancy J. Hafkin and Edna G. Bay. (Stanford, Stanford University Press, 1976), pp. 19-44.

BROUARD, NICOLAS

Brouard, Nicolas. Esperance de vie active, reprise d'activite feminine: un modele. REVUE ECONOMIQUE (PARIS) November 1980, 31:1260-87. With English summary.

BROWN, BARBARA B.

Brown, Barbara B.. Impact of male labour migration on women in Botswana. AFRICAN AFFAIRS (LONDON) July 1983, 82:367-88.

Brown, Barbara B.. Women, migrant labor and social change in Botswana. BOSTON UNIVERSITY. AFRICAN STUDIES CENTER. WORKING PAPERS (BOSTON) 1980, No. 41:1-21.

BROWN, SUSAN E.

Brown, Susan E.. Love unites them and hunger separates them: poor women in the Dominican Republic. In: Toward an anthropology of women. Edited by Rayna R. Reiter. (New York, Monthly Review Press, 1975), pp. 322-31.

Brown, Susan E.. Lower economic sector female mating patterns in the Dominican Republic: a comparative analysis. In: Women cross-culturally: change and challenge. Edited by Ruby Rohrlich-Leavitt. (The Hague, Mouton, 1975), pp. 149-62.

BRUCHHAUS, EVA-MARIA

Bruchhaus, Eva-Maria. Von der Bauerin zur Hilfskraft? E & Z, ENTWICKLUNG UND ZUSAMMENARBEIT (BONN) June 25, 1984, 25:19-21.

BUJRA, JANET

Bujra, Janet. Women and fieldwork. In: Women cross-culturally: change and challenge. Edited by Ruby Rohrlich-Leavitt. (The Hague, Mouton, 1975), pp. 521-557.

BURIC, OLIVERA

Buric, Olivera. Change in the system of social power; conditions for the social equality of women. In: Changing position of women in family and society: a cross-national comparison. Edited by Eugen Lupri. (Leiden, E. J. Brill, 1983), pp. 311-27.

BURKINA FASO

Yoon, Soon-Young. Le barrage des femmes; les femmes mossi du Burkina-Faso. TIERS-MONDE (PARIS) April/June 1985, 26:443-49.

Burma: balance and harmony. By: Khaing, Mi Mi. In: Women in the new Asia; the changing social roles of men and women in South and South-east Asia. Edited by Barbara E. Ward. ([Paris], Unesco, 1963), pp. 104-37.

BURUNDI

Muller-Blattau, Beate and Seibert, Ulrike. Funf Frauen - funf Leben. E & Z, ENTWICKLUNG UND ZUSAMMENARBEIT (BONN) January 1985, 26:16-17.

BUVINIC, MAYRA

Buvinic, Mayra and Lycette, Margaret. Eye-opening survey unlocks doors for low-income women. HORIZONS, U.S. AGENCY FOR INTERNATIONAL DEVELOPMENT (WASHINGTON) Summer 1985, 4:31-33. The authors describe how the International Center for Research on Women (ICRW), with a $120,000 grant from AID, is helping to put home ownership within reach of low-income women, through its experiences with the Solanda low-income housing project in Quito, Ecuador.

Buvinic, Mayra and Leslie, Joanne. Health care for women in Latin America and the Caribbean. STUDIES IN FAMILY PLANNING (NEW YORK) March 1981, 12:112-15.

Buvinic, Mayra. Projects for women in the Third World: explaining their misbehavior. WORLD DEVELOPMENT (OXFORD) May 1986, 14:653-64. Explains why the economic objectives of a large number of income-generation projects for poor women in the Third World have evolved into welfare action during implementation.

BUVINIC, MAYRA, ET AL.

Buvinic, Mayra, et al.. Women and world development: an annotated bibliography. (Washington, Overseas Development Council, 1976), 162 pp. Companion to: Women and world development, edited by Irene Tinker and Michele Bramsen. Product of the AAAs seminar on women in development held in Mexico City in June 1975; prepared under the auspices of the American Association for the Advancement of Science.

CAIN, MEAD

Cain, Mead. Women's status and fertility in developing countries: son preference and economic security. Series: World Bank Staff Working Papers, No. 682. (Washington, World Bank, 1984), 68 pp. Prepared as a background paper for the World Development Report 1984. Also published as No. 7 in the Population and Development Series.

CALLAWAY, BARBARA J.

Callaway, Barbara J.. Ambiguous consequences of the socialisation and seclusion of Hausa women. JOURNAL OF MODERN AFRICAN STUDIES (OXFORD) September 1984, 22:429-50.

CALLAWAY, BARBARA J. AND KLEEMAN, KATHERINE E.

Callaway, Barbara J. and Kleeman, Katherine E.. Three women of Kano: modern women and traditional life. AFRICA REPORT (NEW YORK) March/April 1985, 30:26-29.

CAMBODIA

Boua, Chanthou. Women in today's Cambodia. NEW LEFT REVIEW (LONDON) January/February 1982, No. 131:45-61.

CAMEROON

Bruchhaus, Eva-Maria. Von der Bauerin zur Hilfskraft? E & Z, ENTWICKLUNG UND ZUSAMMENARBEIT (BONN) June 25, 1984, 25:19-21.

Cooksey, Brian. Education and sexual inequality in Cameroun. JOURNAL OF MODERN AFRICAN STUDIES (OXFORD) March 1982, 20:167-77.

Geary, Christraud M. On legal change in Cameroon: women, marriage, and bridewealth. BOSTON UNIVERSITY. AFRICAN STUDIES CENTER. WORKING PAPERS (BOSTON) 1986, No. 113:1-37.

CAMPBELL, CLAUDIA

Steel, William F. and Campbell, Claudia. Women's employment and development: a conceptual framework applied to Ghana. In: Women and work in Africa. Edited by Edna G. Bay. (Boulder, CO, Westview Press, 1982), pp. 225-48.

CAMPOS, ANA AUDILIA MOREIRA DE

Campos, Ana Audilia Moreira de. Our national inferiority complex: a cause for violence? In: Latin American women: the meek speak out. Edited by June H. Turner. (Silver Spring, MD, International Educational Development, 1980), pp. 66-72. A commentary by a rural woman in El Salvador.

CANADA

Robinson, Chris and Tomes, Nigel. More on the labour supply of Canadian women. CANADIAN JOURNAL OF ECONOMICS (TORONTO) February 1985, 18:156-63.

Capitalism and subsistence: rural women in India. By: Mies, Maria. DEVELOPMENT (ROME) 1984, No. 4:18-24.

Capitalist development and women's work: a Nigerian case study. By: Dennis, Carolyne. REVIEW OF AFRICAN POLITICAL ECONOMY (SHEFFIELD) 1984, No. 27/28:109-19.

CARDENAS DE SANZ DE SANTAMARIA, MARIA CONSUELO

Cardenas de Sanz de Santamaria, Maria Consuelo. Epistemologia y sicologia en "la cuestion de la mujer". DESARROLLO Y SOCIEDAD (BOGOTA) January 1984, No. 13:39-55. With English summary.

Career constraints among women graduate students in a developing society: West Pakistan; a study in the changing status of women. By: Korson, J. Henry. In: Women in the family and the economy: an international comparative survey. Edited by George Kurian and Ratna Ghosh. (Westport, CT, Greenwood Press, 1981), pp. 393-411.

Career-housewife in the Philippines. By: Arceo-Ortega, Angelina. In: Women in the new Asia; the changing social roles of men and women in South and South-east Asia. Edited by Barbara E. Ward ([Paris], Unesco, 1963), pp. 365-73.

CAREW, JOY GLEASON

Carew, Joy Gleason. Note on women and agricultural technology in the Third World. LABOUR AND SOCIETY (GENEVA) July/September 1981, 6:279-85.

CARIBBEAN

Antrobus, Peggy. Reaching beyond university walls. DEVELOPMENT (ROME) 1984, No. 4:45-49. Describes International Development have provided me with the encouragement to write about the work of the Women and Development (WAND) Unit of the Extra-Mural Department of the University of the West Indies (UWI): SID's Grassroots Strategies and Initiatives Programme (GRIS), and its sincere attempt to integrate a serious concern for women in development issues within the overall programme.

Arizpe, Lourdes. Women and development in Latin America and the Caribbean; lessons from the seventies and hopes for the future. DEVELOPMENT DIGEST (WASHINGTON) 1982, Vol. 1/2:74-84.

Buvinic, Mayra and Leslie, Joanne. Health care for women in Latin America and the Caribbean. STUDIES IN FAMILY PLANNING (NEW YORK) March 1981, 12:112-15.

Powell, Dorian. Role of women in the Caribbean. SOCIAL AND ECONOMIC STUDIES (MONA, JAMAICA) June 1984, 33:97-122.

Sense of their own effectiveness. CERES, FAO REVIEW ON AGRICULTURE AND DEVELOPMENT (ROME) January/February 1986, 19:44-46. An interview with Peggy Antrobus, coordinator of WAND (Women and Development Unit), a regional organization created in Barbados in 1978 as a part of the Action Plan of the United Nations Decade for Women.

Staudt, Kathleen. Planning-centred approach to project evaluation: women in mainstream development projects. PUBLIC ADMINISTRATION AND DEVELOPMENT (CHICHESTER) January/March 1985, 5:25-37. Describes the process and outcomes of a 'planning-centred' approach to three development projects in the Caribbean.

CARIBBEAN REGIONAL WORKSHOP FOR WOMEN IN SMALL ISLAND STATES (1981: ST. GEORGES, GRENADA)

Caribbean Regional Workshop for Women in Small Island States (1981: St. Georges, Grenada). Report on Caribbean regional workshop for women in small island states: (management, communication and community mobilisation). (London, Commonwealth Secretariat, [1981]), 9 pp.

Caribbean women: the impact of race, sex, and class. By: Joseph, Gloria I.. In: Comparative perspectives of Third World women: the impact of race, sex, and class. Edited by Beverly Lindsay. (New York, Praeger, 1980), pp. 143-61.

CARLIER, ANA BLEYSWYCK DE

Carlier, Ana Bleyswyck de. Only road. In: Latin American women: the meek speak out. Edited by June H. Turner. (Silver Spring, MD, International Educational Development, 1980), pp. 42-50. Describes women in Peru.

CARR, MARILYN

Carr, Marilyn. Technology and rural women in Africa. INTERNATIONAL LABOUR OFFICE. WORLD EMPLOYMENT PROGRAMME RESEARCH. TECHNOLOGY AND EMPLOYMENT PROGRAMME. WORKING PAPERS (GENEVA) July 1980, No. 61:1-45.

Carr, Marilyn. Women and appropriate technology: two essays. INTERMEDIATE TECHNOLOGY DEVELOPMENT GROUP. OCCASIONAL PAPER (LONDON) 1982, No. 5:1-21. CONTENT: Appropriate technology for African women. - 2. Technologies appropriate for women: theory, practice and policy.

Scott, Gloria L. and Carr, Marilyn. Women in rural Bangladesh: policies for their employment and opportunities in crop processing. Series: World Bank Staff Working Papers, No. 731. (Washington, DC, World Bank, 1985), 107 pp. (Forthcoming).

CARROLL, THEODORA FOSTER

Carroll, Theodora Foster. Women, religion, and development in the Third World. (New York, Praeger Publishers, 1983), 292 pp.

CARTER, MARY

Carter, Mary. Women's banking expands; twenty local affiliates now active in 17 countries. DEVELOPMENT, SOCIETY FOR INTERNATIONAL DEVELOPMENT (ROME) July 31, 1984, No. 155:3. Describes the policies, procedures and design of Women's World Banking, which operates as an independent financial institution to provide loan guarantees or other security to banks and other financial institutions, and arranges technical or other advice and assistance to direct and indirect beneficiaries of guarantees.

CASSAVA

Blain, Daniele. Farming system for women: the case of cassava production in Zaire. CERES, FAO REVIEW ON AGRICULTURE AND DEVELOPMENT (ROME) May/June 1985, 18:43-46.

CASTANEDA, TARSICIO

Castaneda, Tarsicio. Los determinantes de la participacion de la mujer casada en el mercado de trabajo urbano en Colombia. ESTUDIOS DE ECONOMIA (SANTIAGO) Second semester 1981, No. 17:111-34. With English summary.

Caste, class, and gender: production and reproduction in North India. By: Sharma, Miriam. JOURNAL OF PEASANT STUDIES (LONDON) July 1985, 12:26-56.

Casual interpretation of the effect of mother's education and employment status on parental decision-making role patterns in the Korean family. By: Kim, On-Jook Lee and Kim, Kyong-Dong. In: Women in the family and the economy: an international comparative survey. Edited by George Kurian and Ratna Ghosh. (Westport, CT, Greenwood Press, 1981), pp. 43-57.

CATLEY-CARLSON, MARGARET

Catley-Carlson, Margaret. Oversights, insights and new sites. DEVELOPMENT (ROME) 1984, No. 4:82-84.

CAUGHMAN, SUSAN

Caughman, Susan. Women at work in Mali: the case of the Markala cooperative. BOSTON UNIVERSITY. AFRICAN STUDIES CENTER. WORKING PAPERS (BOSTON) 1981, No. 50:1-35.

CEESAY-MARENAH, COUMBA

Ceesay-Marenah, Coumba. Women's cooperative thrift and credit societies: an element of women's programs in the Gambia. In: Women and work in Africa. Edited by Edna G. Bay. (Boulder, CO, Westview Press, 1982), pp. 289-95.

Challenges for sub-Saharan Africa. By: McNamara, Robert S.. Sir John Crawford Memorial Lecture. (Washington, World Bank, November 1, 1985), 49 pp. Defines and reviews the critical issues affecting the outlook for economic growth in sub-Saharan Africa and examines how they might best be addressed.

CHAND, RAMESH AND SIDHU, D. S

Chand, Ramesh and Sidhu, D. S. Impact of agricultural modernization on labour: use pattern in Punjab with special reference to women labour. INDIAN JOURNAL OF AGRICULTURAL ECONOMICS (BOMBAY) July/September 1985, 40:252-59.

Chandigarh Women's Conference: women in informal sector; 'to keep on keeping on'. ECONOMIC AND POLITICAL WEEKLY (BOMBAY) December 20, 1986, 21:2216-18.

CHANEY, ELSA M.

Chaney, Elsa M.. Mobilization of women: three societies. In: Women cross-culturally: change and challenge. Edited by Ruby Rohrlich-Leavitt. (The Hague, Mouton, 1975), pp. 472-89.

Chaney, Elsa M.. Women of the world: Latin America and the Caribbean. ((Washington, DC, U.S. Dept. of Commerce, Bureau of the Census, 1984), 173 pp. Prepared under the resources support services agreement with the Office of Women in Development, Bureau for Program and Policy Coordination, U.S. Agency for International Development.

CHANG, MYONGSUE

Chang, MyongSue. Breaking down barriers and getting in step. FAR EASTERN ECONOMIC REVIEW (HONGKONG) January 5, 1984, 123:39-40. Describes how Korean women have steadily improved their status over the past several decades.

Change in the system of social power; conditions for the social equality of women. By: Buric, Olivera. In: Changing position of women in family and society: a cross-national comparison. Edited by Eugen Lupri. (Leiden, E. J. Brill, 1983), pp. 311-27.

Changes in Canadian female labour force participation and some possible implications for conjugal power. By: Pool, D. Ian. In: Women in the family and the economy: an international comparative survey. Edited by George Kurian and Ratna Ghosh. (Westport, CT, Greenwood Press, 1981), pp. 245-56.

Changes in the position of Malay women. By: Roose, Hashimah. In: Women in the new Asia; the changing social roles of men and women in South and South-east Asia. Edited by Barbara E. Ward. ([Paris], Unesco, 1963), pp. 287-94.

Changing maternal role of Ghanaian women: impacts of education, migration and employment. By: Oppong, Christine and Abu, Katharine. INTERNATIONAL LABOUR OFFICE. WORLD EMPLOYMENT PROGRAMME RESEARCH. POPULATION AND LABOUR POLICIES PROGRAMME. WORKING PAPER (GENEVA) February 1984, No. 143:1-184.

Changing patterns of an East Pakistan family. By: Karim, A. K. Nazmul. In: Women in the new Asia; the changing social roles of men and women in South and South-east Asia. Edited by Barbara E. Ward. ([Paris], Unesco, 1963), pp. 296-322. Describes the family's rural background in Tipera district (now in Bangladesh) and its subsequent move to Dacca.

Changing patterns of political involvement among Malay village women. By: Rogers, Marvin L. ASIAN SURVEY (BERKELEY, CALIF.) March 1986, 26:322-44.

Changing position of black women in South Africa. By: Steyn, Anna F. and Uys, J. M.. In: Changing position of women in family and society; a cross-national comparison. Edited by Eugen Lupri. Series: International studies in sociology and social anthropology, vol. 34. (Leiden, E. J. Brill, 1983), pp. 344-70.

Changing position of women in family and society; a cross-national comparison. Edited by Eugen Lupri. Series: International studies in sociology and social anthropology, vol. 34. (Leiden, E. J. Brill, 1983), 462 pp.

Changing role of Arab women. By: Zurayk, Huda. POPULATION BULLETIN OF ECWA (BEIRUT) December 1979, No. 17:18-31.

Changing roles for Tonga's women. By: Faletau, Meleseini. PACIFIC PERSPECTIVE (SUVA) 1983, 11, No. 2:45-55.

Changing sex roles in Bedouin society in Syria and Lebanon. By: Chatty, Dawn. In: Women in the Muslim world. Edited by Lois Beck and Nikki Keddie. (Cambridge, MA, Harvard University Press, 1978), pp. 399-415.

Changing sex roles in the Greek family and society. By: Safilios-Rothschild, Constantina and Dijkers, Marcellinus. In: Changing position of women in family and society: an cross-national comparison. Edited by Eugen Lupri. (Leiden, E. J. Brill, 1983), pp. 190-97.

CHANT, SYLVIA

Chant, Sylvia. Household labour and self-help housing in Queretaro, Mexico. BOLETIN DE ESTUDIOS LATINO-AMERICANOS Y DEL CARIBE (AMSTERDAM) December 1984, No. 37:45-68.

CHAPMAN, BRUCE J

Chapman, Bruce J. Sex and location differences in wages in the Australian public service. AUSTRALIAN ECONOMIC PAPERS (ADELAIDE) December 1985, 24:296-309.

CHAPMAN, BRUCE J.

Chapman, Bruce J. and Harding, J. Ross. Sex differences in earnings: an analysis of Malaysian wage data. HARVARD INSTITUTE FOR INTERNATIONAL DEVELOPMENT, DEVELOPMENT DISCUSSION PAPER (CAMBRIDGE, MASS.) December 1980, No. 112:1-24.

CHAPMAN, BRUCE J. AND HARDING, J. ROSS

Chapman, Bruce J. and Harding, J. Ross. Sex differences in earnings: an analysis of Malaysian wage data. JOURNAL OF DEVELOPMENT STUDIES (LONDON) April 1985, 21:362-76.

Characteristics of female employment; implications of research and policy. By: Sundar, Pushpa. ECONOMIC AND POLITICAL WEEKLY (BOMBAY) May 19, 1981, 16:863-71.

CHARLTON, SUE ELLEN M.

Charlton, Sue Ellen M.. Women in Third world development. (Boulder, Colorado, Westview Press, 1984), 240 pp.

CHATTY, DAWN

Chatty, Dawn. Changing sex roles in Bedouin society in Syria and Lebanon. In: Women in the Muslim world. Edited by Lois Beck and Nikki Keddie. (Cambridge, MA, Harvard University Press, 1978), pp. 399-415.

CHAUDHURY, RAFIQUL HUDA

Chaudhury, Rafiqul Huda. Effect of mother's work on child care, dietary intake, and dietary adequacy of pre-school children. BANGLADESH DEVELOPMENT STUDIES (DACCA) December 1982, 10:33-61.

Chaudhury, Rafiqul Huda. Female labour force status and fertility behaviour in Bangladesh: search for policy interventions. BANGLADESH DEVELOPMENT STUDIES (DACCA) September 1983, 11:59-102.

CHAUDHURY, RAFIQUL HUDA

Chaudhury, Rafiqul Huda. Female labour force status and fertility behaviour; some theoretical, methodical and policy issues. PAKISTAN DEVELOPMENT REVIEW (ISLAMABAD) Winter 1979, 18:341-57. An attempt is made to examine the dynamics of the relationship between female labor force status and fertility behavior and also to evaluate the implication of the relationship for reduction of fertility, particularly with reference to the developing countries of the world.

CHEN, LINCOLN C.

Chen, Lincoln C.. Where have the women gone? Insights from Bangladesh on low sex ratio of India's population. ECONOMIC AND POLITICAL WEEKLY (BOMBAY) March 6, 1982, 17:364-72.

CHEN, MARTY

Chen, Marty. Poverty, gender, and work in Bangladesh. ECONOMIC AND POLITICAL WEEKLY (BOMBAY) February 1, 1986, 21:217-22. Redefines the three broad classes of rural households in terms of women's labour and income and describes the process of impoverishment from the perspective of women.

CHIBA, ATSUKO

Chiba, Atsuko. Trappings of success, but an inner emptiness. FAR EASTERN ECONOMIC REVIEW (HONGKONG) January 5, 1984, 123:30-31. The author discusses Japanes women.

La Chicana: Guadalupe or Malinche. By: Gonzales, Sylvia A.. In: Comparative perspectives of Third World women: the impact of race, sex and class. Edited by Beverly Lindsay. (New York, Praeger, 1980), pp. 229-50.

CHIJUMBA, BEAT J.

Chijumba, Beat J.. Attitudes of Tanzanian husbands toward the employment of their wives. AFRICA DEVELOPMENT (DAKAR) April/June 1983, 8:74-85.

CHILD HEALTH

Gopalan, C.. Mother and child in India. ECONOMIC AND POLITICAL WEEKLY (BOMBAY) January 26, 1985, 20:159-66.

Child quantity and quality in a developing country: family background, endogenous tastes, and biological supply factors. ECONOMIC DEVELOPMENT AND CULTURAL CHANGE (CHICAGO) July 1986, 34:703-20. The data are from a cross-sectional area-stratified random sample of about 4,000 women aged 15-45 collected in Nicaragua in 1977-78 as part of a larger study on the socio-economic roles of women in developing countries.

CHILD WELFARE

Chaudhury, Rafiqul Huda. Effect of mother's work on child care, dietary intake, and dietary adequacy of pre-school children. BANGLADESH DEVELOPMENT STUDIES (DACCA) December 1982, 10:33-61.

Childbirth and collaboration among women in Bijnor district, Uttar Pradesh. By: Jeffery, Patricia and Jeffery, Roger. JOURNAL OF SOCIAL STUDIES (DHAKA) July 1984, No. 25:15-33.

Childcare dilemma of working mothers in African cities: the case of Lagos, Nigeria. By: Fapohunda, Eleanor R.. In: Women and work in Africa. Edited by Edna G. Bay. (Boulder, CO, Westview Press, 1982), pp. 277-88.

CHILDREN

Child quantity and quality in a developing country: family background, endogenous tastes, and biological supply factors. ECONOMIC DEVELOPMENT AND CULTURAL CHANGE (CHICAGO) July 1986, 34:703-20. The data are from a cross-sectional area-stratified random sample of about 4,000 women aged 15-45 collected in Nicaragua in 1977-78 as part of a larger study on the socio-economic roles of women in developing countries.

Jayawardena, Kumari. Plantation sector in Sri Lanka: recent changes in the welfare of children and women. WORLD DEVELOPMENT (OXFORD) March 1984, 12, Special issue:317-28.

CHILE

Kirkwood, Julieta. Women and politics in Chile. INTERNATIONAL SOCIAL SCIENCE JOURNAL (PARIS) 1983, 35, No. 4:625-37.

Paredes, Ricardo. Diferencias de ingreso entre hombres y mujeres en el Gran Santiago 1969 y 1981. ESTUDIOS DE ECONOMIA (SANTIAGO) First semester 1982, No. 18:97-121. With English summary.

China pursues peace and development in 1986-1990. By: Mu, Yuan. WOMEN OF CHINA (BEIJING) January 1986, No. 1:24-25.

CHINA, PEO. REP. OF

Courtship, love, and marriage in contemporary China; a symposium. PACIFIC AFFAIRS (VANCOUVER, B.C.) Summer 1984, 57:209-69. CONTENT: Young, Marilyn B., Introduction. - Wolf, Margery, Marriage, family, and the state in contemporary China. - Hershatter, Gail, Making a friend: changing patterns of courtship in urban China. - Honig, Emily, Private issues, public discourse: the life and times of Yu Luojin. - The marriage law of the People's Republic of China.

Dalsimer, Marlyn and Nisonoff, Laurie. New economic readjustment policies: implications for Chinese urban working women. REVIEW OF RADICAL POLITICAL ECONOMICS (NEW YORK) Spring 1984, 16:17-43.

Elementary education for girls. WOMEN OF CHINA (BEIJING) June 1986, No. 6:6-7.

Hao, Keming and Zhou, Yan. Growth of women's education. WOMEN OF CHINA (BEIJING) April 1985, No. 4:2-3.

Honig, Emily. Contract labor system and women workers; pre-liberation cotton mills of Shanghai. MODERN CHINA (BEVERLY HILLS) October 1983, 9:421-54.

Honig, Emily. Socialist revolution and women's liberation in China -- a review article. JOURNAL OF ASIAN STUDIES (ANN ARBOR, MICH.) February 1985, 44:328-36.

Hooper, Beverley. China's modernization; are young women going to lose out? MODERN CHINA (BEVERLY HILLS) July 1984, 10:317-43. Focuses on two areas that are prerequisites to young women having the opportunity to play an equal role in China's economic development: obtaining education, particularly higher education, and securing employment.

Jianhai, Cao. Marriage and family; single women and men in China. WOMEN OF CHINA (BEIJING) November 1984, No. 11:14-15.

Kelkar, Govind. Women in Mao's China. DEVELOPMENT (ROME) 1984, No. 4:55-58. The author recounts the history of the single most important effort to equalize women's position in society, the quest for egalitarianism in Maoist China.

CHINA, PEO. REP. OF

Li, Yuan. Tibet through our eyes (2); education: opening the door to women. WOMEN OF CHINA (BEIJING) August 1985, No. 8:6-7.

McAllister, Elizabeth J. Women in development. WOMEN OF CHINA (BEIJING) October 1986, No. 10:15-19, 25. Paper presented at a training seminar entitled Women in development. Also included: Zhang, Xiaolan, Enlightened by a project. -- Sun Huilan, Women academics serve rural sisters.

Ming, Xiao. Women in rural economic reform. WOMEN OF CHINA (BEIJING) May 1986, No. 5:3-7.

Ming, Xiao. Women in the special economic zones and open cities (4); a visit to Zhanjiang. WOMEN OF CHINA (BEIJING) January 1986, No. 1:15-18.

Mu, Yuan. China pursues peace and development in 1986-1990. WOMEN OF CHINA (BEIJING) January 1986, No. 1:24-25.

Robinson, Jean C.. Of women and washing machines: employment, housework, and the reproduction of motherhood in socialist China. CHINA QUARTERLY (LONDON) March 1985, No. 101:32-57.

Sun, Mary. Traditional role rules, exceptions are striking. FAR EASTERN ECONOMIC REVIEW (HONGKONG) January 5, 1984, 123:27-28. Discusses the situation of women in China.

Women in the workforce. WOMEN OF CHINA (BEIJING) March 1986, No. 3:13-15.

Wu, Wei. Going to the society. WOMEN OF CHINA (BEIJING) April 1985, No. 4:17-18.

Zhong, Fu. Comrade Mao Zedong's investigations of women's conditions in the countryside. WOMEN OF CHINA (BEIJING) December 1983, No. 12:4-6.

China's modernization; are young women going to lose out? By: Hooper, Beverley. MODERN CHINA (BEVERLY HILLS) July 1984, 10:317-43. Focuses on two areas that are prerequisites to young women having the opportunity to play an equal role in China's economic development: obtaining education, particularly higher education, and securing employment.

Chinese women: the relative influences of ideological revolution, economic growth, and cultural change. By: Wang, Bee-Lan Chan. In: Comparative perspectives of Third World women: the impact of race, sex and class. Edited by Beverly Lindsay. (New York, Praeger, 1980), pp. 96-122.

Chinese women of Singapore: their present status in the family and in marriage. By: Wee, Ann E.. In: Women in the new Asia; the changing social roles of men and women in South and South-east Asia. Edited by Barbara E. Ward. ([Paris], Unesco, 1963), pp. 376-409.

CHIRA, SUSAN

Chira, Susan. Tough ascent for Japanese women. NEW YORK TIMES (NEW YORK) February 24, 1985, Section 3, p. 1-27. Equal employment opportunities for women in Japan remain scarce and male-dominated industries resist women's attempts to change traditional ways.

CHO, UHN

Cho, Uhn and Koo, Hagen. Economic development and women's work in a newly industrializing country: the case of Korea. DEVELOPMENT AND CHANGE (THE HAGUE, etc.) October 1983, 14:515-31. The authors investigate how women's economic activities have changed in relation to the pattern of economic growth in Korea in the past two decades.

Choco woman: agent for change. By: Nimnicht, Marta Arango de. In: Latin American women: the meek speak out. Edited by June H. Turner. (Silver Spring, MD, International Educational Development, 1980), pp. 89-100. Discusses women in Colombia.

CHOPP-TIBON, SHIRA

Shapira, Rina and Etzioni-Halevy, Eva and Chopp-Tibon, Shira. Occupational choice among female academicians -- the Israeli case. In: Women in the family and the economy: an international comparative survey. Edited by George Kurian and Ratna Ghosh. (Westport, CT, Greenwood Press, 1981), pp. 345-58.

CHOUDHURY, S.

Choudhury, S. and Giri, A. K. Nature and extent of female labour use in agriculture - a comparison between progressive and non-progressive area. ECONOMIC AFFAIRS (CALCUTTA) June 1986, 31:81-86.

CHURCH, KATIE

Oppong, Christine and Church, Katie. Field guide to research on seven roles of women: focussed biographies. INTERNATIONAL LABOUR OFFICE. WORLD EMPLOYMENT PROGRAMME RESEARCH. POPULATION AND LABOUR POLICIES PROGRAMME. WORKING PAPER (GENEVA) May 1981, No. 106:1-52.

CLARK, MARI H.

Clark, Mari H.. Household economic strategies and support networks of the poor in Kenya: a literature survey. Series: Discussion Paper; Report No.: UDD-69, Water Supply and Urban Development Dept., Operations Policy Staff, World Bank. (Washington, DC, World Bank, 1985), 117 pp.

Class and gender on the copperbelt: women in Northern Rhodesian copper mining areas 1926-1964. By: Parpart, Jane L.. BOSTON UNIVERSITY. AFRICAN STUDIES CENTER. WORKING PAPERS (BOSTON) 1983, No. 77:1-29.

Class, commodity, and the status of women. By: Leacock, Eleanor. In: Women cross-culturally: change and challenge. Edited by Ruby Rohrlich-Leavitt. (The Hague, Mouton, 1975), pp. 601-16.

COHN, STEVEN

Cohn, Steven and Wood, Robert. U.S. aid and Third World women: the impact of Peace Corps programs. ECONOMIC DEVELOPMENT AND CULTURAL CHANGE (CHICAGO) July 1981, 29:795-811.

COLE, BERNADETTE

Cole, Bernadette. Where to get a loan. WEST AFRICA (LONDON) November 10, 1986, No. 3610:p. 2362. Reports on Women's World Banking (WWB), an independent financial organisation set up to advance and promote entrepreneurship among women within their local economies.

Cole, Bernadette. UN women's decade; preparing the way. WEST AFRICA (LONDON) October 29, 1984, No. 3506:2165-66. Reports from Tanzania on the African regional preparatory meeting which will constitute the 'African position' at the UN End of Women's Decade Conference.

COLE, JOHNNETTA B.

Cole, Johnnetta B.. Women in Cuba: the revolution within the revolution. In: Comparative perspectives of Third World women: the impact of race, sex and class. Edited by Beverly Lindsay. (New York, Praeger, 1980), pp. 162-78.

COLFER, CAROL

Colfer, Carol. On circular migration -- from the distaff side: women left behind in the forests of East Kalimantan. INTERNATIONAL LABOUR OFFICE. WORLD EMPLOYMENT PROGRAMME RESEARCH. POPULATION AND LABOUR POLICIES PROGRAMME. WORKING PAPER (GENEVA) May 1983, No. 132:1-42. Focuses on male circular migration (or migration with the in;tent to return home) and its impact on the women who remain in the villages tending the farm. The area studied is East Kalimantan (Indonesian Borneo).

COLLECTIVE FARMS

Pelzer White, Christine. Collectives and the status of women: the Vietnamese experience. CERES, FAO REVIEW ON AGRICULTURE AND DEVELOPMENT (ROME) July/August 1983, 16:22-26.

Collectivization, kinship, and the status of women in rural China. By: Diamond, Norma. In: Toward an anthropology of women. Edited by Rayna R. Reiter. (New York, Monthly Review Press, 1975), pp. 372-95.

COLOMBIA

Bonilla de Ramos, Elssy. La madre trabajadora. UNIVERSIDAD DE LOS ANDES. CENTRO DE ESTUDIOS SOBRE DESARROLLO ECONOMICO. DOCUMENTO (BOGOTA) September 1981, No. 66:1-139.

Bonilla de Ramos, Elssy. La madre trabajadora: una contradiccion. DESARROLLO Y SOCIEDAD (BOGOTA) September 1982, No. 9:67-84.

Bonilla de Ramos, Elssy. La mujer y su imagen en los medios. UNIVERSIDAD DE LOS ANDES. CENTRO DE ESTUDIOS SOBRE DESARROLLO ECONOMICO. DOCUMENTO (BOGOTA) Arpil 1981, No. 64:1-183.

Castaneda, Tarsicio. Los determinantes de la participacion de la mujer casada en el mercado de trabajo urbano en Colombia. ESTUDIOS DE ECONOMIA (SANTIAGO) Second semester 1981, No. 17:111-34. With English summary.

Rey De Marulanda, Nohra. Las mujeres jefes de hogar. UNIVERSIDAD DE LOS ANDES. CENTRO DE ESTUDIOS SOBRE DESARROLLO ECONOMICO. DOCUMENTO (BOGOTA) September 1982, No. 68:1-66.

COLOMBINO, UGO

Colombino, Ugo. Variabili dipendenti limitate e selezione non casuale delle osservazioni: una applicazione alla stima della funzione di salario e di offerta di lavoro delle donne sposate in Italia. GIORNALE DEGLI ECONOMISTI E ANNALI DI ECONOMIA (MILAN) May/June 1983, 42, N.S.:369-85. With English summary, p. 388.

Colonialism, education, and work: sex differentiation in colonial Zaire. By: Yates, Barbara A.. In: Women and work in Africa. Edited by Edna G. Bay. (Boulder, CO, Westview Press, 1982), pp. 127-52.

Combining marriage and career in Karachi. By: Gani, Amna. In: Women in the new Asia; the changing social roles of men and women in South and South-east Asia. Edited by Barbara E. Ward. ([Paris], Unesco, 1963), pp. 323-39.

Comite de teinturerie dans un quartier de Kinshasa (Zaire). By: Grilly, Catherine. TIERS-MONDE (PARIS) April/June 1985, 26:429-34.

Community characteristics, women's education, and fertility in Peru. By: Tienda, Marta. STUDIES IN FAMILY PLANNING (NEW YORK) July/August 1984, 15:162-69.

COMMUNITY DEVELOPMENT

Jain, Devaki and Singh, Nalini. Role of rural women in community life; a case study from India. ECONOMIC BULLETIN FOR ASIA AND THE PACIFIC (BANGKOK) December 1978, 29:84-126.

Community education training centre (CETC). By: Sue, Mee Kwain. PACIFIC PERSPECTIVE (SUVA) 1983, 11, No. 2:62-4. Describes a regional center established in 1963 to provide a programme of community education for women.

Community forestry depends on women. By: Hoskings, Marilyn W.. UNASYLVA (ROME) 1980, 32, No. 130:27-32.

COMMUNITY PARTICIPATION

van Wijk-Sijbesma, Christine. Helping women to help themselves. WATERLINES (LONDON) April 1986, 4:29-31. Suggests that women's programmes and organizations have great potential to mobilize women to improve their own water supply and sanitation if they are not served by other programmes.

Community response to a pilot farming project in Nigeria. By: Okali, C. and Cassaday, K.. BOSTON UNIVERSITY. AFRICAN-AMERICAN ISSUES CENTER. DISCUSSION PAPER (BOSTON) [1985], No. 10:1-28. The authors report on a preliminary study of farmers' response to alley farming, a technology designed to improve small ruminant (sheep and goat) and arable crop production in the humid zone of West Africa.

Comparative perspective on women in provenicial Iran and Turkey. By: Good, Mary-Jo DelVecchio. In: Women in the Muslim world. Edited by Lois Beck and Nikki Keddie. (Cambridge, MA, Harvard University Press, 1978), pp. 482-500.

Comparison of economic models and empirical results for female labor force participation in Japan and the United State. By: Hill, M. Anne. YALE UNIVERSITY. ECONOMIC GROWTH CENTER. DISCUSSION PAPER (NEW HAVEN, CONN.) July 1982, No. 415:1-36.

Compiling social indicators on the situation of women. Series: Studies in methods. Series F, No. 32. (New York, United Nations, 1984), 94 pp. Documents, ST/ESA/STAT/SER.F/32. Prepared as part of a joint project of the Statistical Office of the United Nations Secretariat and the United Nations International Research and Training Institute for the Advancement of Women.

Comrade Mao Zedong's investigations of women's conditions in the countryside. By: Zhong, Fu. WOMEN OF CHINA (BEIJING) December 1983, No. 12:4-6.

CONABLE, BARBER B.

Conable, Barber B.. Address to the Board of Governors of the World Bank and International Finance Corporation. (Washington, World Bank, September 30, 1986), 11 pp.

Conditions required for women to conduct research on women in the Arab region. By: Oussedik, Fatma. In: Social science research on women in the Arab world. (London, Frances Pinter; Paris, Unesco, 1984), pp. 113-21.

La conference mondiale des femmes et la femme africaine. By: Kratz, Achim. MOIS EN AFRIQUE (PARIS) April/May 1986, 21:160-66.

Confronting the male bias in research priorities. By: Mascarenhas, Ophelia. CERES, FAO REVIEW ON AGRICULTURE AND DEVELOPMENT (ROME) May/June 1985, 18:28-32. Suggests that agricultural research in most formerly colonial countries has two characteristics: the overemphasis of cash crops and the tendency to ignore women in the planning, development, and implementation of such research.

CONKLIN, GEORGE H.

Conklin, George H.. Cultural determinants of power for women within the family: a neglected aspect of family research. In: Women in the family and the economy: an international comparative survey. Edited by George Kurian and Ratna Ghosh. (Westport, CT, Greenwood Press, 1981), pp. 9-27.

CONSEIL NATIONAL DU GHANA

Conseil national du Ghana. Groupements a but economique de femmes solidaires; l'experience du Ghana. TIERS-MONDE (PARIS) April/June 1985, 26:451-56.

Les consequences de l'introduction d'une culture de rente et d'une culture attelee sur la position de la femme wolof a Saloum. By: Venema, Bernhard. TIERS-MONDE (PARIS) July/September 1982, 23:603-16.

Constraints on the organization of women industrial workers. By: Blake, Myrna. In: Women in the urban and industrial workforce; Southeast and East Asia. Edited by Gavin W. Jones. Series: Development Studies Centre. Monograph, No. 33. (Canberra, Australia, Australian National University, 1984), pp. 149-62. Series edited by Helen Hughes.

Constraints to women and development in Africa. By: Due, Jean M. and Summary, Rebecca. JOURNAL OF MODERN AFRICAN STUDIES (OXFORD) March 1982, 20:155-66.

Contract labor system and women workers; pre-liberation cotton mills of Shanghai. By: Honig, Emily. MODERN CHINA (BEVERLY HILLS) October 1983, 9:421-54.

Contributions of women in the labor force to economic development in Taiwan, the Republic of China. By: Li, K. T. INDUSTRY OF FREE CHINA (TAIPEI) August 25, 1985, 64:1-8.

Control of land, labor, and capital in rural southern Sierra Leone. By: MacCormack, Carol P.. In: Women and work in Africa. Edited by Edna G. Bay. (Boulder, CO, Westview Press, 1982), pp. 35-53.

COOKSEY, BRIAN

Cooksey, Brian. Education and sexual inequality in Cameroun. JOURNAL OF MODERN AFRICAN STUDIES (OXFORD) March 1982, 20:167-77.

COOPERATIVE AGRICULTURE

Deere, Carmen Diana. Developpement cooperatif et participation feminine a la reforme agraire nicaraguayenne. TIERS-MONDE (PARIS) April/June 1985, 26:403-08.

COOPERATIVES

Bisilliat, Jeanne. La participation des femmes aux cooperatives mixtes: temps et ideologie. TIERS-MONDE (PARIS) April/June 1985, 26:409-15.

Caughman, Susan. Women at work in Mali: the case of the Markala cooperative. BOSTON UNIVERSITY. AFRICAN STUDIES CENTER. WORKING PAPERS (BOSTON) 1981, No. 50:1-35.

Halatuituia, Lasale and Latu, Sela N.. Women's co-operatives in Tonga. PACIFIC PERSPECTIVE (SUVA) 1983, 11, No. 2:13-17.

Hurwitch-MacDonald, Jan. La incorporacion femenina a las empresas asociativas. DESARROLLO RURAL EN LAS AMERICAS (SAN JOSE) January/June 1983, 15:55-64.

Mavrogiannis, Dionysos. La place des femmes au sein des societes et groupements cooperatifs (enquetes du BIT). TIERS-MONDE (PARIS) April/June 1985, 26:383-92.

COPPER INDUSTRY

Parpart, Jane L.. Class and gender on the copperbelt: women in Northern Rhodesian copper mining areas 1926-1964. BOSTON UNIVERSITY. AFRICAN STUDIES CENTER. WORKING PAPERS (BOSTON) 1983, No. 77:1-29.

CORRIHER, KURT

Berger, Brigitte and Corriher, Kurt. Underground women of the Third world. WALL STREET JOURNAL (NEW YORK) July 26, 1985, p. 20. Authors state that in addition to their role in production and marketing, women are acquiring vital leadership skills because informal institutions are springing up to accompany informal economies.

COSAR, FATMA MANSUR

Cosar, Fatma Mansur. Women in Turkish society. In: Women in the Muslim world. Edited by Lois Beck and Nikki Keddie. (Cambridge, MA, Harvard University Press, 1978), pp. 124-40.

Cost of development projects; women among the 'willing evacuees'. By: Rao, Amiya. ECONOMIC AND POLITICAL WEEKLY (BOMBAY) March 22, 1986, 21:474-76. Describes the heavy price of development paid by India's women.

COSTA RICA

Guzman Stein, Laura. La industria de la maquila y la explotacion de la fuerza de trabajo de la mujer: el caso de Costa Rica. DESARROLLO Y SOCIEDAD (BOGOTA) January 1984, No. 13:161-76. With English summary.

Muller-Blattau, Beate and Seibert, Ulrike. Funf Frauen - funf Leben. E & Z, ENTWICKLUNG UND ZUSAMMENARBEIT (BONN) January 1985, 26:16-17.

COTTER, JIM

Cotter, Jim. Women and water: two UN Decades share goals. HORIZONS, U.S. AGENCY FOR INTERNATIONAL DEVELOPMENT (WASHINGTON) Winter 1985, 4:14-15.

COULSON, NOEL

Coulson, Noel and Hinchcliffe, Doreen. Women and law reform in contemporary Islam. In: Women in the Muslim world. Edited by Lois Beck and Nikki Keddie. (Cambridge, MA, Harvard University Press, 1978), pp. 37-51.

Courtship, love, and marriage in contemporary China; a symposium. PACIFIC AFFAIRS (VANCOUVER, B.C.) Summer 1984, 57:209-69. CONTENT: Young, Marilyn B., Introduction. - Wolf, Margery, Marriage, family, and the state in contemporary China. - Hershatter, Gail, Making a friend: changing patterns of courtship in urban China. - Honig, Emily, Private issues, public discourse: the life and times of Yu Luojin. - The marriage law of the People's Republic of China.

Craftswomen in Kerdassa, Egypt. Household production and reproduction. By: Lynch, Patricia D. and Fahmy, Hoda. Series: Women, work and development, No. 7. (Geneva, International Labour Office, 1984), 91 pp. Undertaken under the auspices of the Center for Egyptian Civilisation Studies and with the financial support of the United Nations Fund for Population Activities (UNFPA).

CREDIT

Barres, Victoria. Deux programmes de credit bien adaptes aux besoins des femmes du Tiers monde. TIERS-MONDE (PARIS) April/June 1985, 26:435-42. Cet article presente deux programmes de credits d'investissement destines a des femmes pauvres du Tiers Monde, l'un en milieu urbain (Madras, Inde) et l'autre en milieu rural (pays yoruba, Nigeria).

Krishnaswami, Lalita. From drudgery to dignity: the SEWA experience. LABOUR AND SOCIETY (GENEVA) September 1985, 10:323-31. Discusses the achievements of the Self-Employed Women's Association (SEWA), which is at once a union, a trust and a credit institution whose basic aim is to provide better living and working conditions for the poor, illiterate women who comprise its membership.

CREHAN, KATE

Crehan, Kate. Women and development in north western Zambia: from producer to housewife. REVIEW OF AFRICAN POLITICAL ECONOMY (SHEFFIELD) 1984, No. 27/28:51-66.

Critical analysis of Latin American programs to integrate women in development. By: Figueroa, Teresa Orrego de. In: Women and world development. Edited by Irene Tinker and Michele Bo Bramsen. ([Washington, DC], Overseas Development Council, 1976), pp. 45-54.

CROCOMBE, MARJORIE TUAINEKORE

Crocombe, Marjorie Tuainekore. Women at the University of the South Pacific. PACIFIC PERSPECTIVE (SUVA) 1983, 11, No. 2:24-8.

CROPPING SYSTEMS

Okali, C. and Cassaday, K.. Community response to a pilot farming project in Nigeria. BOSTON UNIVERSITY. AFRICAN-AMERICAN ISSUES CENTER. DISCUSSION PAPER (BOSTON) [1985], No. 10:1-28. The authors report on a preliminary study of farmers' response to alley farming, a technology designed to improve small ruminant (sheep and goat) and arable crop production in the humid zone of West Africa.

CROPS

Gupta, R. P. and Tewari, S. K. Factors affecting crop diversification: an empirical analysis. INDIAN JOURNAL OF AGRICULTURAL ECONOMICS (BOMBAY) July/September 1985, 40:304-09.

CUBA

Farnos, Alfonso and Gonzalez, Fernando. Role of women and demographic change in Cuba. INTERNATIONAL LABOUR OFFICE. WORLD EMPLOYMENT PROGRAMME RESEARCH. POPULATION AND LABOUR POLICIES PROGRAMME. WORKING PAPER (GENEVA) August 1983, No. 138:1-52.

Cultural determinants of power for women within the family: a neglected aspect of family research. By: Conklin, George H.. In: Women in the family and the economy: an international comparative survey. Edited by George Kurian and Ratna Ghosh. (Westport, CT, Greenwood Press, 1981), pp. 9-27.

CULTURE

LaDuke, Betty. Women, art, and culture in the new Grenada. LATIN AMERICAN PERSPECTIVES (BEVERLY HILLS) Summer 1984, 11:37-52.

Cultuur als camouflage: Westerse weerstanden tegen vrouwen als ontwikkelingsrelevant onderwerp. By: Schrijvers, Joke. INTERNATIONALE SPECTATOR (THE HAGUE) September 1983, 37:556-62.

CYPRUS

House, William J.. Occupational segregation and discriminatory pay: the position of women in the Cyprus labour market. INTERNATIONAL LABOUR REVIEW (GENEVA) January/February 1983, 122:75-93.

D'AMICO, RONALD J

Maxwell, Nan L. and D'Amico, Ronald J. Employment and wage effects of involuntary job separation: male-female differences. AMERICAN ECONOMIC REVIEW, PAPERS AND PROCEEDINGS (NASHVILLE) May 1986, 76:373-77.

DABAT, CHRISTINE

Dabat, Christine and Modak, Marianne. Femmes et controle des naissances; refus, contraintes et vecus. INSTITUT UNIVERSITAIRE D'ETUDES DU DEVELOPPEMENT. ITINERAIRES: NOTES ET TRAVAUX (GENEVA) April 1981, No. 15:1-119.

DAHHAN, OMAYMAH

Dahhan, Omaymah. Examination of the literature on Jordanian women. INTERNATIONAL LABOUR OFFICE. WORLD EMPLOYMENT PROGRAMME RESEARCH. POPULATION AND LABOUR POLICIES: REGIONAL PROGRAMME FOR THE MIDDLE EAST. WORKING PAPER (BEIRUT) March 1981, No. 8:1-146.

DAIRY INDUSTRY

Thorve, P. V. and Galgalikar, V. D. Economics of diversification of farming with dairy enterprise. INDIAN JOURNAL OF AGRICULTURAL ECONOMICS (BOMBAY) July/September 1985, 40:317-23.

Dakar declaration on Another development with women. DEVELOPMENT DIALOGUE (UPPSALA) 1982, No. 1/2:11-16. Consensus reached at the seminar "Another development with women," held in Dakar, Senegal, June 21-25, 1982, jointly organized by the Association of African Women for Research and Development (AAWORD/AFARD) and the Dag Hammarskjold Foundation.

DALSIMER, MARLYN

Dalsimer, Marlyn and Nisonoff, Laurie. New economic readjustment policies: implications for Chinese urban working women. REVIEW OF RADICAL POLITICAL ECONOMICS (NEW YORK) Spring 1984, 16:17-43.

DANDEKAR, HEMALATA C.

Dandekar, Hemalata C.. Impact of Bombay's textile industry on work of women from Sugao village. THIRD WORLD PLANNING REVIEW (LIVERPOOL) November 1983, 5:371-82.

DANDEKAR, KUMUDINI

Dandekar, Kumudini. Employment guarantee scheme: an employment opportunity for women. Series: Gokhale Institute Studies, No. 67. (Pune, Gokhale Institute of Politics and Economics, 1983), 76 pp.

DANFORTH, SANDRA

Danforth, Sandra. Muslim Middle Eastern women's participation in violent political conflict: causes and characteristics. STUDIES IN THIRD WORLD SOCIETIES (WILLIAMSBURG) June 1981, No. 16:49-68.

DATE-BAH, EUGENIA

Date-Bah, Eugenia and Stevens, Yvette. Rural women in Africa and technological change: some issues. LABOUR AND SOCIETY (GENEVA) April/June 1981, 6:149-62.

Daughters of the nightmare: Caribbean women. Series: Change International Reports: Women and Society, No. 9. (London, Change International Reports, [1982?]), 18 pp.

DAVIES, MIRANDA

Davies, Miranda. Women in struggle. THIRD WORLD QUARTERLY (LONDON) October 1983, 5:874-914. CONTENT: Davies, Miranda, An overview. - Sayigh, Rosemary, Palestine. - Unterhalter, Elaine, South Africa. - Silkin, Trish, Eritrea.

DAVIES, WENDY

Davies, Wendy. Slow progress on women's health. NEW AFRICAN (LONDON) August 1985, No. 215:p. 42.

DAVIN, DELIA

Davin, Delia. Women's movement in the People's Republic of China: a study. In: Women cross-culturally: change and challenge. Edited by Ruby Rohrlich-Leavitt. (The Hague, Mouton, 1975), pp. 459-69.

DAVIS, NIRA YUVAL

Davis, Nira Yuval. Israeli women and men: divisions behind the unity. Series: Change International Reports: Women and Society, No. 6. (London, Change International Reports, [1983?]), 27 pp.

DAVIS, SUSAN SCHAEFER

Davis, Susan Schaefer. Working women in a Moroccan village. In: Women in the Muslim world. Edited by Lois Beck and Nikki Keddie. (Cambridge, MA, Harvard University Press, 1978), pp. 416-33.

DE BRITO, ANGELA NEVES-XAVIER

de Brito, Angela Neves-Xavier. Brazilian women in exile; the quest for an identity. LATIN AMERICAN PERSPECTIVES (BEVERLY HILLS) Spring 1986, 13:58-80.

DE SENARCLENS, MARINA

de Senarclens, Marina. Le role de la femme dans la vie economique et sociale. REVUE ECONOMIQUE ET SOCIALE (LAUSANNE) December 1979, 37:200-09.

DE VRIES, MARGARET G.

de Vries, Margaret G.. Women, jobs, and development. FINANCE AND DEVELOPMENT (WASHINGTON) December 1971, 8:4:2-9. Discusses the employment of women in developing countries in the light of recent changes in emphasis on the strategy and objectives of economic development. Also published in French, German, Portuguese, and Spanish.

DEBLE, ISABELLE

Deble, Isabelle. La deuxieme strategie de l'UNESCO a l'egard des femmes. TIERS-MONDE (PARIS) April/June 1985, 26:283-97.

UN Decade for Women conference held in Nairobi. UNITED STATES. DEPARTMENT OF STATE. BULLETIN (WASHINGTON) February 1986, 86:89-92. Contains statements by Maureen Reagan, head of the U.S. delegation, in a plenary session of the conference on July 16 and in UN General Assembly Committee III on November 5.

UN decade for women; 'for, by, about women'. WEST AFRICA (LONDON) July 29, 1985, No. 3544:1542-43. Reports on the Nairobi End of Decade conference.

Decently paid employment -- not more drudgery. By: Ahmad, Zubeida and Loufti, Martha. CERES, FAO REVIEW ON AGRICULTURE AND DEVELOPMENT (ROME) July/August 1983, 16:40-46. The authors conclude that there is an urgent need for improved living and working conditions for many poor rural women.

DECISION-MAKING

Biryukova, Alexandra. Role of the Soviet woman in decision-making in trade union committees and in industry. LABOUR AND SOCIETY (GENEVA) September 1985, 10:307-21.

DEERE, CARMEN DIANA

Deere, Carmen Diana. Developpement cooperatif et participation feminine a la reforme agraire nicaraguayenne. TIERS-MONDE (PARIS) April/June 1985, 26:403-08.

Deere, Carmen Diana. Division of labor by sex in agriculture; a Peruvian case study. ECONOMIC DEVELOPMENT AND CULTURAL CHANGE (CHICAGO) July 1982, 30:795-811.

Deere, Carmen Diana. Rural women and state policy: the Latin American agrarian reform experience. WORLD DEVELOPMENT (OXFORD) September 1985, 13:1037-53.

Demands of work and the human quality of marriage: an exploratory study of professionals in two socialist societies. By: Rueschemeyer, Marilyn. In: Women in the family and the economy: an international comparative survey. Edited by George Kurian and Ratna Ghosh. (Westport, CT, Greenwood Press, 1981), pp. 331-43. Countries discussed in this chapter are the Soviet Union and East Germany.

DEMMER, HILDEGARD

> Demmer, Hildegard and Kupper, Bettina. Arbeitsbelastungen von Frauen im Paketdienst. WSI-MITTEILUNGEN (DUSSELDORF) August 1986, 39:522-28.

DENGLER, IAN C.

> Dengler, Ian C.. Turkish women in the Ottoman Empire: the classical age. In: Women in the Muslim world. Edited by Lois Beck and Nikki Keddie. (Cambridge, MA, Harvard University Press, 1978), pp. 229-44.

DENNIS, CAROLYNE

> Dennis, Carolyne. Capitalist development and women's work: a Nigerian case study. REVIEW OF AFRICAN POLITICAL ECONOMY (SHEFFIELD) 1984, No. 27/28:109-19.

Dependence and autonomy: the economic activities of secluded Hausa women in Kano, Nigeria. By: Schildkrout, Enid. In: Women and work in Africa. Edited by Edna G. Bay. (Boulder, CO, Westview Press, 1982), pp. 55-81.

Desarrollo dependiente y la segregacion ocupacional por sexo. By: Scott, Alison MacEwen. DESARROLLO Y SOCIEDAD (BOGOTA) January 1984, No. 13:99-136. With English summary.

DESERAN, FORREST A

> Acock, Alan C. and Deseran, Forrest A. Off-farm employment by women and marital instability. RURAL SOCIOLOGY (PROVO, UTAH) Fall 1986, 51:314-27. The impact of farm women's paid work experience on the quality and stability of their marriages is examined in the context of two competing frameworks - status competition and status enhancement.

Desexing decision styles. By: Rowe, Alan J. and Bennis, Warren. PERSONNEL (SARANAC LAKE, N.Y.) January/February 1984, 61:43-52. The authors attempt to determine why women are thought of as being different from men in terms of their ability to perform effectively in management positions.

Los determinantes de la participacion de la mujer casada en el mercado de trabajo urbano en Colombia. By: Castaneda, Tarsicio. ESTUDIOS DE ECONOMIA (SANTIAGO) Second semester 1981, No. 17:111-34. With English summary.

Determinants of child health, mortality, and nutrition in a developing country. By: Wolfe, Barbara L. and Behrman, Jere R.. UNIVERSITY OF WISCONSIN-MADISON. INSTITUTE FOR RESEARCH ON POVERTY. DISCUSSION PAPERS (MADISON) January 1981, No. 643-80:1-53. The authors use data collected in a cross-sectional multipurpose survey of women of childbearing age in Nicaragua.

Determinants of female age at marriage in rural Uttar Pradesh. By: Srivastava, J. N.. INDIAN JOURNAL OF ECONOMICS (ALLAHABAD) January 1984, 64:327-44.

Determinants of female employment. By: Eyland, E.A. and Mason, C.A.. ECONOMIC RECORD (MELBOURNE) March 1982, 58:11-17.

Determinants of female labor-force participation. By: Nishikawa, Shunsaku and Higuchi, Yoshio. JAPANESE ECONOMIC STUDIES (ARMONK, N.Y.) Winter 1980/1981, 9:62-87.

Determinants of labour earnings in developing metropoli: estimates from Bogota and Cali, Colombia. By: Mohan, Rakesh. Series: World Bank Staff Working Papers, No. 498. (Washington, DC, World Bank, 1981), 135 pp.

Determinants of labour force participation of urban women in Nigeria: a case study of Benin City. By: Okojie, Christiana E. E.. NIGERIAN JOURNAL OF ECONOMIC AND SOCIAL STUDIES (IBADAN) March 1983, 25:39-59.

Determinants of women's roles and status. By: Smock, Audrey Chapman. In: Women: roles and status in eight countries. Edited by Janet Zollinger Giele and Audrey Chapman Smock. (New York, John Wiley, 1977), pp. 385-421.

Deux programmes de credit bien adaptes aux besoins des femmes du Tiers monde. By: Barres, Victoria. TIERS-MONDE (PARIS) April/June 1985, 26:435-42. Cet article presente deux programmes de credits d'investissement destines a des femmes pauvres du Tiers Monde, l'un en milieu urbain (Madras, Inde) et l'autre en milieu rural (pays yoruba, Nigeria).

La deuxieme strategie de l'UNESCO a l'egard des femmes. By: Deble, Isabelle. TIERS-MONDE (PARIS) April/June 1985, 26:283-97.

DEVELOPING COUNTRIES

> Dwyser, Daisy Hilse. Women and income in the Third world: implications for policy. POPULATION COUNCIL. INTERNATIONAL PROGRAMS. WORKING PAPERS (NEW YORK) June 1983, No. 18:1-39.

DEVELOPING COUNTRIES

Entwicklungshilfe - Fluch oder Segen fur die Frauen? E & Z, ENTWICKLUNG UND ZUSAMMENARBEIT (BONN) January 1985, 26:4-21.

Fischer, Wolfgang E.. Entwicklungshilfe: Fluch oder Segen fur die Frauen? Die bedeutende Rolle der Frauen wird bei der Projektplanung nicht angemessen berucksichtigt. E & Z, ENTWICKLUNG UND ZUSAMMENARBEIT (BONN) January 1985, 26:6-7.

Kvinder, konsrelationer og social forandring. DEN NY VERDEN (COPENHAGEN) 1983, 17, No.4:1-124. Content: Wilson, Fiona, Kvinder og kommercialisering af landbruget: en diskussion af aktuelle tendenser i Mexico. - Odgaard, Rie, and Jens Dahl, Gronlandske bygdekvinder i en okonomisk forandringsproces. - Roberts, Pepe, Kvinder i landomraderne i Vestnigeria. - Thorbek, Susanne, Refleksioner fra en Bangkok slum. - Tarp, Elsebeth, Kvindekamp og kulturkamp i Mexico. - Sjorslev, Inger, Rituel magt og social undertrykkelse; kvinder i Brasilien.

Samman, Mouna Liliane. Activite economique des femmes du Tiers monde et perspectives de baisse de leur fecondite. TIERS-MONDE (PARIS) April/June 1983, 24:367-76.

Developing income generating opportunity for rural women. By: Lewis, Martha. HORIZONS, U.S. AGENCY FOR INTERNATIONAL DEVELOPMENT (WASHINGTON) January 1983, 2:28-31. Describes how bananas, solar-dried and marketed as banana-figs, promise to boost Jamaican farm women's earnings.

Developing labor resources in the Arab world: labor activity effects from school attendance and socioeconomic background among women in the East Jordan valley. By: Stuart, Madeleine Fisher. (University of Southern California, 1981), 536 pp. Thesis (Ph.D.) -- University of Southern California, 1981.

Development as if women mattered: an annotated bibliography with a Third world focus. Compiled by May Rihani and Jody Joy. Series: Overseas Development Council, Washington D.C. Occasional Paper Series, No. 10. (Washington, 1978), 137 pp. Prepared under the auspices of the Secretariat for Women in Development of the New TransCentury Foundation.

Development of educated women in India: reflections of a social psychologist. By: Singhal, Sushila. COMPARATIVE EDUCATION (OXFORD) October 1984, 20:355-70.

Development of women entrepreneurship in India -- problems and prospects. By: Heggade, O. D.. ECONOMIC AFFAIRS (CALCUTTA) January/March 1981, 26:39-50.

Development planning in an oil economy and the role of the woman: the case of Kuwait. By: Al-Sabah, S. M.. (London, Eastlords Publishing, 1983), 380 pp.

Developpement cooperatif et participation feminine a la reforme agraire nicaraguayenne. By: Deere, Carmen Diana . TIERS-MONDE (PARIS) April/June 1985, 26:403-08.

DEVI, D. RADHA AND RAVINDRAN, M.

Devi, D. Radha and Ravindran, M.. Women's work in India. INTERNATIONAL SOCIAL SCIENCE JOURNAL (PARIS) 1983, 35, No. 4:683-701.

DEVON, TONIA K.

Devon, Tonia K.. Up from the harem? The effects of class and sex on political life in northern India. In: Comparative perspectives of Third World women: the impact of race, sex and class. Edited by Beverly Lindsay. (New York, Praeger, 1980), pp. 123-42.

DEWAN, RITU

Sawant, S. D. and Dewan, Ritu. Rural female labour and economic development. ECONOMIC AND POLITICAL WEEKLY (BOMBAY) June 30, 1979, 14:1091-99. This paper, based on a study of a sample of 150 villages in two talukas of Thane district in Maharashtra, attempts to examine the impact of economic development on rural women, particularly on their employment.

DEY, JENNIE

Dey, Jennie. Women in African rice farming systems. FOOD AND AGRICULTURE ORGANIZATION OF THE UNITED NATIONS. INTERNATIONAL RICE COMMISSION NEWSLETTER (ROME) December 1983, 32:1-4.

Diamond in the rough. By: Isralow, Sharon. HORIZONS, U.S. AGENCY FOR INTERNATIONAL DEVELOPMENT (WASHINGTON) Summer 1985, 4:34-37. Examines the achievements of the women and men of Sri Lanka's Kirillapone shanty town.

DIAMOND, NORMA

Diamond, Norma. Collectivization, kinship, and the status of women in rural China. In: Toward an anthropology of women. Edited by Rayna R. Reiter. (New York, Monthly Review Press, 1975), pp. 372-95.

DIAROUMEYE, FATOUMATA AGNES

Diaroumeye, Fatoumata Agnes. Le role comparé de la femme dans les milieux ruraux et urbains en Afrique. MONDES EN DEVELOPPEMENT (PARIS) 1982, No. 40:481-82.

DICKINSON, PRAMUAN

Dickinson, Pramuan. My life history in Thailand. In: Women in the new Asia; the changing social roles of men and women in South and South-east Asia. Edited by Barbara E. Ward. ([Paris], Unesco, 1963), pp. 452-70.

Diferencias de ingreso entre hombres y mujeres en el Gran Santiago 1969 y 1981. By: Paredes, Ricardo. ESTUDIOS DE ECONOMIA (SANTIAGO) First semester 1982, No. 18:97-121. With English summary.

Differentiation by sex among small-scale farming households in Kenya. By: Barnes, Carolyn. RURAL AFRICANA (EAST LANSING) Winter/Spring 1983, No. 15/16:41-63.

DIJKERS, MARCELLINUS

Safilios-Rothschild, Constatina and Dijkers, Marcellinus. Changing sex roles in the Greek family and society. In: Changing position of women in family and society: an cross-national comparison. Edited by Eugen Lupri. (Leiden, E. J. Brill, 1983), pp. 190-97.

Das Dilemma internationaler Frauenforderungspolitik. By: Linnhoff, Ursula. E & Z, ENTWICKLUNG UND ZUSAMMENARBEIT (BONN) January 1985, 26:18-19.

Dilemma of peasant women: a view from a village in Yucatan. By: Elmendorf, Mary. In: Women and world development. Edited by Irene Tinker and Michele Bo Bramsen. ([Washington, DC], Overseas Development Council, 1976), pp. 88-94. Describes the changes that industrialization and modernization have brought for Mexican women in general, and then focuses on the women in the village of Chan Kom.

Discovering self-reliance in Paraty. By: Institute for Cultural Action (IDAC). DEVELOPMENT (ROME) 1984, No. 4:41-44. Describes a project of women's education for self-reliance in Paraty, a rural village in Brazil.

Dispossession and counterstrategies in Zambia 1930-1970. By: Muntemba, Maud Shimwaayi. DEVELOPMENT (ROME) 1984, No. 4:15-17.

Diversification of Punjab agriculture: an econometric analysis. By: Singh, A. S. and Jain, K. K. INDIAN JOURNAL OF AGRICULTURAL ECONOMICS (BOMBAY) July/September 1985, 40:298-303.

Diversifying women's employment: the only road to genuine equality of opportunity. By: Janjic, Marion. INTERNATIONAL LABOUR REVIEW (GENEVA) March/April 1981, 120:149-63.

Division of labor by sex in agriculture; a Peruvian case study. By: Deere, Carmen Diana. ECONOMIC DEVELOPMENT AND CULTURAL CHANGE (CHICAGO) July 1982, 30:795-811.

DIVORCE. ECONOMIC ASPECTS

Johnson, William R. and Skinner, Jonathan. Labor supply and marital separation. AMERICAN ECONOMIC REVIEW (NASHVILLE) June 1986, 76:455-69. A simultaneous model of future divorce probability and current labor supply is estimated for married women. The results support the hypothesis that divorce probabilities increase labor supply.

Dix ans d'irruption des sciences humaines dans le domaine du travail des paysannes. By: Michel, Andree. TIERS-MONDE (PARIS) April/June 1985, 26:261-71.

DIXON, RUTH

Dixon, Ruth. Land, labour, and the sex composition of the agricultural labour force: an international comparison. DEVELOPMENT AND CHANGE (THE HAGUE, etc.) July 1983, 14:347-72.

DIXON, RUTH B.

Dixon, Ruth B.. Rural women at work: strategies for development in South Africa. (Baltimore, published for Resources for the Future by Johns Hopkins Press, 1978), 227 pp.

Documentation and analysis of the invisible work of invisible women: a Nigerian case study. By: Pittin, Renee. INTERNATIONAL LABOUR REVIEW (GENEVA) July/August 1984, 123:473-90. Discusses problems arising in the documentation and analysis of the work of secluded women. Focusing on the Muslim Hausa women of Katsina, Nigeria, the author contends that past surveys and censuses have grossly underestimated these women's economic contribution to the Nigerian economy, and that this neglect is increasing.

DODD, PETER C.

   Dodd, Peter C.. Effect of religious affiliation on woman's role in Middle Eastern Arab society. In: Women in the family and the economy: an international comparative survey. Edited by George Kurian and Ratna Ghosh. (Westport, CT, Greenwood Press, 1981), pp. 117-29.

Domestic social environment of women and girls in Isfahan, Iran. By: Gulick, John and Gulick, Margaret E.. In: Women in the Muslim world. Edited by Lois Beck and Nikki Keddie. (Cambridge, MA, Harvard University Press, 1978), pp. 501-21.

DOMESTIC WORKERS

   Chant, Sylvia. Household labour and self-help housing in Queretaro, Mexico. BOLETIN DE ESTUDIOS LATINO-AMERICANOS Y DEL CARIBE (AMSTERDAM) December 1984, No. 37:45-68.

   Sen, Gita and Sen, Chiranjib. Women's domestic work and economic activity: results from the National Sample Survey. CENTRE FOR DEVELOPMENT STUDIES. WORKING PAPER (ULLOOR, TRIVANDRUM) August 1984, No. 197:1-37.

Domestication of women: discrimination in developing societies. By: Rogers, Barbara. (New York, St. Martin's Press, 1980), 200 pp.

DOMINGUEZ, ANA E.

   Sanchez, Aurelia Guadalupe and Dominguez, Ana E.. Women in Mexico. In: Women cross-culturally: change and challenge. Edited by Ruby Rohrlich-Leavitt. (The Hague, Mouton, 1975), pp. 95-110.

DONNER-REICHLE, CAROLA

   Donner-Reichle, Carola. Nach zehn Jahren Bewusstsein fur Frauen geschaffen. E & Z, ENTWICKLUNG UND ZUSAMMENARBEIT (BONN) January 1985, 26:14-15.

DOW, THOMAS E., JR.

   Dow, Thomas E., Jr. and Werner, Linda H.. Perceptions of family planning among rural Kenyan women. STUDIES IN FAMILY PLANNING (NEW YORK) February 1983, 14:35-43.

DRAPER, ELAINE

   Draper, Elaine. Women's work and development in Latin America. STUDIES IN COMPARATIVE INTERNATIONAL DEVELOPMENT (NEW BRUNSWICK, N.J.) Spring 1985, 20:3-30.

DRAPER, PATRICIA

   Draper, Patricia. Kung women: contrasts in sexual egalitarianism in foraging and sedentary contexts. In: Toward an anthropology of women. Edited by Rayna R. Reiter. (New York, Monthly Review Press, 1975), pp. 77-109.

Dual oppression: to be poor and also a woman. By: Varma, Margaret. RUTGERS UNIVERSITY/COOK COLLEGE INTERNATIONAL AGRICULTURE AND FOOD PROGRAM. WORKING PAPER SERIES (NEW BRUNSWICK, NJ) 1985, No. 5:1-9. Deals with women and poverty, and particularly, with women in extreme povelrty and exclusion--women of the fourth world.

Dual-sex political system in operation: Igbo women and community politics in midwestern Nigeria. By: Okonjo, Kamene. In: Women in Africa: studies in social and economic change. Edited by Nancy J. Hafkin and Edna G. Bay. (Stanford, Stanford University Press, 1976), pp. 45-58.

DUBE, S. C.

   Dube, S. C.. Men's and women's roles in India: a sociological review. In: Women in the new Asia; the changing social roles of men and women in South and South-east Asia. Edited by Barbara E. Ward. ([Paris], Unesco, 1963), pp. 174-203.

DUBOW, WENDY D.

   Dubow, Wendy D.. Women in business: a credit-able investment. HORIZONS, U.S. AGENCY FOR INTERNATIONAL DEVELOPMENT (WASHINGTON) Summer 1985, 4:9-11. Describes the achievements of a creative, new network of businesswomen, Women's World Banking.

DUBROVSKY, SILVIA

   Orlansky, Dora and Dubrovsky, Silvia. Effects of rural-urban migration on women's role and status in Latin America. Series: Reports and papers in the social sciences, No. 41. (Paris, Unesco, 1978), 50 pp.

DUDEN, BARBARA

   Bock, Gisela and Duden, Barbara. Labor of love -- love as labor on the Genesis of housework in the West. DEVELOPMENT (ROME) 1984, No. 4:6-14.

DUE, JEAN M.

   Due, Jean M. and Summary, Rebecca. Constraints to women and development in Africa. JOURNAL OF MODERN AFRICAN STUDIES (OXFORD) March 1982, 20:155-66.

DUE, JEAN M.

Due, Jean M. and Anandajayasekeram, P.. Women and productivity in two contrasting farming areas of Tanzania. UNIVERSITY OF ILLINOIS. DEPT. OF AGRICULTURAL ECONOMICS. STAFF PAPER. SERIES E (URBANA) July 1982, No. 82 E-228:1-23.

DUMOR, ERNEST

Dumor, Ernest. Women in rural development in Ghana. RURAL AFRICANA (EAST LANSING) Fall 1983, No. 17:69-81.

DWYER, DAISY HILSE

Dwyer, Daisy Hilse. Women, Sufism, and decision-making in Moroccan Islam. In: Women in the Muslim world. Edited by Lois Beck and Nikki Keddie. (Cambridge, MA, Harvard University Press, 1978), pp. 585-98.

DWYSER, DAISY HILSE

Dwyser, Daisy Hilse. Women and income in the Third world: implications for policy. POPULATION COUNCIL. INTERNATIONAL PROGRAMS. WORKING PAPERS (NEW YORK) June 1983, No. 18:1-39.

DYES AND DYEING

Grilly, Catherine. Comite de teinturerie dans un quartier de Kinshasa (Zaire). TIERS-MONDE (PARIS) April/June 1985, 26:429-34.

Dynamic models of the labor force behavior of married women which can be estimated using limited amounts of past information. By: Nakamura, Alice and Nakamura, Masao. JOURNAL OF ECONOMETRICS (AMSTERDAM) March 1985, 27:273-98.

Easing the burden of women in a developing society: a host of good intentions. By: Holford, Nicky. NEW AFRICAN (LONDON) December 1981, p. 39-40. Discusses the new UN Convention for the prevention of discrimination against women, which was adopted in September, and suggests that the measure should influence customs and practices all over Africa.

EBANKS, G. E.

George, P. M. and Ebanks, G. E.. Labor force participation and fertility contraceptive knowledge; attitudes and practice of the women of Barbados. In: Women in the family and the economy: an international comparative survey. Edited by George Kurian and Ratna Ghosh. (Westport, CT, Greenwood Press, 1981), pp. 285-96.

L'echappee belle, ou la mobilisation generale des femmes dans l'agriculture en France. By: Salmona, Micheline. TIERS-MONDE (PARIS) April/June 1985, 26:247-60.

ECONOMETRICS

Nakamura, Alice and Nakamura, Masao. Dynamic models of the labor force behavior of married women which can be estimated using limited amounts of past information. JOURNAL OF ECONOMETRICS (AMSTERDAM) March 1985, 27:273-98.

Economic and demographic status of female-headed households in rural Botswana. By: Kossoudji, Sherrie and Mueller, Eva. ECONOMIC DEVELOPMENT AND CULTURAL CHANGE (CHICAGO) July 1983, 31:831-59.

Economic basis of the status of women. By: Larguia, Isabel. In: Women cross-culturally: change and challenge. Edited by Ruby Rohrlich-Leavitt. (The Hague, Mouton, 1975), pp. 281-95.

Economic contribution of women and its effect on the dynamics of the family in two Lebanese villages. By: Lorfing, I. and Khalaf, M.. INTERNATIONAL LABOUR OFFICE. WORLD EMPLOYMENT PROGRAMME RESEARCH. POPULATION AND LABOUR POLICIES PROGRAMME. WORKING PAPER (GENEVA) May 1985, No. 148:1-32.

ECONOMIC DEVELOPMENT

Ahooja-Patel, Krishna. Another development with women. DEVELOPMENT DIALOGUE (UPPSALA) 1982, No. 1/2:17-28. After describing how difficult it was for women to voice their views in the development debate as late as the mid-seventies, the author presents an overview of the contribution women have made and are making in agriculture, industry, health and education.

Brambilla, Francesco. Women and development. GIORNALE DEGLI ECONOMISTI E ANNALI DI ECONOMIA (MILAN) September/December 1979, 38, N.S.:619-67. With English summary.

Dakar declaration on Another development with women. DEVELOPMENT DIALOGUE (UPPSALA) 1982, No. 1/2:11-16. Consensus reached at the seminar "Another development with women," held in Dakar, Senegal, June 21-25, 1982, jointly organized by the Association of African Women for Research and Development (AAWORD/AFARD) and the Dag Hammarskjold Foundation.

ECONOMIC DEVELOPMENT

Davies, Miranda. Women in struggle. THIRD WORLD QUARTERLY (LONDON) October 1983, 5:874-914. CONTENT: Davies, Miranda, An overview. - Sayigh, Rosemary, Palestine. - Unterhalter, Elaine, South Africa. - Silkin, Trish, Eritrea.

de Vries, Margaret G.. Women, jobs, and development. FINANCE AND DEVELOPMENT (WASHINGTON) December 1971, 8:4:2-9. Discusses the employment of women in developing countries in the light of recent changes in emphasis on the strategy and objectives of economic development. Also published in French, German, Portuguese, and Spanish.

Les femmes et le developpement. TIERS-MONDE (PARIS) July/September 1982, 23:577-618.

Kopenhagen: de tweede VN-conferentie voor vrouwen; Vrouwen en ontwikkeling. INTERNATIONALE SPECTATOR (THE HAGUE) June 1980, 34:309-57.

Mignot-Lefebvre, Yvonne. Femmes et developpement; idees et strategies des organisations internationales. TIERS-MONDE (PARIS) October/December 1980, 21:845-62.

Moriarty, Michele. Women in development. BANK'S WORLD (WASHINGTON) March 1983, 2:7-8. Discusses some of the issues raised at the World Bank's third "Workshop on Women in Development," which took place recently in Baltimore.

Postel-Coster, Els. Misverstanden rond de kostwinner in het ontwikkelingsbeleid. INTERNATIONALE SPECTATOR (THE HAGUE) September 1983, 37:549-55.

Purcell, Deborah Ross. Integrating women into development; an investment in human capital. HORIZONS, U.S. AGENCY FOR INTERNATIONAL DEVELOPMENT (WASHINGTON) July/August 1983, 2:20-23. Discusses the work of AID's Office of Women in Development (WID).

Rao, Amiya. Cost of development projects; women among the 'willing evacuees'. ECONOMIC AND POLITICAL WEEKLY (BOMBAY) March 22, 1986, 21:474-76. Describes the heavy price of development paid by India's women.

Rogombe, Rose Francine. Women; equal partners in Africa's development. AFRICA REPORT (NEW YORK) March/April 1985, 30:17-20.

Safilios-Rothschild, Constantina. Socioeconomic development and the status of women in the Third world. POPULATION COUNCIL. CENTER FOR POLICY STUDIES. WORKING PAPERS (NEW YORK) May 1985, No. 112:1-49. Examines the relationship between socioeconomic development and women's status in 75 developing countries.

Schrijvers, Joke. Cultuur als camouflage: Westerse weerstanden tegen vrouwen als ontwikkelingsrelevant onderwerp. INTERNATIONALE SPECTATOR (THE HAGUE) September 1983, 37:556-62.

Schuster, Ilsa. Recent research on women in development; review article. JOURNAL OF DEVELOPMENT STUDIES (LONDON) July 1982, 18:511-35.

van Dam, Andre. Women - what role in development? D & C, DEVELOPMENT AND COOPERATION (BONN) May/June 1981, No. 3:10-13.

Wichterich, Christa. Der Fortschritt drangt die Frauen ins Abseits. E & Z, ENTWICKLUNG UND ZUSAMMENARBEIT (BONN) January 1985, 26:4-5.

Wiese, Eva-Maria. Frauen tragen die Last der Entwicklung; Beispiele aus West-Afrika. E & Z, ENTWICKLUNG UND ZUSAMMENARBEIT (BONN) January 1985, 26:8-10.

Women of Vanuatu. Integration of women in the development process. PACIFIC PERSPECTIVE (SUVA) 1983, 11, No. 2:1-4. Adapted from the paper presented by the Women of Vanuatu to the 21st South Pacific Conference, Vila.

Economic development and women's place: women in Singapore. By: Wong, Aline K.. Series: Change Interantional Reports. Women in Society. No. 1. (London, Change International Reports, 1980), 20 pp.

Economic development and women's work in a newly industrializing country: the case of Korea. By: Cho, Uhn and Koo, Hagen. DEVELOPMENT AND CHANGE (THE HAGUE, etc.) October 1983, 14:515-31. The authors investigate how women's economic activities have changed in relation to the pattern of economic growth in Korea in the past two decades.

ECONOMIC DEVELOPMENT PROJECTS

Buvinic, Mayra. Projects for women in the Third World: explaining their misbehavior. WORLD DEVELOPMENT (OXFORD) May 1986, 14:653-64. Explains why the economic objectives of a large number of income-generation projects for poor women in the Third World have evolved into welfare action during implementation.

Staudt, Kathleen. Planning-centred approach to project evaluation: women in mainstream development projects. PUBLIC ADMINISTRATION AND DEVELOPMENT (CHICHESTER) January/March 1985, 5:25-37. Describes the process and outcomes of a 'planning-centred' approach to three development projects in the Caribbean.

ECONOMIC DEVELOPMENT. FINANCE

Conable, Barber B.. Address to the Board of Governors of the World Bank and International Finance Corporation. (Washington, World Bank, September 30, 1986), 11 pp.

Economic growth and changing female employment structure in the cities of Southeast and East Asia. By: Jones, Gavin W.. In: Women in the urban and industrial workforce; Southeast and East Asia. Edited by Gavin W. Jones. Series: Development Studies Centre. Monograph, No. 33. (Canberra, Australia, Australian National University, 1984), pp. 17-60. Series edited by Helen Hughes.

ECONOMIC PLANNING

Mu, Yuan. China pursues peace and development in 1986-1990. WOMEN OF CHINA (BEIJING) January 1986, No. 1:24-25.

ECONOMIC POLICY

Dalsimer, Marlyn and Nisonoff, Laurie. New economic readjustment policies: implications for Chinese urban working women. REVIEW OF RADICAL POLITICAL ECONOMICS (NEW YORK) Spring 1984, 16:17-43.

Mohammadi, Pari. Women in national planning: false expectations. DEVELOPMENT (ROME) 1984, No. 4:80-81.

Economic role of women: a case of occupational dependency. By: Mohiuddin, Yasmeen. PAKISTAN & GULF ECONOMIST (KARACHI) February 2, 1985, 4:12-15.

Economic role of women in the ECE region. ECONOMIC BULLETIN FOR EUROPE: JOURNAL OF THE UNITED NATIONS ECONOMIC COMMISSION FOR EUROPE (OXFORD) March 1985, 37:1-112. This issue features a number of country papers as well as conclusions and recommendations adopted at the Seminar on the Economic Role of Women held in Vienna, Austria, October 15-19, 1984.

Economic role of women in the ECE region. By: United Nations. Economic Commission for Europe. Series: United Nations [Document], E/ECE/1013. (New York, United Nations, 1980), 122 pp.

Economics of diversification of farming with dairy enterprise. By: Thorve, P. V. and Galgalikar, V. D. INDIAN JOURNAL OF AGRICULTURAL ECONOMICS (BOMBAY) July/September 1985, 40:317-23.

Economische aspecten van een quoterings-maatregel ten behoeve van vrouwen op de arbeidsmarkt. By: Schippers, J. J. and Siegers, J. J.. MAANDSCHRIFT ECONOMIE (TILBURG) 1984, 48, No. 6:484-99.

ECUADOR

Buvinic, Mayra and Lycette, Margaret. Eye-opening survey unlocks doors for low-income women. HORIZONS, U.S. AGENCY FOR INTERNATIONAL DEVELOPMENT (WASHINGTON) Summer 1985, 4:31-33. The authors describe how the International Center for Research on Women (ICRW), with a $120,000 grant from AID, is helping to put home ownership within reach of low-income women, through its experiences with the Solanda low-income housing project in Quito, Ecuador.

EDMUNDS, MARILYN

Edmunds, Marilyn and Helzner, Judith F.. Peru-mujer: women organizing for development. PATHPAPERS, PATHFINDER FUND (CHESTNUT HILL, MASS.) August 1982, No. 9:1-18.

Edmunds, Marilyn and Helzner, Judith F.. Peru-Mujer: women organizing for development. Series: Pathpapers series, No. 9. (Chestnut Hill, MA, Pathfinder Fund, 1982), 18 pp.

EDUCATION

Berliner, Joseph S.. Education, labor-force participation, and fertility in the USSR. JOURNAL OF COMPARATIVE ECONOMICS (NEW YORK) June 1983, 7:131-57. The effect of education on Soviet fertility and female labor participation is analyzed in terms of the neoclassical theory of the household.

EDUCATION

Bowman, Mary Jean and Anderson, C. Arnold. Participation of women in education in the Third World. COMPARATIVE EDUCATION REVIEW (NEW YORK) June 1980, 24:S13-32.

Cooksey, Brian. Education and sexual inequality in Cameroun. JOURNAL OF MODERN AFRICAN STUDIES (OXFORD) March 1982, 20:167-77.

Elliott, Carolyn M. and Kelly, Gail P.. Introduction: perspectives on the education of women in Third World nations. COMPARATIVE EDUCATION REVIEW (NEW YORK) June 1980, 24:S1-12.

Finn, Jeremy D. and Reis, Janet. Sex differences in educational attainment: the process. COMPARATIVE EDUCATION REVIEW (NEW YORK) June 1980, 24:S33-52. Examines various obstacles to women's education.

Gould, Ketayun. Sex inequalities in the dual system of education; the Parsis of Gujarat. ECONOMIC AND POLITICAL WEEKLY (BOMBAY) September 24, 1983, 18:1668-76.

Kalia, Narendra Nath. Images of men and women in Indian textbooks. COMPARATIVE EDUCATION REVIEW (NEW YORK) June 1980, 24:S209-23. Attempts to demonstrate that Indian school textbooks promote an ideology which refuses females equal access to opportunities and rewards even in areas where the sex of a person is totally irrelevant.

Kelly, Gail P. and Lulat, Younus. Women and schooling in the Third World: a bibliography. COMPARATIVE EDUCATION REVIEW (NEW YORK) June 1980, 24:S224-63.

LeVine, Robert A.. Influences of women's schooling on maternal behavior in the Third World. COMPARATIVE EDUCATION REVIEW (NEW YORK) June 1980, 24:S78-105.

Mazumdar, Vina. Women's studies: challenge to educational system. ECONOMIC AND POLITICAL WEEKLY (BOMBAY) May 16, 1981, 16:890-92. Discusses some of the recommendations of the National Conference on Women's Studies, held in Bombay, April 20-24, 1981.

Rohwer, Gertrude. Integration durch Ausbildung; eine Strategie zur Uberwindung sozialer Disparitaten in Oman: Bemerkungen uber die Partizipationschancen von Frauen am gesellschaftlichen Entwicklungsprozess in einem islamischen Land. ORIENT (HAMBURG) September 1984, 25:391-402. With English summary, p. 458.

EDUCATION

Sue, Mee Kwain. Community education training centre (CETC). PACIFIC PERSPECTIVE (SUVA) 1983, 11, No. 2:62-4. Describes a regional center established in 1963 to provide a programme of community education for women.

Taamallah, Lamouria. La scolarisation et la formation professionnelle des femmes en Tunisie. REVUE TUNISIENNE DE SCIENCES SOCIALES (TUNIS) 1982, 19, No. 68/69:107-28.

Wang, Bee-Lan Chan. Sex and ethnic differences in educational investment in Malaysia: the effect of reward structures. COMPARATIVE EDUCATION REVIEW (NEW YORK) June 1980, 24:S140-59.

Education and employment among Kuwaiti women. By: Nath, Kamla. In: Women in the Muslim world. Edited by Lois Beck and Nikki Keddie. (Cambridge, MA, Harvard University Press, 1978), pp. 172-88.

Education and sexual inequality in Cameroun. By: Cooksey, Brian. JOURNAL OF MODERN AFRICAN STUDIES (OXFORD) March 1982, 20:167-77.

Education, labor-force participation, and fertility in the USSR. By: Berliner, Joseph S.. JOURNAL OF COMPARATIVE ECONOMICS (NEW YORK) June 1983, 7:131-57. The effect of education on Soviet fertility and female labor participation is analyzed in terms of the neoclassical theory of the household.

Education of Muslim women: tradition versus modernity. By: Menon, M. Indie. In: Women in the family and the economy: an international comparative survey. Edited by George Kurian and Ratna Ghosh. (Westport, CT, Greenwood Press, 1981), pp. 107-15.

EDUCATION OF WOMEN

Child quantity and quality in a developing country: family background, endogenous tastes, and biological supply factors. ECONOMIC DEVELOPMENT AND CULTURAL CHANGE (CHICAGO) July 1986, 34:703-20. The data are from a cross-sectional area-stratified random sample of about 4,000 women aged 15-45 collected in Nicaragua in 1977-78 as part of a larger study on the socio-economic roles of women in developing countries.

Deble, Isabelle. La deuxieme strategie de l'UNESCO a l'egard des femmes. TIERS-MONDE (PARIS) April/June 1985, 26:283-97.

EDUCATION OF WOMEN

Elementary education for girls. WOMEN OF CHINA (BEIJING) June 1986, No. 6:6-7.

Forray, Katalin R. Bildungswege der Frauen in Ungarn: neue Tendenzen in der Ausbildung und Beschaftigung aus soziologischer Sicht. OSTERREICHISCHE OSTHEFTE (VIENNA) 1986, 28, No. 2:107-25.

Hooper, Beverley. China's modernization; are young women going to lose out? MODERN CHINA (BEVERLY HILLS) July 1984, 10:317-43. Focuses on two areas that are prerequisites to young women having the opportunity to play an equal role in China's economic development: obtaining education, particularly higher education, and securing employment.

Jain, Anrudh K. and Nag, Moni. Female primary education and fertility reduction in India. POPULATION COUNCIL. CENTER FOR POLICY STUDIES. WORKING PAPERS (NEW YORK) September 1985, No. 114:1-57.

Li, Yuan. Tibet through our eyes (2); education: opening the door to women. WOMEN OF CHINA (BEIJING) August 1985, No. 8:6-7.

Maskiell, Michelle. Social change and social control: college-educated Punjabi women 1913 to 1960. MODERN ASIAN STUDIES (LONDON) February 1985, 19:55-83.

Oppong, Christine and Abu, Katharine. Changing maternal role of Ghanaian women: impacts of education, migration and employment. INTERNATIONAL LABOUR OFFICE. WORLD EMPLOYMENT PROGRAMME RESEARCH. POPULATION AND LABOUR POLICIES PROGRAMME. WORKING PAPER (GENEVA) February 1984, No. 143:1-184.

Singhal, Sushila. Development of educated women in India: reflections of a social psychologist. COMPARATIVE EDUCATION (OXFORD) October 1984, 20:355-70.

Taamallah, Lamouria. La scolarisation et la formation professionnelle des femmes en Tunisie. REVUE TUNISIENNE DE SCIENCES SOCIALES (TUNIS) 1982, 19, No. 68/69:107-28.

Trends in women's work, education, and family building; proceedings of the Conference, Chelwood Gate, Sussex, England, May 31 - June 3, 1983. JOURNAL OF LABOR ECONOMICS (CHICAGO) January 1985, 3:S1-S396.

Verheust, Therese. Potraits de femmes: les intellectuelles zairoises. CAHIERS DU CEDAF (BRUSSELS) October 1985, No. 6:1-148.

Women's work may help to make jobs for the girls. PACIFIC ISLANDS MONTHLY (SYDNEY) May 1986, 57:22-23.

EDUCATIONAL POLICY

Jain, Anrudh K. and Nag, Moni. Importance of female primary education for fertility reduction in India. ECONOMIC AND POLITICAL WEEKLY (BOMBAY) September 6, 1986, 21:1602-08.

Effect of female labour force participation on fertility: the case of construction workers in Chiang Mai City. By: Singhanetra-Renard, Anchalee. In: Women in the urban and industrial workforce; Southeast and East Asia. Edited by Gavin W. Jones. Series: Development Studies Centre. Monograph, No. 33. (Canberra, Australia, Australian National University, 1984), pp. 325-38. Series edited by Helen Hughes.

Effect of mother's work on child care, dietary intake, and dietary adequacy of pre-school children. By: Chaudhury, Rafiqul Huda. BANGLADESH DEVELOPMENT STUDIES (DACCA) December 1982, 10:33-61.

Effect of religious affiliation on woman's role in Middle Eastern Arab society. By: Dodd, Peter C.. In: Women in the family and the economy: an international comparative survey. Edited by George Kurian and Ratna Ghosh. (Westport, CT, Greenwood Press, 1981), pp. 117-29.

Effect of sex antidiscriminatory legislation on the variability of female employment in Britian. By: Tzannatos, Z. and Zabalza, A. APPLIED ECONOMICS (LONDON) December 1985, 17:1117-34. The authors attempt to determine whether fluctuations in aggregate employment are reflected in fluctuations in the employment of men and women, and to investigate if the sex antidiscriminatory legislation enacted in Britian during the 1970s has had any effect on the variability of female employment.

Effect of the Equal Rights Amendment on the economic status of women. By: Medoff, Marshall H. ATLANTIC ECONOMIC JOURNAL (WORDEN, IL) September 1985, 13:60-68.

Effect on reported levels of female labour force participation in developing countries of questionnaire design, sex of interviewer and sex/proxy status of respondent: description of a methodological field experiment. By: Anker, Richard. INTERNATIONAL LABOUR OFFICE. WORLD EMPLOYMENT PROGRAMME RESEARCH. POPULATION AND LABOUR POLICIES PROGRAMME. WORKING PAPER (GENEVA) July 1983, No. 137:1-76. The methods test described is conducting household surveys in India (Uttar Pradesh state) and Egypt, using different types of questionnaires; male and female interviewers; self-respondents (female only) and proxy-respondents (male and female).

Effects of rural-urban migration on women's role and status in Latin America. By: Orlansky, Dora and Dubrovsky, Silvia. Series: Reports and papers in the social sciences, No. 41. (Paris, Unesco, 1978), 50 pp.

Effects of the international division of labour on female workers in the textile and clothing industries. By: Robert, Annette. DEVELOPMENT AND CHANGE (THE HAGUE, etc.) January 1983, 14:19-37.

EGYPT

Bach, Rebecca and Gadalla, Saad. Mothers' influence on daughters' orientations toward education: an Egyptian case study. COMPARATIVE EDUCATION REVIEW (NEW YORK) August 1985, 29:374-84.

Khouri-Dagher, Nadia. La participation des femmes a l'economie egyptienne: tendances et evolutions. TIERS-MONDE (PARIS) April/June 1985, 26:335-50.

Lesch, Ann Mosely and Sullivan, Earl L. Women in Egypt; new roles and realities. UNIVERSITIES FIELD STAFF INTERNATIONAL REPORTS, AFRICA (HANOVER, NH) 1986, No. 22:1-9.

Egypt: from seclusion to limited participation. By: Smock, Audrey Chapman and Youssef, Nadia Haggag. In: Women: roles and status in eight countries. Edited by Janet Zollinger Giele and Audrey Chapman Smock. (New York, John Wiley, 1977), pp. 35-79.

EL BELGHITI, MALIKA

El Belghiti, Malika. Role of women in socio-economic development: indicators as instruments of social analysis; the case of Morocco. In: Women and development: indicators of their changing role. Series: Socio-economic studies, No. 3. (Paris, Unesco, 1981), pp. 15-32.

EL-BAKRI AND KAMEIR, E. M.

El-Bakri and Kameir, E. M.. Aspects of women's political participation in Sudan. INTERNATIONAL SOCIAL SCIENCE JOURNAL (PARIS) 1983, 35, No. 4:605-23.

EL-MESSIRI, SAWSAN

El-Messiri, Sawsan. Self-images of traditional urban women in Cairo. In: Women in the Muslim world. Edited by Lois Beck and Nikki Keddie. (Cambridge, MA, Harvard University Press, 1978), pp. 522-40.

Elaboration d'un cadre d'analyse pour les projets agro-alimentaires. By: Weekes-Vagliani, Winifred. TIERS-MONDE (PARIS) April/June 1985, 26:307-16. Etude d'un projet agro-alimentaire indonesien.

Elementary education for girls. WOMEN OF CHINA (BEIJING) June 1986, No. 6:6-7.

ELLIOTT, CAROLYN M.

Elliott, Carolyn M. and Kelly, Gail P.. Introduction: perspectives on the education of women in Third World nations. COMPARATIVE EDUCATION REVIEW (NEW YORK) June 1980, 24:S1-12.

ELMENDORF, M. L.

Elmendorf, M. L.. Mayan woman and change. In: Women cross-culturally: change and challenge. Edited by Ruby Rohrlich-Leavitt. (The Hague, Mouton, 1975), pp. 111-27.

ELMENDORF, MARY

Elmendorf, Mary. Dilemma of peasant women: a view from a village in Yucatan. In: Women and world development. Edited by Irene Tinker and Michele Bo Bramsen. ([Washington, DC], Overseas Development Council, 1976), pp. 88-94. Describes the changes that industrialization and modernization have brought for Mexican women in general, and then focuses on the women in the village of Chan Kom.

Elmendorf, Mary. Mexico: the many worlds of women. In: Women: roles and status in eight countries. Edited by Janet Zollinger Giele and Audrey Chapman Smock. (New York, John Wiley, 1977), pp. 129-72.

ELMENDORF, MARY L.

Elmendorf, Mary L. and Isely, Raymond B.. Role of women in water supply and sanitation. WORLD HEALTH FORUM (GENEVA) 1982, 3, No. 2:227-30.

EMIGRANT REMITTANCES

Griffith, David C. Women, remittances, and reproduction. AMERICAN ETHNOLOGIST (WASHINGTON) November 1985, 12:676-90. Presents and interprets data on how women in Jamaica use remittances from migrating husbands, boyfriends, sons, and so forth, and examines some of the reasons for these uses. The author concludes that seasonal-labor migration aids Jamaican peasant households in meeting the costs of reproducing themselves and their social and economic conditions.

Empirical investigation of female labor-force participation, fertility, age at marriage, and wages in Korea. By: Lee, Bun Song and McElwain, Adrienne M. JOURNAL OF DEVELOPING AREAS (MACOMB, ILL.) July 1985, 19:483-500.

El empleo de la mujer, los cambios sociales y la liberacion femenina; el caso de Africa. By: Savane, Marie Angelique. COMERCIO EXTERIOR (MEXICO, D.F.) August 1980, 30:861-66. Ponencia presentada en la Mesa II, "Recursos humanos y empleo en los paises en desarrollo," del Sexto Congreso Mundial de Economistas.

Emplois "feminins" et emplois "masculins": mesure de la segregation et evolution de la feminisation des emplois. By: Sofer, Catherine. INSTITUT NATIONAL DE LA STATISTIQUE ET DES ETUDES ECONOMIQUES, ANNALES (PARIS) October/December 1983, No. 52:55-85. With English summary.

Employed women in Barbados: a demographic profile, 1946-1970. By: Massiah, Joycelin. Series: Occasional Paper (University of the West Indies. Institute of Social and Economic Research, No. 8. (Cave Hill, Barbados, University of the West Indies, 1984), 131 pp.

EMPLOYMENT

Eyland, E.A. and Mason, C.A.. Determinants of female employment. ECONOMIC RECORD (MELBOURNE) March 1982, 58:11-17.

Ferber, Marianne A. and Green, Carole A. Work power and earnings of women and men. AMERICAN ECONOMIC REVIEW, PAPERS AND PROCEEDINGS (NASHVILLE) May 1986, 76:53-56.

Maxwell, Nan L. and D'Amico, Ronald J. Employment and wage effects of involuntary job separation: male-female differences. AMERICAN ECONOMIC REVIEW, PAPERS AND PROCEEDINGS (NASHVILLE) May 1986, 76:373-77.

EMPLOYMENT

Pulea, Mere. Women, employment and development. PACIFIC PERSPECTIVE (SUVA) 1983, 11, No. 2:18-28.

Sofer, Catherine. Emplois "feminins" et emplois "masculins": mesure de la segregation et evolution de la feminisation des emplois. INSTITUT NATIONAL DE LA STATISTIQUE ET DES ETUDES ECONOMIQUES, ANNALES (PARIS) October/December 1983, No. 52:55-85. With English summary.

Tzannatos, Z. and Zabalza, A. Effect of sex antidiscriminatory legislation on the variability of female employment in Britian. APPLIED ECONOMICS (LONDON) December 1985, 17:1117-34. The authors attempt to determine whether fluctuations in aggregate employment are reflected in fluctuations in the employment of men and women, and to investigate if the sex antidiscriminatory legislation enacted in Britian during the 1970s has had any effect on the variability of female employment.

Employment and unemployment of women in OECD countries. By: Paukert, Liba. (Paris, Organisation for Economic Co-operation and Development, 1984), 88 pp. Prepared for the OECD's Working Party on the Role of Women in the Economy.

Employment and wage effects of involuntary job separation: male-female differences. By: Maxwell, Nan L. and D'Amico, Ronald J. AMERICAN ECONOMIC REVIEW, PAPERS AND PROCEEDINGS (NASHVILLE) May 1986, 76:373-77.

Employment guarantee scheme: an employment opportunity for women. By: Dandekar, Kumudini. Series: Gokhale Institute Studies, No. 67. (Pune, Gokhale Institute of Politics and Economics, 1983), 76 pp.

Employment of women outside agriculture in Third world countries: an overview of occupational statistics. By: Anker, Richard and Hein, Catherine. INTERNATIONAL LABOUR OFFICE. WORLD EMPLOYMENT PROGRAMME RESEARCH. POPULATION AND LABOUR POLICIES PROGRAMME. WORKING PAPER (GENEVA) March 1985, No. 147:1-70.

Employment patterns of educated women in Indonesian cities. By: Raharjo, Yulfita and Hull, Valerie. In: Women in the urban and industrial workforce; Southeast and East Asia. Edited by Gavin W. Jones. Series: Development Studies Centre. Monograph, No. 33. (Canberra, Australia, Australian National University, 1984), pp. 101-28. Series edited by Helen Hughes.

Employment structure of female migrants to the cities in the Philippines. By: Engracia, Luisa and Herrin, Alejandro. In: Women in the urban and industrial workforce; Southeast and East Asia. Edited by Gavin W. Jones. Series: Development Studies Centre. Monograph, No. 33. (Canberra, Australia, Australian National University, 1984), pp. 293-304. Series edited by Helen Hughes.

EMPLOYMENT. WOMEN

Ahmad, Zubeida M.. Women's work and their struggle to organize. DEVELOPMENT (ROME) 1984, No. 4:36-40.

Mies, Maria. Capitalism and subsistence: rural women in India. DEVELOPMENT (ROME) 1984, No. 4:18-24.

Mitter, Swasti. On the global assembly line women and multinationals. DEVELOPMENT (ROME) 1984, No. 4:31-33.

Mohiuddin, Yasmeen. Female handicraft workers; the invisible hand. PAKISTAN & GULF ECONOMIST (KARACHI) July 20, 1985, 4:44-47. The purpose of this study is to investigate the economic role and status of these invisible producers in the all-female handicraft production in Sind, Pakistan.

End of the UN decade: what advances for African women? AFRICA REPORT (NEW YORK) March/April 1985, 30, Special issue p. 4-82..

Endangered sex; neglect of female children in rural north India. By: Miller, Barbara D.. (Ithaca, New York, Cornell University Press, 1981), 201 pp.

Das Ende der Bescheidenheit: Probleme und Perspektiven von Frauenforderplanen. By: Weg, Marianne. WSI-MITTEILUNGEN (DUSSELDORF) August 1986, 39:566-75.

Endless day: some case material on Asian rural women. Edited by T. Scarlett Epstein and Rosemary A. Watts. Series: Women in Development, Vol. 3. (Oxford, England, New York, Pergamon Press, 1981), 179 pp.

Engels revisited: women, the organization of production, and private property. By: Sacks, Karen. In: Toward an anthropology of women. Edited by Rayna R. Reiter. (New York, Monthly Review Press, 1975), pp. 211-34.

Engine of fertility - influenced by interbirth employment? By: Jensen, An-Magritt and Schweder, Tore. NORWAY. STATISTISK SENTRALBYRA. DISCUSSION PAPER (OSLO) June 1986, No. 15:1-33.

ENGINEERING

Pearson, Richard. So few women in engineering. NATURE (LONDON) October 2, 1986, 323:p. 474.

ENGRACIA, LUISA

Engracia, Luisa and Herrin, Alejandro. Employment structure of female migrants to the cities in the Philippines. In: Women in the urban and industrial workforce; Southeast and East Asia. Edited by Gavin W. Jones. Series: Development Studies Centre. Monograph, No. 33. (Canberra, Australia, Australian National University, 1984), pp. 293-304. Series edited by Helen Hughes.

Entwicklungshilfe - Fluch oder Segen fur die Frauen? E & Z, ENTWICKLUNG UND ZUSAMMENARBEIT (BONN) January 1985, 26:4-21.

Entwicklungshilfe: Fluch oder Segen fur die Frauen? Die bedeutende Rolle der Frauen wird bei der Projektplanung nicht angemessen berucksichtigt. By: Fischer, Wolfgang E.. E & Z, ENTWICKLUNG UND ZUSAMMENARBEIT (BONN) January 1985, 26:6-7.

Epistemologia y sicologia en "la cuestion de la mujer". By: Cardenas de Sanz de Santamaria, Maria Consuelo. DESARROLLO Y SOCIEDAD (BOGOTA) January 1984, No. 13:39-55. With English summary.

EQUAL PAY FOR EQUAL WORK

Gaston, Cheryl L. Idea whose time has not come: comparable worth and the market salary problem. POPULATION RESEARCH AND POLICY REVIEW (AMSTERDAM) 1986, 5, No. 1:15-29.

Sorensen, Elaine. Implementing comparable worth: a survey of recent job evaluation studies. AMERICAN ECONOMIC REVIEW, PAPERS AND PROCEEDINGS (NASHVILLE) May 1986, 76:364-72.

Equality of Malay women -- real but restricted. By: Abdullah, Noraini. FAR EASTERN ECONOMIC REVIEW (HONGKONG) April 10, 1986, 132:38-39.

Equality of opportunity and treatment for women workers: eighth item on the agenda. By: International Labor Office. (Geneva, International Labour Office, 1974), 123 pp. Prepared as a basis for discussion at the International Labour Conference, 60th session, 1975, Report VIII.

Equality or protection? Protective legislation for women in Japan. By: Nakanishi, Tamako. INTERNATIONAL LABOUR REVIEW (GENEVA) September/October 1983, 122:609-21.

ERUMSELE, A. AKHIGBE

Erumsele, A. Akhigbe. Women's part in rural development. WEST AFRICA (LONDON) August 18, 1980, No. 3291:1539-40. Discusses some of the findings of a study on "Rural women's participation in development" just published by the United Nations Development Programme (UNDP).

ESMAN, MILTON J. (MILTON JACOB)

Esman, Milton J. (Milton Jacob). Paraprofessionals in rural development: issues in field-level staffing for agricultural projects. Series: World Bank Staff Working Papers, No. 573. (Washington, DC, World Bank, 1983), 55 pp.

Esperance de vie active, reprise d'activite feminine: un modele. By: Brouard, Nicolas. REVUE ECONOMIQUE (PARIS) November 1980, 31:1260-87. With English summary.

Establishing a programme of women and development studies in the University of the West Indies. By: Massiah, Joycelin. SOCIAL AND ECONOMIC STUDIES (MONA, JAMAICA) March 1986, 35:151-97.

Los estudios de la mujer y la critica epistemologica a los paradigmas de las ciencias humanas. By: Bonder, Gloria. DESARROLLO Y SOCIEDAD (BOGOTA) January 1984, No. 13:25-38. With English summary.

ETHICS

Women and morality. SOCIAL RESEARCH (NEW YORK) Autumn 1983, 50, No. 3:487-695. Brings together various perspectives, with specific attention to the "essentially moral" character of women's "felt" experience.

Etude comparative du statut sexuel des femmes dans le monde mediterraneen, berbere et Africain. By: Ben Miled, Emna. REVUE TUNISIENNE DE SCIENCES SOCIALES (TUNIS) 1985, 22, No. 82/83:75-110.

ETZIONI-HALEVY, EVA

Shapira, Rina and Etzioni-Halevy, Eva and Chopp-Tibon, Shira. Occupational choice among female academicians -- the Israeli case. In: Women in the family and the economy: an international comparative survey. Edited by George Kurian and Ratna Ghosh. (Westport, CT, Greenwood Press, 1981), pp. 345-58.

EUROPE

Economic role of women in the ECE region. ECONOMIC BULLETIN FOR EUROPE: JOURNAL OF THE UNITED NATIONS ECONOMIC COMMISSION FOR EUROPE (OXFORD) March 1985, 37:1-112. This issue features a number of country papers as well as conclusions and recommendations adopted at the Seminar on the Economic Role of Women held in Vienna, Austria, October 15-19, 1984.

EVERETT, JANA

Everett, Jana and Savara, Mira. Bank loans to lower class women in Bombay; problems and prospects. ECONOMIC AND POLITICAL WEEKLY (BOMBAY) August 25, 1984, 19:M113-M119. The authors report the results of an exploratory study of bank loans to lower caste women in Bombay. They seek to shed some light on the problems surrounding and the prospects for bank loans as an economic development strategy for poor women.

EVIOTA, ELIZABETH U.

Eviota, Elizabeth U.. Measuring Filipino women's participation in development. In: Women and development, perspectives from South and Southeast Asia. Edited by Rounaq Jahan and Hanna Papanek. (Dacca, The Bangladesh Institute of Law and International Affairs, 1979), pp. 171-201.

Eviota, Elizabeth U. and Smith, Peter C.. Migration of women in the Philippines. In: Women in the cities of Asia: migration and urban adaptation. Edited by James T. Fawcett, Siew-Ean Khoo and Peter C. Smith. (Boulder, CO, Westview Press, 1984), pp. 165-90.

Examination of education, social change, and national development policy: the case of Kenyan women. By: Lindsay, Beverly. STUDIES IN THIRD WORLD SOCIETIES (WILLIAMSBURG) June 1981, No. 16:29-48.

Examination of the literature on Jordanian women. By: Dahhan, Omaymah. INTERNATIONAL LABOUR OFFICE. WORLD EMPLOYMENT PROGRAMME RESEARCH. POPULATION AND LABOUR POLICIES: REGIONAL PROGRAMME FOR THE MIDDLE EAST. WORKING PAPER (BEIRUT) March 1981, No. 8:1-146.

Expected interruptions in labour force participation and sex-related differences in earnings growth. By: Weiss, Yoram and Gronau, Reuben. REVIEW OF ECONOMIC STUDIES (EDINBURGH) October 1981, 48:607-19.

Experience and issues in rural development: selected papers and proceedings of an IBRD/KIT seminar held in Amsterdam, 1 and 2 May, 1979. Edited by Willem Keddeman. (Amsterdam, Koninklijk Instituut voor de Tropen, 1979), 56 pp.

Experience of the Association of African Women for Research and Development (AAWORD); a workshop report prepared for the high-level meeting on the review of technical cooperation among developing countries. DEVELOPMENT DIALOGUE (UPPSALA) 1982, No. 1/2:101-113. Reviews the existing studies on African women and highlights some of their important consequences. The origin and early history of AAWORD is outlined and an account is given of its objectives, policies and programmes.

Eye-opening survey unlocks doors for low-income women. By: Buvinic, Mayra and Lycette, Margaret. HORIZONS, U.S. AGENCY FOR INTERNATIONAL DEVELOPMENT (WASHINGTON) Summer 1985, 4:31-33. The authors describe how the International Center for Research on Women (ICRW), with a $120,000 grant from AID, is helping to put home ownership within reach of low-income women, through its experiences with the Solanda low-income housing project in Quito, Ecuador.

EYLAND, E.A.

Eyland, E.A. and Mason, C.A.. Determinants of female employment. ECONOMIC RECORD (MELBOURNE) March 1982, 58:11-17.

Factoring gender into the development equation. By: Horenstein, Nadine R.. HORIZONS, U.S. AGENCY FOR INTERNATIONAL DEVELOPMENT (WASHINGTON) Summer 1985, 4:26-30.

Factors affecting crop diversification: an empirical analysis. By: Gupta, R. P. and Tewari, S. K. INDIAN JOURNAL OF AGRICULTURAL ECONOMICS (BOMBAY) July/September 1985, 40:304-09.

FAHMY, HODA

Lynch, Patricia D. and Fahmy, Hoda. Craftswomen in Kerdassa, Egypt. Household production and reproduction. Series: Women, work and development, No. 7. (Geneva, International Labour Office, 1984), 91 pp. Undertaken under the auspices of the Center for Egyptian Civilisation Studies and with the financial support of the United Nations Fund for Population Activities (UNFPA).

FALETAU, MELESEINI

Faletau, Meleseini. Changing roles for Tonga's women. PACIFIC PERSPECTIVE (SUVA) 1983, 11, No. 2:45-55.

Families divided: the impact of migrant labour in Lesotho. By: Murray, Colin. Series: African Studies Series, 29. (Cambridge, England, Cambridge University Press, 1981), 219 pp.

FAMILY

Courtship, love, and marriage in contemporary China; a symposium. PACIFIC AFFAIRS (VANCOUVER, B.C.) Summer 1984, 57:209-69. CONTENT: Young, Marilyn B., Introduction. - Wolf, Margery, Marriage, family, and the state in contemporary China. - Hershatter, Gail, Making a friend: changing patterns of courtship in urban China. - Honig, Emily, Private issues, public discourse: the life and times of Yu Luojin. - The marriage law of the People's Republic of China.

Greenhalgh, Susan. Sexual stratification: the other side of "growth with equity" in East Asia. POPULATION AND DEVELOPMENT REVIEW (NEW YORK) June 1985, 11:265-314. This paper explores changes in women's status on Taiwan focussing on how the traditional system of sexual stratification was perpetuated and even intensified with the rapid development of the economy.

Kravchenko, M.. For the mother, for the family. SOVIET REVIEW, A JOURNAL OF TRANSLATIONS (ARMONK, N.Y.) Summer 1984, 25:18-24.

Family and female participation in the labor market in Latin America. By: Recchini de Lattes, Zulma.. LATIN AMERICAN RESEARCH REVIEW (ALBUQUERQUE, NM) 1982, 17, No. 1:101-04.

Family planning programs; the clients' perspective. By: Ainsworth, Martha. Series: World Bank Staff Working Papers, No. 676; Population and Development Series, No. 1. (Washington, DC, World Bank, 1985), 86 pp.

FAMILY SIZE. ECONOMIC ASPECTS

Helmore, Kristin. Family ties: wives and mothers. CHRISTIAN SCIENCE MONITOR (BOSTON) December 18, 1985, p. 17-19. Part 2 of 5-part series entitled: "The neglected resource; women in the developing world." Author looks at marriage and motherhood in various cultures in the less developed countries.

Family status production work: what does it produce? By: Sharma, Ursula M.. JOURNAL OF SOCIAL STUDIES (DHAKA) April 1984, No. 24:74-94. Attempts to develop some issues regarding women's work in the household, using a study of women in urban households in Simla, Himachal Pradesh.

Family ties: wives and mothers. By: Helmore, Kristin. CHRISTIAN SCIENCE MONITOR (BOSTON) December 18, 1985, p. 17-19. Part 2 of 5-part series entitled: "The neglected resource; women in the developing world." Author looks at marriage and motherhood in various cultures in the less developed countries.

FAMILY. ECONOMIC ASPECTS

Geary, Christraud M. On legal change in Cameroon: women, marriage, and bridewealth. BOSTON UNIVERSITY. AFRICAN STUDIES CENTER. WORKING PAPERS (BOSTON) 1986, No. 113:1-37.

FAPOHUNDA, ELEANOR R.

Fapohunda, Eleanor R.. Childcare dilemma of working mothers in African cities: the case of Lagos, Nigeria. In: Women and work in Africa. Edited by Edna G. Bay. (Boulder, CO, Westview Press, 1982), pp. 277-88.

FARM MECHANIZATION

Hye, Hasnat Abdul. Mechanisation in agriculture and women in Bangladesh. JOURNAL OF SOCIAL STUDIES (DHAKA) January 1985, No. 27:78-100.

FARMERS

Koopman Henn, Jeanne. Feeding the cities and feeding the peasants: what role for Africa's women farmers? WORLD DEVELOPMENT (OXFORD) December 1983, 11:1043-55.

Farming system for women: the case of cassava production in Zaire. By: Blain, Daniele. CERES, FAO REVIEW ON AGRICULTURE AND DEVELOPMENT (ROME) May/June 1985, 18:43-46.

FARNOS, ALFONSO

Farnos, Alfonso and Gonzalez, Fernando. Role of women and demographic change in Cuba. INTERNATIONAL LABOUR OFFICE. WORLD EMPLOYMENT PROGRAMME RESEARCH. POPULATION AND LABOUR POLICIES PROGRAMME. WORKING PAPER (GENEVA) August 1983, No. 138:1-52.

FATIMA, BURNAD

Fatima, Burnad. Rural development and women's liberation: caste, class and gender in a grass-roots organisation in Tamil Nadu, South India. IDS BULLETIN, INSTITUTE OF DEVELOPMENT STUDIES AT THE UNIVERSITY OF SUSSEX (BRIGHTON) January 1984, 15:45-50.

FAWCETT, JAMES T.

Fawcett, James T. and Khoo, Siew-Ean and Smith, Peter C.. Urbanization, migration, and the status of women. In: Women in the cities of Asia: migration and urban adaptation. Edited by James T. Fawcett, Siew-Ean Khoo and Peter C. Smith. (Boulder, CO, Westview Press, 1984), pp. 15-35.

Feeding the cities and feeding the peasants: what role for Africa's women farmers? By: Koopman Henn, Jeanne. WORLD DEVELOPMENT (OXFORD) December 1983, 11:1043-55.

FEIJOO, MARIA DEL CARMEN

Feijoo, Maria del Carmen. Research on the status of women, development and population trends in Latin America: an annotated bibliography. In: Bibliographic guide to studies on the status of women: development and population trends. (New York, Bowker, UNIPUB; Paris, Unesco, 1983), pp. 141-82.

FELDMAN, RAYAH

Feldman, Rayah. Women's groups and women's subordination: an analysis of policies towards rural women in Kenya. REVIEW OF AFRICAN POLITICAL ECONOMY (SHEFFIELD) 1984, No. 27/28:67-85.

Female Asian immigrants in Honolulu: adaptation and success. By: Gardner, Robert W. and Wright, Paul A.. In: Women in the cities of Asia: migration and urban adaptation. Edited by James T. Fawcett, Siew-Ean Khoo and Peter C. Smith. (Boulder, CO, Westview Press, 1984), pp. 322-46.

Female domestic servant and social change: Lima, Peru. By: Smith, Margo L.. In: Women cross-culturally: change and challenge. Edited by Ruby Rohrlich-Leavitt. (The Hague, Mouton, 1975), pp. 163-80.

Female domestic servants in Cagayan de Oro, Philippines: social and economic implications of employment in a 'premodern' occupational role. By: Palabrica-Costello, Marilou. In: Women in the urban and industrial workforce; Southeast and East Asia. Edited by Gavin W. Jones. Series: Development Studies Centre. Monograph, No. 33. (Canberra, Australia, Australian National University, 1984), pp. 235-50. Series edited by Helen Hughes.

Female employment and social status; survey. By: Mohiuddin, Yasmeen. PAKISTAN & GULF ECONOMIST (KARACHI) April 6, 1985, 4:30-33. Report based on a survey of 216 female handicraft workers located at major centres of handicraft work in north, middle and south Sind.

Female employment and the family: a case study of the Bataan export processing zone. By: Zosa-Feranil, Imelda. In: Women in the urban and industrial workforce; Southeast and East Asia. Edited by Gavin W. Jones. Series: Development Studies Centre. Monograph, No. 33. (Canberra, Australia, Australian National University, 1984), pp. 387-405. Series edited by Helen Hughes.

Female factor in anthropology. By: Ifeka, Caroline. In: Women cross-culturally: change and challenge. Edited by Ruby Rohrlich-Leavitt. (The Hague, Mouton, 1975), pp. 559-66.

Female handicraft workers; the invisible hand. By: Mohiuddin, Yasmeen. PAKISTAN & GULF ECONOMIST (KARACHI) July 20, 1985, 4:44-47. The purpose of this study is to investigate the economic role and status of these invisible producers in the all-female handicraft production in Sind, Pakistan.

Female labor and capitalism in the United States and Brazil. By: Saffioti, Heleieth Iara Bongiovani. In: Women cross-culturally: change and challenge. Edited by Ruby Rohrlich-Leavitt. (The Hague, Mouton, 1975), pp. 60-94.

Female labor force participation in developing and developed countries -- consideration of the informal sector. By: Hill, M. Anne. REVIEW OF ECONOMICS AND STATISTICS (CAMBRIDGE, MASS.) August 1983, 65:459-68.

Female labor force participation in urban Japan; a trichotomous logit model. By: Hill, M. Anne. YALE UNIVERSITY. ECONOMIC GROWTH CENTER. DISCUSSION PAPER (NEW HAVEN, CONN.) September 1980, No. 362:1-42.

Female labor participation and female seclusion in rural India: a regional view. By: Miller, Barbara D.. ECONOMIC DEVELOPMENT AND CULTURAL CHANGE (CHICAGO) July 1982, 30:777-94.

Female labour force participation in developing countries: a critique of current definitions and data collection methods. By: Anker, Richard. INTERNATIONAL LABOUR REVIEW (GENEVA) November/December 1983, 122:709-23.

Female labour force participation: the enigma of the interwar period. By: Hatton, T. J.. UNIVERSITY OF ESSEX. DEPT. OF ECONOMICS. DISCUSSION PAPER SERIES (COLCHESTER) June 1986, No. 285:1-36.

Female labour force status and fertility behaviour in Bangladesh: search for policy interventions. By: Chaudhury, Rafiqul Huda. BANGLADESH DEVELOPMENT STUDIES (DACCA) September 1983, 11:59-102.

Female labour force status and fertility behaviour; some theoretical, methodical and policy issues. By: Chaudhury, Rafiqul Huda. PAKISTAN DEVELOPMENT REVIEW (ISLAMABAD) Winter 1979, 18:341-57. An attempt is made to examine the dynamics of the relationship between female labor force status and fertility behavior and also to evaluate the implication of the relationship for reduction of fertility, particularly with reference to the developing countries of the world.

Female labour participation in rice farming system of Chhattisgarh region. By: Marothia, D. K. and Sharma, S. K. INDIAN JOURNAL OF AGRICULTURAL ECONOMICS (BOMBAY) July/September 1985, 40:235-39.

Female migrant in Pakistan. By: Shah, Nasra M.. In: Women in the cities of Asia: migration and urban adaptation. Edited by James T. Fawcett, Siew-Ean Khoo and Peter C. Smith. (Boulder, CO, Westview Press, 1984), pp. 108-24.

Female migrants in Bangkok metropolis. By: Piampiti, Suwanlee. In: Women in the cities of Asia: migration and urban adaptation. Edited by James T. Fawcett, Siew-Ean Khoo and Peter C. Smith. (Boulder, CO, Westview Press, 1984), pp. 227-46.

Female migration: a conceptual framework. By: Thadani, Veena N. and Todaro, Michael P.. In: Women in the cities of Asia: migration and urban adaptation. Edited by James T. Fawcett, Siew-Ean Khoo and Peter C. Smith. (Boulder, CO, Westview Press, 1984), pp. 36-59.

Female migration in Thailand. By: Arnold, Fred and Piampiti, Suwanlee. In: Women in the cities of Asia: migration and urban adaptation. Edited by James T. Fawcett, Siew-Ean Khoo and Peter C. Smith. (Boulder, CO, Westview Press, 1984), pp. 143-64.

Female primary education and fertility reduction in India. By: Jain, Anrudh K. and Nag, Moni. POPULATION COUNCIL. CENTER FOR POLICY STUDIES. WORKING PAPERS (NEW YORK) September 1985, No. 114:1-57.

Female rural-to-urban migration in peninsular Malaysia. By: Khoo, Siew-Ean and Pirie, Peter. In: Women in the cities of Asia: migration and urban adaptation. Edited by James T. Fawcett, Siew-Ean Khoo and Peter C. Smith. (Boulder, CO, Westview Press, 1984), pp. 125-42.

Female work participation and fertility in a Philippine setting: a test of alternative models. By: Herrin, Alejandro N.. UNIVERSITY OF THE PHILIPPINES. SCHOOL OF ECONOMICS. DISCUSSION PAPER (QUEZON) October 1980, No. 8005:1-99.

Female workers as described in a help-wanted information magazine. By: Shinotsuka, Eiko. JAPANESE ECONOMIC STUDIES (ARMONK, N.Y.) Spring 1984, 12:3-20.

Female-headed households and domestic organization in San Isidro, Guatemala: a test of Hammel and Laslett's comparative typology. By: Kendall, Carl. In: Women in the family and the economy: an international comparative survey. Edited by George Kurian and Ratna Ghosh. (Westport, CT, Greenwood Press, 1981), pp. 29-41.

Females in the agricultural labour force and non-formal education for rural development in Ghana. By: Greenstreet, Miranda. INSTITUTE OF SOCIAL STUDIES. OCCASIONAL PAPERS (THE HAGUE) August 1981, No. 90:1-22.

FEMINISM

de Brito, Angela Neves-Xavier. Brazilian women in exile; the quest for an identity. LATIN AMERICAN PERSPECTIVES (BEVERLY HILLS) Spring 1986, 13:58-80.

FEMINISM

Haug, Frigga. Women's movement in West Germany. NEW LEFT REVIEW (LONDON) January/February 1986, No. 155:50-74.

Feminism and nationalist politics in Egypt. By: Philipp, Thomas. In: Women in the Muslim world. Edited by Lois Beck and Nikki Keddie. (Cambridge, MA, Harvard University Press, 1978), pp. 277-94.

Feminism at work. By: Maroney, Heather Jon. NEW LEFT REVIEW (LONDON) September/October 1983, No. 141:51-71.

La femme malaise, productrice et gestionnaire. By: Massard, Josiane. TIERS-MONDE (PARIS) April/June 1985, 26:359-70.

Les femmes dans l'economie, de l'invisibilite a de nouveaux modes d'organisation. By: Mignot-Lefebvre, Yvonne. TIERS-MONDE (PARIS) April/June 1985, 26:247-60.

Femmes et controle des naissances; refus, contraintes et vecus. By: Dabat, Christine and Modak, Marianne. INSTITUT UNIVERSITAIRE D'ETUDES DU DEVELOPPEMENT. ITINERAIRES: NOTES ET TRAVAUX (GENEVA) April 1981, No. 15:1-119.

Femmes et developpement apres Nairobi; ideologie et enjeux internationaux d'une decennie. By: Mignot-Lefebvre, Yvonne. TIERS-MONDE (PARIS) January/March 1986, 27:129-42.

Femmes et developpement en Afrique sahelienne: l'experience nigerienne d'animation feminine (1966-1976). By: Belloncle, Guy. Series: Collection Developpement et Civilisations. (Paris, Editions Ouvrieres, 1980), 212 pp.

Femmes et developpement; idees et strategies des organisations internationales. By: Mignot-Lefebvre, Yvonne. TIERS-MONDE (PARIS) October/December 1980, 21:845-62.

Les femmes et le developpement. TIERS-MONDE (PARIS) July/September 1982, 23:577-618.

Les femmes et les programmes de developpement rural; avec reference aux programmes-femmes finances par le Fonds Europeen de Developpement au Kenya. By: Roberts, Penelope. TIERS-MONDE (PARIS) April/June 1985, 26:299-305.

Femmes musulmanes entre "l'etat sauvage" et les "cultures civilisees". By: Moatassime, Ahmed. TIERS-MONDE (PARIS) January/March 1984, 25:139-54.

Les femmes paysannes et la crise agraire en Amerique latine. By: Arizpe, Lourdes. TIERS-MONDE (PARIS) April/June 1985, 26:325-34.

FERBER, MARIANNE A.

Ferber, Marianne A. and Green, Carole A. Work power and earnings of women and men. AMERICAN ECONOMIC REVIEW, PAPERS AND PROCEEDINGS (NASHVILLE) May 1986, 76:53-56.

Fertility and employment: an assessment of role incompatibility among African urban women. By: Lewis, Barbara. In: Women and work in Africa. Edited by Edna G. Bay. (Boulder, CO, Westview Press, 1982), pp. 249-76.

Fertility and family economy in the Iranian rural communities. By: Aghajanian, Akbar. In: Women in the family and the economy: an international comparative survey. Edited by George Kurian and Ratna Ghosh. (Westport, CT, Greenwood Press, 1981), pp. 297-305.

Fertility and labor force participation of married women: empirical evidence from the 1980 population census of Japan. By: Yamada, Tadashi and Yamada, Tetsuji. QUARTERLY REVIEW OF ECONOMICS AND BUSINESS (URBANA, ILL.) Summer 1986, 26:35-46.

Fertility, female employment and policy measures in Hungary. By: Barta, Barnabas and Klinger, Andras. Series: Women, Work and Development, No. 6. (Geneva, International Labour Organisation, 1984), 88 pp. Published with the financial support of the United Nations Fund for Population Activities (UNFPA).

FIEGE, KARIN

Kranz, Jutta and Fiege, Karin. Work never ends; problems of women in the farm economy of the Ivory Coast. D & C, DEVELOPMENT AND COOPERATION (BONN) November/December 1983, No. 6:12-13.

Field guide to research on seven roles of women: focussed biographies. By: Oppong, Christine and Church, Katie. INTERNATIONAL LABOUR OFFICE. WORLD EMPLOYMENT PROGRAMME RESEARCH. POPULATION AND LABOUR POLICIES PROGRAMME. WORKING PAPER (GENEVA) May 1981, No. 106:1-52.

Fighting two colonialisms. By: Urdang, Stephanie. (New York, Monthly Review Press, 1979), 320 pp. The author discusses the situation of women in Guinea-Bissau.

FIGUEROA, BLANCA

Figueroa, Blanca and Anderson, Jeanine. Women in Peru. Series: Change International Reports: Women in Society, No. 5. (London, Change International Reports, 1981), 16 pp.

FIGUEROA, TERESA ORREGO DE

Figueroa, Teresa Orrego de. Critical analysis of Latin American programs to integrate women in development. In: Women and world development. Edited by Irene Tinker and Michele Bo Bramsen. ([Washington, DC], Overseas Development Council, 1976), pp. 45-54.

FIJI

Kamikamica, Esiteri. Fiji women on the move. PACIFIC PERSPECTIVE (SUVA) 1983, 11, No. 2:40-44.

FINN, JEREMY D.

Finn, Jeremy D. and Reis, Janet. Sex differences in educational attainment: the process. COMPARATIVE EDUCATION REVIEW (NEW YORK) June 1980, 24:S33-52. Examines various obstacles to women's education.

FISCHER, MICHAEL M. J.

Fischer, Michael M. J.. On changing the concept and position of Persian women. In: Women in the Muslim world. Edited by Lois Beck and Nikki Keddie. (Cambridge, MA, Harvard University Press, 1978), pp. 189-215.

FISCHER, WOLFGANG E.

Fischer, Wolfgang E.. Entwicklungshilfe: Fluch oder Segen fur die Frauen? Die bedeutende Rolle der Frauen wird bei der Projektplanung nicht angemessen berücksichtigt. E & Z, ENTWICKLUNG UND ZUSAMMENARBEIT (BONN) January 1985, 26:6-7.

FISH INDUSTRY

Gulati, Leela. Fishing, technology and women. CENTRE FOR DEVELOPMENT STUDIES. WORKING PAPER (ULLOOR, TRIVANDRUM) January 1983, No. 155:1-253. Attempts to discover and document how changes in the technology of fishing and fish preservation in Kerala communities have affected women of fishing households, not only in general economic terms, but also in terms, specifically, of demographic behaviour. CONTENT: Pt. 1 - Pt. 2: Case studies.

FISH INDUSTRY

Gulati, Leela. Technological change and women's work; participation and demographic behaviour: a case study of three fishing villages. ECONOMIC AND POLITICAL WEEKLY (BOMBAY) December 8, 1984, 19:2089-94.

Gulati, Leela. Women in fishing villages on the Kerala coast: demographic and socio-economic impacts of a fisheries development project. INTERNATIONAL LABOUR OFFICE. WORLD EMPLOYMENT PROGRAMME RESEARCH. POPULATION AND LABOUR POLICIES PROGRAMME. WORKING PAPER (GENEVA) March 1983, No. 128:1-143.

Fishing, technology and women. By: Gulati, Leela. CENTRE FOR DEVELOPMENT STUDIES. WORKING PAPER (ULLOOR, TRIVANDRUM) January 1983, No. 155:1-253. Attempts to discover and document how changes in the technology of fishing and fish preservation in Kerala communities have affected women of fishing households, not only in general economic terms, but also in terms, specifically, of demographic behaviour. CONTENT: Pt. 1 - Pt. 2: Case studies.

FISHING VILLAGES

Gulati, Leela. Women in fishing villages on the Kerala coast: demographic and socio-economic impacts of a fisheries development project. INTERNATIONAL LABOUR OFFICE. WORLD EMPLOYMENT PROGRAMME RESEARCH. POPULATION AND LABOUR POLICIES PROGRAMME. WORKING PAPER (GENEVA) March 1983, No. 128:1-143.

Five studies on the situation of women in Latin America. Series: Estudios e Informes de la Cepal, [No.] 16. (Santiago, Chile, United Nations, 1983), 188 pp. Position paper for the Second Conference on the Integration of Women into Latin american Economic and Social Development, held at Macuto, Venezuela, November 1979. Originally published in Spanish with title: Cinco estudios sobre la situacion de la mujer en America Latina (Santiago de Chile, Naciones Unidas, 1982). 178 pp.

FLEMING, VICTORIA

Fleming, Victoria. Women and development. WEST AFRICA (LONDON) December 7, 1981, No. 3358:2921-22. Discusses the progress and the pitfalls halfway through the International Decade for Women.

FLORA, CORNELIA BUTLER

Flora, Cornelia Butler. Social policy and women in Latin America: the need for a new model. STUDIES IN THIRD WORLD SOCIETIES (WILLIAMSBURG) March 1981, No. 15:91-105.

FLORMAN, SAMUEL C.

Florman, Samuel C.. Where are the women engineers? ACROSS THE BOARD (NEW YORK) January 1982, 19:56-61. A male engineer writes: 'The ultimate feminist dream will never be realized as long as women would rather supervise the world than help build it.'

FLOUR-MILLS

Nath, Kamla. Labor-saving techniques in food processing: rural women and technological change in the Gambia. BOSTON UNIVERSITY. AFRICAN STUDIES CENTER. WORKING PAPERS (BOSTON) 1985, No. 108:1-26. Describes the methodology used in developing a project design for the introduction of sorghum and millet decorticators and flour milling units in rural areas of the Gambia in West Africa.

Focusing on women for water and sanitation: the case of Mapo community in Ibadan, Nigeria. By: Olaseha, I. O. and Namanja, Gracian Bazilious. INTERNATIONAL QUARTERLY OF COMMUNITY HEALTH EDUCATION (FARMINGDALE, N.Y.) 1985/1986, 6, No. 4:335-43.

FOOD

Brandtzaeg, Brita. Role and status of women in post-harvest food conservation. FOOD AND NUTRITION BULLETIN (TOKYO) January 1982, 4:33-40.

FOOD AID

Katona-Apte, Judit. Women and food aid; a developmental perspective. FOOD POLICY (GUILDFORD, ENG.) August 1986, 11:216-22.

FOOD PROCESSING

Nath, Kamla. Labor-saving techniques in food processing: rural women and technological change in the Gambia. BOSTON UNIVERSITY. AFRICAN STUDIES CENTER. WORKING PAPERS (BOSTON) 1985, No. 108:1-26. Describes the methodology used in developing a project design for the introduction of sorghum and millet decorticators and flour milling units in rural areas of the Gambia in West Africa.

FOOD SUPPLY

Vellenga, Dorothy Dee. Women, households, and food commodity chains in southern Ghana: contradictions between the search for profit and the struggle for survival. REVIEW, FERNAND BRAUDEL CENTER (BINGHAMTON, N.Y.) Winter 1985, 8:293-318.

For the mother, for the family. By: Kravchenko, M.. SOVIET REVIEW, A JOURNAL OF TRANSLATIONS (ARMONK, N.Y.) Summer 1984, 25:18-24.

FOREIGN AID

Cohn, Steven and Wood, Robert. U.S. aid and Third World women: the impact of Peace Corps programs. ECONOMIC DEVELOPMENT AND CULTURAL CHANGE (CHICAGO) July 1981, 29:795-811.

Entwicklungshilfe - Fluch oder Segen fur die Frauen? E & Z, ENTWICKLUNG UND ZUSAMMENARBEIT (BONN) January 1985, 26:4-21.

Fischer, Wolfgang E.. Entwicklungshilfe: Fluch oder Segen fur die Frauen? Die bedeutende Rolle der Frauen wird bei der Projektplanung nicht angemessen berucksichtigt. E & Z, ENTWICKLUNG UND ZUSAMMENARBEIT (BONN) January 1985, 26:6-7.

FOREST ECOLOGY

Jain, Shobhita. Women and people's ecological movement; a case study of women's role in the Chipko movement in Uttar Pradesh. ECONOMIC AND POLITICAL WEEKLY (BOMBAY) October 13, 1984, 19:1788-93.

FORESTS AND FORESTRY

Hoskings, Marilyn W.. Community forestry depends on women. UNASYLVA (ROME) 1980, 32, No. 130:27-32.

Formal or nonformal education? Entrepreneurial women in Ghana. By: Robertson, Claire C.. COMPARATIVE EDUCATION REVIEW (NEW YORK) November 1984, 28:639-58.

FORRAY, KATALIN R

Forray, Katalin R. Bildungswege der Frauen in Ungarn: neue Tendenzen in der Ausbildung und Beschaftigung aus soziologischer Sicht. OSTERREICHISCHE OSTHEFTE (VIENNA) 1986, 28, No. 2:107-25.

FORTMANN, LOUISE

Fortmann, Louise and Rocheleau, Dianne. Women and agroforestry: four myths and three case studies. AGROFORESTRY SYSTEMS (THE HAGUE) 1985, 2, No. 4:253-72. The involvement of women in agroforestry projects and activities is examined in case studies from the Dominican Republic, India and Kenya. Consideration for including women in agroforestry projects are discussed.

Fortmann, Louise. Women's work in a communal setting: the Tanzanian policy of Ujamaa. In: Women and work in Africa. Edited by Edna G. Bay. (Boulder, CO, Westview Press, 1982), pp. 191-205.

Fortmann, Louise. Women's involvement in high risk arable agriculture, the Botswana case. (Washington, Office of Women in Development, Agency for International Development, International Development Cooperation Agency, 1980), 27 pp. Prepared for presentation at Ford Foundation workshop on women in agriculture in Eastern and Southern Africa. Nairobi, 9-11 April, 1980.

Der Fortschritt drangt die Frauen ins Abseits. By: Wichterich, Christa. E & Z, ENTWICKLUNG UND ZUSAMMENARBEIT (BONN) January 1985, 26:4-5.

Four women's organizations of Calcutta. By: Fruzzetti, Lina M. UNIVERSITIES FIELD STAFF INTERNATIONAL REPORTS, ASIA (HANOVER, NH) 1986, No. 4:1-5.

FOX, ROBERT

Fox, Robert. Men and women in the Philippines. In: Women in the new Asia, the changing social roles of men and women in South and South-east Asia. Edited by Barbara E. Ward. ([Paris], Unesco, 1963), pp. 342-64.

FRANCE

Salmona, Micheline. L'echappee belle, ou la mobilisation generale des femmes dans l'agriculture en France. TIERS-MONDE (PARIS) April/June 1985, 26:247-60.

France: contrasts in familial and societal roles. By: Bodard Silver, Catherine. In: Women: roles and status in eight countries. Edited by Janet Zollinger Giele and Audrey Chapman Smock. (New York, John Wiley, 1977), pp. 259-99.

Frauen auf dem Arbeitsmarkt: Verdrangung statt Integration? By: Gottschall, Karin. WSI-MITTEILUNGEN (DUSSELDORF) August 1986, 39:514-21.

Frauen tragen die Last der Entwicklung; Beispiele aus West-Afrika. By: Wiese, Eva-Maria. E & Z, ENTWICKLUNG UND ZUSAMMENARBEIT (BONN) January 1985, 26:8-10.

Frauenarbeit: ein Beitrag zur gewerkschaftlichen Technikdebatte. By: Metzner, Ulrike and Stahn-Willig, Brigitte. WSI-MITTEILUNGEN (DUSSELDORF) August 1986, 39:529-36.

FREE PORTS AND ZONES

Gothoskar, Sujata. Free trade zones: pitting women against women. ECONOMIC AND POLITICAL WEEKLY (BOMBAY) August 23, 1986, 21:1489-92.

FRIEDL, ERIKA

Friedl, Erika. Women in contemporary Persian folktales. In: Women in the Muslim world. Edited by Lois Beck and Nikki Keddie. (Cambridge, MA, Harvard University Press, 1978), pp. 629-50.

From drudgery to dignity: the SEWA experience. By: Krishnaswami, Lalita. LABOUR AND SOCIETY (GENEVA) September 1985, 10:323-31. Discusses the achievements of the Self-Employed Women's Association (SEWA), which is at once a union, a trust and a credit institution whose basic aim is to provide better living and working conditions for the poor, illiterate women who comprise its membership.

From Lelemama to lobbying: women's associations in Mombasa, Kenya. By: Strobel, Margaret. In: Women in Africa: studies in social and economic change. Edited by Nancy J. Hafkin and Edna G. Bay. (Stanford, Stanford University Press, 1976), pp. 183-211.

From the village to the slum. By: Helmore, Kristin. CHRISTIAN SCIENCE MONITOR (BOSTON) December 17, 1985, p. 17-20. Part 1 of 5-part series entitled: "The neglected resource; women in the developing world." After spending three months in Africa, Asia and Latin America the author examines the plight of women and what can be done to ease their burdens.

FRUZZETTI, LINA M

Fruzzetti, Lina M. Four women's organizations of Calcutta. UNIVERSITIES FIELD STAFF INTERNATIONAL REPORTS, ASIA (HANOVER, NH) 1986, No. 4:1-5.

FUEL

Batliwala, Srilatha. Women and cooking energy. ECONOMIC AND POLITICAL WEEKLY (BOMBAY) December 24, 1983, 18:2227-30. Describes how a woman in poverty has low access to cooking fuel, spends the longest time obtaining it, and puts it to use in stoves which are not only fuel-inefficient, but which also subject her to serious or fatal disease.

Ki-Zerbo, Jacqueline. Women and the energy crisis in the Sahel. UNASYLVA (ROME) 1981, 33, No. 133:5-10.

Funf Frauen - funf Leben. By: Muller-Blattau, Beate and Seibert, Ulrike. E & Z, ENTWICKLUNG UND ZUSAMMENARBEIT (BONN) January 1985, 26:16-17.

G. K. T. Chiepe, Minister of Foreign Affairs, Botswana. By: Novicki, Margaret A.. AFRICA REPORT (NEW YORK) March/April 1985, 30:14-16. An interview with Dr. G. K. T. Chiepe, Botswans's first woman university graduate and first female cabinet minister who discusses the advances of women over the UN Decade and the significance of women's contributions to the economic development of her country.

Ga women and socioeconomic change in Accra, Ghana. By: Robertson, Claire. In: Women in Africa: studies in social and economic change. Edited by Nancy J. Hafkin and Edna G. Bay. (Stanford, Stanford University Press, 1976), pp. 111-33.

GADALLA, SAAD

Bach, Rebecca and Gadalla, Saad. Mothers' influence on daughters' orientations toward education: an Egyptian case study. COMPARATIVE EDUCATION REVIEW (NEW YORK) August 1985, 29:374-84.

GAMBIA

Badoe, Yaba Mangela. Gambia; rice and dependency. WEST AFRICA (LONDON) October 24, 1983, No. 3454:2484. Discusses the sexual politics of rice production and concludes that women are the prime losers but the cost to national food production is enormous.

Nath, Kamla. Labor-saving techniques in food processing: rural women and technological change in the Gambia. BOSTON UNIVERSITY. AFRICAN STUDIES CENTER. WORKING PAPERS (BOSTON) 1985, No. 108:1-26. Describes the methodology used in developing a project design for the introduction of sorghum and millet decorticators and flour milling units in rural areas of the Gambia in West Africa.

GAMBIA

Nath, Kamla. National machineries for integration of women in development: a strategy for The Gambia. BOSTON UNIVERSITY. AFRICAN STUDIES CENTER. WORKING PAPERS (BOSTON) 1985, No. 104:1-17.

Nath, Kamla. Women and technological change in The Gambia: a case study of the salt industry. BOSTON UNIVERSITY. AFRICAN STUDIES CENTER. WORKING PAPERS (BOSTON) 1985, No. 107:1-15.

Nath, Kamla. Women and vegetable gardens in the Gambia: Action AID and rural development. BOSTON UNIVERSITY. AFRICAN STUDIES CENTER. WORKING PAPERS (BOSTON) 1985, No. 109:1-13. Examines Action Aid's program for improving the capacity of rural women to produce garden vegetables and to introduce marketing infrastructures.

Gambia; rice and dependency. By: Badoe, Yaba Mangela. WEST AFRICA (LONDON) October 24, 1983, No. 3454:2484. Discusses the sexual politics of rice production and concludes that women are the prime losers but the cost to national food production is enormous.

Gandhi's philosophy; an inspiration for women. By: Jain, Devaki. DEVELOPMENT (ROME) 1984, No. 4:71-74.

GANI, AMNA

Gani, Amna. Combining marriage and career in Karachi. In: Women in the new Asia; the changing social roles of men and women in South and South-east Asia. Edited by Barbara E. Ward. ([Paris], Unesco, 1963), pp. 323-39.

GARABAGHI, NINOU K.

Garabaghi, Ninou K.. New approach to women's participation in the economy. INTERNATIONAL SOCIAL SCIENCE JOURNAL (PARIS) 1983, 35, No. 4:659-82.

GARDNER, ROBERT W.

Gardner, Robert W. and Wright, Paul A.. Female Asian immigrants in Honolulu: adaptation and success. In: Women in the cities of Asia: migration and urban adaptation. Edited by James T. Fawcett, Siew-Ean Khoo and Peter C. Smith. (Boulder, CO, Westview Press, 1984), pp. 322-46.

GASTON, CHERYL L

Gaston, Cheryl L. Idea whose time has not come: comparable worth and the market salary problem. POPULATION RESEARCH AND POLICY REVIEW (AMSTERDAM) 1986, 5, No. 1:15-29.

GAUFFENIC, ARMELLE

Gauffenic, Armelle. Le statut social de la femme; pour un nouvel ordre mondial. TIERS-MONDE (PARIS) April/June 1985, 26:273-81.

GAY, JUDITH S.

Gay, Judith S.. Women and development in Lesotho. (Washington, Lesotho, USAID, Bureau for Africa, 1982), 84 pp. (Mimeographed)

GEARY, CHRISTRAUD M

Geary, Christraud M. On legal change in Cameroon: women, marriage, and bridewealth. BOSTON UNIVERSITY. AFRICAN STUDIES CENTER. WORKING PAPERS (BOSTON) 1986, No. 113:1-37.

GEIGER, SUSAN

Geiger, Susan. Umoja wa wanawake wa Tanzania and the needs of the rural poor. AFRICAN STUDIES REVIEW (WALTHAM, MASS.) June/September 1982, 25:45-65. Describes the national women's organization of Tanzania.

Gender and organizations: a selective review and a critique of a neglected area. By: Hearn, Jeff and Parkin, P. Wendy. ORGANIZATION STUDIES (BERLIN) 1983, 4, No. 3:219-42.

Gender basis of American social policy. By: Sapiro, Virginia. POLITICAL SCIENCE QUARTERLY (NEW YORK) 1986, 101, No. 2:221-38.

Gender, politics and modernization: the Indian case. By: Mukhopadhyay, Carol C. and Bald, Suresht R.. STUDIES IN THIRD WORLD SOCIETIES (WILLIAMSBURG) June 1981, No. 16:91-121.

Generational differences in female occupational attainment -- have the 1970's changed women's opportunities? By: Zalokar, Nadja. AMERICAN ECONOMIC REVIEW, PAPERS AND PROCEEDINGS (NASHVILLE) May 1986, 76:378-81.

GEORGE, P. M.

George, P. M. and Ebanks, G. E.. Labor force participation and fertility contraceptive knowledge; attitudes and practice of the women of Barbados. In: Women in the family and the economy: an international comparative survey. Edited by George Kurian and Ratna Ghosh. (Westport, CT, Greenwood Press, 1981), pp. 285-96.

GERMANY, FED. REP.

Becker-Schmidt, Regina and Knapp, Gudrun-Axeli. Wertewandel und Widerspruche; Erziehungsorientierungen und -probleme von Arbeiterinnen im Vergleich zweier Generationen. WSI-MITTEILUNGEN (DUSSELDORF) August 1986, 39:558-66.

Demmer, Hildegard and Kupper, Bettina. Arbeitsbelastungen von Frauen im Paketdienst. WSI-MITTEILUNGEN (DUSSELDORF) August 1986, 39:522-28.

Gottschall, Karin. Frauen auf dem Arbeitsmarkt: Verdrangung statt Integration? WSI-MITTEILUNGEN (DUSSELDORF) August 1986, 39:514-21.

Haug, Frigga. Women's movement in West Germany. NEW LEFT REVIEW (LONDON) January/February 1986, No. 155:50-74.

Kurz-Scherf, Ingrid. Von der Emanzipation des Brunnenmadchens in Heilbadern; Frauendiskriminierung, Frauenforderung durch Tarifvertrag und Tarifpolitik. WSI-MITTEILUNGEN (DUSSELDORF) August 1986, 39:537-49.

Metz-Gockel, Sigrid and Muller, Ursula. Die Partnerschaft der Manner ist (noch) nicht die Partnerschaft der Frauen; empirische Befunde zum Geschlechterverhaltnis aus der Frauenperspektive. WSI-MITTEILUNGEN (DUSSELDORF) August 1986, 39:549-58.

Metzner, Ulrike and Stahn-Willig, Brigitte. Frauenarbeit: ein Beitrag zur gewerkschaftlichen Technikdebatte. WSI-MITTEILUNGEN (DUSSELDORF) August 1986, 39:529-36.

Raasch, Sibylle. Mindestens die Halfte aller Arbeits- und Ausbildungsplatze fur Frauen? Zur Quotierungsforderung in dem Entwurf eines Antidiscriminierungsgesetzes der Grunen. WSI-MITTEILUNGEN (DUSSELDORF) August 1986, 39:575-82.

Weg, Marianne. Das Ende der Bescheidenheit: Probleme und Perspektiven von Frauenforderplanen. WSI-MITTEILUNGEN (DUSSELDORF) August 1986, 39:566-75.

GHANA

Conseil national du Ghana. Groupements a but economique de femmes solidaires; l'experience du Ghana. TIERS-MONDE (PARIS) April/June 1985, 26:451-56.

Dumor, Ernest. Women in rural development in Ghana. RURAL AFRICANA (EAST LANSING) Fall 1983, No. 17:69-81.

GHANA

Greenstreet, Miranda. Females in the agricultural labour force and non-formal education for rural development in Ghana. INSTITUTE OF SOCIAL STUDIES. OCCASIONAL PAPERS (THE HAGUE) August 1981, No. 90:1-22.

Novicki, Margaret A.. Interview: Joyce Aryee, Secretary for Education, Ghana. AFRICA REPORT (NEW YORK) March/April 1985, 30:55-8.

Oppong, Christine and Abu, Katharine. Changing maternal role of Ghanaian women: impacts of education, migration and employment. INTERNATIONAL LABOUR OFFICE. WORLD EMPLOYMENT PROGRAMME RESEARCH. POPULATION AND LABOUR POLICIES PROGRAMME. WORKING PAPER (GENEVA) February 1984, No. 143:1-184.

Robertson, Claire C.. Formal or nonformal education? Entrepreneurial women in Ghana. COMPARATIVE EDUCATION REVIEW (NEW YORK) November 1984, 28:639-58.

Vellenga, Dorothy Dee. Women, households, and food commodity chains in southern Ghana: contradictions between the search for profit and the struggle for survival. REVIEW, FERNAND BRAUDEL CENTER (BINGHAMTON, N.Y.) Winter 1985, 8:293-318.

Ghana: from autonomy to subordination. By: Smock, Audrey Chapman. In: Women: roles and status in eight countries. Edited by Janet Zollinger Giele and Audrey Chapman Smock. (New York, John Wiley, 1977), pp. 175-216.

GHANDI, LAPIAN

Ghandi, Lapian. Status of women in Indonesian marriage law. In: Women and development, perspectives from South and Southeast Asia. Edited by Rounaq Jahan and Hanna Papanek. (Dacca, Bangladesh Institute of Law and International Affairs, 1979), pp. 71-94.

GHOSH, RATNA

Ghosh, Ratna. Minority within minority -- on being south Asian and female in Canada. In: Women in the family and the economy: an international comparative survey. Edited by George Kurian and Ratna Ghosh. (Westport, CT, Greenwood Press, 1981), pp. 413-26.

Ghosh, Ratna. Social and economic integration of south Asian women in Montreal, Canada. In: Women in the family and the economy: an international comparative survey. Edited by George Kurian and Ratna Ghosh. (Westport, CT, Greenwood Press, 1981), pp. 59-80.

GINAT, JOSEPH

Ginat, Joseph. Women in Muslim rural society: status and role in family and community. Series: The Monograph Series, Shiloah Center for Middle Eastern and African Studies, Tel Aviv University. (New Brunswick, NJ, Transaction Books, 1982), 268 pp.

GIRI, A. K

Choudhury, S. and Giri, A. K. Nature and extent of female labour use in agriculture - a comparison between progressive and non-progressive area. ECONOMIC AFFAIRS (CALCUTTA) June 1986, 31:81-86.

GNANADASON, ARUNA

Gnanadason, Aruna. Women's health: plea for a new approach. ECONOMIC AND POLITICAL WEEKLY (BOMBAY) September 13, 1986, 21:1630-30.

Going to the society. By: Wu, Wei. WOMEN OF CHINA (BEIJING) April 1985, No. 4:17-18.

GOLDIN, CLAUDIA

Goldin, Claudia. Maximum hours legislation and female employment in the 1920s: a reassessment. NATIONAL BUREAU OF ECONOMIC RESEARCH. WORKING PAPER SERIES (CAMBRIDGE, MASS.) June 1986, No. 1949:1-27.

GONCET, ODETTE

Goncet, Odette. Technologies appropriees pour les femmes africaines. MONDES EN DEVELOPPEMENT (PARIS) 1985, 13, No. 49:193-99.

GONZALES, SYLVIA A.

Gonzales, Sylvia A.. La Chicana: Guadalupe or Malinche. In: Comparative perspectives of Third World women: the impact of race, sex and class. Edited by Beverly Lindsay. (New York, Praeger, 1980), pp. 229-50.

GONZALEZ, FERNANDO

Farnos, Alfonso and Gonzalez, Fernando. Role of women and demographic change in Cuba. INTERNATIONAL LABOUR OFFICE. WORLD EMPLOYMENT PROGRAMME RESEARCH. POPULATION AND LABOUR POLICIES PROGRAMME. WORKING PAPER (GENEVA) August 1983, No. 138:1-52.

GOOD, MARY-JO DELVECCHIO

Good, Mary-Jo DelVecchio. Comparative perspective on women in provenicial Iran and Turkey. In: Women in the Muslim world. Edited by Lois Beck and Nikki Keddie. (Cambridge, MA, Harvard University Press, 1978), pp. 482-500.

GOODMAN, MATTHEW

Goodman, Matthew. Japanese women in finance. TOKYO BUSINESS TODAY (TOKYO) May 1986, p. 19-23.

GOPALAN, C.

Gopalan, C.. Mother and child in India. ECONOMIC AND POLITICAL WEEKLY (BOMBAY) January 26, 1985, 20:159-66.

GOTHOSKAR, SUJATA

Gothoskar, Sujata. Free trade zones: pitting women against women. ECONOMIC AND POLITICAL WEEKLY (BOMBAY) August 23, 1986, 21:1489-92.

Gothoskar, Sujata and Banaji, Rohini. Women, work, organisation and struggle. ECONOMIC AND POLITICAL WEEKLY (BOMBAY) March 5, 1983, 18:339-44. Article based on the conclusions of the authors' forthcoming book "My life is one long struggle... women, work, organisation and struggle".

GOTTSCHALL, KARIN

Gottschall, Karin. Frauen auf dem Arbeitsmarkt: Verdrangung statt Integration? WSI-MITTEILUNGEN (DUSSELDORF) August 1986, 39:514-21.

GOUGH, KATHLEEN

Gough, Kathleen. Origin of the family. In: Toward an anthropology of women. Edited by Rayna R. Reiter. (New York, Monthly Review Press, 1975), pp. 51-76.

GOULD, KETAYUN

Gould, Ketayun. Sex inequalities in the dual system of education; the Parsis of Gujarat. ECONOMIC AND POLITICAL WEEKLY (BOMBAY) September 24, 1983, 18:1668-76.

GOVERNMENT OFFICIALS AND EMPLOYEES. SALARIES

Chapman, Bruce J. Sex and location differences in wages in the Australian public service. AUSTRALIAN ECONOMIC PAPERS (ADELAIDE) December 1985, 24:296-309.

GRAVES, NANCY B.

Graves, Nancy B.. Adaptation of Polynesian female migrants in New Zealand. In: Women in the cities of Asia: migration and urban adaptation. Edited by James T. Fawcett, Siew-Ean Khoo and Peter C. Smith. (Boulder, CO, Westview Press, 1984), pp. 365-93.

GRAWE, ROGER

Grawe, Roger. Ability in pre-schoolers, earnings and home-environment. Series: World Bank Staff Working Papers, No. 322. (Washington, DC, World Bank, 1979), 92 pp.

GREECE

Kanellopoulos, Costas N.. Male-female pay differentials in Greece. GREEK ECONOMIC REVIEW (ATHENS) August 1982, 4:222-41.

GREEN, CAROLE A

Ferber, Marianne A. and Green, Carole A. Work power and earnings of women and men. AMERICAN ECONOMIC REVIEW, PAPERS AND PROCEEDINGS (NASHVILLE) May 1986, 76:53-56.

GREENHALGH, CHRISTINE A.

Stewart, Mark B. and Greenhalgh, Christine A.. Work history patterns and the occupational attainment of women. ECONOMIC JOURNAL (LONDON) September 1984, 94:493-519.

GREENHALGH, SUSAN

Greenhalgh, Susan. Sexual stratification: the other side of "growth with equity" in East Asia. POPULATION AND DEVELOPMENT REVIEW (NEW YORK) June 1985, 11:265-314. This paper explores changes in women's status on Taiwan focussing on how the traditional system of sexual stratification was perpetuated and even intensified with the rapid development of the economy.

GREENSTREET, MIRANDA

Greenstreet, Miranda. Females in the agricultural labour force and non-formal education for rural development in Ghana. INSTITUTE OF SOCIAL STUDIES. OCCASIONAL PAPERS (THE HAGUE) August 1981, No. 90:1-22.

GRENADA

LaDuke, Betty. Women, art, and culture in the new Grenada. LATIN AMERICAN PERSPECTIVES (BEVERLY HILLS) Summer 1984, 11:37-52.

GREWAL, R. S. AND NANDAL, D. S

Grewal, R. S. and Nandal, D. S. Impact of rural development programme on rural women in Bhiwani district of Haryana. INDIAN JOURNAL OF AGRICULTURAL ECONOMICS (BOMBAY) July/September 1985, 40:259-62.

GRIFFITH, DAVID C

Griffith, David C. Women, remittances, and reproduction. AMERICAN ETHNOLOGIST (WASHINGTON) November 1985, 12:676-90. Presents and interprets data on how women in Jamaica use remittances from migrating husbands, boyfriends, sons, and so forth, and examines some of the reasons for these uses. The author concludes that seasonal-labor migration aids Jamaican peasant households in meeting the costs of reproducing themselves and their social and economic conditions.

GRILLY, CATHERINE

Grilly, Catherine. Comite de teinturerie dans un quartier de Kinshasa (Zaire). TIERS-MONDE (PARIS) April/June 1985, 26:429-34.

GRONAU, REUBEN

Weiss, Yoram and Gronau, Reuben. Expected interruptions in labour force participation and sex-related differences in earnings growth. REVIEW OF ECONOMIC STUDIES (EDINBURGH) October 1981, 48:607-19.

GROSHEIDE-VAN DE RIET, M.F.F.

Grosheide-Van de Riet, M.F.F.. Vrouwen in de Sovjetunie. INTERNATIONALE SPECTATOR (THE HAGUE) January 1982, 37:12-20.

GROSSAT, BERNARD

Weekes-Vagliani, Winifred and Grossat, Bernard. Women in development at the right time for the right reasons. Series: Development Centre studies. (Paris, Development Centre of the Organization for Economic Co-operation and Development, 1980), 330 pp.

Groupements a but economique de femmes solidaires; l'experience du Ghana. By: Conseil national du Ghana. TIERS-MONDE (PARIS) April/June 1985, 26:451-56.

Growth of female employment in Brazilian manufacturing industry in the 1970s. By: Humphrey, John. JOURNAL OF DEVELOPMENT STUDIES (LONDON) July 1984, 20:224-47.

Growth of the bazaar economy and its significance for women's employment: trends of the 1970's in Davao City, Philippines. By: Hackenberg, Beverly and Barth, Gerald. In: Women in the urban and industrial workforce; Southeast and East Asia. Edited by Gavin W. Jones. Series: Development Studies Centre. Monograph, No. 33. (Canberra, Australia, Australian National University, 1984), pp. 259-76. Series edited by Helen Hughes.

Growth of women's education. By: Hao, Keming and Zhou, Yan. WOMEN OF CHINA (BEIJING) April 1985, No. 4:2-3.

GULATI, LEELA

Gulati, Leela. Fishing, technology and women. CENTRE FOR DEVELOPMENT STUDIES. WORKING PAPER (ULLOOR, TRIVANDRUM) January 1983, No. 155:1-253. Attempts to discover and document how changes in the technology of fishing and fish preservation in Kerala communities have affected women of fishing households, not only in general economic terms, but also in terms, specifically, of demographic behaviour. CONTENT: Pt. 1 - Pt. 2: Case studies.

Gulati, Leela. Images and image makers: some insights from work with working women. CENTRE FOR DEVELOPMENT STUDIES. WORKING PAPER (ULLOOR, TRIVANDRUM) January 1983, No. 154:1-26.

Gulati, Leela. Role of women from fishing households: case study of a Kerala fishing village. CENTRE FOR DEVELOPMENT STUDIES. WORKING PAPER (ULLOOR, TRIVANDRUM) July 1981, No. 144:1-11.

Gulati, Leela. Technological change and women's work; participation and demographic behaviour: a case study of three fishing villages. ECONOMIC AND POLITICAL WEEKLY (BOMBAY) December 8, 1984, 19:2089-94.

Gulati, Leela. Women and technological change -- a case study of three fishing villages. CENTRE FOR DEVELOPMENT STUDIES. WORKING PAPER (ULLOOR, TRIVANDRUM) [1982?], No. 143:1-26.

Gulati, Leela. Women in fishing villages on the Kerala coast: demographic and socio-economic impacts of a fisheries development project. INTERNATIONAL LABOUR OFFICE. WORLD EMPLOYMENT PROGRAMME RESEARCH. POPULATION AND LABOUR POLICIES PROGRAMME. WORKING PAPER (GENEVA) March 1983, No. 128:1-143.

GULATI, LEELA

Gulati, Leela. Women in the unorganised sector with special reference to Kerala. CENTRE FOR DEVELOPMENT STUDIES. WORKING PAPER (ULLOOR, TRIVANDRUM) [July 1983]?, No. 172:1-22.

GULICK, JOHN

Gulick, John and Gulick, Margaret E.. Domestic social environment of women and girls in Isfahan, Iran. In: Women in the Muslim world. Edited by Lois Beck and Nikki Keddie. (Cambridge, MA, Harvard University Press, 1978), pp. 501-21.

GUPTA, A. R.

Gupta, A. R.. Women in Hindu society: a study of tradition and transition. (New Delhi, Jyotsna Prakashan, 2nd ed., 1982), 257 pp.

GUPTA, R. P.

Gupta, R. P.. Rural women and economic development. ECONOMIC AFFAIRS (CALCUTTA) July-Sept. 1983, 28:784-90.

GUPTA, R. P. AND TEWARI, S. K

Gupta, R. P. and Tewari, S. K. Factors affecting crop diversification: an empirical analysis. INDIAN JOURNAL OF AGRICULTURAL ECONOMICS (BOMBAY) July/September 1985, 40:304-09.

GUSTMAN, ALAN

Gustman, Alan and Steinmeier, Thomas L. Wages, employment, training and job attachment in low wage labor markets for women. NATIONAL BUREAU OF ECONOMIC RESEARCH. WORKING PAPER SERIES (CAMBRIDGE, MASS.) October 1986, No. 2037:1-52. The authors analyze economic behaviour and the effects of training and income support policies in the low wage labor market for women.

GUYER, JANE I.

Guyer, Jane I.. Raw, the cooked, and the half-baked: a note on the division of labor by sex. BOSTON UNIVERSITY. AFRICAN STUDIES CENTER. WORKING PAPERS (BOSTON) 1981, No. 48:1-12.

Guyer, Jane I.. Women's work in the food economy of the cocoa belt: a comparison. BOSTON UNIVERSITY. AFRICAN STUDIES CENTER. WORKING PAPERS (BOSTON) 1978, No. 7:1-35.

GUZMAN STEIN, LAURA

Guzman Stein, Laura. La industria de la maquila y la explotacion de la fuerza de trabajo de la mujer: el caso de Costa Rica. DESARROLLO Y SOCIEDAD (BOGOTA) January 1984, No. 13:161-76. With English summary.

GWARADZIMBA, FADZAI

Gwaradzimba, Fadzai. Heroines find it hard; Zimbabwe, a special report. GUARDIAN (LONDON) August 23, 1985, p. 15. Author states that the assessment of the gains made by women since independence clearly indicates that emancipation does not automatically follow the establishment of a socialist society, nor does participation in the liberation struggle guarantee equality and full integration.

GYI, NI NI

Gyi, Ni Ni. Patterns of social change in a Burmese family. In: Women in the new Asia; the changing social roles of men and women in South and South-east Asia. Edited by Barbara E. Ward. ([Paris], Unesco, 1963), pp. 138-48.

HACKENBERG, BEVERLY

Hackenberg, Beverly and Barth, Gerald. Growth of the bazaar economy and its significance for women's employment: trends of the 1970's in Davao City, Philippines. In: Women in the urban and industrial workforce; Southeast and East Asia. Edited by Gavin W. Jones. Series: Development Studies Centre. Monograph, No. 33. (Canberra, Australia, Australian National University, 1984), pp. 259-76. Series edited by Helen Hughes.

HADORN, VERENA

Hadorn, Verena. Une place au marche de Sopocachi; travail de femmes en Bolivie. ENTWICKLUNG, DEVELOPPEMENT (BERNE) 1985, No. 19:14-16.

HAFNER, ANNEMARIE

Hafner, Annemarie. Working women, their problems and trade unions in India. JOURNAL OF SOCIAL STUDIES (DHAKA) October 1985, No. 30:57-76.

HAHN, NATALIE D.

Hahn, Natalie D.. Losing the land. DEVELOPMENT (ROME) 1984, No. 4:26-29.

HAKIKI, FATIHA

Hakiki, Fatiha and Talahite, Claude. Human sciences research on Algerian women. In: Social science research on women in the Arab world. (London, Frances Pinter; Paris, Unesco, 1984), pp. 82-89.

HAKIKI-TALAHITE, FATIHA

Hakiki-Talahite, Fatiha. Paro e inactividad de las mujeres en Argelia: lo visible y lo invisible. DESARROLLO Y SOCIEDAD (BOGOTA) January 1984, No. 13:139-59. With English summary.

HALATUITUIA, LASALE

Halatuituia, Lasale and Latu, Sela N.. Women's co-operatives in Tonga. PACIFIC PERSPECTIVE (SUVA) 1983, 11, No. 2:13-17.

HALIM, FATIMAH

Halim, Fatimah. Workers' resistance and management control: a comparative case study of male and female workers in West Malaysia. JOURNAL OF CONTEMPORARY ASIA (LONDON) 1983, 13, No. 2:131-50.

HALL, MARJORIE J.

Hall, Marjorie J. and Ismail, Bathita Amin. Sisters under the sun: the story of Sudanese women. (London, New York, Longman, 1981), 264 pp.

HAMID, RIZU

Hamid, Rizu. Why women are wasted. NEW AFRICAN (LONDON) July 1983, No. 190:48. Describes some of the objectives and activities of the Commonwealth Women and Development Unit set up in the Commonwealth Secretariat in 1980.

HANDICRAFT

Mohiuddin, Yasmeen. Female employment and social status; survey. PAKISTAN & GULF ECONOMIST (KARACHI) April 6, 1985, 4:30-33. Report based on a survey of 216 female handicraft workers located at major centres of handicraft work in north, middle and south Sind.

Mohiuddin, Yasmeen. Female handicraft workers; the invisible hand. PAKISTAN & GULF ECONOMIST (KARACHI) July 20, 1985, 4:44-47. The purpose of this study is to investigate the economic role and status of these invisible producers in the all-female handicraft production in Sind, Pakistan.

HAO, KEMING

Hao, Keming and Zhou, Yan. Growth of women's education. WOMEN OF CHINA (BEIJING) April 1985, No. 4:2-3.

HARA, KIMI

Hara, Kimi. Research on the status of women, development and population trends in Asia: an annotated bibliography. In: Bibliographic guide to studies on the status of women: development and population trends. (New York, Bowker, UNIPUB; Paris, Unesco, 1983), [pp. 82-111].

HARDING, J. ROSS

Chapman, Bruce J. and Harding, J. Ross. Sex differences in earnings: an analysis of Malaysian wage data. HARVARD INSTITUTE FOR INTERNATIONAL DEVELOPMENT, DEVELOPMENT DISCUSSION PAPER (CAMBRIDGE, MASS.) December 1980, No. 112:1-24.

HARDING, SUSAN

Harding, Susan. Women and words in a Spanish village. In: Toward an anthropology of women. Edited by Rayna R. Reiter. (New York, Monthly Review Press, 1975), pp. 283-308.

HARRIS, JOAN

Harris, Joan. Women in Kenya; revolution or evolution? AFRICA REPORT (NEW YORK) March/April 1985, 30:30-32.

HARRISON, CHARLES

Harrison, Charles. Plight of Africa's women. TIMES (LONDON) August 1, 1985, p. 4. Suggests that female workers' lack of status can be blamed for much of the famine crisis.

HATTON, T. J.

Hatton, T. J.. Female labour force participation: the enigma of the interwar period. UNIVERSITY OF ESSEX. DEPT. OF ECONOMICS. DISCUSSION PAPER SERIES (COLCHESTER) June 1986, No. 285:1-36.

HAUG, FRIGGA

Haug, Frigga. Women's movement in West Germany. NEW LEFT REVIEW (LONDON) January/February 1986, No. 155:50-74.

HAY, MARGARET JEAN

Hay, Margaret Jean. Luo women and economic change during the colonial period. In: Women in Africa: studies in social and economic change. Edited by Nancy J. Hafkin and Edna G. Bay. (Stanford, Stanford University Press, 1976), pp. 87-109.

HEALTH

Davies, Wendy. Slow progress on women's health. NEW AFRICAN (LONDON) August 1985, No. 215:p. 42.

Health care for women in Latin America and the Caribbean. By: Buvinic, Mayra and Leslie, Joanne. STUDIES IN FAMILY PLANNING (NEW YORK) March 1981, 12:112-15.

Health care for women in the Sudan. By: Naisho, Joyce. WORLD HEALTH FORUM (GENEVA) 1982, 3,No.2:164-65.

HEARN, JEFF

Hearn, Jeff and Parkin, P. Wendy. Gender and organizations: a selective review and a critique of a neglected area. ORGANIZATION STUDIES (BERLIN) 1983, 4, No. 3:219-42.

HEATH, KATHRYN G.

Heath, Kathryn G.. Legislation: an aid in eliminating sex bias in education in the United States. In: Women cross-culturally: change and challenge. Edited by Ruby Rohrlich-Leavitt. (The Hague, Mouton, 1975), pp. 327-60.

HEGGADE, O. D.

Heggade, O. D.. Development of women entrepreneurship in India -- problems and prospects. ECONOMIC AFFAIRS (CALCUTTA) January/March 1981, 26:39-50.

HEIDE, RICHTER

Heide, Richter. Unter uns Frauen - Sudan, parteiisch gesehen. E & Z, ENTWICKLUNG UND ZUSAMMENARBEIT (BONN) March 1984, 25:11-13.

HEIN, CATHERINE

Anker, Richard and Hein, Catherine. Employment of women outside agriculture in Third world countries: an overview of occupational statistics. INTERNATIONAL LABOUR OFFICE. WORLD EMPLOYMENT PROGRAMME RESEARCH. POPULATION AND LABOUR POLICIES PROGRAMME. WORKING PAPER (GENEVA) March 1985, No. 147:1-70.

HELM, LESLIE AND TAKAHASHI, KYOKO

Helm, Leslie and Takahashi, Kyoko. Japan's secret economic weapon: exploited women. BUSINESS WEEK (NEW YORK) March 4, 1985, No. 2883:54-55.

HELMORE, KRISTIN

Helmore, Kristin. Awareness and action. CHRISTIAN SCIENCE MONITOR (BOSTON) December 23, 1985, p. 14-16. Part 5 of 5-part series entitled: "The neglected resource; women in the developing world." Discusses increasing awareness among women in the less developed countries of their inferior economic status and of the value of collective action.

Helmore, Kristin. Breezes of social change sweep slowly through Senegal. CHRISTIAN SCIENCE MONITOR (BOSTON) March 31, 1986, p. 23. Second in a series entitled: "Voices from the Third world." An interview with Marie-Angelique Savane, president of the Association of African Women for Research and Development.

Helmore, Kristin. Family ties: wives and mothers. CHRISTIAN SCIENCE MONITOR (BOSTON) December 18, 1985, p. 17-19. Part 2 of 5-part series entitled: "The neglected resource; women in the developing world." Author looks at marriage and motherhood in various cultures in the less developed countries.

Helmore, Kristin. From the village to the slum. CHRISTIAN SCIENCE MONITOR (BOSTON) December 17, 1985, p. 17-20. Part 1 of 5-part series entitled: "The neglected resource; women in the developing world." After spending three months in Africa, Asia and Latin America the author examines the plight of women and what can be done to ease their burdens.

Helmore, Kristin. Learning and unlearning. CHRISTIAN SCIENCE MONITOR (BOSTON) December 20, 1985, p. 15-17. Part four of 5-part series entitled: "The neglected resource; women in the developing world." Discusses education of women in the less developed countries, particularly the contrast between opportunities for education for men and for women.

Helmore, Kristin. Working for survival; working for cash. CHRISTIAN SCIENCE MONITOR (BOSTON) December 19, 1985, p.18-20. Part three of a 5-part series entitled: "The neglected resource; women in the developing world," focusses on women's work in the agricultural sector as main provider of family sustenance. Also examines the deleterious effects of some development policies for women in the rural areas.

Helping women to help themselves. By: van Wijk-Sijbesma, Christine. WATERLINES (LONDON) April 1986, 4:29-31. Suggests that women's programmes and organizations have great potential to mobilize women to improve their own water supply and sanitation if they are not served by other programmes.

HELZNER, JUDITH F.

Edmunds, Marilyn and Helzner, Judith F.. Peru-mujer: women organizing for development. PATHPAPERS, PATHFINDER FUND (CHESTNUT HILL, MASS.) August 1982, No. 9:1-18.

Wiarda, Ieda Siqueira and Helzner, Judith F.. Women, population and international development in Latin America: persistent legacies and new perceptions for the 1980's. UNIVERSITY OF MASSACHUSETTS AT AMHERST. PROGRAM IN LATIN AMERICAN STUDIES. OCCASIONAL PAPERS SERIES (AMHERST) April 1981, No. 13:1-40.

Edmunds, Marilyn and Helzner, Judith F.. Peru-Mujer: women organizing for development. Series: Pathpapers series, No. 9. (Chestnut Hill, MA, Pathfinder Fund, 1982), 18 pp.

HELZNER, JUDITH FRYE

Siqueira Wiarda, Ieda and Helzner, Judith Frye. Women, population, and international development in Latin America: a 1984 assessment. MANAGING INTERNATIONAL DEVELOPMENT (ARMONK, N.Y.) September/October 1984, 1:84-106.

HEMMINGS-GAPIHAN, GRACE S.

Hemmings-Gapihan, Grace S.. International development and the evolution of women's economic roles: a case study from northern Gulma, Upper Volta. In: Women and work in Africa. Edited by Edna G. Bay. (Boulder, CO, Westview Press, 1982), pp. 171-89.

Heroines find it hard; Zimbabwe, a special report. By: Gwaradzimba, Fadzai. GUARDIAN (LONDON) August 23, 1985, p. 15. Author states that the assessment of the gains made by women since independence clearly indicates that emancipation does not automatically follow the establishment of a socialist society, nor does participation in the liberation struggle guarantee equality and full integration.

HERRIN, ALEJANDRO

Engracia, Luisa and Herrin, Alejandro. Employment structure of female migrants to the cities in the Philippines. In: Women in the urban and industrial workforce; Southeast and East Asia. Edited by Gavin W. Jones. Series: Development Studies Centre. Monograph, No. 33. (Canberra, Australia, Australian National University, 1984), pp. 293-304. Series edited by Helen Hughes.

HERRIN, ALEJANDRO N.

Herrin, Alejandro N.. Female work participation and fertility in a Philippine setting: a test of alternative models. UNIVERSITY OF THE PHILIPPINES. SCHOOL OF ECONOMICS. DISCUSSION PAPER (QUEZON) October 1980, No. 8005:1-99.

Hidden face of Eve: women in the Arab world. By: Sa'adawi, Naw'al. (Boston, MA, Beacon Press, 1982), 212 pp.

Hidden sun: women of modern Japan. By: Robins-Mowry, Dorothy. (Boulder, Colorado, Westview Press, 1982), 394 pp.

HIGHER EDUCATION

Crocombe, Marjorie Tuainekore. Women at the University of the South Pacific. PACIFIC PERSPECTIVE (SUVA) 1983, 11, No. 2:24-8.

Hao, Keming and Zhou, Yan. Growth of women's education. WOMEN OF CHINA (BEIJING) April 1985, No. 4:2-3.

HIGUCHI, YOSHIO

Nishikawa, Shunsaku and Higuchi, Yoshio. Determinants of female labor-force participation. JAPANESE ECONOMIC STUDIES (ARMONK, N.Y.) Winter 1980/1981, 9:62-87.

HILL, M. ANNE

Hill, M. Anne. Comparison of economic models and empirical results for female labor force participation in Japan and the United State. YALE UNIVERSITY. ECONOMIC GROWTH CENTER. DISCUSSION PAPER (NEW HAVEN, CONN.) July 1982, No. 415:1-36.

Hill, M. Anne. Female labor force participation in developing and developed countries -- consideration of the informal sector. REVIEW OF ECONOMICS AND STATISTICS (CAMBRIDGE, MASS.) August 1983, 65:459-68.

HILL, M. ANNE

Hill, M. Anne. Female labor force participation in urban Japan; a trichotomous logit model. YALE UNIVERSITY. ECONOMIC GROWTH CENTER. DISCUSSION PAPER (NEW HAVEN, CONN.) September 1980, No. 362:1-42.

HINCHCLIFFE, DOREEN

Coulson, Noel and Hinchcliffe, Doreen. Women and law reform in contemporary Islam. In: Women in the Muslim world. Edited by Lois Beck and Nikki Keddie. (Cambridge, MA, Harvard University Press, 1978), pp. 37-51.

HING, AI YUN

Hing, Ai Yun. Women and work in West Malaysia. JOURNAL OF CONTEMPORARY ASIA (LONDON) 1984, 14, No. 2:204-18.

History, development, organization and position of women's studies in the Sudan. By: Kashif-Badri, Hagga. In: Social science research on women in the Arab world. (London, Frances Pinter; Paris, Unesco, 1984), pp. 94-105.

HO, SUK-CHING

Ho, Suk-ching. Position of women in the labour market in Hong Kong: a content analysis of the recruitment advertisements. LABOUR AND SOCIETY (GENEVA) September 1985, 10:333-44.

Hohola: the significance of social networks in urban adaptation of women in Papua-New Guinea's first low-cost housing estate. By: Oeser, Lynn. Series: Bulletin, New Guinea Research Unit, Research School of Pacific Studies, Australian National University, Canberra, No. 29. (Canberra, New Guinea Research Unit, Australian National University, 1969), 120 pp.

HOLFORD, NICKY

Holford, Nicky. Easing the burden of women in a developing society: a host of good intentions. NEW AFRICAN (LONDON) December 1981, p. 39-40. Discusses the new UN Convention for the prevention of discrimination against women, which was adopted in September, and suggests that the measure should influence customs and practices all over Africa.

HOLLAND, JANET

Holland, Janet. Selected studies on the status of women, changes and continuities in the sexual division of labour in family and society, women's education/labour force participation and demographic trends in Northern America and Western Europe from 1975: ... In: Bibliographic guide to studies on the status of women: development and population trends. (New York, Bowker, UNIPUB; Paris, Unesco, 1983), pp. 183-267.

HOLMSTROM, NANCY

Holmstrom, Nancy. "Women's work," the family and capitalism. SCIENCE & SOCIETY (NEW YORK) Summer 1981, 45:186-211.

Home economics and agriculture in Third World countries. By: Seltzer, Miriam, ed.. (St. Paul, Center for Youth Development and Research, College of Home Economics, University of Minnesota, [1980?]), 103 pp. Seminar held in St. Paul, Minnesota on May 14, 16, 23, 1980. The seminar led to recognition that women's roles in developing areas may need to be acknowledged and dealt with directly in any attack on the food problems of the poor.

HONG KONG

Ho, Suk-ching. Position of women in the labour market in Hong Kong: a content analysis of the recruitment advertisements. LABOUR AND SOCIETY (GENEVA) September 1985, 10:333-44.

Ng, Margaret. Social ascendancy without the fanfare. FAR EASTERN ECONOMIC REVIEW (HONGKONG) January 5, 1984, 123:28-29. Discusses the status of women in Hongkong.

HONG, SAWON

Hong, Sawon. Urban migrant women in the Republic of Korea. In: Women in the cities of Asia: migration and urban adaptation. Edited by James T. Fawcett, Siew-Ean Khoo and Peter C. Smith. (Boulder, CO, Westview Press, 1984), pp. 191-210.

HONIG, EMILY

Honig, Emily. Contract labor system and women workers; pre-liberation cotton mills of Shanghai. MODERN CHINA (BEVERLY HILLS) October 1983, 9:421-54.

Honig, Emily. Socialist revolution and women's liberation in China -- a review article. JOURNAL OF ASIAN STUDIES (ANN ARBOR, MICH.) February 1985, 44:328-36.

HOON, LEE SIEW

Hoon, Lee Siew. Occupational health hazards of female industrial workers in Malaysia. In: Women in the urban and industrial workforce; Southeast and East Asia. Edited by Gavin W. Jones. Series: Development Studies Centre. Monograph, No. 33. (Canberra, Australia, Australian National University, 1984), pp. 175-88. Series edited by Helen Hughes.

HOOPER, BEVERLEY

Hooper, Beverley. China's modernization; are young women going to lose out? MODERN CHINA (BEVERLY HILLS) July 1984, 10:317-43. Focuses on two areas that are prerequisites to young women having the opportunity to play an equal role in China's economic development: obtaining education, particularly higher education, and securing employment.

HORENSTEIN, NADINE R.

Horenstein, Nadine R.. Factoring gender into the development equation. HORIZONS, U.S. AGENCY FOR INTERNATIONAL DEVELOPMENT (WASHINGTON) Summer 1985, 4:26-30.

HORN, ROBERT V.

Horn, Robert V.. Workers and work: an activities approach. LABOUR AND SOCIETY (GENEVA) April/June 1981, 6:111-25. Concludes that the activities approach helps to give a more balanced view of women at work and of the relation between paid and unpaid work of individuals and the household.

HOSKINGS, MARILYN W.

Hoskings, Marilyn W.. Community forestry depends on women. UNASYLVA (ROME) 1980, 32, No. 130:27-32.

HOTTINGER, ARNOLD

Hottinger, Arnold. Women in Islam. SWISS REVIEW OF WORLD AFFAIRS (ZURICH) October 1980, 30:8-14.

HOURS OF LABOR

Goldin, Claudia. Maximum hours legislation and female employment in the 1920s: a reassessment. NATIONAL BUREAU OF ECONOMIC RESEARCH. WORKING PAPER SERIES (CAMBRIDGE, MASS.) June 1986, No. 1949:1-27.

HOUSE, WILLIAM J.

House, William J.. Occupational segregation and discriminatory pay: the position of women in the Cyprus labour market. INTERNATIONAL LABOUR REVIEW (GENEVA) January/February 1983, 122:75-93.

Household economic strategies and support networks of the poor in Kenya: a literature survey. By: Clark, Mari H.. Series: Discussion Paper; Report No.: UDD-69, Water Supply and Urban Development Dept., Operations Policy Staff, World Bank. (Washington, DC, World Bank, 1985), 117 pp.

Household labour and self-help housing in Queretaro, Mexico. By: Chant, Sylvia. BOLETIN DE ESTUDIOS LATINO-AMERICANOS Y DEL CARIBE (AMSTERDAM) December 1984, No. 37:45-68.

HOUSEHOLD SURVEYS

Anker, Richard. Effect on reported levels of female labour force participation in developing countries of questionnaire design, sex of interviewer and sex/proxy status of respondent: description of a methodological field experiment. INTERNATIONAL LABOUR OFFICE. WORLD EMPLOYMENT PROGRAMME RESEARCH. POPULATION AND LABOUR POLICIES PROGRAMME. WORKING PAPER (GENEVA) July 1983, No. 137:1-76. The methods test described is conducting household surveys in India (Uttar Pradesh state) and Egypt, using different types of questionnaires; male and female interviewers; self-respondents (female only) and proxy-respondents (male and female).

HOUSEHOLDS

Review of women studies. ECONOMIC AND POLITICAL WEEKLY (BOMBAY) April 27, 1985, 20:WS1-WS56. CONTENT: Ortiz, Bobbye Suckle, Changing consciousness of Central American women. -- Thorner, Alice, and Jyoti Ranadive, Household as a first stage in a study of urban working-class women. -- Levi, Luisa Accati, Wife-husband relations: differences between peasant households and modern professional-class families in North-Eastern Italy. -- Standing, Hilary, Women's employment and the household: some findings from Calcutta. -- Kelkar, Govind, Impact of household contract system on women in rural India. -- Sen, Gita and Charanjib Sen, Women's domestic work and economic activity results from national sample survey.

Sharma, Ursula. Unmarried women and the household economy: a research note. JOURNAL OF SOCIAL STUDIES (DHAKA) October 1985, No. 30:1-12.

HOUSING

Buvinic, Mayra and Lycette, Margaret. Eye-opening survey unlocks doors for low-income women. HORIZONS, U.S. AGENCY FOR INTERNATIONAL DEVELOPMENT (WASHINGTON) Summer 1985, 4:31-33. The authors describe how the International Center for Research on Women (ICRW), with a $120,000 grant from AID, is helping to put home ownership within reach of low-income women, through its experiences with the Solanda low-income housing project in Quito, Ecuador.

How Kenyan peasants, pastoralists and peri-urban women see water problems. By: Bifani, Patricia. WATERLINES (LONDON) January 1986, 4:16-19.

HOWARD-MERRIAM, KATHLEEN

Howard-Merriam, Kathleen. Women's political participation in Morocco's development: how much and for whom? MAGHREB REVIEW (LONDON) January/April 1984, 9:12-25.

HOWE, GARY NIGEL

Howe, Gary Nigel. Upgrading women in Yemen: a matter of dollars and sense. HORIZONS, U.S. AGENCY FOR INTERNATIONAL DEVELOPMENT (WASHINGTON) Summer 1985, 4:41-42.

HUANG, NORA CHIANG

Huang, Nora Chiang. Migration of rural women to Taipei. In: Women in the cities of Asia: migration and urban adaptation. Edited by James T. Fawcett, Siew-Ean Khoo and Peter C. Smith. (Boulder, CO, Westview Press, 1984), pp. 247-68.

HUGHES, MARIJA MATICH

Hughes, Marija Matich. Sexual barrier: legal, medical, economic and social aspects of sex discrimination. (Washington, Hughes Press, 1977), 843 pp. An enlarged and reissued edition of the author's original bibliography on women, entitled The Sexual barrier: legal and economic aspects of employment, published in 1970, with supplements in 1971 and 1972.

HULL, VALERIE

Raharjo, Yulfita and Hull, Valerie. Employment patterns of educated women in Indonesian cities. In: Women in the urban and industrial workforce; Southeast and East Asia. Edited by Gavin W. Jones. Series: Development Studies Centre. Monograph, No. 33. (Canberra, Australia, Australian National University, 1984), pp. 101-28. Series edited by Helen Hughes.

HUMAN FERTILITY

Bach, Rebecca and Gadalla, Saad. Mothers' influence on daughters' orientations toward education: an Egyptian case study. COMPARATIVE EDUCATION REVIEW (NEW YORK) August 1985, 29:374-84.

Jensen, An-Magritt and Schweder, Tore. Engine of fertility - influenced by interbirth employment? NORWAY. STATISTISK SENTRALBYRA. DISCUSSION PAPER (OSLO) June 1986, No. 15:1-33.

Lee, Bun Song and McElwain, Adrienne M. Empirical investigation of female labor-force participation, fertility, age at marriage, and wages in Korea. JOURNAL OF DEVELOPING AREAS (MACOMB, ILL.) July 1985, 19:483-500.

Osawa, Machiko. Working mothers: changing patterns of employment and fertility in Japan. ECONOMICS RESEARCH CENTER. NORC [NATIONAL OPINION RESEARCH CENTER] DISCUSSION PAPER SERIES (CHICAGO) June 1986, No. 86-5:1-58. In this paper the differential fertility rates between paid women workers in the formal sector and family workers in the informal sector are featured to analyze the reasons why the Japanese fertility trend in the post-World War II period differs from other nations.

Sprague, Alison. Post-war fertility and female labour force participation rates. OXFORD UNIVERSITY. INSTITUTE OF ECONOMICS AND STATISTICS. APPLIED ECONOMICS DISCUSSION PAPER (OXFORD) June 1986, No. 9:1-35.

Yamada, Tadashi and Yamada, Tetsuji. Fertility and labor force participation of married women: empirical evidence from the 1980 population census of Japan. QUARTERLY REVIEW OF ECONOMICS AND BUSINESS (URBANA, ILL.) Summer 1986, 26:35-46.

Human sciences research on Algerian women. By: Hakiki, Fatiha and Talahite, Claude. In: Social science research on women in the Arab world. (London, Frances Pinter; Paris, Unesco, 1984), pp. 82-89.

HUMPHREY, JOHN

Humphrey, John. Growth of female employment in Brazilian manufacturing industry in the 1970s. JOURNAL OF DEVELOPMENT STUDIES (LONDON) July 1984, 20:224-47.

HUNGARY

Forray, Katalin R. Bildungswege der Frauen in Ungarn: neue Tendenzen in der Ausbildung und Beschaftigung aus soziologischer Sicht. OSTERREICHISCHE OSTHEFTE (VIENNA) 1986, 28, No. 2:107-25.

HURTADO, MARIA ELENA

Hurtado, Maria Elena. Struggling women and feminist struggle. SOUTH; THE THIRD WORLD MAGAZINE (LONDON) October 1985, No. 60:44-45. Reports on the UN women's conference in Nairobi.

HURWITCH-MACDONALD, JAN

Hurwitch-MacDonald, Jan. La incorporacion femenina a las empresas asociativas. DESARROLLO RURAL EN LAS AMERICAS (SAN JOSE) January/June 1983, 15:55-64.

HUSTON, PERDITA

Huston, Perdita. Third world women speak out: interviews in six countries on change, development, and basic needs. (New York, published in cooperation with the Overseas Development Council by Praeger, 1979), 153 pp. Countries discussed are: Tunisia, Egypt, Sudan, Kenya, Sri Lanka and Mexico.

HYE, HASNAT ABDUL

Hye, Hasnat Abdul. Mechanisation in agriculture and women in Bangladesh. JOURNAL OF SOCIAL STUDIES (DHAKA) January 1985, No. 27:78-100.

Idea whose time has not come: comparable worth and the market salary problem. By: Gaston, Cheryl L. POPULATION RESEARCH AND POLICY REVIEW (AMSTERDAM) 1986, 5, No. 1:15-29.

IFEKA, CAROLINE

Ifeka, Caroline. Female factor in anthropology. In: Women cross-culturally: change and challenge. Edited by Ruby Rohrlich-Leavitt. (The Hague, Mouton, 1975), pp. 559-66.

ILO TRIPARTITE ASIAN REGIONAL SEMINAR (1981: MAHABALESHWAR, INDIA)

ILO Tripartite Asian Regional Seminar (1981: Mahabaleshwar, India). Rural development and women in Asia: proceedings and conclusions of the ILO Tripartite Asian Regional Seminar, Mahabaleshwar, Maharashtra, India, 6-11 April 1981. Series: A WEP study. (Geneva, International Labour Office, 1982), 88 pp.

Images and image makers: some insights from work with working women. By: Gulati, Leela. CENTRE FOR DEVELOPMENT STUDIES. WORKING PAPER (ULLOOR, TRIVANDRUM) January 1983, No. 154:1-26.

Images of men and women in Indian textbooks. By: Kalia, Narendra Nath. COMPARATIVE EDUCATION REVIEW (NEW YORK) June 1980, 24:S209-23. Attempts to demonstrate that Indian school textbooks promote an ideology which refuses females equal access to opportunities and rewards even in areas where the sex of a person is totally irrelevant.

Impact of agricultural modernization on labour: use pattern in Punjab with special reference to women labour. By: Chand, Ramesh and Sidhu, D. S. INDIAN JOURNAL OF AGRICULTURAL ECONOMICS (BOMBAY) July/September 1985, 40:252-59.

Impact of Bombay's textile industry on work of women from Sugao village. By: Dandekar, Hemalata C.. THIRD WORLD PLANNING REVIEW (LIVERPOOL) November 1983, 5:371-82.

Impact of demographic changes on income distribution in a developing country. By: Wolfe, Barbara L. and Behrman, Jere R.. JOURNAL OF DEVELOPMENT ECONOMICS (AMSTERDAM) December 1982, 11:355-77. The authors use data from a stratified random sample of about 4,000 women aged 15 to 45 in Nicaragua.

Impact of diversification on income, employment and credit needs of small farmers in Punjab. By: Saini, Amrik S. and Singh, Raj Vir. INDIAN JOURNAL OF AGRICULTURAL ECONOMICS (BOMBAY) July/September 1985, 40:310-16.

Impact of female employment on household management. By: Miralao, Virginia A.. In: Women in the urban and industrial workforce; Southeast and East Asia. Edited by Gavin W. Jones. Series: Development Studies Centre. Monograph, No. 33. (Canberra, Australia, Australian National University, 1984), pp. 369-86. Series edited by Helen Hughes.

Impact of Ghod irrigation project on employment of female agricultural labour. By: Suryawanshi, S. D. and Kapase, P. M. INDIAN JOURNAL OF AGRICULTURAL ECONOMICS (BOMBAY) July/September 1985, 40:240-44.

Impact of male labour migration on women in Botswana. By: Brown, Barbara B.. AFRICAN AFFAIRS (LONDON) July 1983, 82:367-88.

Impact of rural development programme on rural women in Bhiwani district of Haryana. By: Grewal, R. S. and Nandal, D. S. INDIAN JOURNAL OF AGRICULTURAL ECONOMICS (BOMBAY) July/September 1985, 40:259-62.

Impact of technological changes on economic status of female labour. By: Ray, A. K. and Rangarao, I. V. INDIAN JOURNAL OF AGRICULTURAL ECONOMICS (BOMBAY) July/September 1985, 40:244-52.

Implementing comparable worth: a survey of recent job evaluation studies. By: Sorensen, Elaine. AMERICAN ECONOMIC REVIEW, PAPERS AND PROCEEDINGS (NASHVILLE) May 1986, 76:364-72.

Importance of female primary education for fertility reduction in India. By: Jain, Anrudh K. and Nag, Moni. ECONOMIC AND POLITICAL WEEKLY (BOMBAY) September 6, 1986, 21:1602-08.

Improving women's access to credit in the Third World: policy and project recommendations. By: Lycette, Margaret A.. Series: ICRW occasional paper, No. 1. (Washington, DC, International Center for Research on Women, 1984), 23 pp.

In poor families, women's income is the lifeline. By: Jain, Devaki. CERES, FAO REVIEW ON AGRICULTURE AND DEVELOPMENT (ROME) July/August 1984, 17:35-38. Presents an interview with the director of the Institute of Social Studies, New Delhi, describing the pressures on landless female agricultural laborers.

In the footsteps of Indira. By: Nicholson, Louise. TIMES (LONDON) July 12, 1985, p. 11. Concludes that, once in power, Mrs. Gandhi made little difference to the lives of poor rural women, but there has been some progress recently for what the West would call middle-class women.

INCOME DISTRIBUTION

Dwyser, Daisy Hilse. Women and income in the Third world: implications for policy. POPULATION COUNCIL. INTERNATIONAL PROGRAMS. WORKING PAPERS (NEW YORK) June 1983, No. 18:1-39.

Wolfe, Barbara L. and Behrman, Jere R.. Impact of demographic changes on income distribution in a developing country. JOURNAL OF DEVELOPMENT ECONOMICS (AMSTERDAM) December 1982, 11:355-77. The authors use data from a stratified random sample of about 4,000 women aged 15 to 45 in Nicaragua.

Income distribution, poverty and employment. By: Kurian, Rachel. INSTITUTE OF SOCIAL STUDIES. OCCASIONAL PAPERS (THE HAGUE) September 1979, No. 73:1-55. Examines the marginalization of women in theory and in reality, with examples from studies carried out in Sri Lanka and Yugoslavia.

La incorporacion femenina a las empresas asociativas. By: Hurwitch-MacDonald, Jan. DESARROLLO RURAL EN LAS AMERICAS (SAN JOSE) January/June 1983, 15:55-64.

INDIA

Agarwal, Bina. Women, poverty and agricultural growth in India. INSTITUTE OF ECONOMIC GROWTH. [PAPERS] (DELHI) June 1985, No. E/112/85:1-101.

Agarwal, Nina. Women, poverty and agricultural growth in India. JOURNAL OF PEASANT STUDIES (LONDON) July 1986, 13:165-220.

Ahmad, Karuna. Women's life cycle and identity. ECONOMIC AND POLITICAL WEEKLY (BOMBAY) January 2, 1982, 17:15-17. Discusses a seminar on women, organized by the Indian Council of Social Science Research, New Delhi, Centre for Women's Development Studies, New Delhi, Tata Institute of Social Sciences, Bombay, and Ford Foundation, New Delhi.

Banerjee, Nirmala. Women and poverty; report on a workshop. ECONOMIC AND POLITICAL WEEKLY (BOMBAY) October 1, 1983, 18:1693-98.

Bardhan, Kalpana. Women's work, welfare and status; forces of tradition and change in India, pt. 1. ECONOMIC AND POLITICAL WEEKLY (BOMBAY) December 14, 1985, 20:2207-20.

Bardhan, Kalpana. Women's work, welfare and status; forces of tradition and change in India, pt. 2. ECONOMIC AND POLITICAL WEEKLY (BOMBAY) December 21, 1985, 20:2262-69.

Barres, Victoria. Deux programmes de credit bien adaptes aux besoins des femmes du Tiers monde. TIERS-MONDE (PARIS) April/June 1985, 26:435-42. Cet article presente deux programmes de credits d'investissement destines a des femmes pauvres du Tiers Monde, l'un en milieu urbain (Madras, Inde) et l'autre en milieu rural (pays yoruba, Nigeria).

INDIA

Batliwala, Srilatha. Women and cooking energy. ECONOMIC AND POLITICAL WEEKLY (BOMBAY) December 24, 1983, 18:2227-30. Describes how a woman in poverty has low access to cooking fuel, spends the longest time obtaining it, and puts it to use in stoves which are not only fuel-inefficient, but which also subject her to serious or fatal disease.

Chand, Ramesh and Sidhu, D. S. Impact of agricultural modernization on labour: use pattern in Punjab with special reference to women labour. INDIAN JOURNAL OF AGRICULTURAL ECONOMICS (BOMBAY) July/September 1985, 40:252-59.

Chandigarh Women's Conference: women in informal sector; 'to keep on keeping on'. ECONOMIC AND POLITICAL WEEKLY (BOMBAY) December 20, 1986, 21:2216-18.

Chen, Lincoln C.. Where have the women gone? Insights from Bangladesh on low sex ratio of India's population. ECONOMIC AND POLITICAL WEEKLY (BOMBAY) March 6, 1982, 17:364-72.

Choudhury, S. and Giri, A. K. Nature and extent of female labour use in agriculture - a comparison between progressive and non-progressive area. ECONOMIC AFFAIRS (CALCUTTA) June 1986, 31:81-86.

Colfer, Carol. On circular migration -- from the distaff side: women left behind in the forests of East Kalimantan. INTERNATIONAL LABOUR OFFICE. WORLD EMPLOYMENT PROGRAMME RESEARCH. POPULATION AND LABOUR POLICIES PROGRAMME. WORKING PAPER (GENEVA) May 1983, No. 132:1-42. Focuses on male circular migration (or migration with the in;tent to return home) and its impact on the women who remain in the villages tending the farm. The area studied is East Kalimantan (Indonesian Borneo).

Dandekar, Hemalata C.. Impact of Bombay's textile industry on work of women from Sugao village. THIRD WORLD PLANNING REVIEW (LIVERPOOL) November 1983, 5:371-82.

Devi, D. Radha and Ravindran, M.. Women's work in India. INTERNATIONAL SOCIAL SCIENCE JOURNAL (PARIS) 1983, 35, No. 4:683-701.

INDIA

Everett, Jana and Savara, Mira. Bank loans to lower class women in Bombay; problems and prospects. ECONOMIC AND POLITICAL WEEKLY (BOMBAY) August 25, 1984, 19:M113-M119. The authors report the results of an exploratory study of bank loans to lower caste women in Bombay. They seek to shed some light on the problems surrounding and the prospects for bank loans as an economic development strategy for poor women.

Fatima, Burnad. Rural development and women's liberation: caste, class and gender in a grass-roots organisation in Tamil Nadu, South India. IDS BULLETIN, INSTITUTE OF DEVELOPMENT STUDIES AT THE UNIVERSITY OF SUSSEX (BRIGHTON) January 1984, 15:45-50.

Fruzzetti, Lina M. Four women's organizations of Calcutta. UNIVERSITIES FIELD STAFF INTERNATIONAL REPORTS, ASIA (HANOVER, NH) 1986, No. 4:1-5.

Gnanadason, Aruna. Women's health: plea for a new approach. ECONOMIC AND POLITICAL WEEKLY (BOMBAY) September 13, 1986, 21:1630-30.

Gopalan, C.. Mother and child in India. ECONOMIC AND POLITICAL WEEKLY (BOMBAY) January 26, 1985, 20:159-66.

Gothoskar, Sujata and Banaji, Rohini. Women, work, organisation and struggle. ECONOMIC AND POLITICAL WEEKLY (BOMBAY) March 5, 1983, 18:339-44. Article based on the conclusions of the authors' forthcoming book "My life is one long struggle... women, work, organisation and struggle".

Gould, Ketayun. Sex inequalities in the dual system of education; the Parsis of Gujarat. ECONOMIC AND POLITICAL WEEKLY (BOMBAY) September 24, 1983, 18:1668-76.

Grewal, R. S. and Nandal, D. S. Impact of rural development programme on rural women in Bhiwani district of Haryana. INDIAN JOURNAL OF AGRICULTURAL ECONOMICS (BOMBAY) July/September 1985, 40:259-62.

INDIA

Gulati, Leela. Fishing, technology and women. CENTRE FOR DEVELOPMENT STUDIES. WORKING PAPER (ULLOOR, TRIVANDRUM) January 1983, No. 155:1-253. Attempts to discover and document how changes in the technology of fishing and fish preservation in Kerala communities have affected women of fishing households, not only in general economic terms, but also in terms, specifically, of demographic behaviour. CONTENT: Pt. 1 - Pt. 2: Case studies.

Gulati, Leela. Images and image makers: some insights from work with working women. CENTRE FOR DEVELOPMENT STUDIES. WORKING PAPER (ULLOOR, TRIVANDRUM) January 1983, No. 154:1-26.

Gulati, Leela. Role of women from fishing households: case study of a Kerala fishing village. CENTRE FOR DEVELOPMENT STUDIES. WORKING PAPER (ULLOOR, TRIVANDRUM) July 1981, No. 144:1-11.

Gulati, Leela. Technological change and women's work; participation and demographic behaviour: a case study of three fishing villages. ECONOMIC AND POLITICAL WEEKLY (BOMBAY) December 8, 1984, 19:2089-94.

Gulati, Leela. Women and technological change -- a case study of three fishing villages. CENTRE FOR DEVELOPMENT STUDIES. WORKING PAPER (ULLOOR, TRIVANDRUM) [1982?], No. 143:1-26.

Gulati, Leela. Women in fishing villages on the Kerala coast: demographic and socio-economic impacts of a fisheries development project. INTERNATIONAL LABOUR OFFICE. WORLD EMPLOYMENT PROGRAMME RESEARCH. POPULATION AND LABOUR POLICIES PROGRAMME. WORKING PAPER (GENEVA) March 1983, No. 128:1-143.

Gulati, Leela. Women in the unorganised sector with special reference to Kerala. CENTRE FOR DEVELOPMENT STUDIES. WORKING PAPER (ULLOOR, TRIVANDRUM) [July 1983]?, No. 172:1-22.

Gupta, R. P.. Rural women and economic development. ECONOMIC AFFAIRS (CALCUTTA) July-Sept. 1983, 28:784-90.

Gupta, R. P. and Tewari, S. K. Factors affecting crop diversification: an empirical analysis. INDIAN JOURNAL OF AGRICULTURAL ECONOMICS (BOMBAY) July/September 1985, 40:304-09.

INDIA

Hafner, Annemarie. Working women, their problems and trade unions in India. JOURNAL OF SOCIAL STUDIES (DHAKA) October 1985, No. 30:57-76.

Heggade, O. D.. Development of women entrepreneurship in India -- problems and prospects. ECONOMIC AFFAIRS (CALCUTTA) January/March 1981, 26:39-50.

Jain, Anrudh K. and Nag, Moni. Female primary education and fertility reduction in India. POPULATION COUNCIL. CENTER FOR POLICY STUDIES. WORKING PAPERS (NEW YORK) September 1985, No. 114:1-57.

Jain, Anrudh K. and Nag, Moni. Importance of female primary education for fertility reduction in India. ECONOMIC AND POLITICAL WEEKLY (BOMBAY) September 6, 1986, 21:1602-08.

Jain, Devaki. In poor families, women's income is the lifeline. CERES, FAO REVIEW ON AGRICULTURE AND DEVELOPMENT (ROME) July/August 1984, 17:35-38. Presents an interview with the director of the Institute of Social Studies, New Delhi, describing the pressures on landless female agricultural laborers.

Jain, Devaki and Singh, Nalini. Role of rural women in community life; a case study from India. ECONOMIC BULLETIN FOR ASIA AND THE PACIFIC (BANGKOK) December 1978, 29:84-126.

Jain, Shobhita. Women and people's ecological movement; a case study of women's role in the Chipko movement in Uttar Pradesh. ECONOMIC AND POLITICAL WEEKLY (BOMBAY) October 13, 1984, 19:1788-93.

Jeffery, Patricia and Jeffery, Roger. Childbirth and collaboration among women in Bijnor district, Uttar Pradesh. JOURNAL OF SOCIAL STUDIES (DHAKA) July 1984, No. 25:15-33.

Kalia, Narendra Nath. Images of men and women in Indian textbooks. COMPARATIVE EDUCATION REVIEW (NEW YORK) June 1980, 24:S209-23. Attempts to demonstrate that Indian school textbooks promote an ideology which refuses females equal access to opportunities and rewards even in areas where the sex of a person is totally irrelevant.

Kelkar, Govind. Tractors against women. DEVELOPMENT (ROME) 1985, No. 3:18-21. Concludes that the Green Revolution has brought in its wake the all-India trend of pauperization and marginalization and the increased inequality between the sexes.

INDIA

Krishnaswami, Lalita. From drudgery to dignity: the SEWA experience. LABOUR AND SOCIETY (GENEVA) September 1985, 10:323-31. Discusses the achievements of the Self-Employed Women's Association (SEWA), which is at once a union, a trust and a credit institution whose basic aim is to provide better living and working conditions for the poor, illiterate women who comprise its membership.

Kynch, Jocelyn and Sen, Amartya. Indian women: well-being and survival. CAMBRIDGE JOURNAL OF ECONOMICS (LONDON) September/December 1983, 7:363-80.

Laufer, Leslie A.. Substitution between male and female labor in rural Indian agricultural production. YALE UNIVERSITY. ECONOMIC GROWTH CENTER. DISCUSSION PAPER (NEW HAVEN, CONN.) April 1985, No 472:1-24.

Leonard, Karen. Women in India; some recent perspectives; research note. PACIFIC AFFAIRS (VANCOUVER, B.C.) Spring 1979, 52:95-107.

Marothia, D. K. and Sharma, S. K. Female labour participation in rice farming system of Chhattisgarh region. INDIAN JOURNAL OF AGRICULTURAL ECONOMICS (BOMBAY) July/September 1985, 40:235-39.

Maskiell, Michelle. Social change and social control: college-educated Punjabi women 1913 to 1960. MODERN ASIAN STUDIES (LONDON) February 1985, 19:55-83.

Mazumdar, Vina. Women's studies: challenge to educational system. ECONOMIC AND POLITICAL WEEKLY (BOMBAY) May 16, 1981, 16:890-92. Discusses some of the recommendations of the National Conference on Women's Studies, held in Bombay, April 20-24, 1981.

Mencher, Joan P. and Saradamoni, K.. Muddy feet, dirty hands; rice production and female agricultural labour. ECONOMIC AND POLITICAL WEEKLY (BOMBAY) December 25, 1982, 17:A149-A167.

Mies, Maria. Capitalism and subsistence: rural women in India. DEVELOPMENT (ROME) 1984, No. 4:18-24.

Mies, Maria. Indian women in subsistence and agricultural labour. INTERNATIONAL LABOUR OFFICE. WORLD EMPLOYMENT PROGRAMME RESEARCH. RURAL EMPLOYMENT POLICY RESEARCH PROGRAMME. WORKING PAPER (GENEVA) (GENEVA) May 1984, No. 34:1-243.

INDIA

Miller, Barbara D.. Female labor participation and female seclusion in rural India: a regional view. ECONOMIC DEVELOPMENT AND CULTURAL CHANGE (CHICAGO) July 1982, 30:777-94.

Mukhopadhyay, Carol C. and Bald, Suresht R.. Gender, politics and modernization: the Indian case. STUDIES IN THIRD WORLD SOCIETIES (WILLIAMSBURG) June 1981, No. 16:91-121.

Nicholson, Louise. In the footsteps of Indira. TIMES (LONDON) July 12, 1985, p. 11. Concludes that, once in power, Mrs. Gandhi made little difference to the lives of poor rural women, but there has been some progress recently for what the West would call middle-class women.

Omvedt, Gail. Women and rural revolt in India. JOURNAL OF PEASANT STUDIES (LONDON) April 1978, 5:370-403. It is argued that in India, increasingly during the last decade, capitalism has developed in the countryside, and that, with the changing social relations of production, there has emerged a mass-based and militant women's movement ... This is illustrated ... especially for the state of Maharashtra.

Pani, Dharani K. Women; dew does well. BUSINESS INDIA (BOMBAY) January 26, 1987, No. 232:p. 34. Discusses the work of Tamilnadu Corporation for the Development of Women Ltd (DEW) in bringing economic independence to women belonging to the economically weaker sections of society.

Papola, T. S.. Women workers in an Indian urban labour market. INTERNATIONAL LABOUR OFFICE. WORLD EMPLOYMENT PROGRAMME RESEARCH. POPULATION AND LABOUR POLICIES PROGRAMME. WORKING PAPER (GENEVA) September 1983, No. 141:1-67.

Patel, I. G.. Promotion of credit to women entrepreneurs. RESERVE BANK OF INDIA, BULLETIN (BOMBAY) December 1981, 35:1059-64. Address at the International Workshop of Women's Banking at Bhaikaka Bhavan, Ahmedabad on December 1, 1981.

Patel, Vibhuti. Les organisations feminines en Inde. TIERS-MONDE (PARIS) April/June 1985, 26:351-57.

Patel, Vibhuti. Women's liberation in India. NEW LEFT REVIEW (LONDON) September/October 1985, No. 153:75-86.

Pettigrew, Joyce. Problems concerning tubectomy operations in rural areas of Punjab. ECONOMIC AND POLITICAL WEEKLY (BOMBAY) June 30, 1984, 19:995-1002.

Ramachandran, P. and Shastri, P. P.. Intercensal urban Indian female participation rates and their variations, 1961-71: a census analysis. ECONOMIC AFFAIRS (CALCUTTA) October/December 1983, 28:816-28.

Rao, Amiya. Cost of development projects; women among the 'willing evacuees'. ECONOMIC AND POLITICAL WEEKLY (BOMBAY) March 22, 1986, 21:474-76. Describes the heavy price of development paid by India's women.

Ray, A. K. and Rangarao, I. V. Impact of technological changes on economic status of female labour. INDIAN JOURNAL OF AGRICULTURAL ECONOMICS (BOMBAY) July/September 1985, 40:244-52.

Reveiw of women studies. ECONOMIC AND POLITICAL WEEKLY (BOMBAY) October 25, 1986, 21:WS 53-WS 104.

Review in women studies. ECONOMIC AND POLITICAL WEEKLY (BOMBAY) October 26, 1985, 20:WS-57 - WS-96.

Saini, Amrik S. and Singh, Raj Vir. Impact of diversification on income, employment and credit needs of small farmers in Punjab. INDIAN JOURNAL OF AGRICULTURAL ECONOMICS (BOMBAY) July/September 1985, 40:310-16.

Saradamoni, K.. Women's status in changing agrarian relations; a Kerala experience. ECONOMIC AND POLITICAL WEEKLY (BOMBAY) January 30, 1982, 17:155-62.

Sawant, S. D. and Dewan, Ritu. Rural female labour and economic development. ECONOMIC AND POLITICAL WEEKLY (BOMBAY) June 30, 1979, 14:1091-99. This paper, based on a study of a sample of 150 villages in two talukas of Thane district in Maharashtra, attempts to examine the impact of economic development on rural women, particularly on their employment.

Scriabine, Raisa. Self-employed women: visible and valuable. HORIZONS, U.S. AGENCY FOR INTERNATIONAL DEVELOPMENT (WASHINGTON) Summer 1985, 4:38-40. Describes the Self-Employed Women's Association (SEWA), a trade union of more than 8,000 poor women workers in Ahmedabad, India. Members include small enterpreneurs, home-based producers, and manual laborers.

INDIA

Sen, Gita. Paddy production, processing and women workers in India - the south versus the northeast. CENTRE FOR DEVELOPMENT STUDIES. WORKING PAPER (ULLOOR, TRIVANDRUM) December 1983, No. 186.

Sen, Gita. Women agricultural labourers -- regional variations in incidence and employment. CENTRE FOR DEVELOPMENT STUDIES. WORKING PAPER (ULLOOR, TRIVANDRUM) April 1983, No. 168:1-28.

Sen, Gita and Sen, Chiranjib. Women's domestic work and economic activity: results from the National Sample Survey. CENTRE FOR DEVELOPMENT STUDIES. WORKING PAPER (ULLOOR, TRIVANDRUM) August 1984, No. 197:1-37.

Sen, Gita. Women's work and women agricultural labourers: a study of the Indian Census. CENTRE FOR DEVELOPMENT STUDIES. WORKING PAPER (ULLOOR, TRIVANDRUM) February 1983, No. 159:1-43.

Sharma, Miriam. Caste, class, and gender: production and reproduction in North India. JOURNAL OF PEASANT STUDIES (LONDON) July 1985, 12:26-56.

Sharma, Ursula. Unmarried women and the household economy: a research note. JOURNAL OF SOCIAL STUDIES (DHAKA) October 1985, No. 30:1-12.

Sharma, Ursula M.. Family status production work: what does it produce? JOURNAL OF SOCIAL STUDIES (DHAKA) April 1984, No. 24:74-94. Attempts to develop some issues regarding women's work in the household, using a study of women in urban households in Simla, Himachal Pradesh.

Singh, A. S. and Jain, K. K. Diversification of Punjab agriculture: an econometric analysis. INDIAN JOURNAL OF AGRICULTURAL ECONOMICS (BOMBAY) July/September 1985, 40:298-303.

Singh, Geetanjali. Trying to throw off the shackles of the past. FAR EASTERN ECONOMIC REVIEW (HONGKONG) January 5, 1984, 123:29-30. Examines the situation of women in India.

Singhal, Sushila. Development of educated women in India: reflections of a social psychologist. COMPARATIVE EDUCATION (OXFORD) October 1984, 20:355-70.

Sisodia, J. S. Role of farm women in agriculture: a study of Chambal command area of Madhya Pradesh. INDIAN JOURNAL OF AGRICULTURAL ECONOMICS (BOMBAY) July/September 1985, 40:223-34.

Srivastava, J. N.. Determinants of female age at marriage in rural Uttar Pradesh. INDIAN JOURNAL OF ECONOMICS (ALLAHABAD) January 1984, 64:327-44.

Structural changes in the employment of women: 1971-1981; an analysis of the changing distribution of women's employment. QUARTERLY ECONOMIC REPORT, INDIAN INSTITUTE OF PUBLIC OPINION (NEW DELHI) May/August 1986, 30:24-33.

Sundar, Pushpa. Characteristics of female employment; implications of research and policy. ECONOMIC AND POLITICAL WEEKLY (BOMBAY) May 19, 1981, 16:863-71.

Sundar, Pushpa. Women's employment and organisation modes. ECONOMIC AND POLITICAL WEEKLY: REVIEW OF MANAGEMENT (BOMBAY) November 26, 1983, 18:M171-M176.

Suryawanshi, S. D. and Kapase, P. M. Impact of Ghod irrigation project on employment of female agricultural labour. INDIAN JOURNAL OF AGRICULTURAL ECONOMICS (BOMBAY) July/September 1985, 40:240-44.

Thorve, P. V. and Galgalikar, V. D. Economics of diversification of farming with dairy enterprise. INDIAN JOURNAL OF AGRICULTURAL ECONOMICS (BOMBAY) July/September 1985, 40:317-23.

Tilak, Jandhyala B. G.. Inequality by sex in human labour market discrimination and returns to education. MARGIN; QUARTERLY JOURNAL OF THE NATIONAL COUNCIL OF APPLIED ECONOMIC RESEARCH (NEW DELHI) January 1980, 12:57-80. Examines some economic aspects of discrimination against women in India.

Wichterich, Christa. Der Fortschritt drangt die Frauen ins Abseits. E & Z, ENTWICKLUNG UND ZUSAMMENARBEIT (BONN) January 1985, 26:4-5.

Wichterich, Christa. Progress in India - but not for women. D & C, DEVELOPMENT AND COOPERATION (BONN) March/April 1985, No. 2:18, 20. Looks at the impact of a wave of revolutions -- the "Green Revolution", which has increased rice and wheat yields, the "White Revolution", which turned traditional milk production upside down, and a "Blue" one, which modernized fish production.

INDIA

Working class women and working class families in Bombay; report of a survey. ECONOMIC AND POLITICAL WEEKLY (BOMBAY) July 22, 1978, 13:1168-73.

Indian women: well-being and survival. By: Kynch, Jocelyn and Sen, Amartya. CAMBRIDGE JOURNAL OF ECONOMICS (LONDON) September/December 1983, 7:363-80.

Indian women in subsistence and agricultural labour. By: Mies, Maria. INTERNATIONAL LABOUR OFFICE. WORLD EMPLOYMENT PROGRAMME RESEARCH. RURAL EMPLOYMENT POLICY RESEARCH PROGRAMME. WORKING PAPER (GENEVA) (GENEVA) May 1984, No. 34:1-243.

INDONESIA

Colfer, Carol. On circular migration -- from the distaff side: women left behind in the forests of East Kalimantan. INTERNATIONAL LABOUR OFFICE. WORLD EMPLOYMENT PROGRAMME RESEARCH. POPULATION AND LABOUR POLICIES PROGRAMME. WORKING PAPER (GENEVA) May 1983, No. 132:1-42. Focuses on male circular migration (or migration with the in;tent to return home) and its impact on the women who remain in the villages tending the farm. The area studied is East Kalimantan (Indonesian Borneo).

Weekes-Vagliani, Winifred. Elaboration d'un cadre d'analyse pour les projets agro-alimentaires. TIERS-MONDE (PARIS) April/June 1985, 26:307-16. Etude d'un projet agro-alimentaire indonesien.

La industria de la maquila y la explotacion de la fuerza de trabajo de la mujer: el caso de Costa Rica. By: Guzman Stein, Laura. DESARROLLO Y SOCIEDAD (BOGOTA) January 1984, No. 13:161-76. With English summary.

INDUSTRIAL RELATIONS

Halim, Fatimah. Workers' resistance and management control: a comparative case study of male and female workers in West Malaysia. JOURNAL OF CONTEMPORARY ASIA (LONDON) 1983, 13, No. 2:131-50.

INDUSTRIALIZATION

Scott, Alison MacEwen. Women and industrialisation: examining the "female marginalisation" thesis. JOURNAL OF DEVELOPMENT STUDIES (LONDON) July 1986, 22:649-80. The article argues for attention to be paid to the micro-level processes which give rise to women's marginalisation.

Inequality by sex in human labour market discrimination and returns to education. By: Tilak, Jandhyala B. G.. MARGIN; QUARTERLY JOURNAL OF THE NATIONAL COUNCIL OF APPLIED ECONOMIC RESEARCH (NEW DELHI) January 1980, 12:57-80. Examines some economic aspects of discrimination against women in India.

INFANTS. NUTRITION

Gopalan, C.. Mother and child in India. ECONOMIC AND POLITICAL WEEKLY (BOMBAY) January 26, 1985, 20:159-66.

Influences of women's schooling on maternal behavior in the Third World. By: LeVine, Robert A.. COMPARATIVE EDUCATION REVIEW (NEW YORK) June 1980, 24:S78-105.

INFORMAL SECTOR

Ahmad, Zubeida. Advancement of rural women: the emerging networks. CERES, FAO REVIEW ON AGRICULTURE AND DEVELOPMENT (ROME) March/April 1986, 19:31-35.

Babb, Florence E.. Women in the marketplace: petty commerce in Peru. REVIEW OF RADICAL POLITICAL ECONOMICS (NEW YORK) Spring 1984, 16:45-59.

Chandigarh Women's Conference: women in informal sector; 'to keep on keeping on'. ECONOMIC AND POLITICAL WEEKLY (BOMBAY) December 20, 1986, 21:2216-18.

Gulati, Leela. Women in the unorganised sector with special reference to Kerala. CENTRE FOR DEVELOPMENT STUDIES. WORKING PAPER (ULLOOR, TRIVANDRUM) [July 1983]?, No. 172:1-22.

Hill, M. Anne. Female labor force participation in developing and developed countries -- consideration of the informal sector. REVIEW OF ECONOMICS AND STATISTICS (CAMBRIDGE, MASS.) August 1983, 65:459-68.

Inside Libya today. By: Kitchener, Julie. NEW AFRICAN (LONDON) October 1983, No. 193:10-14. Examines the strange paradoxes that give Libya its distinctive character, including the emancipation of Libyan women.

INSTITUTE FOR CULTURAL ACTION (IDAC)

Institute for Cultural Action (IDAC). Discovering self-reliance in Paraty. DEVELOPMENT (ROME) 1984, No. 4:41-44. Describes a project of women's education for self-reliance in Paraty, a rural village in Brazil.

Integrating women into development; an investment in human capital. By: Purcell, Deborah Ross. HORIZONS, U.S. AGENCY FOR INTERNATIONAL DEVELOPMENT (WASHINGTON) July/August 1983, 2:20-23. Discusses the work of AID's Office of Women in Development (WID).

Integrating women into rural cooperatives: pluses and minuses. By: Arellano, Bambi Eddy de. In: Latin American women: the meek speak out. Edited by June H. Turner. (Silver Spring, MD, International Educational Development, 1980), pp. 114-25. Discusses women in Bolivia.

Integration durch Ausbildung; eine Strategie zur Uberwindung sozialer Disparitaten in Oman: Bemerkungen uber die Partizipationschancen von Frauen am gesellschaftlichen Entwicklungsprozess in einem islamischen Land. By: Rohwer, Gertrude. ORIENT (HAMBURG) September 1984, 25:391-402. With English summary, p. 458.

Integration of women in Philippine development. By: Tidalgo, Rosa Linda P. UNIVERSITY OF THE PHILIPPINES. SCHOOL OF ECONOMICS. DISCUSSION PAPER (QUEZON) April 1985, No. 8502:1-82.

Integration of women in the development process. By: Women of Vanuatu. PACIFIC PERSPECTIVE (SUVA) 1983, 11, No. 2:1-4. Adapted from the paper presented by the Women of Vanuatu to the 21st South Pacific Conference, Vila.

Intercensal urban Indian female participation rates and their variations, 1961-71: a census analysis. By: Ramachandran, P. and Shastri, P. P.. ECONOMIC AFFAIRS (CALCUTTA) October/December 1983, 28:816-28.

International development and the evolution of women's economic roles: a case study from northern Gulma, Upper Volta. By: Hemmings-Gapihan, Grace S.. In: Women and work in Africa. Edited by Edna G. Bay. (Boulder, CO, Westview Press, 1982), pp. 171-89.

INTERNATIONAL FINANCE

Bowring, Philip. Attack on the symptoms. FAR EASTERN ECONOMIC REVIEW (HONGKONG) October 24, 1985, 130:62-64. Reviews the World Bank / IMF meetings in Seoul and suggests it left many questions unanswered.

INTERNATIONAL LABOR OFFICE

International Labor Office. Equality of opportunity and treatment for women workers: eighth item on the agenda. (Geneva, International Labour Office, 1974), 123 pp. Prepared as a basis for discussion at the International Labour Conference, 60th session, 1975, Report VIII.

INTERNATIONAL LABOUR OFFICE

International Labour Office. Report on the ILO/ECA/YWCA/SIDA workshop on participation of women in handicrafts and small industries, Kitwe, Zambia, 9-20 December, 1974. Series: Document ILO/Tf/AFR/R.19 (Geneva, [1974]), 190 pp. At head of title: International Labour Office. Swedish International Development Authority. (Mimeographed).

International Labour Office. Selected standards and policy statements of special interest to women workers adopted under the auspices of the International Labour Office. (Geneva, International Labour Office, 1980), 132 pp.

International labour office programme on rural women. By: Ahmad, Zubeida M. and Loutfi, Martha F.. (Geneva, International Labour Office, 1981), 28 pp.

INTERNATIONAL MONETARY ECONOMICS

Bowring, Philip. Attack on the symptoms. FAR EASTERN ECONOMIC REVIEW (HONGKONG) October 24, 1985, 130:62-64. Reviews the World Bank / IMF meetings in Seoul and suggests it left many questions unanswered.

INTERNATIONAL SYMPOSIUM ON WOMEN AND INDUSTRIAL RELATIONS (1978: VIENNA, AUSTRIA)

International Symposium on Women and Industrial Relations (1978: Vienna, Austria). Women and industrial relations: working papers of an international symposium, Vienna, September 1978. 2 vols. Series: Women, Work and Society; International Institute for Labour Studies, Research Series, No. 56/57. (Geneva, International Institute for Labour Studies, 1980), In English, French or German, with summaries in the other languages.

INTERREGIONAL MEETING OF EXPERTS ON THE INTEGRATION OF WOMEN IN DEVELOPMENT, NEW YORK, 1972

Interregional Meeting of Experts on the Integration of Women in Development, New York, 1972. Report. Series: United Nations Publication sales no. E.73.IV.12, United Nations Document ST/SOA/120. (New York, United Nations, 1973), 77 pp. At head of title: Department of Economic and Social Affairs.

Interview: Joyce Aryee, Secretary for Education, Ghana. By: Novicki, Margaret A.. AFRICA REPORT (NEW YORK) March/April 1985, 30:55-8.

Introduction: Arab women; the status of research in the social science and the status of women. By: Rassam, Amal. In: Social science research on women in the Arab world. (London, Frances Pinter; Paris, Unesco, 1984), pp. 1-13.

Introduction: perspectives on the education of women in Third World nations. By: Elliott, Carolyn M. and Kelly, Gail P.. COMPARATIVE EDUCATION REVIEW (NEW YORK) June 1980, 24:S1-12.

Investments in child nutrition and women's allocation of time in developing countries. By: Blau, David M.. YALE UNIVERSITY. ECONOMIC GROWTH CENTER. DISCUSSION PAPER (NEW HAVEN, CONN.) March 1981, No. 371:1-41. The purpose of this study is to investigate the determinants of fertility and home investments in the human capital of children in a context in which women have the option of working in the informal sector as well as the formal sector or no market work. The empirical analysis presented in section III uses data from a 1977-78 survey of households in Nicaragua.

IRAN

Afshar, Haleh. Women, state and ideology in Iran. THIRD WORLD QUARTERLY (LONDON) April 1985, 7:256-78.

Iranian women in family alliance and sexual politics. By: Vieille, Paul. In: Women in the Muslim world. Edited by Lois Beck and Nikki Keddie. (Cambridge, MA, Harvard University Press, 1978), pp. 451-72.

IRAQ

Joseph, Suad. Mobilization of Iraqi women into the wage labor force. STUDIES IN THIRD WORLD SOCIETIES (WILLIAMSBURG) June 1981, No. 16:69-90.

IRRIGATION

Suryawanshi, S. D. and Kapase, P. M. Impact of Ghod irrigation project on employment of female agricultural labour. INDIAN JOURNAL OF AGRICULTURAL ECONOMICS (BOMBAY) July/September 1985, 40:240-44.

Is "Women in Development" working? By: Viveros-Long, Anamaria and Krueger, Christine. HORIZONS, U.S. AGENCY FOR INTERNATIONAL DEVELOPMENT (WASHINGTON) Summer 1985, 4:15-17. The authors describe how AID's Center for Development Information and Evaluation (CDIE) is making the first systematic assessment of the progress AID has made in integrating women into development activities at the project level.

ISAACMAN, BARBARA

Isaacman, Barbara and Stephen, June. Mozambique: women, the law and agrarian reform. Series: [African Training and Research Centre for Women] Research Series, No. 01/80. ([Addis Ababa], United Nations Economic Commission for Africa, 1980), 148 pp. "ATRCWSDD/RES01/80"

ISELY, RAYMOND B.

Elmendorf, Mary L. and Isely, Raymond B.. Role of women in water supply and sanitation. WORLD HEALTH FORUM (GENEVA) 1982, 3, No. 2:227-30.

ISLAM, MAHMUDA

Islam, Mahmuda. Bibliography on Bangladesh women with annotation. (Dacca, Women for Women Research and Study Group, [1979]), 63 pp.

Islamic attitudes to female employment in industrializing economies: some notes from Malaysia. By: Siraj, Mehrun. In: Women in the urban and industrial workforce; Southeast and East Asia. Edited by Gavin W. Jones. Series: Development Studies Centre. Monograph, No. 33. (Canberra, Australia, Australian National University, 1984), pp. 163-74. Series edited by Helen Hughes.

ISMAIL, BATHITA AMIN

Hall, Marjorie J. and Ismail, Bathita Amin. Sisters under the sun: the story of Sudanese women. (London, New York, Longman, 1981), 264 pp.

ISMAIL-SCHMIDT, ELLEN

Ismail-Schmidt, Ellen. Sudan - Frauen zwischen Tradition und Moderne. E & Z, ENTWICKLUNG UND ZUSAMMENARBEIT (BONN) January 1985, 26:11-13, 20.

ISRAEL

Katzir, Yael. Yemenite Jewish women in Israeli rural development: female power versus male authority. ECONOMIC DEVELOPMENT AND CULTURAL CHANGE (CHICAGO) October 1983, 32:45-61.

Israeli women and men: divisions behind the unity. By: Davis, Nira Yuval. Series: Change International Reports: Women and Society, No. 6. (London, Change International Reports, [1983?]), 27 pp.

ISRALOW, SHARON

Isralow, Sharon. Diamond in the rough. HORIZONS, U.S. AGENCY FOR INTERNATIONAL DEVELOPMENT (WASHINGTON) Summer 1985, 4:34-37. Examines the achievements of the women and men of Sri Lanka's Kirillapone shanty town.

Issues confronting professional African women: illustrations from Kenya. By: Lindsay, Beverly. In: Comparative perspectives of Third World women: the impact of race, sex and class. Edited by Beverly Lindsay. (New York, Praeger, 1980), pp. 78-95.

Italian women; between family and feminism. By: Wieser, Theodore. SWISS REVIEW OF WORLD AFFAIRS (ZURICH) May 1982, 32:12-13.

ITALY

Colombino, Ugo. Variabili dipendenti limitate e selezione non casuale delle osservazioni: una applicazione alla stima della funzione di salario e di offerta di lavoro delle donne sposate in Italia. GIORNALE DEGLI ECONOMISTI E ANNALI DI ECONOMIA (MILAN) May/June 1983, 42, N.S.:369-85. With English summary, p. 388.

Wieser, Theodore. Italian women; between family and feminism. SWISS REVIEW OF WORLD AFFAIRS (ZURICH) May 1982, 32:12-13.

It's a man's Third world. By: Beasley, Julia. GUARDIAN (LONDON) November 5, 1984, p. 12. The author indicates that "Across the cultural divide, sexism is the only thing countries have in common."

IVORY COAST

Kranz, Jutta and Fiege, Karin. Work never ends; problems of women in the farm economy of the Ivory Coast. D & C, DEVELOPMENT AND COOPERATION (BONN) November/December 1983, No. 6:12-13.

IVORY COAST

Yaccob, May. Ahmadiyya and urbanization: migrant women in Abidjan. BOSTON UNIVERSITY. AFRICAN STUDIES CENTER. WORKING PAPERS (BOSTON) 1983, No. 75:1-16.

JACKSON, ROBERTA H.

Jackson, Roberta H.. Some aspirations of lower class black mothers. In: Women in the family and the economy: an international comparative survey. Edited by George Kurian and Ratna Ghosh. (Westport, CT, Greenwood Press, 1981), pp. 273-83.

JACOBS, SUSIE

Jacobs, Susie. Women and land resettlement in Zimbabwe. REVIEW OF AFRICAN POLITICAL ECONOMY (SHEFFIELD) 1984, No. 27/28:33-50.

JAHAN, FARIDA AKHTER

Khan, Atiqur Rahman and Jahan, Farida Akhter. Maternal mortality in rural Bangladesh: the Jamalpur district. STUDIES IN FAMILY PLANNING (NEW YORK) January/February 1986, 17:7-12.

JAHAN, ROUNAQ

Jahan, Rounaq. Women in Bangladesh. In: Women cross-culturally: change and challenge. Edited by Ruby Rohrlich-Leavitt. (The Hague, Mouton, 1975), pp. 5-30.

JAHANGIR, B. K

Jahangir, B. K. Women and property in rural Bangladesh. JOURNAL OF SOCIAL STUDIES (DHAKA) October 1986, No. 34:87-95.

JAIN, ANRUDH K.

Jain, Anrudh K. and Nag, Moni. Female primary education and fertility reduction in India. POPULATION COUNCIL. CENTER FOR POLICY STUDIES. WORKING PAPERS (NEW YORK) September 1985, No. 114:1-57.

Jain, Anrudh K. and Nag, Moni. Importance of female primary education for fertility reduction in India. ECONOMIC AND POLITICAL WEEKLY (BOMBAY) September 6, 1986, 21:1602-08.

JAIN, DEVAKI

Jain, Devaki. Gandhi's philosophy; an inspiration for women. DEVELOPMENT (ROME) 1984, No. 4:71-74.

JAIN, DEVAKI

Jain, Devaki. In poor families, women's income is the lifeline. CERES, FAO REVIEW ON AGRICULTURE AND DEVELOPMENT (ROME) July/August 1984, 17:35-38. Presents an interview with the director of the Institute of Social Studies, New Delhi, describing the pressures on landless female agricultural laborers.

Jain, Devaki and Singh, Nalini. Role of rural women in community life; a case study from India. ECONOMIC BULLETIN FOR ASIA AND THE PACIFIC (BANGKOK) December 1978, 29:84-126.

JAIN, SHOBHITA

Jain, Shobhita. Women and people's ecological movement; a case study of women's role in the Chipko movement in Uttar Pradesh. ECONOMIC AND POLITICAL WEEKLY (BOMBAY) October 13, 1984, 19:1788-93.

JAKUBSON, GEORGE

Jakubson, George. Sensitivity of labor supply parameter estimates to unobserved individual effects: fixed and random effects estimates in a nonlinear model using panel data. PRINCETON UNIVERSITY. INDUSTRIAL RELATIONS SECTION. WORKING PAPER (PRINCETON) August 1986, No. 210:1-37; A1-A4 (various pagings).

JAMAICA

Griffith, David C. Women, remittances, and reproduction. AMERICAN ETHNOLOGIST (WASHINGTON) November 1985, 12:676-90. Presents and interprets data on how women in Jamaica use remittances from migrating husbands, boyfriends, sons, and so forth, and examines some of the reasons for these uses. The author concludes that seasonal-labor migration aids Jamaican peasant households in meeting the costs of reproducing themselves and their social and economic conditions.

Lewis, Martha. Developing income generating opportunity for rural women. HORIZONS, U.S. AGENCY FOR INTERNATIONAL DEVELOPMENT (WASHINGTON) January 1983, 2:28-31. Describes how bananas, solar-dried and marketed as banana-figs, promise to boost Jamaican farm women's earnings.

JANJIC, MARION

Janjic, Marion. Diversifying women's employment: the only road to genuine equality of opportunity. INTERNATIONAL LABOUR REVIEW (GENEVA) March/April 1981, 120:149-63.

JAPAN

Chiba, Atsuko. Trappings of success, but an inner emptiness. FAR EASTERN ECONOMIC REVIEW (HONGKONG) January 5, 1984, 123:30-31. The author discusses Japanes women.

Chira, Susan. Tough ascent for Japanese women. NEW YORK TIMES (NEW YORK) February 24, 1985, Section 3, p. 1-27. Equal employment opportunities for women in Japan remain scarce and male-dominated industries resist women's attempts to change traditional ways.

Goodman, Matthew. Japanese women in finance. TOKYO BUSINESS TODAY (TOKYO) May 1986, p. 19-23.

Helm, Leslie and Takahashi, Kyoko. Japan's secret economic weapon: exploited women. BUSINESS WEEK (NEW YORK) March 4, 1985, No. 2883:54-55.

Hill, M. Anne. Comparison of economic models and empirical results for female labor force participation in Japan and the United State. YALE UNIVERSITY. ECONOMIC GROWTH CENTER. DISCUSSION PAPER (NEW HAVEN, CONN.) July 1982, No. 415:1-36.

Hill, M. Anne. Female labor force participation in urban Japan; a trichotomous logit model. YALE UNIVERSITY. ECONOMIC GROWTH CENTER. DISCUSSION PAPER (NEW HAVEN, CONN.) September 1980, No. 362:1-42.

Nakanishi, Tamako. Equality or protection? Protective legislation for women in Japan. INTERNATIONAL LABOUR REVIEW (GENEVA) September/October 1983, 122:609-21.

Nishikawa, Shunsaku and Higuchi, Yoshio. Determinants of female labor-force participation. JAPANESE ECONOMIC STUDIES (ARMONK, N.Y.) Winter 1980/1981, 9:62-87.

Nishimura, Namiko. Women at work. JOURNAL OF JAPANESE TRADE & INDUSTRY (TOKYO) May/June 1986, 5:46-47.

Osawa, Machiko. Wage gap in Japan: changing patterns of labor force participation, schooling and tenure. ECONOMICS RESEARCH CENTER. NORC [NATIONAL OPINION RESEARCH CENTER] DISCUSSION PAPER SERIES (CHICAGO) April 1986, No. 86-1:1-29. Examines how changes in schooling and work experience over time between men and women workers have affected wage differentials observed in the post-WWII period in Japan.

JAPAN

    Osawa, Machiko. Working mothers: changing patterns of employment and fertility in Japan. ECONOMICS RESEARCH CENTER. NORC [NATIONAL OPINION RESEARCH CENTER] DISCUSSION PAPER SERIES (CHICAGO) June 1986, No. 86-5:1-58. In this paper the differential fertility rates between paid women workers in the formal sector and family workers in the informal sector are featured to analyze the reasons why the Japanese fertility trend in the post-World War II period differs from other nations.

    Shinotsuka, Eiko. Female workers as described in a help-wanted information magazine. JAPANESE ECONOMIC STUDIES (ARMONK, N.Y.) Spring 1984, 12:3-20.

    Shinotsuka, Eiko. Women at work; equality and care of the species. FAR EASTERN ECONOMIC REVIEW (HONGKONG) Dec. 3, 1982, 118:87-90.

    Woronoff, Jon. Wasting Japan's women workers. ORIENTAL ECONOMIST (TOKYO) November 1980, 48:22-24.

    Yamada, Tadashi and Yamada, Tetsuji. Fertility and labor force participation of married women: empirical evidence from the 1980 population census of Japan. QUARTERLY REVIEW OF ECONOMICS AND BUSINESS (URBANA, ILL.) Summer 1986, 26:35-46.

    Yashiro, Naohiro. Male-female wage differentials in Japan: a rational explanation. JAPANESE ECONOMIC STUDIES (ARMONK, N.Y.) Winter 1980/1981, 9:28-61.

Japan: historical and contemporary perspectives. By: Pharr, Susan J.. In: Women: roles and status in eight countries. Edited by Janet Zollinger Giele and Audrey Chapman Smock. (New York, John Wiley, 1977), pp. 219-55.

Japanese women in finance. By: Goodman, Matthew. TOKYO BUSINESS TODAY (TOKYO) May 1986, p. 19-23.

Japan's secret economic weapon: exploited women. By: Helm, Leslie and Takahashi, Kyoko. BUSINESS WEEK (NEW YORK) March 4, 1985, No. 2883:54-55.

JAYAWARDENA, KUMARI

    Jayawardena, Kumari. Plantation sector in Sri Lanka: recent changes in the welfare of children and women. WORLD DEVELOPMENT (OXFORD) March 1984, 12, Special issue:317-28.

JEFFERY, PATRICIA

    Jeffery, Patricia and Jeffery, Roger. Childbirth and collaboration among women in Bijnor district, Uttar Pradesh. JOURNAL OF SOCIAL STUDIES (DHAKA) July 1984, No. 25:15-33.

JENSEN, AN-MAGRITT

    Jensen, An-Magritt and Schweder, Tore. Engine of fertility - influenced by interbirth employment? NORWAY. STATISTISK SENTRALBYRA. DISCUSSION PAPER (OSLO) June 1986, No. 15:1-33.

JIANHAI, CAO

    Jianhai, Cao. Marriage and family; single women and men in China. WOMEN OF CHINA (BEIJING) November 1984, No. 11:14-15.

JIMENEZ BUTRAGUENO, MARIA DE LOS ANGELES

    Jimenez Butragueno, Maria de los Angeles. Protective legislation and equal opportunity and treatment for women in Spain. INTERNATIONAL LABOUR REVIEW (GENEVA) March/April 1982, 121:185-98.

Job equality for women: Progress, problems and perspectives. By: Sarfati, Hedva. LABOUR AND SOCIETY (GENEVA) September 1985, 10:273-88.

JOB EVALUATION

    Sorensen, Elaine. Implementing comparable worth: a survey of recent job evaluation studies. AMERICAN ECONOMIC REVIEW, PAPERS AND PROCEEDINGS (NASHVILLE) May 1986, 76:364-72.

JOHN, MIRIAM

    Kurian, George and John, Miriam. Attitudes of women towards certain selected cultural practices in Kerala State, India. In: Women in the family and the economy: an international comparative survey. Edited by George Kurian and Ratna Ghosh. (Westport, CT, Greenwood Press, 1981), pp. 131-64.

JOHNSON, WILLIAM R.

    Johnson, William R. and Skinner, Jonathan. Labor supply and marital separation. AMERICAN ECONOMIC REVIEW (NASHVILLE) June 1986, 76:455-69. A simultaneous model of future divorce probability and current labor supply is estimated for married women. The results support the hypothesis that divorce probabilities increase labor supply.

JONES, GAVIN W.

Jones, Gavin W.. Economic growth and changing female employment structure in the cities of Southeast and East Asia. In: Women in the urban and industrial workforce; Southeast and East Asia. Edited by Gavin W. Jones. Series: Development Studies Centre. Monograph, No. 33. (Canberra, Australia, Australian National University, 1984), pp. 17-60. Series edited by Helen Hughes.

JORDAN

Dahhan, Omaymah. Examination of the literature on Jordanian women. INTERNATIONAL LABOUR OFFICE. WORLD EMPLOYMENT PROGRAMME RESEARCH. POPULATION AND LABOUR POLICIES: REGIONAL PROGRAMME FOR THE MIDDLE EAST. WORKING PAPER (BEIRUT) March 1981, No. 8:1-146.

JOSEPH, GLORIA I.

Joseph, Gloria I.. Caribbean women: the impact of race, sex, and class. In: Comparative perspectives of Third World women: the impact of race, sex and class. Edited by Beverly Lindsay. (New York, Praeger, 1980), pp. 143-61.

JOSEPH, SUAD

Joseph, Suad. Mobilization of Iraqi women into the wage labor force. STUDIES IN THIRD WORLD SOCIETIES (WILLIAMSBURG) June 1981, No. 16:69-90.

Joseph, Suad. Women and the neighborhood street in Barj Hammoud, Lebanon. In: Women in the Muslim world. Edited by Lois Beck and Nikki Keddie. (Cambridge, MA, Harvard University Press, 1978), pp. 541-57.

JOUFFREY, ROGER

Jouffrey, Roger. La paysanne africaine au travail. AFRIQUE CONTEMPORAINE, DOCUMENTS D'AFRIQUE NOIRE ET DE MADAGASCAR (PARIS) April/June 1983, 22:23-29.

KABEER, NAILA

Kabeer, Naila. Minus lives: women of Bangladesh. Series: Change International Reports: Women and Society, No. 10. (London, Change International Reports , [1983?]), 16 pp.

KAGITCIBASI, CIGDEM

Kagitcibasi, Cigdem. Status of women in Turkey: cross-cultural perspectives. INTERNATIONAL JOURNAL OF MIDDLE EAST STUDIES (CAMBRIDGE) November 1986, 18:485-99.

KALIA, NARENDRA NATH

Kalia, Narendra Nath. Images of men and women in Indian textbooks. COMPARATIVE EDUCATION REVIEW (NEW YORK) June 1980, 24:S209-23. Attempts to demonstrate that Indian school textbooks promote an ideology which refuses females equal access to opportunities and rewards even in areas where the sex of a person is totally irrelevant.

KAMIKAMICA, ESITERI

Kamikamica, Esiteri. Fiji women on the move. PACIFIC PERSPECTIVE (SUVA) 1983, 11, No. 2:40-44.

KANELLOPOULOS, COSTAS N.

Kanellopoulos, Costas N.. Male-female pay differentials in Greece. GREEK ECONOMIC REVIEW (ATHENS) August 1982, 4:222-41.

KARAOSMANOGLU, ATTILA

Karaosmanoglu, Attila. U.N. Decade for Women. BANK'S WORLD (WASHINGTON) September 1985, 4:11-12. The World Bank's statement at the world conference reviewing and appraising the achievements of the U.N. Decade for Women in Nairobi, Kenya, in July.

KARIM, A. K. NAZMUL

Karim, A. K. Nazmul. Changing patterns of an East Pakistan family. In: Women in the new Asia; the changing social roles of men and women in South and South-east Asia. Edited by Barbara E. Ward. ([Paris], Unesco, 1963), pp. 296-322. Describes the family's rural background in Tipera district (now in Bangladesh) and its subsequent move to Dacca.

KASHIF-BADRI, HAGGA

Kashif-Badri, Hagga. History, development, organization and position of women's studies in the Sudan. In: Social science research on women in the Arab world. (London, Frances Pinter; Paris, Unesco, 1984), pp. 94-105.

KATONA-APTE, JUDIT

Katona-Apte, Judit. Women and food aid; a developmental perspective. FOOD POLICY (GUILDFORD, ENG.) August 1986, 11:216-22.

KATZIR, YAEL

Katzir, Yael. Yemenite Jewish women in Israeli rural development: female power versus male authority. ECONOMIC DEVELOPMENT AND CULTURAL CHANGE (CHICAGO) October 1983, 32:45-61.

KEARNEY, ROBERT N.

   Kearney, Robert N.. Women in politics in Sri Lanka. ASIAN SURVEY (BERKELEY, CALIF.) July 1981, 21:729-46.

KELKAR, GOVIND

   Kelkar, Govind. Tractors against women. DEVELOPMENT (ROME) 1985, No. 3:18-21. Concludes that the Green Revolution has brought in its wake the all-India trend of pauperization and marginalization and the increased inequality between the sexes.

   Kelkar, Govind. Women in Mao's China. DEVELOPMENT (ROME) 1984, No. 4:55-58. The author recounts the history of the single most important effort to equalize women's position in society, the quest for egalitarianism in Maoist China.

KELLY, DEIRDRE

   Kelly, Deirdre. St. Lucia's female electronics factory workers: key components in an export-oriented industrialization strategy. WORLD DEVELOPMENT (OXFORD) July 1986, 14:823-38.

KELLY, GAIL P.

   Elliott, Carolyn M. and Kelly, Gail P.. Introduction: perspectives on the education of women in Third World nations. COMPARATIVE EDUCATION REVIEW (NEW YORK) June 1980, 24:S1-12.

   Kelly, Gail P.. Schooling of Vietnamese immigrants: internal colonialism and its impact on women. In: Comparative perspectives of Third World women: the impact of race, sex and class. Edited by Beverly Lindsay. (New York, Praeger, 1980), pp. 276-96.

   Kelly, Gail P. and Lulat, Younus. Women and schooling in the Third World: a bibliography. COMPARATIVE EDUCATION REVIEW (NEW YORK) June 1980, 24:S224-63.

KENDALL, CARL

   Kendall, Carl. Female-headed households and domestic organization in San Isidro, Guatemala: a test of Hammel and Laslett's comparative typology. In: Women in the family and the economy: an international comparative survey. Edited by George Kurian and Ratna Ghosh. (Westport, CT, Greenwood Press, 1981), pp. 29-41.

KENYA

   Barnes, Carolyn. Differentiation by sex among small-scale farming households in Kenya. RURAL AFRICANA (EAST LANSING) Winter/Spring 1983, No. 15/16:41-63.

KENYA

   Donner-Reichle, Carola. Nach zehn Jahren Bewusstsein fur Frauen geschaffen. E & Z, ENTWICKLUNG UND ZUSAMMENARBEIT (BONN) January 1985, 26:14-15.

   Dow, Thomas E., Jr. and Werner, Linda H.. Perceptions of family planning among rural Kenyan women. STUDIES IN FAMILY PLANNING (NEW YORK) February 1983, 14:35-43.

   Feldman, Rayah. Women's groups and women's subordination: an analysis of policies towards rural women in Kenya. REVIEW OF AFRICAN POLITICAL ECONOMY (SHEFFIELD) 1984, No. 27/28:67-85.

   Harris, Joan. Women in Kenya; revolution or evolution? AFRICA REPORT (NEW YORK) March/April 1985, 30:30-32.

   Lindsay, Beverly. Examination of education, social change, and national development policy: the case of Kenyan women. STUDIES IN THIRD WORLD SOCIETIES (WILLIAMSBURG) June 1981, No. 16:29-48.

   Roberts, Penelope. Les femmes et les programmes de developpement rural; avec reference aux programmes-femmes finances par le Fonds Europeen de Developpement au Kenya. TIERS-MONDE (PARIS) April/June 1985, 26:299-305.

   van Buren, Linda. KWFT steps in to make African women bankable. AFRICAN BUSINESS (LONDON) July 1985, No. 83:10-12. Describes the Kenya Women Finance Trust.

   Ventura-Dias, V.. Technological change, production organisation and rural women in Kenya. INTERNATIONAL LABOUR OFFICE. WORLD EMPLOYMENT PROGRAMME RESEARCH. TECHNOLOGY AND EMPLOYMENT PROGRAMME. WORKING PAPERS (GENEVA) November 1982, No. 101:1-64.

KERMOND, LESLEY

   Kermond, Lesley. Women -- the 25 hour day, women in development. A book exhibition, 15 October - 28 November 1982. (London, Library & Resource Centre, Commonwealth Institute, 1982), 19 pp. With supplement.

KHAING, MI MI

   Khaing, Mi Mi. Burma: balance and harmony. In: Women in the new Asia; the changing social roles of men and women in South and South-east Asia. Edited by Barbara E. Ward. ([Paris], Unesco, 1963), pp. 104-37.

KHALAF, M.

Lorfing, I. and Khalaf, M.. Economic contribution of women and its effect on the dynamics of the family in two Lebanese villages. INTERNATIONAL LABOUR OFFICE. WORLD EMPLOYMENT PROGRAMME RESEARCH. POPULATION AND LABOUR POLICIES PROGRAMME. WORKING PAPER (GENEVA) May 1985, No. 148:1-32.

KHAN, ATIQUR RAHMAN

Khan, Atiqur Rahman and Jahan, Farida Akhter. Maternal mortality in rural Bangladesh: the Jamalpur district. STUDIES IN FAMILY PLANNING (NEW YORK) January/February 1986, 17:7-12.

KHAN, NIGHAT S

Khan, Nighat S. Women Pakistan: position, status and movement. JOURNAL OF SOCIAL STUDIES (DHAKA) October 1985, No. 30:27-40.

KHAN, ZARINA RAHMAN

Khan, Zarina Rahman. Women's economic role: insights from a village in Bangladesh. JOURNAL OF SOCIAL STUDIES (DHAKA) October 1985, No. 30:13-26.

KHANDKER, SHAHIDUR R

Khandker, Shahidur R. Women's role in household productive activities and fertility in Bangladesh. YALE UNIVERSITY. ECONOMIC GROWTH CENTER. DISCUSSION PAPER (NEW HAVEN, CONN.) July 1985, No. 488:1-35. Seeks to identify the factors that may affect the role of women in the rural areas of a developing country and the possible impact of these factors on fertility.

KHODJA, SOUAD

Khodja, Souad. Women's work as viewed in present-day Algerian society. INTERNATIONAL LABOUR REVIEW (GENEVA) July/August 1982, 121:481-87.

KHOO, SIEW-EAN

Fawcett, James T. and Khoo, Siew-Ean and Smith, Peter C.. Urbanization, migration, and the status of women. In: Women in the cities of Asia: migration and urban adaptation. Edited by James T. Fawcett, Siew-Ean Khoo and Peter C. Smith. (Boulder, CO, Westview Press, 1984), pp. 15-35.

Khoo, Siew-Ean and Pirie, Peter. Female rural-to-urban migration in peninsular Malaysia. In: Women in the cities of Asia: migration and urban adaptation. Edited by James T. Fawcett, Siew-Ean Khoo and Peter C. Smith. (Boulder, CO, Westview Press, 1984), pp. 125-42.

KHOO, SIEW-EAN

Khoo, Siew-Ean. Urbanward migration and employment of women in Southeast and East Asian cities: patterns and policy issues. In: Women in the urban and industrial workforce; Southeast and East Asia. Edited by Gavin W. Jones. Series: Development Studies Centre. Monograph, No. 33. (Canberra, Australia, Australian National University, 1984), pp. 277-92. Series edited by Helen Hughes.

KHOURI-DAGHER, NADIA

Khouri-Dagher, Nadia. La participation des femmes a l'economie egyptienne: tendances et evolutions. TIERS-MONDE (PARIS) April/June 1985, 26:335-50.

KI-ZERBO, JACQUELINE

Ki-Zerbo, Jacqueline. Women and the energy crisis in the Sahel. UNASYLVA (ROME) 1981, 33, No. 133:5-10.

KIM, KYONG-DONG

Kim, On-Jook Lee and Kim, Kyong-Dong. Casual interpretation of the effect of mother's education and employment status on parental decision-making role patterns in the Korean family. In: Women in the family and the economy: an international comparative survey. Edited by George Kurian and Ratna Ghosh. (Westport, CT, Greenwood Press, 1981), pp. 43-57.

KIM, LE KWANG

Kim, Le Kwang. Woman of Viet-Nam in a changing world. In: Women in the new Asia; the changing social roles of men and women in South and South-east Asia. Edited by Barbara E. Ward. ([Paris], Unesco, 1963), pp. 462-70.

KIM, ON-JOOK LEE

Kim, On-Jook Lee and Kim, Kyong-Dong. Casual interpretation of the effect of mother's education and employment status on parental decision-making role patterns in the Korean family. In: Women in the family and the economy: an international comparative survey. Edited by George Kurian and Ratna Ghosh. (Westport, CT, Greenwood Press, 1981), pp. 43-57.

KINZER, NORA SCOTT

Kinzer, Nora Scott. Sociocultural factors mitigating role conflict of Buenos Aires professional women. In: Women cross-culturally: change and challenge. Edited by Ruby Rohrlich-Leavitt. (The Hague, Mouton, 1975), pp. 181-97.

KIRKWOOD, JULIETA

Kirkwood, Julieta. Women and politics in Chile. INTERNATIONAL SOCIAL SCIENCE JOURNAL (PARIS) 1983, 35, No. 4:625-37.

KISEKKA, MERE

Kisekka, Mere. Research of the status of women, development and population trends in Africa: an annotated bibliography. In: Bibliographic guide to studies on the status of women: development and population trends. (New York, Bowker, UNIPUB; Paris, Unesco, 1983), pp. 41-66.

KITCHENER, JULIE

Kitchener, Julie. Inside Libya today. NEW AFRICAN (LONDON) October 1983, No. 193:10-14. Examines the strange paradoxes that give Libya its distinctive character, including the emancipation of Libyan women.

KLINGER, ANDRAS

Barta, Barnabas and Klinger, Andras. Fertility, female employment and policy measures in Hungary. Series: Women, Work and Development, No. 6. (Geneva, International Labour Organisation, 1984), 88 pp. Published with the financial support of the United Nations Fund for Population Activities (UNFPA).

KNAPP, GUDRUN-AXELI

Becker-Schmidt, Regina and Knapp, Gudrun-Axeli. Wertewandel und Widerspruche; Erziehungsorientierungen und -probleme von Arbeiterinnen im Vergleich zweier Generationen. WSI-MITTEILUNGEN (DUSSELDORF) August 1986, 39:558-66.

KONIE, GWENDOLINE

Konie, Gwendoline. Women in southern Africa; gaining political power. AFRICA REPORT (NEW YORK) March/April 1983, 28:11-14.

KOO, HAGEN

Cho, Uhn and Koo, Hagen. Economic development and women's work in a newly industrializing country: the case of Korea. DEVELOPMENT AND CHANGE (THE HAGUE, etc.) October 1983, 14:515-31. The authors investigate how women's economic activities have changed in relation to the pattern of economic growth in Korea in the past two decades.

KOO, SUNG-YEAL

Koo, Sung-Yeal. Trends in female labour force participation and occupational shifts in urban Korea. In: Women in the urban and industrial workforce; Southeast and East Asia. Edited by Gavin W. Jones. Series: Development Studies Centre. Monograph, No. 33. (Canberra, Australia, Australian National University, 1984), pp. 61-73. Series edited by Helen Hughes.

KOOPMAN HENN, JEANNE

Koopman Henn, Jeanne. Feeding the cities and feeding the peasants: what role for Africa's women farmers? WORLD DEVELOPMENT (OXFORD) December 1983, 11:1043-55.

Kopenhagen: de tweede VN-conferentie voor vrouwen; Vrouwen en ontwikkeling. INTERNATIONALE SPECTATOR (THE HAGUE) June 1980, 34:309-57.

KOREA

Chang, MyongSue. Breaking down barriers and getting in step. FAR EASTERN ECONOMIC REVIEW (HONGKONG) January 5, 1984, 123:39-40. Describes how Korean women have steadily improved their status over the past several decades.

Cho, Uhn and Koo, Hagen. Economic development and women's work in a newly industrializing country: the case of Korea. DEVELOPMENT AND CHANGE (THE HAGUE, etc.) October 1983, 14:515-31. The authors investigate how women's economic activities have changed in relation to the pattern of economic growth in Korea in the past two decades.

Lee, Bun Song and McElwain, Adrienne M. Empirical investigation of female labor-force participation, fertility, age at marriage, and wages in Korea. JOURNAL OF DEVELOPING AREAS (MACOMB, ILL.) July 1985, 19:483-500.

KORSON, J. HENRY

Korson, J. Henry. Career constraints among women graduate students in a developing society: West Pakistan; a study in the changing status of women. In: Women in the family and the economy: an international comparative survey. Edited by George Kurian and Ratna Ghosh. (Westport, CT, Greenwood Press, 1981), pp. 393-411.

KOSSOUDJI, SHERRIE

Kossoudji, Sherrie and Mueller, Eva. Economic and demographic status of female-headed households in rural Botswana. ECONOMIC DEVELOPMENT AND CULTURAL CHANGE (CHICAGO) July 1983, 31:831-59.

Koumbidia (Senegal); developpement d'une activite maraichere villageoise. TIERS-MONDE (PARIS) April/June 1985, 26:421-28.

KRANZ, JUTTA

Kranz, Jutta and Fiege, Karin. Work never ends; problems of women in the farm economy of the Ivory Coast. D & C, DEVELOPMENT AND COOPERATION (BONN) November/December 1983, No. 6:12-13.

KRATZ, ACHIM

Kratz, Achim. La conference mondiale des femmes et la femme africaine. MOIS EN AFRIQUE (PARIS) April/May 1986, 21:160-66.

KRAVCHENKO, M.

Kravchenko, M.. For the mother, for the family. SOVIET REVIEW, A JOURNAL OF TRANSLATIONS (ARMONK, N.Y.) Summer 1984, 25:18-24.

KRISHNASWAMI, LALITA

Krishnaswami, Lalita. From drudgery to dignity: the SEWA experience. LABOUR AND SOCIETY (GENEVA) September 1985, 10:323-31. Discusses the achievements of the Self-Employed Women's Association (SEWA), which is at once a union, a trust and a credit institution whose basic aim is to provide better living and working conditions for the poor, illiterate women who comprise its membership.

KRUEGER, CHRISTINE

Viveros-Long, Anamaria and Krueger, Christine. Is "Women in Development" working? HORIZONS, U.S. AGENCY FOR INTERNATIONAL DEVELOPMENT (WASHINGTON) Summer 1985, 4:15-17. The authors describe how AID's Center for Development Information and Evaluation (CDIE) is making the first systematic assessment of the progress AID has made in integrating women into development activities at the project level.

KUMAR, MANJU

Kumar, Manju. Social equality: the constitutional experiment in India. (New Delhi, S. Chand, 1982), 264 pp.

Kung women: contrasts in sexual egalitarianism in foraging and sedentary contexts. By: Draper, Patricia. In: Toward an anthropology of women. Edited by Rayna R. Reiter. (New York, Monthly Review Press, 1975), pp. 77-109.

KUNIANSKY, ANNA

Kuniansky, Anna. Soviet fertility, labor-force participation, and marital instabililty. JOURNAL OF COMPARATIVE ECONOMICS (NEW YORK) June 1983, 7:114-30.

KUPPER, BETTINA

Demmer, Hildegard and Kupper, Bettina. Arbeitsbelastungen von Frauen im Paketdienst. WSI-MITTEILUNGEN (DUSSELDORF) August 1986, 39:522-28.

KURIAN, GEORGE

Kurian, George and John, Miriam. Attitudes of women towards certain selected cultural practices in Kerala State, India. In: Women in the family and the economy: an international comparative survey. Edited by George Kurian and Ratna Ghosh. (Westport, CT, Greenwood Press, 1981), pp. 131-64.

KURIAN, RACHEL

Kurian, Rachel. Income distribution, poverty and employment. INSTITUTE OF SOCIAL STUDIES. OCCASIONAL PAPERS (THE HAGUE) September 1979, No. 73:1-55. Examines the marginalization of women in theory and in reality, with examples from studies carried out in Sri Lanka and Yugoslavia.

KURZ-SCHERF, INGRID

Kurz-Scherf, Ingrid. Von der Emanzipation des Brunnenmadchens in Heilbadern; Frauendiskriminierung, Frauenforderung durch Tarifvertrag und Tarifpolitik. WSI-MITTEILUNGEN (DUSSELDORF) August 1986, 39:537-49.

Kvinder, konsrelationer og social forandring. DEN NY VERDEN (COPENHAGEN) 1983, 17, No.4:1-124. Content: Wilson, Fiona, Kvinder og kommercialisering af landbruget: en diskussion af aktuelle tendenser i Mexico. - Odgaard, Rie, and Jens Dahl, Gronlandske bygdekvinder i en okonomisk forandringsproces. - Roberts, Pepe, Kvinder i landomraderne i Vestnigeria. - Thorbek, Susanne, Refleksioner fra en Bangkok slum. - Tarp, Elsebeth, Kvindekamp og kulturkamp i Mexico. - Sjorslev, Inger, Rituel magt og social undertrykkelse; kvinder i Brasilien.

KWFT steps in to make African women bankable. By: van Buren, Linda. AFRICAN BUSINESS (LONDON) July 1985, No. 83:10-12. Describes the Kenya Women Finance Trust.

KYNCH, JOCELYN

Kynch, Jocelyn and Sen, Amartya. Indian women: well-being and survival. CAMBRIDGE JOURNAL OF ECONOMICS (LONDON) September/December 1983, 7:363-80.

LABOR DISPUTES

Wehkamp, Andy. Luchas colectivas de las obreras peruanas: los motivos de participacion y alejamiento. BOLETIN DE ESTUDIOS LATINO-AMERICANOS Y DEL CARIBE (AMSTERDAM) December 1984, No. 37:69-83.

LABOR ECONOMICS

Ahmad, Perveen. Unsung heroines: Bangladesh's unrecognized workforce gains a new self-awareness. FAR EASTERN ECONOMIC REVIEW (HONGKONG) January 5, 1984, 123:26-27.

Azzam, Henry T.. Participation of Arab women in the labour force: development factors and policies. INTERNATIONAL LABOUR OFFICE. WORLD EMPLOYMENT PROGRAMME RESEARCH. POPULATION AND EMPLOYMENT PROJECT. WORKING PAPERS (GENEVA) 1979, No. 80:1-83.

Bonilla de Ramos, Elssy. La madre trabajadora. UNIVERSIDAD DE LOS ANDES. CENTRO DE ESTUDIOS SOBRE DESARROLLO ECONOMICO. DOCUMENTO (BOGOTA) September 1981, No. 66:1-139.

Brouard, Nicolas. Esperance de vie active, reprise d'activite feminine: un modele. REVUE ECONOMIQUE (PARIS) November 1980, 31:1260-87. With English summary.

Castaneda, Tarsicio. Los determinantes de la participacion de la mujer casada en el mercado de trabajo urbano en Colombia. ESTUDIOS DE ECONOMIA (SANTIAGO) Second semester 1981, No. 17:111-34. With English summary.

Chapman, Bruce J. and Harding, J. Ross. Sex differences in earnings: an analysis of Malaysian wage data. HARVARD INSTITUTE FOR INTERNATIONAL DEVELOPMENT, DEVELOPMENT DISCUSSION PAPER (CAMBRIDGE, MASS.) December 1980, No. 112:1-24.

LABOR ECONOMICS

Chaudhury, Rafiqul Huda. Female labour force status and fertility behaviour: some theoretical, methodical and policy issues. PAKISTAN DEVELOPMENT REVIEW (ISLAMABAD) Winter 1979, 18:341-57. An attempt is made to examine the dynamics of the relationship between female labor force status and fertility behavior and also to evaluate the implication of the relationship for reduction of fertility, particularly with reference to the developing countries of the world.

Chira, Susan. Tough ascent for Japanese women. NEW YORK TIMES (NEW YORK) February 24, 1985, Section 3, p. 1-27. Equal employment opportunities for women in Japan remain scarce and male-dominated industries resist women's attempts to change traditional ways.

de Vries, Margaret G.. Women, jobs, and development. FINANCE AND DEVELOPMENT (WASHINGTON) December 1971, 8:4:2-9. Discusses the employment of women in developing countries in the light of recent changes in emphasis on the strategy and objectives of economic development. Also published in French, German, Portuguese, and Spanish.

Due, Jean M. and Summary, Rebecca. Constraints to women and development in Africa. JOURNAL OF MODERN AFRICAN STUDIES (OXFORD) March 1982, 20:155-66.

Florman, Samuel C.. Where are the women engineers? ACROSS THE BOARD (NEW YORK) January 1982, 19:56-61. A male engineer writes: 'The ultimate feminist dream will never be realized as long as women would rather supervise the world than help build it.'

Guyer, Jane I.. Raw, the cooked, and the half-baked: a note on the division of labor by sex. BOSTON UNIVERSITY. AFRICAN STUDIES CENTER. WORKING PAPERS (BOSTON) 1981, No. 48:1-12.

Guyer, Jane I.. Women's work in the food economy of the cocoa belt: a comparison. BOSTON UNIVERSITY. AFRICAN STUDIES CENTER. WORKING PAPERS (BOSTON) 1978, No. 7:1-35.

Heggade, O. D.. Development of women entrepreneurship in India -- problems and prospects. ECONOMIC AFFAIRS (CALCUTTA) January/March 1981, 26:39-50.

LABOR ECONOMICS

Hill, M. Anne. Comparison of economic models and empirical results for female labor force participation in Japan and the United State. YALE UNIVERSITY. ECONOMIC GROWTH CENTER. DISCUSSION PAPER (NEW HAVEN, CONN.) July 1982, No. 415:1-36.

Hill, M. Anne. Female labor force participation in urban Japan; a trichotomous logit model. YALE UNIVERSITY. ECONOMIC GROWTH CENTER. DISCUSSION PAPER (NEW HAVEN, CONN.) September 1980, No. 362:1-42.

Holmstrom, Nancy. "Women's work," the family and capitalism. SCIENCE & SOCIETY (NEW YORK) Summer 1981, 45:186-211.

Horn, Robert V.. Workers and work: an activities approach. LABOUR AND SOCIETY (GENEVA) April/June 1981, 6:111-25. Concludes that the activities approach helps to give a more balanced view of women at work and of the relation between paid and unpaid work of individuals and the household.

Janjic, Marion. Diversifying women's employment: the only road to genuine equality of opportunity. INTERNATIONAL LABOUR REVIEW (GENEVA) March/April 1981, 120:149-63.

Jimenez Butragueno, Maria de los Angeles. Protective legislation and equal opportunity and treatment for women in Spain. INTERNATIONAL LABOUR REVIEW (GENEVA) March/April 1982, 121:185-98.

Leonard, Karen. Women in India; some recent perspectives; research note. PACIFIC AFFAIRS (VANCOUVER, B.C.) Spring 1979, 52:95-107.

Levine, Victor and Moock, Peter R.. Labor force experience and earnings: women with children. ECONOMICS OF EDUCATION REVIEW (OXFORD) 1984, 3, No. 3:183-93. Acknowledging that married women with children are observed to earn less than men, and less also than women without children, the authors examine the impact of hours worked in all past periods on the current wage rate. They find that differences in the intensity of prior work experience account for approximately half of the observed sex-related wage gap.

Miller, Barbara D.. Female labor participation and female seclusion in rural India: a regional view. ECONOMIC DEVELOPMENT AND CULTURAL CHANGE (CHICAGO) July 1982, 30:777-94.

Newland, Kathleen. Women, men, and the division of labor. WORLDWATCH PAPER (WASHINGTON) 1980, No. 37:1-43.

LABOR ECONOMICS

Nishikawa, Shunsaku and Higuchi, Yoshio. Determinants of female labor-force participation. JAPANESE ECONOMIC STUDIES (ARMONK, N.Y.) Winter 1980/1981, 9:62-87.

Novikova, E. E.. Scientific and technical progress and women's work in the USSR. LABOUR AND SOCIETY (GENEVA) January/March 1982, 7:13-22.

Paredes, Ricardo. Diferencias de ingreso entre hombres y mujeres en el Gran Santiago 1969 y 1981. ESTUDIOS DE ECONOMIA (SANTIAGO) First semester 1982, No. 18:97-121. With English summary.

Paukert, Liba. Personal preference, social change or economic necessity? Why women work. LABOUR AND SOCIETY (GENEVA) October/December 1982, 7:311-31.

Recchini de Lattes, Zulma.. Family and female participation in the labor market in Latin America. LATIN AMERICAN RESEARCH REVIEW (ALBUQUERQUE, NM) 1982, 17, No. 1:101-04.

Robert, Annette. Effects of the international division of labour on female workers in the textile and clothing industries. DEVELOPMENT AND CHANGE (THE HAGUE, etc.) January 1983, 14:19-37.

Rothschild, K. W.. Note on female labour supply. KYKLOS (BASLE) 1980, 33, No. 2:246-60.

Sanderson, Warren C.. Nonutilitarian economic model of fertility and female labor force participation. REVUE ECONOMIQUE (PARIS) November 1980, 31:1045-80.

Savane, Marie Angelique. El empleo de la mujer, los cambios sociales y la liberacion femenina; el caso de Africa. COMERCIO EXTERIOR (MEXICO, D.F.) August 1980, 30:861-66. Ponencia presentada en la Mesa II, "Recursos humanos y empleo en los paises en desarrollo," del Sexto Congreso Mundial de Economistas.

Sawant, S. D. and Dewan, Ritu. Rural female labour and economic development. ECONOMIC AND POLITICAL WEEKLY (BOMBAY) June 30, 1979, 14:1091-99. This paper, based on a study of a sample of 150 villages in two talukas of Thane district in Maharashtra, attempts to examine the impact of economic development on rural women, particularly on their employment.

LABOR ECONOMICS

Shinotsuka, Eiko. Women at work; equality and care of the species. FAR EASTERN ECONOMIC REVIEW (HONGKONG) Dec. 3, 1982, 118:87-90.

Sundar, Pushpa. Characteristics of female employment; implications of research and policy. ECONOMIC AND POLITICAL WEEKLY (BOMBAY) May 19, 1981, 16:863-71.

Tilak, Jandhyala B. G.. Inequality by sex in human labour market discrimination and returns to education. MARGIN; QUARTERLY JOURNAL OF THE NATIONAL COUNCIL OF APPLIED ECONOMIC RESEARCH (NEW DELHI) January 1980, 12:57-80. Examines some economic aspects of discrimination against women in India.

Weiss, Yoram and Gronau, Reuben. Expected interruptions in labour force participation and sex-related differences in earnings growth. REVIEW OF ECONOMIC STUDIES (EDINBURGH) October 1981, 48:607-19.

Women and the informal sector. IDS BULLETIN, INSTITUTE OF DEVELOPMENT STUDIES AT THE UNIVERSITY OF SUSSEX (BRIGHTON) July 1981, 12:1-62. CONTENT: Heyzer, Noeleen, Towards a framework of analysis. - Bienefeld, Manfred, The informal sector and women's oppression. - Greenstreet, Miriam, When education is unequal. - Moser, Caroline, Surviving in the suburbios. - Goddard, Victoria, The leather trade in the Bassi of Naples. - Banerjee, Nirmala, The weakest link. - Allen, Sheila, Invisible threads. - Savara, Mira, Organising the Annapurna. - Moser, Caroline, and Kate Young, Women of the working poor.

Working class women and working class families in Bombay; report of a survey. ECONOMIC AND POLITICAL WEEKLY (BOMBAY) July 22, 1978, 13:1168-73.

Woronoff, Jon. Wasting Japan's women workers. ORIENTAL ECONOMIST (TOKYO) November 1980, 48:22-24.

Yashiro, Naohiro. Male-female wage differentials in Japan: a rational explanation. JAPANESE ECONOMIC STUDIES (ARMONK, N.Y.) Winter 1980/1981, 9:28-61.

Labor force experience and earnings: women with children. By: Levine, Victor and Moock, Peter R.. ECONOMICS OF EDUCATION REVIEW (OXFORD) 1984, 3, No. 3:183-93. Acknowledging that married women with children are observed to earn less than men, and less also than women without children, the authors examine the impact of hours worked in all past periods on the current wage rate. They find that differences in the intensity of prior work experience account for approximately half of the observed sex-related wage gap.

Labor force participation and earnings determinants for women in the special conditions of developing countries. By: Behrman, Jere R. and Wolfe, Barbara L.. JOURNAL OF DEVELOPMENT ECONOMICS (AMSTERDAM) May/August 1984, 15:259-88. The authors focus on labor market conditions for women in Nicaragua.

Labor force participation and fertility contraceptive knowledge; attitudes and practice of the women of Barbados. By: George, P. M. and Ebanks, G. E.. In: Women in the family and the economy: an international comparative survey. Edited by George Kurian and Ratna Ghosh. (Westport, CT, Greenwood Press, 1981), pp. 285-96.

Labor of love -- love as labor on the Genesis of housework in the West. By: Bock, Gisela and Duden, Barbara. DEVELOPMENT (ROME) 1984, No. 4:6-14.

LABOR SUPPLY

Greenstreet, Miranda. Females in the agricultural labour force and non-formal education for rural development in Ghana. INSTITUTE OF SOCIAL STUDIES. OCCASIONAL PAPERS (THE HAGUE) August 1981, No. 90:1-22.

Herrin, Alejandro N.. Female work participation and fertility in a Philippine setting: a test of alternative models. UNIVERSITY OF THE PHILIPPINES. SCHOOL OF ECONOMICS. DISCUSSION PAPER (QUEZON) October 1980, No. 8005:1-99.

Joseph, Suad. Mobilization of Iraqi women into the wage labor force. STUDIES IN THIRD WORLD SOCIETIES (WILLIAMSBURG) June 1981, No. 16:69-90.

Khodja, Souad. Women's work as viewed in present-day Algerian society. INTERNATIONAL LABOUR REVIEW (GENEVA) July/August 1982, 121:481-87.

Kuniansky, Anna. Soviet fertility, labor-force participation, and marital instabililty. JOURNAL OF COMPARATIVE ECONOMICS (NEW YORK) June 1983, 7:114-30.

LABOR SUPPLY

Macarthy, Peter. Notes on inequalities in male-female shares in the labour market, occupations, wages, overtime, and hours of work - Mexico, 1940-1980. PAISLEY COLLEGE OF TECHNOLOGY. DEPT. OF ECONOMICS AND MANAGEMENT. SOCIAL SCIENCE WORKING PAPER (PAISLEY) June 1984, No. 61:1-38.

Mies, Maria. Social origins of the sexual division of labour. INSTITUTE OF SOCIAL STUDIES. OCCASIONAL PAPERS (THE HAGUE) January 1981, No. 85:1-49.

Labor supply and marital separation. By: Johnson, William R. and Skinner, Jonathan. AMERICAN ECONOMIC REVIEW (NASHVILLE) June 1986, 76:455-69. A simultaneous model of future divorce probability and current labor supply is estimated for married women. The results support the hypothesis that divorce probabilities increase labor supply.

LABOR UNIONS

Biryukova, Alexandra. Role of the Soviet woman in decision-making in trade union committees and in industry. LABOUR AND SOCIETY (GENEVA) September 1985, 10:307-21.

Hafner, Annemarie. Working women, their problems and trade unions in India. JOURNAL OF SOCIAL STUDIES (DHAKA) October 1985, No. 30:57-76.

Metzner, Ulrike and Stahn-Willig, Brigitte. Frauenarbeit: ein Beitrag zur gewerkschaftlichen Technikdebatte. WSI-MITTEILUNGEN (DUSSELDORF) August 1986, 39:529-36.

Labor-saving techniques in food processing: rural women and technological change in the Gambia. By: Nath, Kamla. BOSTON UNIVERSITY. AFRICAN STUDIES CENTER. WORKING PAPERS (BOSTON) 1985, No. 108:1-26. Describes the methodology used in developing a project design for the introduction of sorghum and millet decorticators and flour milling units in rural areas of the Gambia in West Africa.

LADERMAN, CAROL

Laderman, Carol. Politics of healing in Malaysia. STUDIES IN THIRD WORLD SOCIETIES (WILLIAMSBURG) June 1981, No. 16:143-58. Discusses varying governmental attitudes towards midwives (bidan), who, with few exceptions, are women, and to native doctors (bomoh), who may be either male or female.

LADUKE, BETTY

LaDuke, Betty. Women, art, and culture in the new Grenada. LATIN AMERICAN PERSPECTIVES (BEVERLY HILLS) Summer 1984, 11:37-52.

LAMYA' AL-FARUQI, LOIS

Lamya' al-Faruqi, Lois. Women in a Qur'anic society. AL-TAWHID; A QUARTERLY JOURNAL OF ISLAMIC THOUGHT AND CULTURE (TEHRAN) July 1984, 1, No. 4:36-49.

Land, labour, and the sex composition of the agricultural labour force: an international comparison. By: Dixon, Ruth. DEVELOPMENT AND CHANGE (THE HAGUE, etc.) July 1983, 14:347-72.

LAND REFORM

Deere, Carmen Diana. Developpement cooperatif et participation feminine a la reforme agraire nicaraguayenne. TIERS-MONDE (PARIS) April/June 1985, 26:403-08.

Deere, Carmen Diana. Rural women and state policy: the Latin American agrarian reform experience. WORLD DEVELOPMENT (OXFORD) September 1985, 13:1037-53.

LARGUIA, ISABEL

Larguia, Isabel. Economic basis of the status of women. In: Women cross-culturally: change and challenge. Edited by Ruby Rohrlich-Leavitt. (The Hague, Mouton, 1975), pp. 281-95.

Last transition? Women and development in Mozambique. By: Urdang, Stephanie. REVIEW OF AFRICAN POLITICAL ECONOMY (SHEFFIELD) 1984, No. 27/28:8-32.

LATIN AMERICA

Aguiar, Neuma. La mujer en la fuerza de trabajo en la America Latina: un resumen introductorio. DESARROLLO Y SOCIEDAD (BOGOTA) January 1984, No. 13:57-79. With English summary.

Arizpe, Lourdes. Les femmes paysannes et la crise agraire en Amerique latine. TIERS-MONDE (PARIS) April/June 1985, 26:325-34.

Arizpe, Lourdes. Women and development in Latin America and the Caribbean; lessons from the seventies and hopes for the future. DEVELOPMENT DIGEST (WASHINGTON) 1982, Vol. 1/2:74-84.

Bonder, Gloria. Study of politics from the standpoint of women. INTERNATIONAL SOCIAL SCIENCE JOURNAL (PARIS) 1983, 35, No. 4:569-83.

LATIN AMERICA

Buvinic, Mayra and Leslie, Joanne. Health care for women in Latin America and the Caribbean. STUDIES IN FAMILY PLANNING (NEW YORK) March 1981, 12:112-15.

Deere, Carmen Diana. Rural women and state policy: the Latin American agrarian reform experience. WORLD DEVELOPMENT (OXFORD) September 1985, 13:1037-53.

Draper, Elaine. Women's work and development in Latin America. STUDIES IN COMPARATIVE INTERNATIONAL DEVELOPMENT (NEW BRUNSWICK, N.J.) Spring 1985, 20:3-30.

Flora, Cornelia Butler. Social policy and women in Latin America: the need for a new model. STUDIES IN THIRD WORLD SOCIETIES (WILLIAMSBURG) March 1981, No. 15:91-105.

Recchini de Lattes, Zulma.. Family and female participation in the labor market in Latin America. LATIN AMERICAN RESEARCH REVIEW (ALBUQUERQUE, NM) 1982, 17, No. 1:101-04.

Schmidt, Steffen W.. Research on women in Latin America: problems of networking and comparative analysis in the last decade. STUDIES IN THIRD WORLD SOCIETIES (WILLIAMSBURG) March 1981, No. 15:107-33.

Schmidt, Steffen W.. Women, politics and development; a review essay. LATIN AMERICAN RESEARCH REVIEW (ALBUQUERQUE, NM) 1983, 18, No. 1:210-27.

Siqueira Wiarda, Ieda and Helzner, Judith Frye. Women, population, and international development in Latin America: a 1984 assessment. MANAGING INTERNATIONAL DEVELOPMENT (ARMONK, N.Y.) September/October 1984, 1:84-106.

Taylor, Frank. Women grab management power in home of machismo. INTERNATIONAL MANAGEMENT (MAIDENHEAD) February 1984, 39:24-27. Describes how Latin American women are starting to make inroads into business.

Wiarda, Ieda Siqueira and Helzner, Judith F.. Women, population and international development in Latin America: persistent legacies and new perceptions for the 1980's. UNIVERSITY OF MASSACHUSETTS AT AMHERST. PROGRAM IN LATIN AMERICAN STUDIES. OCCASIONAL PAPERS SERIES (AMHERST) April 1981, No. 13:1-40.

LATIN AMERICA

Wilson, Fiona. Women and agricultural change in Latin America: some concepts guiding research. WORLD DEVELOPMENT (OXFORD) September 1985, 13:1017-35.

Women and politics in twentieth century Latin America. STUDIES IN THIRD WORLD SOCIETIES (WILLIAMSBURG) March 1981, no. 15:1-136.

Yudelman, Sally W. After Nairobi: A retrospective of women's development organizations in Latin America. GRASSROOTS DEVELOPMENT (ROSSLYN, VA.) 1986, 10, No. 1:20-29.

Latin American woman: the meek speak out. Edited by June H. Turner. (Silver Spring, MD, International Educational Development, 1980), 174 pp.

LATU, SELA N.

Halatuituia, Lasale and Latu, Sela N.. Women's co-operatives in Tonga. PACIFIC PERSPECTIVE (SUVA) 1983, 11, No. 2:13-17.

LAUBJERG, KRISTIAN

Laubjerg, Kristian. Training village women as health promoters in Tanzania. WATERLINES (LONDON) January 1986, 4:29-31.

LAUFER, LESLIE A.

Laufer, Leslie A.. Substitution between male and female labor in rural Indian agricultural production. YALE UNIVERSITY. ECONOMIC GROWTH CENTER. DISCUSSION PAPER (NEW HAVEN, CONN.) April 1985, No 472:1-24.

LAYOFFS

Maxwell, Nan L. and D'Amico, Ronald J. Employment and wage effects of involuntary job separation: male-female differences. AMERICAN ECONOMIC REVIEW, PAPERS AND PROCEEDINGS (NASHVILLE) May 1986, 76:373-77.

LEACOCK, ELEANOR

Leacock, Eleanor. Class, commodity, and the status of women. In: Women cross-culturally: change and challenge. Edited by Ruby Rohrlich-Leavitt. (The Hague, Mouton, 1975), pp. 601-16.

LEAN, LIM LIN

Lean, Lim Lin. Towards meeting the needs of urban female factory workers in peninsular Malaysia. In: Women in the urban and industrial workforce; Southeast and East Asia. Edited by Gavin W. Jones. Series: Development Studies Centre. Monograph, No. 33. (Canberra, Australia, Australian National University, 1984), pp. 129-48. Series edited by Helen Hughes.

Learning and unlearning. By: Helmore, Kristin. CHRISTIAN SCIENCE MONITOR (BOSTON) December 20, 1985, p. 15-17. Part four of 5-part series entitled: "The neglected resource; women in the developing world." Discusses education of women in the less developed countries, particularly the contrast between opportunities for education for men and for women.

Learning from rural women: village-level success cases of rural women's group income-raising activities. (Bangkok, ESCAP/FAO Inter-Country Project for the Promotion and Training of Rural Women in Income-raising Group Activities, [1979]), 120 pp.

LEBANON

Azzam, Henry T. and Shaib, Diana. Women left behind: a study of the wives of Lebanese migrant workers in the oil rich countries of the region. INTERNATIONAL LABOUR OFFICE. WORLD EMPLOYMENT PROGRAMME RESEARCH. POPULATION AND LABOUR POLICIES: REGIONAL PROGRAMME FOR THE MIDDLE EAST. WORKING PAPER (BEIRUT) September 1980, No. 3:1-56.

Lorfing, I. and Khalaf, M.. Economic contribution of women and its effect on the dynamics of the family in two Lebanese villages. INTERNATIONAL LABOUR OFFICE. WORLD EMPLOYMENT PROGRAMME RESEARCH. POPULATION AND LABOUR POLICIES PROGRAMME. WORKING PAPER (GENEVA) May 1985, No. 148:1-32.

LEE, BUN SONG

Lee, Bun Song and McElwain, Adrienne M. Empirical investigation of female labor-force participation, fertility, age at marriage, and wages in Korea. JOURNAL OF DEVELOPING AREAS (MACOMB, ILL.) July 1985, 19:483-500.

Legal and social positions of Iranian women. By: Pakizegi, Behnaz. In: Women in the Muslim world. Edited by Lois Beck and Nikki Keddie. (Cambridge, MA, Harvard University Press, 1978), pp. 216-26.

Legal reform as an indicator of women's status in Muslim nations. By: White, Elizabeth H.. In: Women in the Muslim world. Edited by Lois Beck and Nikki Keddie. (Cambridge, MA, Harvard University Press, 1978), pp. 52-68.

Legislation: an aid in eliminating sex bias in education in the United States. By: Heath, Kathryn G.. In: Women cross-culturally: change and challenge. Edited by Ruby Rohrlich-Leavitt. (The Hague, Mouton, 1975), pp. 327-60.

LEIBOWITZ, LILA

Leibowitz, Lila. Perspectives on the evolution of sex differences. In: Toward an anthropology of women. Edited by Rayna R. Reiter. (New York, Monthly Review Press, 1975), pp. 20-35.

LELE, UMA

Lele, Uma. Women and structural transformation. ECONOMIC DEVELOPMENT AND CULTURAL CHANGE (CHICAGO) January 1986, 34:195-221. The primary objective of this article is to explore women's distinguishing role as economic actors in traditional societies under quite different social and production-organization systems.

LEONARD, KAREN

Leonard, Karen. Women in India; some recent perspectives; research note. PACIFIC AFFAIRS (VANCOUVER, B.C.) Spring 1979, 52:95-107.

LEPPEL, KAREN

Leppel, Karen. Relations among child quality, family structure, and the value of the mother's time in Malaysia. MALAYAN ECONOMIC REVIEW (SINGAPORE) October 1982, 27:61-70.

LESCH, ANN MOSELY

Lesch, Ann Mosely and Sullivan, Earl L. Women in Egypt; new roles and realities. UNIVERSITIES FIELD STAFF INTERNATIONAL REPORTS, AFRICA (HANOVER, NH) 1986, No. 22:1-9.

LESLIE, JOANNE

Buvinic, Mayra and Leslie, Joanne. Health care for women in Latin America and the Caribbean. STUDIES IN FAMILY PLANNING (NEW YORK) March 1981, 12:112-15.

Less than second-class: women in rural settlement schemes in Tanzania. By: Brain, James L.. In: Women in Africa: studies in social and economic change. Edited by Nancy J. Hafkin and Edna G. Bay. (Stanford, Stanford University Press, 1976), pp. 265-82.

LEVINE, ROBERT A.

LeVine, Robert A.. Influences of women's schooling on maternal behavior in the Third World. COMPARATIVE EDUCATION REVIEW (NEW YORK) June 1980, 24:S78-105.

LEVINE, VICTOR AND MOOCK, PETER R.

Levine, Victor and Moock, Peter R.. Labor force experience and earnings: women with children. ECONOMICS OF EDUCATION REVIEW (OXFORD) 1984, 3, No. 3:183-93. Acknowledging that married women with children are observed to earn less than men, and less also than women without children, the authors examine the impact of hours worked in all past periods on the current wage rate. They find that differences in the intensity of prior work experience account for approximately half of the observed sex-related wage gap.

LEVY, BANYEN PHIMMASONE

Levy, Banyen Phimmasone. Yesterday and today in Laos: a girl's autobiographical notes. In: Women in the new Asia; the changing social roles of men and women in South and South-east Asia. Edited by Barbara E. Ward. ([Paris], Unesco, 1963), pp. 244-65.

LEWIS, BARBARA

Lewis, Barbara. Fertility and employment: an assessment of role incompatibility among African urban women. In: Women and work in Africa. Edited by Edna G. Bay. (Boulder, CO, Westview Press, 1982), pp. 249-76.

LEWIS, BARBARA C.

Lewis, Barbara C.. Limitations of group action among entrepreneurs: the market women of Abidjan, Ivory Coast. In: Women in Africa: studies in social and economic change. Edited by Nancy J. Hafkin and Edna G. Bay. (Stanford, Stanford University Press, 1976), pp. 135-56.

LEWIS, DONALD E

Lewis, Donald E. Sources of changes in the occupational segregation of Australian women. ECONOMIC RECORD (MELBOURNE) December 1985, 61:719-36.

LEWIS, DONALD E.

Lewis, Donald E.. Measurement of the occupational and industrial segregation of women. JOURNAL OF INDUSTRIAL RELATIONS (SYDNEY) September 1982, 24:406-23.

LEWIS, MARTHA

Lewis, Martha. Developing income generating opportunity for rural women. HORIZONS, U.S. AGENCY FOR INTERNATIONAL DEVELOPMENT (WASHINGTON) January 1983, 2:28-31. Describes how bananas, solar-dried and marketed as banana-figs, promise to boost Jamaican farm women's earnings.

LEWIS, SHELBY

Lewis, Shelby. African women and national development. In: Comparative perspectives of Third World women: the impact of race, sex and class. Edited by Beverly Lindsay. (New York, Praeger, 1980), pp. 31-54.

LI, K. T

Li, K. T. Contributions of women in the labor force to economic development in Taiwan, the Republic of China. INDUSTRY OF FREE CHINA (TAIPEI) August 25, 1985, 64:1-8.

LI, YUAN

Li, Yuan. Tibet through our eyes (2); education: opening the door to women. WOMEN OF CHINA (BEIJING) August 1985, No. 8:6-7.

Liberated -- but tied to the old loyalties. By: Ocampo-Kalfors, Sheilah. FAR EASTERN ECONOMIC REVIEW (HONGKONG) January 5, 1984, 123:32-34. Describes how women in the Philippines have progressed rapidly in most fields, despite existing laws and traditions that discriminate against them.

Liberation de la femme et marche matrimonial en Tunisie. By: Beaujot, Roderic. POPULATION (PARIS) July/October 1986, 41:853-59.

LIBYA

Kitchener, Julie. Inside Libya today. NEW AFRICAN (LONDON) October 1983, No. 193:10-14. Examines the strange paradoxes that give Libya its distinctive character, including the emancipation of Libyan women.

Life and labor of the woman textile worker in Mexico City. By: Piho, Virve. In: Women cross-culturally: change and challenge. Edited by Ruby Rohrlich-Leavitt. (The Hague, Mouton, 1975), pp. 199-245.

Life crises as a clue to social function: the case of Italy. By: Silverman, Sydel F.. In: Toward an anthropology of women. Edited by Rayna R. Reiter. (New York, Monthly Review Press, 1975), pp. 309-21.

Life of Ceylon women. By: Siriwardena, B. S.. In: Women in the new Asia; the changing social roles of men and women in South and South-east Asia. Edited by Barbara E. Ward. ([Paris], Unesco, 1963), pp. 150-72.

LIM, LINDA

Lim, Linda. New order with some old prejudices. FAR EASTERN ECONOMIC REVIEW (HONGKONG) January 5, 1984, 123:37-38. The position of Singapore's women throughout its brief history has been defined by traditional outlines, male dominance and female subordination.

Limitations of group action among entrepreneurs: the market women of Abidjan, Ivory Coast. By: Lewis, Barbara C.. In: Women in Africa: studies in social and economic change. Edited by Nancy J. Hafkin and Edna G. Bay. (Stanford, Stanford University Press, 1976), pp. 135-56.

LINDSAY, BEVERLY

Lindsay, Beverly. Examination of education, social change, and national development policy: the case of Kenyan women. STUDIES IN THIRD WORLD SOCIETIES (WILLIAMSBURG) June 1981, No. 16:29-48.

Lindsay, Beverly. Issues confronting professional African women: illustrations from Kenya. In: Comparative perspectives of Third World women: the impact of race, sex and class. Edited by Beverly Lindsay. (New York, Praeger, 1980), pp. 78-95.

Lindsay, Beverly. Perspectives of Third World women: an introduction. In: Comparative perspectives of Third World women: the impact of race, sex and class. Edited by Beverly Lindsay. (New York, Praeger, 1980), pp. 1-30.

Lindsay, Beverly. Third World women and social reality: a conclusion. In: Comparative perspectives of Third World women: the impact of race, sex and class. Edited by Beverly Lindsay. (New York, Praeger, 1980), pp. 297-310.

LINNHOFF, URSULA

Linnhoff, Ursula. Das Dilemma internationaler Frauenforderungspolitik. E & Z, ENTWICKLUNG UND ZUSAMMENARBEIT (BONN) January 1985, 26:18-19.

Liste de questions sur le role des femmes dans les projets de developpement agricole. By: Bergmann, Hellmuth and Schul, Jean-Jacques. TIERS-MONDE (PARIS) October/December 1980, 21:833-44.

LITTLE, KENNETH

Little, Kenneth. Women in African towns south of the Sahara: the urbanization dilemma. In: Women and world development. Edited by Irene Tinker and Michele Bo Bramsen. ([Washington, DC], Overseas Development Council, 1976), pp. 78-87.

LIU, PAUL K. C.

Liu, Paul K. C.. Trends in female labour force participation in Taiwan: the transition toward higher technology activities. In: Women in the urban and industrial workforce; Southeast and East Asia. Edited by Gavin W. Jones. Series: Development Studies Centre. Monograph, No. 33. (Canberra, Australia, Australian National University, 1984), pp. 75-100. Series edited by Helen Hughes.

Lives, Chinese working women. Edited by Mary Sheridan and Janet W. Salaff. (Bloomington, Indiana University Press, 1984), 258 pp. Published in association with University of Toronto/York University Joint Centre on Modern East Asia.

LIVESTOCK

Okali, C. and Cassaday, K.. Community response to a pilot farming project in Nigeria. BOSTON UNIVERSITY. AFRICAN-AMERICAN ISSUES CENTER. DISCUSSION PAPER (BOSTON) [1985], No. 10:1-28. The authors report on a preliminary study of farmers' response to alley farming, a technology designed to improve small ruminant (sheep and goat) and arable crop production in the humid zone of West Africa.

Spring, Anita. Men and women smallholder participants in a stall-feeder livestock program in Malawi. HUMAN ORGANIZATION (WASHINGTON) Summer 1986, 45:154-62.

LORFING, I.

Lorfing, I. and Khalaf, M.. Economic contribution of women and its effect on the dynamics of the family in two Lebanese villages. INTERNATIONAL LABOUR OFFICE. WORLD EMPLOYMENT PROGRAMME RESEARCH. POPULATION AND LABOUR POLICIES PROGRAMME. WORKING PAPER (GENEVA) May 1985, No. 148:1-32.

Losing the land. By: Hahn, Natalie D.. DEVELOPMENT (ROME) 1984, No. 4:26-29.

LOUFTI, MARTHA

Ahmad, Zubeida and Loufti, Martha. Decently paid employment -- not more drudgery. CERES, FAO REVIEW ON AGRICULTURE AND DEVELOPMENT (ROME) July/August 1983, 16:40-46. The authors conclude that there is an urgent need for improved living and working conditions for many poor rural women.

LOUTFI, MARTHA F.

Ahmad, Zubeida M. and Loutfi, Martha F.. International labour office programme on rural women. (Geneva, International Labour Office, 1981), 28 pp.

Loutfi, Martha F.. Rural women: unequal partners in development. Series: A WEP study. (Geneva, International Labor Office, 1980), 81 pp.

Love unites them and hunger separates them: poor women in the Dominican Republic. By: Brown, Susan E.. In: Toward an anthropology of women. Edited by Rayna R. Reiter. (New York, Monthly Review Press, 1975), pp. 322-31.

Lower economic sector female mating patterns in the Dominican Republic: a comparative analysis. By: Brown, Susan E.. In: Women cross-culturally: change and challenge. Edited by Ruby Rohrlich-Leavitt. (The Hague, Mouton, 1975), pp. 149-62.

LU, YU-HSIA

Lu, Yu-Hsia. Women, work and the family in a developing society: Taiwan. In: Women in the urban and industrial workforce; Southeast and East Asia. Edited by Gavin W. Jones. Series: Development Studies Centre. Monograph, No. 33. (Canberra, Australia, Australian National University, 1984), pp. 339-68. Series edited by Helen Hughes.

LUBIN, NANCY

Lubin, Nancy. Women in Soviet Central Asia: progress and contradictions. SOVIET STUDIES (GLASGOW) April 1981, 33:182-203.

Luchas colectivas de las obreras peruanas: los motivos de participacion y alejamiento. By: Wehkamp, Andy. BOLETIN DE ESTUDIOS LATINO-AMERICANOS Y DEL CARIBE (AMSTERDAM) December 1984, No. 37:69-83.

LULAT, YOUNUS

Kelly, Gail P. and Lulat, Younus. Women and schooling in the Third World: a bibliography. COMPARATIVE EDUCATION REVIEW (NEW YORK) June 1980, 24:S224-63.

Luo women and economic change during the colonial period. By: Hay, Margaret Jean. In: Women in Africa: studies in social and economic change. Edited by Nancy J. Hafkin and Edna G. Bay. (Stanford, Stanford University Press, 1976), pp. 87-109.

LUZURIAGA NAJERA, LUZ VICENTA

Luzuriaga Najera, Luz Vicenta. Only you men have your needs satisfied. In: Latin American women: the meek speak out. Edited by June H. Turner. (Silver Spring, MD, International Educational Development, 1980), pp. 76-83. Discusses women of Ecuador.

LYCETTE, MARGARET

Buvinic, Mayra and Lycette, Margaret. Eye-opening survey unlocks doors for low-income women. HORIZONS, U.S. AGENCY FOR INTERNATIONAL DEVELOPMENT (WASHINGTON) Summer 1985, 4:31-33. The authors describe how the International Center for Research on Women (ICRW), with a $120,000 grant from AID, is helping to put home ownership within reach of low-income women, through its experiences with the Solanda low-income housing project in Quito, Ecuador.

LYCETTE, MARGARET A.

Lycette, Margaret A.. Improving women's access to credit in the Third World: policy and project recommendations. Series: ICRW occasional paper, No. 1. (Washington, DC, International Center for Research on Women, 1984), 23 pp.

LYNCH, PATRICIA D.

Lynch, Patricia D. and Fahmy, Hoda. Craftswomen in Kerdassa, Egypt. Household production and reproduction. Series: Women, work and development, No. 7. (Geneva, International Labour Office, 1984), 91 pp. Undertaken under the auspices of the Center for Egyptian Civilisation Studies and with the financial support of the United Nations Fund for Population Activities (UNFPA).

MACARTHY, PETER

Macarthy, Peter. Notes on inequalities in male-female shares in the labour market, occupations, wages, overtime, and hours of work - Mexico, 1940-1980. PAISLEY COLLEGE OF TECHNOLOGY. DEPT. OF ECONOMICS AND MANAGEMENT. SOCIAL SCIENCE WORKING PAPER (PAISLEY) June 1984, No. 61:1-38.

MACCORMACK, CAROL P.

MacCormack, Carol P.. Control of land, labor, and capital in rural southern Sierra Leone. In: Women and work in Africa. Edited by Edna G. Bay. (Boulder, CO, Westview Press, 1982), pp. 35-53.

MACK, BEVERLY B.

Mack, Beverly B.. Technical assistants gain experience, improve projects. HORIZONS, U.S. AGENCY FOR INTERNATIONAL DEVELOPMENT (WASHINGTON) Summer 1985, 4:12-14. Examines the International Technical Assistance Fellowship Program funded by AID through the Center for Women in Development (SECID).

La madre trabajadora. By: Bonilla de Ramos, Elssy. UNIVERSIDAD DE LOS ANDES. CENTRO DE ESTUDIOS SOBRE DESARROLLO ECONOMICO. DOCUMENTO (BOGOTA) September 1981, No. 66:1-139.

La madre trabajadora: una contradiccion. By: Bonilla de Ramos, Elssy. DESARROLLO Y SOCIEDAD (BOGOTA) September 1982, No. 9:67-84.

MAHER, MARY

Maher, Mary. Women at the top. DEVELOPMENT FORUM BUSINESS EDITION (NEW YORK) August 18, 1980, No. 60:p. 6.

MAHER, VANESSA

Maher, Vanessa. Women and social change in Morocco. In: Women in the Muslim world. Edited by Lois Beck and Nikki Keddie. (Cambridge, MA, Harvard University Press, 1978), pp. 100-23.

Maher, Vanessa. Women and property in Morocco; their changing relation to the process of social stratification in the middle Atlas. Series: Cambridge Studies in Social Anthropology, No. 10. (London, New York, Cambridge University Press, 1974), 238 pp.

Major theories of the labour market and women's place within it. By: O'Donnell, Carol. JOURNAL OF INDUSTRIAL RELATIONS (SYDNEY) June 1984, 26:147-65. Looks at theories of the labour market with reference to the situation of women workers who tend to be concentrated in particular industries and particular occupations, and whose average wage is lower than that of males.

Make money not babies; changing status markers of northern Thai women. By: Muecke, Marjorie A.. ASIAN SURVEY (BERKELEY, CALIF.) April 1984, 24:459-70.

Making our own way: women working in Lourenco Marques, 1900-1933. By: Penvenne, Jeanne. BOSTON UNIVERSITY. AFRICAN STUDIES CENTER. WORKING PAPERS (BOSTON) 1986, No. 114:1-20.

Making the bread and bringing it home: female factory workers and the family economy in rural Java. By: Wolf, Diane L.. In: Women in the urban and industrial workforce; Southeast and East Asia. Edited by Gavin W. Jones. Series: Development Studies Centre. Monograph, No. 33. (Canberra, Australia, Australian National University, 1984), pp. 215-35. Series edited by Helen Hughes.

MALAWI

Spring, Anita. Men and women smallholder participants in a stall-feeder livestock program in Malawi. HUMAN ORGANIZATION (WASHINGTON) Summer 1986, 45:154-62.

MALAYSIA

Abdullah, Lashidah. Subordination right across the board. FAR EASTERN ECONOMIC REVIEW (HONGKONG) January 5, 1984, 123:31-32. Discusses the status of women in Malaysia.

Abdullah, Noraini. Equality of Malay women -- real but restricted. FAR EASTERN ECONOMIC REVIEW (HONGKONG) April 10, 1986, 132:38-39.

Chapman, Bruce J. and Harding, J. Ross. Sex differences in earnings: an analysis of Malaysian wage data. HARVARD INSTITUTE FOR INTERNATIONAL DEVELOPMENT, DEVELOPMENT DISCUSSION PAPER (CAMBRIDGE, MASS.) December 1980, No. 112:1-24.

Chapman, Bruce J. and Harding, J. Ross. Sex differences in earnings: an analysis of Malaysian wage data. JOURNAL OF DEVELOPMENT STUDIES (LONDON) April 1985, 21:362-76.

MALAYSIA

Halim, Fatimah. Workers' resistance and management control: a comparative case study of male and female workers in West Malaysia. JOURNAL OF CONTEMPORARY ASIA (LONDON) 1983, 13, No. 2:131-50.

Hing, Ai Yun. Women and work in West Malaysia. JOURNAL OF CONTEMPORARY ASIA (LONDON) 1984, 14, No. 2:204-18.

Laderman, Carol. Politics of healing in Malaysia. STUDIES IN THIRD WORLD SOCIETIES (WILLIAMSBURG) June 1981, No. 16:143-58. Discusses varying governmental attitudes towards midwives (bidan), who, with few exceptions, are women, and to native doctors (bomoh), who may be either male or female.

Leppel, Karen. Relations among child quality, family structure, and the value of the mother's time in Malaysia. MALAYAN ECONOMIC REVIEW (SINGAPORE) October 1982, 27:61-70.

Massard, Josiane. La femme malaise, productrice et gestionnaire. TIERS-MONDE (PARIS) April/June 1985, 26:359-70.

Rogers, Marvin L. Changing patterns of political involvement among Malay village women. ASIAN SURVEY (BERKELEY, CALIF.) March 1986, 26:322-44.

Wang, Bee-Lan Chan. Sex and ethnic differences in educational investment in Malaysia: the effect of reward structures. COMPARATIVE EDUCATION REVIEW (NEW YORK) June 1980, 24:S140-59.

Male-female pay differentials in Greece. By: Kanellopoulos, Costas N.. GREEK ECONOMIC REVIEW (ATHENS) August 1982, 4:222-41.

Male-female wage differentials in Japan: a rational explanation. By: Yashiro, Naohiro. JAPANESE ECONOMIC STUDIES (ARMONK, N.Y.) Winter 1980/1981, 9:28-61.

MALI

Caughman, Susan. Women at work in Mali: the case of the Markala cooperative. BOSTON UNIVERSITY. AFRICAN STUDIES CENTER. WORKING PAPERS (BOSTON) 1981, No. 50:1-35.

MANAGEMENT

Rowe, Alan J. and Bennis, Warren. Desexing decision styles. PERSONNEL (SARANAC LAKE, N.Y.) January/February 1984, 61:43-52. The authors attempt to determine why women are thought of as being different from men in terms of their ability to perform effectively in management positions.

Marginal lives: conflict and contradiction in the position of female traders in Lusaka, Zambia. By: Schuster, Ilsa. In: Women and work in Africa. Edited by Edna G. Bay. (Boulder, CO, Westview Press, 1982), pp. 105-26.

Marital status and sexual identity; the position of women in a Mexican peasant society. By: Slade, Doren L.. In: Women cross-culturally: change and challenge. Edited by Ruby Rohrlich-Leavitt. (The Hague, Mouton, 1975), pp. 129-48.

MARKET GARDENING

Koumbidia (Senegal); developpement d'une activite maraichere villageoise. TIERS-MONDE (PARIS) April/June 1985, 26:421-28.

MARKETS

Hadorn, Verena. Une place au marche de Sopocachi; travail de femmes en Bolivie. ENTWICKLUNG, DEVELOPPEMENT (BERNE) 1985, No. 19:14-16.

MARKS, JON

Marks, Jon. Algeria thinks of itself as a radical society; women declare war on the power of the patriach. GUARDIAN (LONDON) August 10, 1984, p. 15.

MARONEY, HEATHER JON

Maroney, Heather Jon. Feminism at work. NEW LEFT REVIEW (LONDON) September/October 1983, No. 141:51-71.

MAROTHIA, D. K. AND SHARMA, S. K

Marothia, D. K. and Sharma, S. K. Female labour participation in rice farming system of Chhattisgarh region. INDIAN JOURNAL OF AGRICULTURAL ECONOMICS (BOMBAY) July/September 1985, 40:235-39.

MARRIAGE

Acock, Alan C. and Deseran, Forrest A. Off-farm employment by women and marital instability. RURAL SOCIOLOGY (PROVO, UTAH) Fall 1986, 51:314-27. The impact of farm women's paid work experience on the quality and stability of their marriages is examined in the context of two competing frameworks - status competition and status enhancement.

Beaujot, Roderic. Liberation de la femme et marche matrimonial en Tunisie. POPULATION (PARIS) July/October 1986, 41:853-59.

Courtship, love, and marriage in contemporary China; a symposium. PACIFIC AFFAIRS (VANCOUVER, B.C.) Summer 1984, 57:209-69. CONTENT: Young, Marilyn B., Introduction. - Wolf, Margery, Marriage, family, and the state in contemporary China. - Hershatter, Gail, Making a friend: changing patterns of courtship in urban China. - Honig, Emily, Private issues, public discourse: the life and times of Yu Luojin. - The marriage law of the People's Republic of China.

Helmore, Kristin. Family ties: wives and mothers. CHRISTIAN SCIENCE MONITOR (BOSTON) December 18, 1985, p. 17-19. Part 2 of 5-part series entitled: "The neglected resource; women in the developing world." Author looks at marriage and motherhood in various cultures in the less developed countries.

Marriage and family; single women and men in China. By: Jianhai, Cao. WOMEN OF CHINA (BEIJING) November 1984, No. 11:14-15.

MARRIAGE LAW

Geary, Christraud M. On legal change in Cameroon: women, marriage, and bridewealth. BOSTON UNIVERSITY. AFRICAN STUDIES CENTER. WORKING PAPERS (BOSTON) 1986, No. 113:1-37.

MARSHALL, SUSAN E.

Marshall, Susan E.. Politics and female status in North Africa: a reconsideration of development theory. ECONOMIC DEVELOPMENT AND CULTURAL CHANGE (CHICAGO) April 1984, 32:499-524. Assesses the applicability of two major theoretical perspectives for explaining national differences in female status among the five North African Muslim states of Morocco, Algeria, Tunisia, Libya, and Egypt, utilizing a composite female modernity index derived from secondary sources. The author also proposes an alternative theoretical framework to explain these divergent national patterns of female participation, highlights the central role of political elites in the late-developing states and suggests an empirical relationship between government policy toward women and female access to the modern sector in North Africa.

Marshall, Susan E. and Stokes, Randall G.. Tradition and the veil: female status in Tunisia and Algeria. JOURNAL OF MODERN AFRICAN STUDIES (OXFORD) December 1981, 19:625-46.

MARTIUS VON HARDER, GUDRUN

Martius von Harder, Gudrun. Le role des services nationaux d'animation rurale et de vulgarisation agricole aupres des femmes. TIERS-MONDE (PARIS) April/June 1985, 26:317-24.

MASCARENHAS, OPHELIA

Mascarenhas, Ophelia. Confronting the male bias in research priorities. CERES, FAO REVIEW ON AGRICULTURE AND DEVELOPMENT (ROME) May/June 1985, 18:28-32. Suggests that agricultural research in most formerly colonial countries has two characteristics: the overemphasis of cash crops and the tendency to ignore women in the planning, development, and implementation of such research.

Mascarenhas, Ophelia and Mbilinyi, Marjorie J.. Women in Tanzania: an analytical bibliography. (Uppsala, Scandinavian Institute of African Studies; Stockholm, Swedish International Development Authority, 1983), 256 pp.

MASKIELL, MICHELLE

Maskiell, Michelle. Social change and social control: college-educated Punjabi women 1913 to 1960. MODERN ASIAN STUDIES (LONDON) February 1985, 19:55-83.

MASON, C.A.

Eyland, E.A. and Mason, C.A.. Determinants of female employment. ECONOMIC RECORD (MELBOURNE) March 1982, 58:11-17.

MASSARD, JOSIANE

Massard, Josiane. La femme malaise, productrice et gestionnaire. TIERS-MONDE (PARIS) April/June 1985, 26:359-70.

MASSIAH, JOYCELIN

Massiah, Joycelin. Establishing a programme of women and development studies in the University of the West Indies. SOCIAL AND ECONOMIC STUDIES (MONA, JAMAICA) March 1986, 35:151-97.

Massiah, Joycelin. Participation of women in socio-economic development: indicators as tools for development planning; the case of the Commonwealth Caribbean. In: Women and development: indicators of their changing role. Series: Socio-economic studies, No. 3. (Paris, Unesco, 1981), pp. 71-100.

Massiah, Joycelin. Women in the Caribbean: an annotated bibliography; a guide to material available in Barbados. Compiled by Joycelin Massiah, with the assistance of Audine Wilkinson and Norma Shorey. Series: University of the West Indies, Cave Hill, Barbados. Institute of Social and Economic Research. Occasional bibliography series, No. 5. (Cave Hill, Barbados, Institute of Social and Economic Research (Eastern Caribbean), University of the West Indies, 1979), 133 pp.

Massiah, Joycelin. Employed women in Barbados: a demographic profile, 1946-1970. Series: Occasional Paper (University of the West Indies. Institute of Social and Economic Research, No. 8. (Cave Hill, Barbados, University of the West Indies, 1984), 131 pp.

Maternal mortality in rural Bangladesh: the Jamalpur district. By: Khan, Atiqur Rahman and Jahan, Farida Akhter. STUDIES IN FAMILY PLANNING (NEW YORK) January/February 1986, 17:7-12.

Maternal mortality in rural Bangladesh: the Tangail district. By: Alauddin, Mohammad. STUDIES IN FAMILY PLANNING (NEW YORK) January/February 1986, 17:13-21.

Matriarchy: a vision of power. By: Webster, Paula. In: Toward an anthropology of women. Edited by Rayna R. Reiter. (New York, Monthly Review Press, 1975), pp. 141-56.

MATSEPE-CASABURRI, IVY

Matsepe-Casaburri, Ivy. Women in southern Africa; legacy of exclusion. AFRICA REPORT (NEW YORK) March/April 1983, 28:7-10. Presents a brief overview of the position of women, with a focus on those belonging to disadvantaged groups.

MAVROGIANNIS, DIONYSOS

Mavrogiannis, Dionysos. La place des femmes au sein des societes et groupements cooperatifs (enquetes du BIT). TIERS-MONDE (PARIS) April/June 1985, 26:383-92.

Maximum hours legislation and female employment in the 1920s: a reassessment. By: Goldin, Claudia. NATIONAL BUREAU OF ECONOMIC RESEARCH. WORKING PAPER SERIES (CAMBRIDGE, MASS.) June 1986, No. 1949:1-27.

MAXWELL, NAN L.

Maxwell, Nan L. and D'Amico, Ronald J. Employment and wage effects of involuntary job separation: male-female differences. AMERICAN ECONOMIC REVIEW, PAPERS AND PROCEEDINGS (NASHVILLE) May 1986, 76:373-77.

Mayan woman and change. By: Elmendorf, M. L.. In: Women cross-culturally: change and challenge. Edited by Ruby Rohrlich-Leavitt. (The Hague, Mouton, 1975), pp. 111-27.

MAZUMDAR, VINA

Mazumdar, Vina. Another development with women: a view from Asia. DEVELOPMENT DIALOGUE (UPPSALA) 1982, No. 1/2:65-73.

Mazumdar, Vina. Women's studies: challenge to educational system. ECONOMIC AND POLITICAL WEEKLY (BOMBAY) May 16, 1981, 16:890-92. Discusses some of the recommendations of the National Conference on Women's Studies, held in Bombay, April 20-24, 1981.

MBILINYI, MARJORIE J.

Mbilinyi, Marjorie J.. Participation of women in African economies. UNIVERSITY OF DAR ES SALAAM. ECONOMIC RESEARCH BUREAU. PAPER (DAR-ES-SALAAM) 1971, No. 71.12:1-32.

Mascarenhas, Ophelia and Mbilinyi, Marjorie J.. Women in Tanzania: an analytical bibliography. (Uppsala, Scandinavian Institute of African Studies; Stockholm, Swedish International Development Authority, 1983), 256 pp.

MCALLISTER, ELIZABETH J

McAllister, Elizabeth J. Women in development. WOMEN OF CHINA (BEIJING) October 1986, No. 10:15-19, 25. Paper presented at a training seminar entitled Women in development. Also included: Zhang, Xiaolan, Enlightened by a project. -- Sun Huilan, Women academics serve rural sisters.

MCANDREW, MAGGIE

McAndrew, Maggie and Peers, Jo. New Soviet woman: model or myth. Series: Change International Reports: Women and Society, No. 3. (London, Change International Reports, 1981), 28 pp.

MCCORMICK, JOHN

McCormick, John and Akello, Grace. Africa's population crisis. NEW AFRICAN (LONDON) January 1984, No. 196:21-23. Discusses the causes of Africa's runaway population growth, and asks how womeen could benefit from population control.

MCELWAIN, ADRIENNE M

Lee, Bun Song and McElwain, Adrienne M. Empirical investigation of female labor-force participation, fertility, age at marriage, and wages in Korea. JOURNAL OF DEVELOPING AREAS (MACOMB, ILL.) July 1985, 19:483-500.

MCGRATH, PATRICIA L.

McGrath, Patricia L.. Unfinished assignment: equal education for women. Series: Worldwatch Paper, 7. ([Washington], Worldwatch Institute, 1976), 47 pp.

MCKIE, DAVID

McKie, David. Third World women and development. INTERNATIONAL PERSPECTIVES (OTTAWA) July/August 1984, p. 13-16.

MCNAMARA, ROBERT S.

McNamara, Robert S.. Challenges for sub-Saharan Africa. Sir John Crawford Memorial Lecture. (Washington, World Bank, November 1, 1985), 49 pp. Defines and reviews the critical issues affecting the outlook for economic growth in sub-Saharan Africa and examines how they might best be addressed.

Measurement of the occupational and industrial segregation of women. By: Lewis, Donald E.. JOURNAL OF INDUSTRIAL RELATIONS (SYDNEY) September 1982, 24:406-23.

Measuring female labour activities in Asian developing countries: a time-allocation approach. By: Tomoda, Shizue. INTERNATIONAL LABOUR REVIEW (GENEVA) November/December 1985, 124:661-76.

Measuring Filipino women's participation in development. By: Eviota, Elizabeth U.. In: Women and development, perspectives from South and Southeast Asia. Edited by Rounaq Jahan and Hanna Papanek. (Dacca, The Bangladesh Institute of Law and International Affairs, 1979), pp. 171-201.

Mechanisation in agriculture and women in Bangladesh. By: Hye, Hasnat Abdul. JOURNAL OF SOCIAL STUDIES (DHAKA) January 1985, No. 27:78-100.

MECHANIZATION

Scott, Joan Wallach. Mechanization of women's work. SCIENTIFIC AMERICAN (NEW YORK) September 1982, 247:166-87.

MEDICAL CARE

Gnanadason, Aruna. Women's health: plea for a new approach. ECONOMIC AND POLITICAL WEEKLY (BOMBAY) September 13, 1986, 21:1630-30.

MEDOFF, MARSHALL H

Medoff, Marshall H. Effect of the Equal Rights Amendment on the economic status of women. ATLANTIC ECONOMIC JOURNAL (WORDEN, IL) September 1985, 13:60-68.

Meet an African farmer ... and her husband. By: Willis, David K.. CHRISTIAN SCIENCE MONITOR (BOSTON) July 5, 1985, p. 9-10. Discusses the role of women in producing food and the need for greater focus on rural women.

MEGHDESSIAN, SAMIRA RAFIDI

Meghdessian, Samira Rafidi. Status of the Arab woman: a select bibliography. Compiled by Samira Rafidi Meghdessian. (Westport, Connecticut, Greenwood Press, 1980), 176 pp. A bibliography compiled under the auspices of the Institute for Women's Studies in the Arab World, Beirut, University College, Lebanon.

MELEISEA, PENELOPE SCHOEFFEL

Meleisea, Penelope Schoeffel. Women's associations and rural development: Western Samoa and East New Britain. PACIFIC PERSPECTIVE (SUVA) 1983, 11, No. 2:56-61.

Men and women in Malay society. By: Swift, Michael. In: Women in the new Asia; the changing social roles of men and women in South and South-east Asia. Edited by Barbara E. Ward. ([Paris], Unesco, 1963), pp. 268-86.

Men and women in the Philippines. By: Fox, Robert. In: Women in the new Asia, the changing social roles of men and women in South and South-east Asia. Edited by Barbara E. Ward. ([Paris], Unesco, 1963), pp. 342-64.

Men and women in the south of France: public and private domains. By: Reiter, Rayna R.. In: Toward an anthropology of women. Edited by Rayna R. Reiter. (New York, Monthly Review Press, 1975), pp. 252-82.

Men and women smallholder participants in a stall-feeder livestock program in Malawi. By: Spring, Anita. HUMAN ORGANIZATION (WASHINGTON) Summer 1986, 45:154-62.

MENCHER, JOAN P.

Mencher, Joan P. and Saradamoni, K.. Muddy feet, dirty hands; rice production and female agricultural labour. ECONOMIC AND POLITICAL WEEKLY (BOMBAY) December 25, 1982, 17:A149-A167.

MENON, M. INDIE

Menon, M. Indie. Education of Muslim women: tradition versus modernity. In: Women in the family and the economy: an international comparative survey. Edited by George Kurian and Ratna Ghosh. (Westport, CT, Greenwood Press, 1981), pp. 107-15.

Men's and women's roles in India: a sociological review. By: Dube, S. C.. In: Women in the new Asia; the changing social roles of men and women in South and South-east Asia. Edited by Barbara E. Ward. ([Paris], Unesco, 1963), pp. 174-203.

MERNISSI, FATIMA

Mernissi, Fatima. Moslem world: women excluded from development. In: Women and world development. Edited by Irene Tinker and Michele Bo Bramsen. ([Washington, DC], Overseas Development Council, 1976), pp. 35-44.

METZ-GOCKEL, SIGRID

Metz-Gockel, Sigrid and Muller, Ursula. Die Partnerschaft der Manner ist (noch) nicht die Partnerschaft der Frauen; empirische Befunde zum Geschlechterverhaltnis aus der Frauenperspektive. WSI-MITTEILUNGEN (DUSSELDORF) August 1986, 39:549-58.

METZNER, ULRIKE

Metzner, Ulrike and Stahn-Willig, Brigitte. Frauenarbeit: ein Beitrag zur gewerkschaftlichen Technikdebatte. WSI-MITTEILUNGEN (DUSSELDORF) August 1986, 39:529-36.

MEXICO

Chant, Sylvia. Household labour and self-help housing in Queretaro, Mexico. BOLETIN DE ESTUDIOS LATINO-AMERICANOS Y DEL CARIBE (AMSTERDAM) December 1984, No. 37:45-68.

Macarthy, Peter. Notes on inequalities in male-female shares in the labour market, occupations, wages, overtime, and hours of work - Mexico, 1940-1980. PAISLEY COLLEGE OF TECHNOLOGY. DEPT. OF ECONOMICS AND MANAGEMENT. SOCIAL SCIENCE WORKING PAPER (PAISLEY) June 1984, No. 61:1-38.

Oliveira, Orlandina de. Migracion femenina, organizacion familiar y mercados laborales en Mexico. COMERCIO EXTERIOR (MEXICO, D.F.) July 1984, 34:676-87.

Mexico: the many worlds of women. By: Elmendorf, Mary. In: Women: roles and status in eight countries. Edited by Janet Zollinger Giele and Audrey Chapman Smock. (New York, John Wiley, 1977), pp. 129-72.

MICHEL, ANDREE

Michel, Andree. Dix ans d'irruption des sciences humaines dans le domaine du travail des paysannes. TIERS-MONDE (PARIS) April/June 1985, 26:261-71.

Michel, Andree. El trabajo invisible de las campesinas del Tercer Mundo. DESARROLLO Y SOCIEDAD (BOGOTA) January 1984, No. 13:81-97. With English summary.

MIDDLE EAST

Danforth, Sandra. Muslim Middle Eastern women's participation in violent political conflict: causes and characteristics. STUDIES IN THIRD WORLD SOCIETIES (WILLIAMSBURG) June 1981, No. 16:49-68.

Hottinger, Arnold. Women in Islam. SWISS REVIEW OF WORLD AFFAIRS (ZURICH) October 1980, 30:8-14.

Ramazani, Nesta. Arab women in the Gulf. MIDDLE EAST JOURNAL (WASHINGTON) Spring 1985, 39:258-76.

Zurayk, Huda. Changing role of Arab women. POPULATION BULLETIN OF ECWA (BEIRUT) December 1979, No. 17:18-31.

Mideast odyssey. By: Miller, Judith. NEW YORK TIMES (NEW YORK) August 12, 1984, section 6:36, 40, 63-65, 72-73.

MIES, MARIA

Mies, Maria. Capitalism and subsistence: rural women in India. DEVELOPMENT (ROME) 1984, No. 4:18-24.

Mies, Maria. Indian women in subsistence and agricultural labour. INTERNATIONAL LABOUR OFFICE. WORLD EMPLOYMENT PROGRAMME RESEARCH. RURAL EMPLOYMENT POLICY RESEARCH PROGRAMME. WORKING PAPER (GENEVA) (GENEVA) May 1984, No. 34:1-243.

Mies, Maria. Social origins of the sexual division of labour. INSTITUTE OF SOCIAL STUDIES. OCCASIONAL PAPERS (THE HAGUE) January 1981, No. 85:1-49.

Mies, Maria. Towards a methodology of women's studies. INSTITUTE OF SOCIAL STUDIES. OCCASIONAL PAPERS (THE HAGUE) November 1979, No. 77:1-23. Attempts to lay down some methodological guidelines, which may be further discussed and developed into a new methodological approach which would be consistent with the social, economic and political aims of the women's movement.

MIGNOT-LEFEBVRE, YVONNE

Mignot-Lefebvre, Yvonne. Les femmes dans l'economie, de l'invisibilite a de nouveaux modes d'organisation. TIERS-MONDE (PARIS) April/June 1985, 26:247-60.

Mignot-Lefebvre, Yvonne. Femmes et developpement apres Nairobi; ideologie et enjeux internationaux d'une decennie. TIERS-MONDE (PARIS) January/March 1986, 27:129-42.

Mignot-Lefebvre, Yvonne. Femmes et developpement; idees et strategies des organisations internationales. TIERS-MONDE (PARIS) October/December 1980, 21:845-62.

Migracion femenina, organizacion familiar y mercados laborales en Mexico. By: Oliveira, Orlandina de. COMERCIO EXTERIOR (MEXICO, D.F.) July 1984, 34:676-87.

MIGRANT LABOR

Azzam, Henry T. and Shaib, Diana. Women left behind: a study of the wives of Lebanese migrant workers in the oil rich countries of the region. INTERNATIONAL LABOUR OFFICE. WORLD EMPLOYMENT PROGRAMME RESEARCH. POPULATION AND LABOUR POLICIES: REGIONAL PROGRAMME FOR THE MIDDLE EAST. WORKING PAPER (BEIRUT) September 1980, No. 3:1-56.

MIGRANT LABOR

Brown, Barbara B.. Women, migrant labor and social change in Botswana. BOSTON UNIVERSITY. AFRICAN STUDIES CENTER. WORKING PAPERS (BOSTON) 1980, No. 41:1-21.

Colfer, Carol. On circular migration -- from the distaff side: women left behind in the forests of East Kalimantan. INTERNATIONAL LABOUR OFFICE. WORLD EMPLOYMENT PROGRAMME RESEARCH. POPULATION AND LABOUR POLICIES PROGRAMME. WORKING PAPER (GENEVA) May 1983, No. 132:1-42. Focuses on male circular migration (or migration with the in;tent to return home) and its impact on the women who remain in the villages tending the farm. The area studied is East Kalimantan (Indonesian Borneo).

Griffith, David C. Women, remittances, and reproduction. AMERICAN ETHNOLOGIST (WASHINGTON) November 1985, 12:676-90. Presents and interprets data on how women in Jamaica use remittances from migrating husbands, boyfriends, sons, and so forth, and examines some of the reasons for these uses. The author concludes that seasonal-labor migration aids Jamaican peasant households in meeting the costs of reproducing themselves and their social and economic conditions.

Migrant women at work in Asia. By: Shah, Nasra M. and Smith, Peter C.. In: Women in the cities of Asia: migration and urban adaptation. Edited by James T. Fawcett, Siew-Ean Khoo and Peter C. Smith. (Boulder, CO, Westview Press, 1984), pp. 297-322.

MIGRATION

Women in migration. INTERNATIONAL MIGRATION REVIEW (STATEN ISLAND, N.Y.) Winter 1984, 18:881-1314, special issue. PARTIAL CONTENT: Khoo, Siew-Ean, and Peter C. Smith, Migration of women to cities: the Asian situation in comparative research. - Trager, Lilian, Family strategies and the migration of women; emigrants to Dagupan City, Philippines. - Drakakis-Smith, D. W., The Changing economic role of women in the urbanization process: a preliminary report from Zimbabwe. - Pittin, Renee, Migration of women in Nigeria: the Hausa case.

Migration of rural women to Taipei. By: Huang, Nora Chiang. In: Women in the cities of Asia: migration and urban adaptation. Edited by James T. Fawcett, Siew-Ean Khoo and Peter C. Smith. (Boulder, CO, Westview Press, 1984), pp. 247-68.

Migration of women in the Philippines. By: Eviota, Elizabeth U. and Smith, Peter C.. In: Women in the cities of Asia: migration and urban adaptation. Edited by James T. Fawcett, Siew-Ean Khoo and Peter C. Smith. (Boulder, CO, Westview Press, 1984), pp. 165-90.

Migration of women workers in peninsular Malaysia: impact and implications. By: Ariffin, Jamilah. In: Women in the cities of Asia: migration and urban adaptation. Edited by James T. Fawcett, Siew-Ean Khoo and Peter C. Smith. (Boulder, CO, Westview Press, 1984), pp. 213-26.

Military ideology and the dissolution of democracy: women in Chile. Series: Change International Reports: Women in Society, No. 4 . (London, Change International Reports, 1981), 24 pp.

MILLER, BARBARA D.

Miller, Barbara D.. Female labor participation and female seclusion in rural India: a regional view. ECONOMIC DEVELOPMENT AND CULTURAL CHANGE (CHICAGO) July 1982, 30:777-94.

Miller, Barbara D.. Endangered sex; neglect of female children in rural north India. (Ithaca, New York, Cornell University Press, 1981), 201 pp.

MILLER, JUDITH

Miller, Judith. Mideast odyssey. NEW YORK TIMES (NEW YORK) August 12, 1984, section 6:36, 40, 63-65, 72-73.

MILLER, LINDA

Miller, Linda. Patrons, politics, and schools; an arena for Brazilian women. STUDIES IN THIRD WORLD SOCIETIES (WILLIAMSBURG) March 1981 , No. 15:67-89.

Mindestens die Halfte aller Arbeits- und Ausbildungsplatze fur Frauen? Zur Quotierungsforderung in dem Entwurf eines Antidiscriminierungsgesetzes der Grunen. By: Raasch, Sibylle. WSI-MITTEILUNGEN (DUSSELDORF) August 1986, 39:575-82.

MING, XIAO

Ming, Xiao. Women in rural economic reform. WOMEN OF CHINA (BEIJING) May 1986, No. 5:3-7.

Ming, Xiao. Women in the special economic zones and open cities (4); a visit to Zhanjiang. WOMEN OF CHINA (BEIJING) January 1986, No. 1:15-18.

Minority within minority -- on being south Asian and female in Canada. By: Ghosh, Ratna. In: Women in the family and the economy: an international comparative survey. Edited by George Kurian and Ratna Ghosh. (Westport, CT, Greenwood Press, 1981), pp. 413-26.

Minus lives: women of Bangladesh. By: Kabeer, Naila. Series: Change International Reports: Women and Society, No. 10. (London, Change International Reports , [1983?]), 16 pp.

MIRALAO, VIRGINIA A.

Miralao, Virginia A.. Impact of female employment on household management. In: Women in the urban and industrial workforce; Southeast and East Asia. Edited by Gavin W. Jones. Series: Development Studies Centre. Monograph, No. 33. (Canberra, Australia, Australian National University, 1984), pp. 369-86. Series edited by Helen Hughes.

Misverstanden rond de kostwinner in het ontwikkelingsbeleid. By: Postel-Coster, Els. INTERNATIONALE SPECTATOR (THE HAGUE) September 1983, 37:549-55.

MITRA, ASOK

Mitra, Asok. Participation of women in socio-economic development: indicators as tools for development planning; the case of India. In: Women and development: indicators of their changing role. Series: Socio-economic studies, No. 3. (Paris, Unesco, 1981), pp. 49-69.

MITTER, SWASTI

Mitter, Swasti. On the global assembly line women and multinationals. DEVELOPMENT (ROME) 1984, No. 4:31-33.

MOATASSIME, AHMED

Moatassime, Ahmed. Femmes musulmanes entre "l'etat sauvage" et les "cultures civilisees". TIERS-MONDE (PARIS) January/March 1984, 25:139-54.

Mobilization of Iraqi women into the wage labor force. By: Joseph, Suad. STUDIES IN THIRD WORLD SOCIETIES (WILLIAMSBURG) June 1981, No. 16:69-90.

Mobilization of women: three societies. By: Chaney, Elsa M.. In: Women cross-culturally: change and challenge. Edited by Ruby Rohrlich-Leavitt. (The Hague, Mouton, 1975), pp. 472-89.

MODAK, MARIANNE

Dabat, Christine and Modak, Marianne. Femmes et controle des naissances; refus, contraintes et vecus. INSTITUT UNIVERSITAIRE D'ETUDES DU DEVELOPPEMENT. ITINERAIRES: NOTES ET TRAVAUX (GENEVA) April 1981, No. 15:1-119.

MOHAMMADI, PARI

Mohammadi, Pari. Women in national planning: false expectations. DEVELOPMENT (ROME) 1984, No. 4:80-81.

MOHAN, RAKESH

Mohan, Rakesh. Determinants of labour earnings in developing metropoli: estimates from Bogota and Cali, Colombia. Series: World Bank Staff Working Papers, No. 498. (Washington, DC, World Bank, 1981), 135 pp.

Mohan, Rakesh. People of Bogota: who they are, what they earn, where they live. Series: World Bank. City Study Research Project. City Study Project Paper, No. 6; World Bank Staff Working Paper, No. 390. (Washington, DC, World Bank, 1980), 1980.

MOHIUDDIN, YASMEEN

Mohiuddin, Yasmeen. Economic role of women: a case of occupational dependency. PAKISTAN & GULF ECONOMIST (KARACHI) February 2, 1985, 4:12-15.

Mohiuddin, Yasmeen. Female employment and social status; survey. PAKISTAN & GULF ECONOMIST (KARACHI) April 6, 1985, 4:30-33. Report based on a survey of 216 female handicraft workers located at major centres of handicraft work in north, middle and south Sind.

Mohiuddin, Yasmeen. Female handicraft workers; the invisible hand. PAKISTAN & GULF ECONOMIST (KARACHI) July 20, 1985, 4:44-47. The purpose of this study is to investigate the economic role and status of these invisible producers in the all-female handicraft production in Sind, Pakistan.

MOLYNEUX, MAXINE

Molyneux, Maxine. Movilizacion sin emancipacion? Los intereses de la mujer, estado y revolucion en Nicaragua. DESARROLLO Y SOCIEDAD (BOGOTA) January 1984, No. 13:177-95. With English summary.

MOLYNEUX, MAXINE

Molyneux, Maxine. Women's emancipation under socialism: a model for the Third World? WORLD DEVELOPMENT (OXFORD) September/October 1981, 9:1019-37. Examines the policies adopted by socialist states to improve the position of women and traces some of these inequalities to the policies themselves, and to the theoretical assumptions underlying them.

More on the labour supply of Canadian women. By: Robinson, Chris and Tomes, Nigel. CANADIAN JOURNAL OF ECONOMICS (TORONTO) February 1985, 18:156-63.

MORIARTY, MICHELE

Moriarty, Michele. Women in development. BANK'S WORLD (WASHINGTON) March 1983, 2:7-8. Discusses some of the issues raised at the World Bank's third "Workshop on Women in Development," which took place recently in Baltimore.

MOROCCO

Howard-Merriam, Kathleen. Women's political participation in Morocco's development: how much and for whom? MAGHREB REVIEW (LONDON) January/April 1984, 9:12-25.

MORSY, SOHEIR A.

Morsy, Soheir A.. Sex differences and folk illness in an Egyptian village. In: Women in the Muslim world. Edited by Lois Beck and Nikki Keddie. (Cambridge, MA, Harvard University Press, 1978), pp. 599-616.

Moslem world: women excluded from development. By: Mernissi, Fatima. In: Women and world development. Edited by Irene Tinker and Michele Bo Bramsen. ([Washington, DC], Overseas Development Council, 1976), pp. 35-44.

Mother and child in India. By: Gopalan, C.. ECONOMIC AND POLITICAL WEEKLY (BOMBAY) January 26, 1985, 20:159-66.

Mothers' influence on daughters' orientations toward education: an Egyptian case study. By: Bach, Rebecca and Gadalla, Saad. COMPARATIVE EDUCATION REVIEW (NEW YORK) August 1985, 29:374-84.

MOTHERS. MORTALITY

Alauddin, Mohammad. Maternal mortality in rural Bangladesh: the Tangail district. STUDIES IN FAMILY PLANNING (NEW YORK) January/February 1986, 17:13-21.

MOTHERS. MORTALITY

    Khan, Atiqur Rahman and Jahan, Farida Akhter. Maternal mortality in rural Bangladesh: the Jamalpur district. STUDIES IN FAMILY PLANNING (NEW YORK) January/February 1986, 17:7-12.

MOTROSHILOVA, NELYA V.

    Motroshilova, Nelya V.. Soviet women in the life of society: achievements and problems. INTERNATIONAL SOCIAL SCIENCE JOURNAL (PARIS) 1983, 35, No. 4:733-46.

    Movilizacion sin emancipacion? Los intereses de la mujer, estado y revolucion en Nicaragua. By: Molyneux, Maxine. DESARROLLO Y SOCIEDAD (BOGOTA) January 1984, No. 13:177-95. With English summary.

MOZAMBIQUE

    Penvenne, Jeanne. Making our own way: women working in Lourenco Marques, 1900-1933. BOSTON UNIVERSITY. AFRICAN STUDIES CENTER. WORKING PAPERS (BOSTON) 1986, No. 114:1-20.

    Urdang, Stephanie. Last transition? Women and development in Mozambique. REVIEW OF AFRICAN POLITICAL ECONOMY (SHEFFIELD) 1984, No. 27/28:8-32.

    Urdang, Stephanie. Women in Mozambique; rural transformations: women in the new society. AFRICA REPORT (NEW YORK) March/April 1985, 30:66-70.

    Mozambique: women, the law and agrarian reform. By: Isaacman, Barbara and Stephen, June. Series: [African Training and Research Centre for Women] Research Series, No. 01/80. ([Addis Ababa], United Nations Economic Commission for Africa, 1980), 148 pp. "ATRCWSDD/RES01/80"

MU, YUAN

    Mu, Yuan. China pursues peace and development in 1986-1990. WOMEN OF CHINA (BEIJING) January 1986, No. 1:24-25.

MUCHENA, OLIVIA

    Muchena, Olivia. Women in southern Africa; are women integrated into development? AFRICA REPORT (NEW YORK) March/April 1983, 28:4-6.

    Muddy feet, dirty hands; rice production and female agricultural labour. By: Mencher, Joan P. and Saradamoni, K.. ECONOMIC AND POLITICAL WEEKLY (BOMBAY) December 25, 1982, 17:A149-A167.

MUECKE, MARJORIE A.

    Muecke, Marjorie A.. Make money not babies; changing status markers of northern Thai women. ASIAN SURVEY (BERKELEY, CALIF.) April 1984, 24:459-70.

MUELLER, EVA

    Kossoudji, Sherrie and Mueller, Eva. Economic and demographic status of female-headed households in rural Botswana. ECONOMIC DEVELOPMENT AND CULTURAL CHANGE (CHICAGO) July 1983, 31:831-59.

    La mujer en la fuerza de trabajo en la America Latina: un resumen introductorio. By: Aguiar, Neuma. DESARROLLO Y SOCIEDAD (BOGOTA) January 1984, No. 13:57-79. With English summary.

    La mujer y su imagen en los medios. By: Bonilla de Ramos, Elssy. UNIVERSIDAD DE LOS ANDES. CENTRO DE ESTUDIOS SOBRE DESARROLLO ECONOMICO. DOCUMENTO (BOGOTA) Arpil 1981, No. 64:1-183.

    Las mujeres jefes de hogar. By: Rey De Marulanda, Nohra. UNIVERSIDAD DE LOS ANDES. CENTRO DE ESTUDIOS SOBRE DESARROLLO ECONOMICO. DOCUMENTO (BOGOTA) September 1982, No. 68:1-66.

MUKHOPADHYAY, CAROL C.

    Mukhopadhyay, Carol C. and Bald, Suresht R.. Gender, politics and modernization: the Indian case. STUDIES IN THIRD WORLD SOCIETIES (WILLIAMSBURG) June 1981, No. 16:91-121.

MULLER, URSULA

    Metz-Gockel, Sigrid and Muller, Ursula. Die Partnerschaft der Manner ist (noch) nicht die Partnerschaft der Frauen; empirische Befunde zum Geschlechterverhaltnis aus der Frauenperspektive. WSI-MITTEILUNGEN (DUSSELDORF) August 1986, 39:549-58.

MULLER-BLATTAU, BEATE AND SEIBERT, ULRIKE

    Muller-Blattau, Beate and Seibert, Ulrike. Funf Frauen - funf Leben. E & Z, ENTWICKLUNG UND ZUSAMMENARBEIT (BONN) January 1985, 26:16-17.

MULLINGS, LEITH

    Mullings, Leith. Women and economic change in Africa. In: Women in Africa: studies in social and economic change. Edited by Nancy J. Hafkin and Edna G. Bay. (Stanford, Stanford University Press, 1976), pp. 239-64.

MULTINATIONAL ENTERPRISE

Gothoskar, Sujata. Free trade zones: pitting women against women. ECONOMIC AND POLITICAL WEEKLY (BOMBAY) August 23, 1986, 21:1489-92.

Mitter, Swasti. On the global assembly line women and multinationals. DEVELOPMENT (ROME) 1984, No. 4:31-33.

MUNTEMBA, MAUD SHIMWAAYI

Muntemba, Maud Shimwaayi. Dispossession and counterstrategies in Zambia 1930-1970. DEVELOPMENT (ROME) 1984, No. 4:15-17.

Muntemba, Maud Shimwaayi. Women and agricultural change in the railway region of Zambia: dispossession and counterstrategies, 1930-1970. In: Women and work in Africa. Edited by Edna G. Bay. (Boulder, CO, Westview Press, 1982), pp. 83-103.

MUNTEMBA, SHIMWAAYI

Muntemba, Shimwaayi. Women as food producers and suppliers in the twentieth century; the case of Zambia. DEVELOPMENT DIALOGUE (UPPSALA) 1982, No. 1/2:29-50.

MURRAY, COLIN

Murray, Colin. Families divided: the impact of migrant labour in Lesotho. Series: African Studies Series, 29. (Cambridge, England, Cambridge University Press, 1981), 219 pp.

Muslim Middle Eastern women's participation in violent political conflict: causes and characteristics. By: Danforth, Sandra. STUDIES IN THIRD WORLD SOCIETIES (WILLIAMSBURG) June 1981, No. 16:49-68.

MUSLIM WOMEN

Abdullah, Noraini. Equality of Malay women -- real but restricted. FAR EASTERN ECONOMIC REVIEW (HONGKONG) April 10, 1986, 132:38-39.

Ali, Ausaf. Status of women. ARABIA; THE ISLAMIC WORLD REVIEW (EAST BURNHAM) October 1986, 6:56-57. Views on the place of women in Islam.

Lamya' al-Faruqi, Lois. Women in a Qur'anic society. AL-TAWHID; A QUARTERLY JOURNAL OF ISLAMIC THOUGHT AND CULTURE (TEHRAN) July 1984, 1, No. 4:36-49.

Moatassime, Ahmed. Femmes musulmanes entre "l'etat sauvage" et les "cultures civilisees". TIERS-MONDE (PARIS) January/March 1984, 25:139-54.

MUSLIM WOMEN

Osman, Fathi. Muslim women's role in society. ARABIA; THE ISLAMIC WORLD REVIEW (EAST BURNHAM) April 1986, 5:11-12.

Yaccob, May. Ahmadiyya and urbanization: migrant women in Abidjan. BOSTON UNIVERSITY. AFRICAN STUDIES CENTER. WORKING PAPERS (BOSTON) 1983, No. 75:1-16.

Muslim women's role in society. By: Osman, Fathi. ARABIA; THE ISLAMIC WORLD REVIEW (EAST BURNHAM) April 1986, 5:11-12.

My life history in Thailand. By: Dickinson, Pramuan. In: Women in the new Asia; the changing social roles of men and women in South and South-east Asia. Edited by Barbara E. Ward. ([Paris], Unesco, 1963), pp. 452-70.

Nach zehn Jahren Bewusstsein fur Frauen geschaffen. By: Donner-Reichle, Carola. E & Z, ENTWICKLUNG UND ZUSAMMENARBEIT (BONN) January 1985, 26:14-15.

NAG, MONI

Jain, Anrudh K. and Nag, Moni. Female primary education and fertility reduction in India. POPULATION COUNCIL. CENTER FOR POLICY STUDIES. WORKING PAPERS (NEW YORK) September 1985, No. 114:1-57.

Jain, Anrudh K. and Nag, Moni. Importance of female primary education for fertility reduction in India. ECONOMIC AND POLITICAL WEEKLY (BOMBAY) September 6, 1986, 21:1602-08.

Nairobi '85; the decade NGO forum. By: Barrow, Nita. AFRICA REPORT (NEW YORK) March/April 1985, 30:9-12.

Nairobi '85:African women at the end of the decade. By: Steady, Filomina Chioma. AFRICA REPORT (NEW YORK) March/April 1985, 30:4-8. Discusses the World Conference on the United Nations Decade for Women, to be held in Nairobi, Kenya, July 15-26, 1985.

NAISHO, JOYCE

Naisho, Joyce. Health care for women in the Sudan. WORLD HEALTH FORUM (GENEVA) 1982, 3,No.2:164-65.

NAKAMURA, ALICE

Nakamura, Alice and Nakamura, Masao. Dynamic models of the labor force behavior of married women which can be estimated using limited amounts of past information. JOURNAL OF ECONOMETRICS (AMSTERDAM) March 1985, 27:273-98.

NAKANISHI, TAMAKO

Nakanishi, Tamako. Equality or protection? Protective legislation for women in Japan. INTERNATIONAL LABOUR REVIEW (GENEVA) September/October 1983, 122:609-21.

NAMANJA, GRACIAN BAZILIOUS

Olaseha, I. O. and Namanja, Gracian Bazilious. Focusing on women for water and sanitation: the case of Mapo community in Ibadan, Nigeria. INTERNATIONAL QUARTERLY OF COMMUNITY HEALTH EDUCATION (FARMINGDALE, N.Y.) 1985/1986, 6, No. 4:335-43.

NASH, JUNE

Nash, June. Resistance as protest: women in the struggle of Bolivian tin-mining communities. In: Women cross-culturally: change and challenge. Edited by Ruby Rohrlich-Leavitt. (The Hague, Mouton, 1975), pp. 261-71.

NATH, KAMLA

Nath, Kamla. Education and employment among Kuwaiti women. In: Women in the Muslim world. Edited by Lois Beck and Nikki Keddie. (Cambridge, MA, Harvard University Press, 1978), pp. 172-88.

Nath, Kamla. Labor-saving techniques in food processing: rural women and technological change in the Gambia. BOSTON UNIVERSITY. AFRICAN STUDIES CENTER. WORKING PAPERS (BOSTON) 1985, No. 108:1-26. Describes the methodology used in developing a project design for the introduction of sorghum and millet decorticators and flour milling units in rural areas of the Gambia in West Africa.

Nath, Kamla. National machineries for integration of women in development: a strategy for The Gambia. BOSTON UNIVERSITY. AFRICAN STUDIES CENTER. WORKING PAPERS (BOSTON) 1985, No. 104:1-17.

Nath, Kamla. Women and technological change in The Gambia: a case study of the salt industry. BOSTON UNIVERSITY. AFRICAN STUDIES CENTER. WORKING PAPERS (BOSTON) 1985, No. 107:1-15.

Nath, Kamla. Women and vegetable gardens in the Gambia: Action AID and rural development. BOSTON UNIVERSITY. AFRICAN STUDIES CENTER. WORKING PAPERS (BOSTON) 1985, No. 109:1-13. Examines Action Aid's program for improving the capacity of rural women to produce garden vegetables and to introduce marketing infrastructures.

National machineries for integration of women in development: a strategy for The Gambia. By: Nath, Kamla. BOSTON UNIVERSITY. AFRICAN STUDIES CENTER. WORKING PAPERS (BOSTON) 1985, No. 104:1-17.

NATIONALE ADVIES RAAD VOOR ONTWIKKELINGSSAMENWERKING (NETHERLANDS)

Nationale Advies Raad Voor Ontwikkelingssamenwerking (Netherlands). Recommendation on women in developing countries: aspects of development cooperation. Series: Publication of the National Advisory Council for Development Corporation, No. 67. (The Hague, Ministry of Foreign Affairs, 1980), 73 pp.

NATO SYMPOSIUM ON WOMEN AND THE WORLD OF WORK (1980: LISBON, PORTUGAL)

Nato Symposium on Women and the World of Work (1980: Lisbon, Portugal). Women and the world of work. Edited by Anne Hoiberg. Series: Nato Conference Series, III, Human Factors, Vol. 18. (New York, Published in cooperation with the Nato Scientific Affairs Division [by] Plenum Press, 1982), 390 pp. Proceedings of a NATO Symposium on Women and the World of Work held August 4-8, 1980, in Lisbon, Portugal.

Nature and extent of female labour use in agriculture - a comparison between progressive and non-progressive area. By: Choudhury, S. and Giri, A. K. ECONOMIC AFFAIRS (CALCUTTA) June 1986, 31:81-86.

NAYER, SUSHILLA

Nayer, Sushilla. Our changing life in India. In: Women in the new Asia; the changing social roles of men and women in South and South-east Asia. Edited by Barbara E. Ward. ([Paris], Unesco, 1963), pp. 204-16.

Negotiation of reality: male-female relations in Sefrou, Morocco. By: Rosen, Lawrence. In: Women in the Muslim world. Edited by Lois Beck and Nikki Keddie. (Cambridge, MA, Harvard University Press, 1978), pp. 561-83.

NELSON, NICI

Nelson, Nici. Why has development neglected rural women? A review of the South Asian literature. Series: Women in Development, Vol. 1. (Oxford, New York, Pergamon Press, 1979), 108 pp. Reviews the literature available on the role of women in rural development in Bangladesh, India, Pakistan and Sri Lanka.

NEPAL

Pradhan, Bina. Women and development: the overlooked link. JOURNAL OF DEVELOPMENT AND ADMINISTRATIVE STUDIES (KATHMANDU) June/December 1981, 3:172-202.

Schroeder, Robert and Schroeder, Elaine. Women in Nepali agriculture: all work and no power. JOURNAL OF DEVELOPMENT AND ADMINISTRATIVE STUDIES (KATHMANDU) January 1979, 1:178-92.

NETHERLANDS

Schippers, Joop J. and Siegers, Jacques J. Women's relative wage rate in the Netherlands, 1950-1983: a test of alternative discrimination theories. DE ECONOMIST (LEIDEN) 1986, 134, No. 2:165-80.

New approach to women's participation in the economy. By: Garabaghi, Ninou K.. INTERNATIONAL SOCIAL SCIENCE JOURNAL (PARIS) 1983, 35, No. 4:659-82.

New economic readjustment policies: implications for Chinese urban working women. By: Dalsimer, Marlyn and Nisonoff, Laurie. REVIEW OF RADICAL POLITICAL ECONOMICS (NEW YORK) Spring 1984, 16:17-43.

New models and traditional networks: migrant women in Tehran. By: Bauer, Janet. In: Women in the cities of Asia: migration and urban adaptation. Edited by James T. Fawcett, Siew-Ean Khoo and Peter C. Smith. (Boulder, CO, Westview Press, 1984), pp. 269-93.

New order with some old prejudices. By: Lim, Linda. FAR EASTERN ECONOMIC REVIEW (HONGKONG) January 5, 1984, 123:37-38. The position of Singapore's women throughout its brief history has been defined by traditional outlines, male dominance and female subordination.

The new Samoan businesswoman. By: Thomas, Pamela and Simi, Noumea. PACIFIC PERSPECTIVE (SUVA) 1983, 11, No. 2:5-12.

New Soviet woman: model or myth. By: McAndrew, Maggie and Peers, Jo. Series: Change International Reports: Women and Society, No. 3. (London, Change International Reports, 1981), 28 pp.

NEWLAND, KATHLEEN

Newland, Kathleen. Women and population growth: choice beyond child-bearing. WORLDWATCH PAPER (WASHINGTON) December 1977, No. 16:1-32.

NEWLAND, KATHLEEN

Newland, Kathleen. Women, men, and the division of labor. WORLDWATCH PAPER (WASHINGTON) 1980, No. 37:1-43.

Newland, Kathleen. Sisterhood of man. (New York, London, W. W. Norton & Company, 1979), 242 pp. A Worldwatch Institute Book.

NG, MARGARET

Ng, Margaret. Social ascendancy without the fanfare. FAR EASTERN ECONOMIC REVIEW (HONGKONG) January 5, 1984, 123:28-29. Discusses the status of women in Hongkong.

NICARAGUA

Behrman, Jere R. and Wolfe, Barbara L.. Labor force participation and earnings determinants for women in the special conditions of developing countries. JOURNAL OF DEVELOPMENT ECONOMICS (AMSTERDAM) May/August 1984, 15:259-88. The authors focus on labor market conditions for women in Nicaragua.

Child quantity and quality in a developing country: family background, endogenous tastes, and biological supply factors. ECONOMIC DEVELOPMENT AND CULTURAL CHANGE (CHICAGO) July 1986, 34:703-20. The data are from a cross-sectional area-stratified random sample of about 4,000 women aged 15-45 collected in Nicaragua in 1977-78 as part of a larger study on the socio-economic roles of women in developing countries.

Deere, Carmen Diana. Developpement cooperatif et participation feminine a la reforme agraire nicaraguayenne. TIERS-MONDE (PARIS) April/June 1985, 26:403-08.

Molyneux, Maxine. Movilizacion sin emancipacion? Los intereses de la mujer, estado y revolucion en Nicaragua. DESARROLLO Y SOCIEDAD (BOGOTA) January 1984, No. 13:177-95. With English summary.

Wolfe, Barbara L. and Behrman, Jere R.. Determinants of child health, mortality, and nutrition in a developing country. UNIVERSITY OF WISCONSIN-MADISON. INSTITUTE FOR RESEARCH ON POVERTY. DISCUSSION PAPERS (MADISON) January 1981, No. 643-80:1-53. The authors use data collected in a cross-sectional multipurpose survey of women of childbearing age in Nicaragua.

NICARAGUA

Wolfe, Barbara L. and Behrman, Jere R.. Impact of demographic changes on income distribution in a developing country. JOURNAL OF DEVELOPMENT ECONOMICS (AMSTERDAM) December 1982, 11:355-77. The authors use data from a stratified random sample of about 4,000 women aged 15 to 45 in Nicaragua.

Wolfe, Barbara L. and Behrman, Jere R.. Socioeconomic characteristics of women in a developing country and the degree of urbanization. UNIVERSITY OF WISCONSIN-MADISON. INSTITUTE FOR RESEARCH ON POVERTY. DISCUSSION PAPERS (MADISON) September 1980, 655-81:1-53. The study is based on a stratified random sample of over 4,000 women aged 15-45 in Nicaragua.

NICHOLSON, LOUISE

Nicholson, Louise. In the footsteps of Indira. TIMES (LONDON) July 12, 1985, p. 11. Concludes that, once in power, Mrs. Gandhi made little difference to the lives of poor rural women, but there has been some progress recently for what the West would call middle-class women.

NIGERIA

Barres, Victoria. Deux programmes de credit bien adaptes aux besoins des femmes du Tiers monde. TIERS-MONDE (PARIS) April/June 1985, 26:435-42. Cet article presente deux programmes de credits d'investissement destines a des femmes pauvres du Tiers Monde, l'un en milieu urbain (Madras, Inde) et l'autre en milieu rural (pays yoruba, Nigeria).

Callaway, Barbara J.. Ambiguous consequences of the socialisation and seclusion of Hausa women. JOURNAL OF MODERN AFRICAN STUDIES (OXFORD) September 1984, 22:429-50.

Callaway, Barbara J. and Kleeman, Katherine E.. Three women of Kano: modern women and traditional life. AFRICA REPORT (NEW YORK) March/April 1985, 30:26-29.

Dennis, Carolyne. Capitalist development and women's work: a Nigerian case study. REVIEW OF AFRICAN POLITICAL ECONOMY (SHEFFIELD) 1984, No. 27/28:109-19.

NIGERIA

Okali, C. and Cassaday, K.. Community response to a pilot farming project in Nigeria. BOSTON UNIVERSITY. AFRICAN-AMERICAN ISSUES CENTER. DISCUSSION PAPER (BOSTON) [1985], No. 10:1-28. The authors report on a preliminary study of farmers' response to alley farming, a technology designed to improve small ruminant (sheep and goat) and arable crop production in the humid zone of West Africa.

Okojie, Christiana E. E.. Determinants of labour force participation of urban women in Nigeria: a case study of Benin City. NIGERIAN JOURNAL OF ECONOMIC AND SOCIAL STUDIES (IBADAN) March 1983, 25:39-59.

Okorji, Eugene C. Role of women in arable cropping enterprises in farming communities of South-Eastern Nigeria: a case study. DEVELOPMENT AND PEACE (BUDAPEST) Autumn 1985, 6:165-73.

Olaseha, I. O. and Namanja, Gracian Bazilious. Focusing on women for water and sanitation: the case of Mapo community in Ibadan, Nigeria. INTERNATIONAL QUARTERLY OF COMMUNITY HEALTH EDUCATION (FARMINGDALE, N.Y.) 1985/1986, 6, No. 4:335-43.

Pittin, Renee. Documentation and analysis of the invisible work of invisible women: a Nigerian case study. INTERNATIONAL LABOUR REVIEW (GENEVA) July/August 1984, 123:473-90. Discusses problems arising in the documentation and analysis of the work of secluded women. Focusing on the Muslim Hausa women of Katsina, Nigeria, the author contends that past surveys and censuses have grossly underestimated these women's economic contribution to the Nigerian economy, and that this neglect is increasing.

NIMNICHT, MARTA ARANGO DE

Nimnicht, Marta Arango de. Choco woman: agent for change. In: Latin American women: the meek speak out. Edited by June H. Turner. (Silver Spring, MD, International Educational Development, 1980), pp. 89-100. Discusses women in Colombia.

NISEKKA, MERE

Nisekka, Mere. Role of women in socio-economic development: indicators as instruments of social analysis; the case of Nigeria and Uganda. In: Women and development: indicators of their changing role. Series: Socio-economic studies, No. 3. (Paris, Unesco, 1981), pp. 33-47.

NISHIKAWA, SHUNSAKU

Nishikawa, Shunsaku and Higuchi, Yoshio. Determinants of female labor-force participation. JAPANESE ECONOMIC STUDIES (ARMONK, N.Y.) Winter 1980/1981, 9:62-87.

NISHIMURA, NAMIKO

Nishimura, Namiko. Women at work. JOURNAL OF JAPANESE TRADE & INDUSTRY (TOKYO) May/June 1986, 5:46-47.

NISONOFF, LAURIE

Dalsimer, Marlyn and Nisonoff, Laurie. New economic readjustment policies: implications for Chinese urban working women. REVIEW OF RADICAL POLITICAL ECONOMICS (NEW YORK) Spring 1984, 16:17-43.

NOMADS

Tavakolian, Bahram. Women and socioeconomic change among Sheikhanzai nomads of western Afghanistan. MIDDLE EAST JOURNAL (WASHINGTON) Summer 1984, 38:433-53. Based on observations made in 1976-1977.

NON-GOVERNMENTAL ORGANIZATIONS

Barrow, Nita. Nairobi '85; the decade NGO forum. AFRICA REPORT (NEW YORK) March/April 1985, 30:9-12.

Nonutilitarian economic model of fertility and female labor force participation. By: Sanderson, Warren C.. REVUE ECONOMIQUE (PARIS) November 1980, 31:1045-80.

NORWAY

Jensen, An-Magritt and Schweder, Tore. Engine of fertility - influenced by interbirth employment? NORWAY. STATISTISK SENTRALBYRA. DISCUSSION PAPER (OSLO) June 1986, No. 15:1-33.

Not just a pretty decade. ECONOMIST DEVELOPMENT REPORT (LONDON) July 1985, 2:1-4, 8-9. Offers a review of women and development, which includes: UN women; Indian credit; African women farmers; women's world banking and a project brief: female circumcision.

Note on female labour supply. By: Rothschild, K. W.. KYKLOS (BASLE) 1980, 33, No. 2:246-60.

Note on women and agricultural technology in the Third World. By: Carew, Joy Gleason. LABOUR AND SOCIETY (GENEVA) July/September 1981, 6:279-85.

Notes on determinants of paid employment for women in Pakistan. By: Oureshi, Sarfraz Khan. In: Women and development, perspectives from South and Southeast Asia. Edited by Rounaq Jahan and Hanna Papanek. (Dacca, Bangladesh Institute of Law and International Affairs, 1979), pp. 219-27.

Notes on inequalities in male-female shares in the labour market, occupations, wages, overtime, and hours of work - Mexico, 1940-1980. By: Macarthy, Peter. PAISLEY COLLEGE OF TECHNOLOGY. DEPT. OF ECONOMICS AND MANAGEMENT. SOCIAL SCIENCE WORKING PAPER (PAISLEY) June 1984, No. 61:1-38.

NOVICKI, MARGARET A.

Novicki, Margaret A.. G. K. T. Chiepe, Minister of Foreign Affairs, Botswana. AFRICA REPORT (NEW YORK) March/April 1985, 30:14-16. An interview with Dr. G. K. T. Chiepe, Botswans's first woman university graduate and first female cabinet minister who discusses the advances of women over the UN Decade and the significance of women's contributions to the economic development of her country.

Novicki, Margaret A.. Interview: Joyce Aryee, Secretary for Education, Ghana. AFRICA REPORT (NEW YORK) March/April 1985, 30:55-8.

NOVIKOVA, E. E.

Novikova, E. E.. Scientific and technical progress and women's work in the USSR. LABOUR AND SOCIETY (GENEVA) January/March 1982, 7:13-22.

Numero special: radioscopie du chomage. L'ECONOMIE DE LA REUNION (STE-CLOTILDE) September/October 1986, No. 25:1-32.

NUTRITION

Basse, Marie-Therese. Women, food and nutrition in Africa: perspective from Senegal. FOOD AND NUTRITION (ROME) 1984, 10, No. 1:65-79. Also includes: Economic change and the outlook for nutrition, prepared by the Food and Agriculture Organization of the United Nations.

NUTRITION

Blau, David M.. Investments in child nutrititon and women's allocation of time in developing countries. YALE UNIVERSITY. ECONOMIC GROWTH CENTER. DISCUSSION PAPER (NEW HAVEN, CONN.) March 1981, No. 371:1-41. The purpose of this study is to investigate the determinants of fertility and home investments in the human capital of children in a context in which women have the option of working in the informal sector as well as the formal sector or no market work. The empirical analysis presented in section III uses data from a 1977-78 survey of households in Nicaragua.

O'DONNELL, CAROL

O'Donnell, Carol. Major theories of the labour market and women's place within it. JOURNAL OF INDUSTRIAL RELATIONS (SYDNEY) June 1984, 26:147-65. Looks at theories of the labour market with reference to the situation of women workers who tend to be concentrated in particular industries and particular occupations, and whose average wage is lower than that of males.

O'KELLY, ELIZABETH

O'Kelly, Elizabeth. Simple technologies for rural women in Bangladesh. (Dacca, UNICEF, Women's Development Programme, 1977), 48 pp. Annexure VI to the Feasibility Survey of Productive Income Generating Activities for Women.

OBBO, CHRISTINE

Obbo, Christine. African women; their struggle for economic independence. Series: Women in the Third World series. (London, Zed Press, 1981), 166 pp.

OBENG, LETITIA

Obeng, Letitia. Women's decade; an opportunity lost. August 21, 1985, p. 17A. Author claims that the U.N. Women's Decade has failed to reach the women most in need, the absolute poor, whose voices are not heard in international fora.

OCAMPO-KALFORS, SHEILAH

Ocampo-Kalfors, Sheilah. Liberated -- but tied to the old loyalties. FAR EASTERN ECONOMIC REVIEW (HONGKONG) January 5, 1984, 123:32-34. Describes how women in the Philippines have progressed rapidly in most fields, despite existing laws and traditions that discriminate against them.

Occupational choice among female academicians -- the Israeli case. By: Shapira, Rina and Etzioni-Halevy, Eva and Chopp-Tibon, Shira. In: Women in the family and the economy: an international comparative survey. Edited by George Kurian and Ratna Ghosh. (Westport, CT, Greenwood Press, 1981), pp. 345-58.

Occupational health hazards of female industrial workers in Malaysia. By: Hoon, Lee Siew. In: Women in the urban and industrial workforce; Southeast and East Asia. Edited by Gavin W. Jones. Series: Development Studies Centre. Monograph, No. 33. (Canberra, Australia, Australian National University, 1984), pp. 175-88. Series edited by Helen Hughes.

Occupational segregation and discriminatory pay: the position of women in the Cyprus labour market. By: House, William J.. INTERNATIONAL LABOUR REVIEW (GENEVA) January/February 1983, 122:75-93.

OCCUPATIONS

Bielby, William T. and Baron, James N. Sex segregation within occupations. AMERICAN ECONOMIC REVIEW, PAPERS AND PROCEEDINGS (NASHVILLE) May 1986, 76:43-47.

Lewis, Donald E. Sources of changes in the occupational segregation of Australian women. ECONOMIC RECORD (MELBOURNE) December 1985, 61:719-36.

Zalokar, Nadja. Generational differences in female occupational attainment -- have the 1970's changed women's opportunities? AMERICAN ECONOMIC REVIEW, PAPERS AND PROCEEDINGS (NASHVILLE) May 1986, 76:378-81.

OCEANIA

Bolabola, Cema. Women in villages: femininity, food and freedom. PACIFIC PERSPECTIVE (SUVA) 1983, 11, No. 2:65-7.

Crocombe, Marjorie Tuainekore. Women at the University of the South Pacific. PACIFIC PERSPECTIVE (SUVA) 1983, 11, No. 2:24-8.

Meleisea, Penelope Schoeffel. Women's associations and rural development: Western Samoa and East New Britain. PACIFIC PERSPECTIVE (SUVA) 1983, 11, No. 2:56-61.

Pulea, Mere. Women, employment and development. PACIFIC PERSPECTIVE (SUVA) 1983, 11, No. 2:18-28.

OCEANIA

Sue, Mee Kwain. Community education training centre (CETC). PACIFIC PERSPECTIVE (SUVA) 1983, 11, No. 2:62-4. Describes a regional center established in 1963 to provide a programme of community education for women.

OESER, LYNN

Oeser, Lynn. Hohola: the significance of social networks in urban adaptation of women in Papua-New Guinea's first low-cost housing estate. Series: Bulletin, New Guinea Research Unit, Research School of Pacific Studies, Australian National University, Canberra, No. 29. (Canberra, New Guinea Research Unit, Australian National University, 1969), 120 pp.

Of women and washing machines: employment, housework, and the reproduction of motherhood in socialist China. By: Robinson, Jean C.. CHINA QUARTERLY (LONDON) March 1985, No. 101:32-57.

Off-farm employment by women and marital instability. By: Acock, Alan C. and Deseran, Forrest A. RURAL SOCIOLOGY (PROVO, UTAH) Fall 1986, 51:314-27. The impact of farm women's paid work experience on the quality and stability of their marriages is examined in the context of two competing frameworks - status competition and status enhancement.

OKALI, C. AND CASSADAY, K.

Okali, C. and Cassaday, K.. Community response to a pilot farming project in Nigeria. BOSTON UNIVERSITY. AFRICAN-AMERICAN ISSUES CENTER. DISCUSSION PAPER (BOSTON) [1985], No. 10:1-28. The authors report on a preliminary study of farmers' response to alley farming, a technology designed to improve small ruminant (sheep and goat) and arable crop production in the humid zone of West Africa.

OKOJIE, CHRISTIANA E. E.

Okojie, Christiana E. E.. Determinants of labour force participation of urban women in Nigeria: a case study of Benin City. NIGERIAN JOURNAL OF ECONOMIC AND SOCIAL STUDIES (IBADAN) March 1983, 25:39-59.

OKONJO, KAMENE

Okonjo, Kamene. Dual-sex political system in operation: Igbo women and community politics in midwestern Nigeria. In: Women in Africa: studies in social and economic change. Edited by Nancy J. Hafkin and Edna G. Bay. (Stanford, Stanford University Press, 1976), pp. 45-58.

Okonjo, Kamene. Role of women in the development of culture in Nigeria. In: Women cross-culturally: change and challenge. Edited by Ruby Rohrlich-Leavitt. (The Hague, Mouton, 1975), pp. 31-40.

OKORJI, EUGENE C

Okorji, Eugene C. Role of women in arable cropping enterprises in farming communities of South-Eastern Nigeria: a case study. DEVELOPMENT AND PEACE (BUDAPEST) Autumn 1985, 6:165-73.

OLASEHA, I. O.

Olaseha, I. O. and Namanja, Gracian Bazilious. Focusing on women for water and sanitation: the case of Mapo community in Ibadan, Nigeria. INTERNATIONAL QUARTERLY OF COMMUNITY HEALTH EDUCATION (FARMINGDALE, N.Y.) 1985/1986, 6, No. 4:335-43.

OLIVEIRA, ORLANDINA DE

Oliveira, Orlandina de. Migracion femenina, organizacion familiar y mercados laborales en Mexico. COMERCIO EXTERIOR (MEXICO, D.F.) July 1984, 34:676-87.

OMAN

Rohwer, Gertrude. Integration durch Ausbildung; eine Strategie zur Uberwindung sozialer Disparitaten in Oman: Bemerkungen uber die Partizipationschancen von Frauen am gesellschaftlichen Entwicklungsprozess in einem islamischen Land. ORIENT (HAMBURG) September 1984, 25:391-402. With English summary, p. 458.

OMVEDT, GAIL

Omvedt, Gail. Women and rural revolt in India. JOURNAL OF PEASANT STUDIES (LONDON) April 1978, 5:370-403. It is argued that in India, increasingly during the last decade, capitalism has developed in the countryside, and that, with the changing social relations of production, there has emerged a mass-based and militant women's movement ... This is illustrated ... especially for the state of Maharashtra.

On changing the concept and position of Persian women. By: Fischer, Michael M. J.. In: Women in the Muslim world. Edited by Lois Beck and Nikki Keddie. (Cambridge, MA, Harvard University Press, 1978), pp. 189-215.

On circular migration -- from the distaff side: women left behind in the forests of East Kalimantan. By: Colfer, Carol. INTERNATIONAL LABOUR OFFICE. WORLD EMPLOYMENT PROGRAMME RESEARCH. POPULATION AND LABOUR POLICIES PROGRAMME. WORKING PAPER (GENEVA) May 1983, No. 132:1-42. Focuses on male circular migration (or migration with the in;tent to return home) and its impact on the women who remain in the villages tending the farm. The area studied is East Kalimantan (Indonesian Borneo).

On legal change in Cameroon: women, marriage, and bridewealth. By: Geary, Christraud M. BOSTON UNIVERSITY. AFRICAN STUDIES CENTER. WORKING PAPERS (BOSTON) 1986, No. 113:1-37.

On the global assembly line women and multinationals. By: Mitter, Swasti. DEVELOPMENT (ROME) 1984, No. 4:31-33.

On the road to Nairobi '85. By: Shahani, Letizia R.. DEVELOPMENT (ROME) 1984, No. 4:85-86.

Only road. By: Carlier, Ana Bleyswyck de. In: Latin American women: the meek speak out. Edited by June H. Turner. (Silver Spring, MD, International Educational Development, 1980), pp. 42-50. Describes women in Peru.

Only you men have your needs satisfied. By: Luzuriaga Najera, Luz Vicenta. In: Latin American women: the meek speak out. Edited by June H. Turner. (Silver Spring, MD, International Educational Development, 1980), pp. 76-83. Discusses women of Ecuador.

OPPONG, CHRISTINE

Oppong, Christine and Abu, Katharine. Changing maternal role of Ghanaian women: impacts of education, migration and employment. INTERNATIONAL LABOUR OFFICE. WORLD EMPLOYMENT PROGRAMME RESEARCH. POPULATION AND LABOUR POLICIES PROGRAMME. WORKING PAPER (GENEVA) February 1984, No. 143:1-184.

Oppong, Christine and Church, Katie. Field guide to research on seven roles of women: focussed biographies. INTERNATIONAL LABOUR OFFICE. WORLD EMPLOYMENT PROGRAMME RESEARCH. POPULATION AND LABOUR POLICIES PROGRAMME. WORKING PAPER (GENEVA) May 1981, No. 106:1-52.

OPPONG, CHRISTINE

Oppong, Christine. Women's role and conjugal family system in Ghana. In: Changing position of women in family and society; a cross-national comparison. Edited by Eugen Lupri. Series: International studies in sociology and social anthropology, Vol. 34. (Leiden, E. J. Brill, 1983), pp. 331-43.

Les organisations feminines en Inde. By: Patel, Vibhuti. TIERS-MONDE (PARIS) April/June 1985, 26:351-57.

ORGANIZATION

Hearn, Jeff and Parkin, P. Wendy. Gender and organizations: a selective review and a critique of a neglected area. ORGANIZATION STUDIES (BERLIN) 1983, 4, No. 3:219-42.

Origin of the family. By: Gough, Kathleen. In: Toward an anthropology of women. Edited by Rayna R. Reiter. (New York, Monthly Review Press, 1975), pp. 51-76.

ORLANSKY, DORA

Orlansky, Dora and Dubrovsky, Silvia. Effects of rural-urban migration on women's role and status in Latin America. Series: Reports and papers in the social sciences, No. 41. (Paris, Unesco, 1978), 50 pp.

OSAWA, MACHIKO

Osawa, Machiko. Wage gap in Japan: changing patterns of labor force participation, schooling and tenure. ECONOMICS RESEARCH CENTER. NORC [NATIONAL OPINION RESEARCH CENTER] DISCUSSION PAPER SERIES (CHICAGO) April 1986, No. 86-1:1-29. Examines how changes in schooling and work experience over time between men and women workers have affected wage differentials observed in the post-WWII period in Japan.

Osawa, Machiko. Working mothers: changing patterns of employment and fertility in Japan. ECONOMICS RESEARCH CENTER. NORC [NATIONAL OPINION RESEARCH CENTER] DISCUSSION PAPER SERIES (CHICAGO) June 1986, No. 86-5:1-58. In this paper the differential fertility rates between paid women workers in the formal sector and family workers in the informal sector are featured to analyze the reasons why the Japanese fertility trend in the post-World War II period differs from other nations.

OSMAN, FATHI

Osman, Fathi. Muslim women's role in society. ARABIA; THE ISLAMIC WORLD REVIEW (EAST BURNHAM) April 1986, 5:11-12.

Our changing life in India. By: Nayer, Sushilla. In: Women in the new Asia; the changing social roles of men and women in South and South-east Asia. Edited by Barbara E. Ward. ([Paris], Unesco, 1963), pp. 204-16.

Our national inferiority complex: a cause for violence? By: Campos, Ana Audilia Moreira de. In: Latin American women: the meek speak out. Edited by June H. Turner. (Silver Spring, MD, International Educational Development, 1980), pp. 66-72. A commentary by a rural woman in El Salvador.

OURESHI, SARFRAZ KHAN

Oureshi, Sarfraz Khan. Notes on determinants of paid employment for women in Pakistan. In: Women and development, perspectives from South and Southeast Asia. Edited by Rounaq Jahan and Hanna Papanek. (Dacca, Bangladesh Institute of Law and International Affairs, 1979), pp. 219-27.

OUSSEDIK, FATMA

Oussedik, Fatma. Conditions required for women to conduct research on women in the Arab region. In: Social science research on women in the Arab world. (London, Frances Pinter; Paris, Unesco, 1984), pp. 113-21.

Oversights, insights and new sites. By: Catley-Carlson, Margaret. DEVELOPMENT (ROME) 1984, No. 4:82-84.

PACIFIC IS.-GENERAL

Pacific women on the move. PACIFIC PERSPECTIVE (SUVA) 1983, 11, No. 2:1-84.

Women's work may help to make jobs for the girls. PACIFIC ISLANDS MONTHLY (SYDNEY) May 1986, 57:22-23.

Pacific women on the move. PACIFIC PERSPECTIVE (SUVA) 1983, 11, No. 2:1-84.

Paddy production, processing and women workers in India - the south versus the northeast. By: Sen, Gita. CENTRE FOR DEVELOPMENT STUDIES. WORKING PAPER (ULLOOR, TRIVANDRUM) December 1983, No. 186.

PAKISTAN

Khan, Nighat S. Women Pakistan: position, status and movement. JOURNAL OF SOCIAL STUDIES (DHAKA) October 1985, No. 30:27-40.

Mohiuddin, Yasmeen. Economic role of women: a case of occupational dependency. PAKISTAN & GULF ECONOMIST (KARACHI) February 2, 1985, 4:12-15.

PAKISTAN

Mohiuddin, Yasmeen. Female employment and social status; survey. PAKISTAN & GULF ECONOMIST (KARACHI) April 6, 1985, 4:30-33. Report based on a survey of 216 female handicraft workers located at major centres of handicraft work in north, middle and south Sind.

Mohiuddin, Yasmeen. Female handicraft workers; the invisible hand. PAKISTAN & GULF ECONOMIST (KARACHI) July 20, 1985, 4:44-47. The purpose of this study is to investigate the economic role and status of these invisible producers in the all-female handicraft production in Sind, Pakistan.

Pakistan: mor and tor; binary and opposing models of Pukhtun womanhood. By: Akbar, S. and Ahmed, Zeenat. In: The endless day: some case material on Asian rural women. Edited by T. Scarlett Epstein and Rosemary A. Watts. Series: Women in development, Vol. 3. (Oxford, England, New York, Pergamon Press, 1981), pp. 31-46.

PAKIZEGI, BEHNAZ

Pakizegi, Behnaz. Legal and social positions of Iranian women. In: Women in the Muslim world. Edited by Lois Beck and Nikki Keddie. (Cambridge, MA, Harvard University Press, 1978), pp. 216-26.

PALABRICA-COSTELLO, MARILOU

Palabrica-Costello, Marilou. Female domestic servants in Cagayan de Oro, Philippines: social and economic implications of employment in a 'premodern' occupational role. In: Women in the urban and industrial workforce; Southeast and East Asia. Edited by Gavin W. Jones. Series: Development Studies Centre. Monograph, No. 33. (Canberra, Australia, Australian National University, 1984), pp. 235-50. Series edited by Helen Hughes.

PALMER, INGRID

Palmer, Ingrid. Women's issues and project appraisal. IDS BULLETIN, INSTITUTE OF DEVELOPMENT STUDIES AT THE UNIVERSITY OF SUSSEX (BRIGHTON) October 1981, 12:32-39.

PAN AMERICAN HEALTH ORGANIZATION

Pan American Health Organization. Women, health and development in the Americas; an annotated bibliography. Series: Scientific publication, No. 464. (Washington, Pan American Health Organization, Pan American Sanitary Bureau, Regional Office of the World Health Organization, 1984), 106 pp.

PANEL ANALYSIS

Jakubson, George. Sensitivity of labor supply parameter estimates to unobserved individual effects: fixed and random effects estimates in a nonlinear model using panel data. PRINCETON UNIVERSITY. INDUSTRIAL RELATIONS SECTION. WORKING PAPER (PRINCETON) August 1986, No. 210:1-37; A1-A4 (various pagings).

PANI, DHARANI K

Pani, Dharani K. Women; dew does well. BUSINESS INDIA (BOMBAY) January 26, 1987, No. 232:p. 34. Discusses the work of Tamilnadu Corporation for the Development of Women Ltd (DEW) in bringing economic independence to women belonging to the economically weaker sections of society.

PAPOLA, T. S.

Papola, T. S.. Women workers in an Indian urban labour market. INTERNATIONAL LABOUR OFFICE. WORLD EMPLOYMENT PROGRAMME RESEARCH. POPULATION AND LABOUR POLICIES PROGRAMME. WORKING PAPER (GENEVA) September 1983, No. 141:1-67.

Paraprofessionals in rural development: issues in field-level staffing for agricultural projects. By: Esman, Milton J. (Milton Jacob). Series: World Bank Staff Working Papers, No. 573. (Washington, DC, World Bank, 1983), 55 pp.

PAREDES, RICARDO

Paredes, Ricardo. Diferencias de ingreso entre hombres y mujeres en el Gran Santiago 1969 y 1981. ESTUDIOS DE ECONOMIA (SANTIAGO) First semester 1982, No. 18:97-121. With English summary.

PARKIN, P. WENDY

Hearn, Jeff and Parkin, P. Wendy. Gender and organizations: a selective review and a critique of a neglected area. ORGANIZATION STUDIES (BERLIN) 1983, 4, No. 3:219-42.

Paro e inactividad de las mujeres en Argelia: lo visible y lo invisible. By: Hakiki-Talahite, Fatiha. DESARROLLO Y SOCIEDAD (BOGOTA) January 1984, No. 13:139-59. With English summary.

PARPART, JANE L.

Parpart, Jane L.. Class and gender on the copperbelt: women in Northern Rhodesian copper mining areas 1926-1964. BOSTON UNIVERSITY. AFRICAN STUDIES CENTER. WORKING PAPERS (BOSTON) 1983, No. 77:1-29.

La participation des femmes a l'economie egyptienne: tendances et evolutions. By: Khouri-Dagher, Nadia. TIERS-MONDE (PARIS) April/June 1985, 26:335-50.

La participation des femmes aux cooperatives mixtes: temps et ideologie. By: Bisilliat, Jeanne. TIERS-MONDE (PARIS) April/June 1985, 26:409-15.

Participation of Arab women in the labour force: development factors and policies. By: Azzam, Henry T.. INTERNATIONAL LABOUR OFFICE. WORLD EMPLOYMENT PROGRAMME RESEARCH. POPULATION AND EMPLOYMENT PROJECT. WORKING PAPERS (GENEVA) 1979, No. 80:1-83.

Participation of women in African economies. By: Mbilinyi, Marjorie J.. UNIVERSITY OF DAR ES SALAAM. ECONOMIC RESEARCH BUREAU. PAPER (DAR-ES-SALAAM) 1971, No. 71.12:1-32.

Participation of women in education in the Third World. By: Bowman, Mary Jean and Anderson, C. Arnold. COMPARATIVE EDUCATION REVIEW (NEW YORK) June 1980, 24:S13-32.

Participation of women in socio-economic development: indicators as tools for development planning; the case of India. By: Mitra, Asok. In: Women and development: indicators of their changing role. Series: Socio-economic studies, No. 3. (Paris, Unesco, 1981), pp. 49-69.

Participation of women in socio-economic development: indicators as tools for development planning; the case of the Commonwealth Caribbean. By: Massiah, Joycelin. In: Women and development: indicators of their changing role. Series: Socio-economic studies, No. 3. (Paris, Unesco, 1981), pp. 71-100.

Participation of women in the economic and social development of their countries. Report of the Secretary-General. By: United Nations. Secretary-General. (New York, United Nations, 1970), 104 pp. United Nations Publication. Sales no.: E.70.IV.4.

Die Partnerschaft der Manner ist (noch) nicht die Partnerschaft der Frauen; empirische Befunde zum Geschlechterverhaltnis aus der Frauenperspektive. By: Metz-Gockel, Sigrid and Muller, Ursula. WSI-MITTEILUNGEN (DUSSELDORF) August 1986, 39:549-58.

PASTNER, CARROLL MCC.

Pastner, Carroll McC.. Status of women and property on a Baluchistan oasis in Pakistan. In: Women in the Muslim world. Edited by Lois Beck and Nikki Keddie. (Cambridge, MA, Harvard University Press, 1978), pp. 434-50.

PATEL, I. G.

Patel, I. G.. Promotion of credit to women entrepreneurs. RESERVE BANK OF INDIA, BULLETIN (BOMBAY) December 1981, 35:1059-64. Address at the International Workshop of Women's Banking at Bhaikaka Bhavan, Ahmedabad on December 1, 1981.

PATEL, VIBHUTI

Patel, Vibhuti. Les organisations feminines en Inde. TIERS-MONDE (PARIS) April/June 1985, 26:351-57.

Patel, Vibhuti. Women's liberation in India. NEW LEFT REVIEW (LONDON) September/October 1985, No. 153:75-86.

Patrons, politics, and schools; an arena for Brazilian women. By: Miller, Linda. STUDIES IN THIRD WORLD SOCIETIES (WILLIAMSBURG) March 1981, No. 15:67-89.

Patterns of social change in a Burmese family. By: Gyi, Ni Ni. In: Women in the new Asia; the changing social roles of men and women in South and South-east Asia. Edited by Barbara E. Ward. ([Paris], Unesco, 1963), pp. 138-48.

PAUKERT, LIBA

Paukert, Liba. Personal preference, social change or economic necessity? Why women work. LABOUR AND SOCIETY (GENEVA) October/December 1982, 7:311-31.

Paukert, Liba. Employment and unemployment of women in OECD countries. (Paris, Organisation for Economic Co-operation and Development, 1984), 88 pp. Prepared for the OECD's Working Party on the Role of Women in the Economy.

La paysanne africaine au travail. By: Jouffrey, Roger. AFRIQUE CONTEMPORAINE, DOCUMENTS D'AFRIQUE NOIRE ET DE MADAGASCAR (PARIS) April/June 1983, 22:23-29.

PEARSON, RICHARD

Pearson, Richard. So few women in engineering. NATURE (LONDON) October 2, 1986, 323:p. 474.

PEASANTRY

Bifani, Patricia. How Kenyan peasants, pastoralists and peri-urban women see water problems. WATERLINES (LONDON) January 1986, 4:16-19.

PEBLEY, ANNE R.

Trussell, James and Pebley, Anne R.. Potential impact of changes in fertility on infant, child, and maternal mortality. Series: World Bank Staff Working Papers, No. 698; Population and Development Series, No. 23. (Washington, DC, World Bank, 1984), 44 pp.

PEERS, JO

McAndrew, Maggie and Peers, Jo. New Soviet woman: model or myth. Series: Change International Reports: Women and Society, No. 3. (London, Change International Reports, 1981), 28 pp.

PELZER WHITE, CHRISTINE

Pelzer White, Christine. Collectives and the status of women: the Vietnamese experience. CERES, FAO REVIEW ON AGRICULTURE AND DEVELOPMENT (ROME) July/August 1983, 16:22-26.

PENVENNE, JEANNE

Penvenne, Jeanne. Making our own way: women working in Lourenco Marques, 1900-1933. BOSTON UNIVERSITY. AFRICAN STUDIES CENTER. WORKING PAPERS (BOSTON) 1986, No. 114:1-20.

People of Bogota: who they are, what they earn, where they live. By: Mohan, Rakesh. Series: World Bank. City Study Research Project. City Study Project Paper, No. 6; World Bank Staff Working Paper, No. 390. (Washington, DC, World Bank, 1980), 1980.

Perceptions of family planning among rural Kenyan women. By: Dow, Thomas E., Jr. and Werner, Linda H.. STUDIES IN FAMILY PLANNING (NEW YORK) February 1983, 14:35-43.

PERRY, ALISON

Perry, Alison. Bearing the burden. WEST AFRICA (LONDON) April 22, 1985, No. 3530:785-86. Looks at the important role women playin the agricultural sector and at the severe handicpas they face, due to their double work-load and a discriminatory system.

PERRY, ALISON

Perry, Alison. Women's decade; plotting ways for women. WEST AFRICA (LONDON) August 5, 1985, No. 3545:p. 1596. Reports on the final document adopted at the United Nations' women's conference in Nairobi, Kenya.

Persistence of women's invisibility in agriculture: theoretical and policy lessons from Lesotho and Sierra Leone. By: Safilios-Rothschild, Constantina. POPULATION COUNCIL. CENTER FOR POLICY STUDIES. WORKING PAPERS (NEW YORK) September 1982, No.88:1-31.

Personal preference, social change or economic necessity? Why women work. By: Paukert, Liba. LABOUR AND SOCIETY (GENEVA) October/December 1982, 7:311-31.

Perspective: United Nations Decade for Women 1976-1985; 'really only a beginning... UNITED NATIONS. UN CHRONICLE (NEW YORK) July/August 1985, 22: Special survey, p. i-xxiv.

Perspectives of Third World women: an introduction. By: Lindsay, Beverly. In: Comparative perspectives of Third World women: the impact of race, sex and class. Edited by Beverly Lindsay. (New York, Praeger, 1980), pp. 1-30.

Perspectives on the evolution of sex differences. By: Leibowitz, Lila. In: Toward an anthropology of women. Edited by Rayna R. Reiter. (New York, Monthly Review Press, 1975), pp. 20-35.

PERU

Babb, Florence E.. Women in the marketplace: petty commerce in Peru. REVIEW OF RADICAL POLITICAL ECONOMICS (NEW YORK) Spring 1984, 16:45-59.

Deere, Carmen Diana. Division of labor by sex in agriculture; a Peruvian case study. ECONOMIC DEVELOPMENT AND CULTURAL CHANGE (CHICAGO) July 1982, 30:795-811.

Edmunds, Marilyn and Helzner, Judith F.. Peru-mujer: women organizing for development. PATHPAPERS, PATHFINDER FUND (CHESTNUT HILL, MASS.) August 1982, No. 9:1-18.

Scott, Alison MacEwen. Desarrollo dependiente y la segregacion ocupacional por sexo. DESARROLLO Y SOCIEDAD (BOGOTA) January 1984, No. 13:99-136. With English summary.

PERU

Scott, Alison MacEwen. Women and industrialisation: examining the "female marginalisation" thesis. JOURNAL OF DEVELOPMENT STUDIES (LONDON) July 1986, 22:649-80. The article argues for attention to be paid to the micro-level processes which give rise to women's marginalisation.

Smith, Michael L.. Women of Peru's slums raise sights with communal kitchens. WASHINGTON POST (WASHINGTON) September 16, 1984, p. A13.

Tienda, Marta. Community characteristics, women's education, and fertility in Peru. STUDIES IN FAMILY PLANNING (NEW YORK) July/August 1984, 15:162-69.

Wehkamp, Andy. Luchas colectivas de las obreras peruanas: los motivos de participacion y alejamiento. BOLETIN DE ESTUDIOS LATINO-AMERICANOS Y DEL CARIBE (AMSTERDAM) December 1984, No. 37:69-83.

Peru-Mujer: women organizing for development. By: Edmunds, Marilyn and Helzner, Judith F.. Series: Pathpapers series, No. 9. (Chestnut Hill, MA, Pathfinder Fund, 1982), 18 pp.

Peru-mujer: women organizing for development. By: Edmunds, Marilyn and Helzner, Judith F.. PATHPAPERS, PATHFINDER FUND (CHESTNUT HILL, MASS.) August 1982, No. 9:1-18.

PETERS, EMRYS L.

Peters, Emrys L.. Status of women in four Middle East communities. In: Women in the Muslim world. Edited by Lois Beck and Nikki Keddie. (Cambridge, MA, Harvard University Press, 1978), pp. 311-50. The four communities examined here include the Bedouin of Cyrenaica (Libya), a horticultural community of Shiite Muslims in south Lebanon, olive farmers, Sunni Muslims, in Tripolitania (Libya), and a Maronite Christian village in central Lebanon.

PETTIGREW, JOYCE

Pettigrew, Joyce. Problems concerning tubectomy operations in rural areas of Punjab. ECONOMIC AND POLITICAL WEEKLY (BOMBAY) June 30, 1984, 19:995-1002.

PHARR, SUSAN J.

Pharr, Susan J.. Japan: historical and contemporary perspectives. In: Women: roles and status in eight countries. Edited by Janet Zollinger Giele and Audrey Chapman Smock. (New York, John Wiley, 1977), pp. 219-55.

PHILIPP, THOMAS

Philipp, Thomas. Feminism and nationalist politics in Egypt. In: Women in the Muslim world. Edited by Lois Beck and Nikki Keddie. (Cambridge, MA, Harvard University Press, 1978), pp. 277-94.

PHILIPPINES

Herrin, Alejandro N.. Female work participation and fertility in a Philippine setting: a test of alternative models. UNIVERSITY OF THE PHILIPPINES. SCHOOL OF ECONOMICS. DISCUSSION PAPER (QUEZON) October 1980, No. 8005:1-99.

Ocampo-Kalfors, Sheilah. Liberated -- but tied to the old loyalties. FAR EASTERN ECONOMIC REVIEW (HONGKONG) January 5, 1984, 123:32-34. Describes how women in the Philippines have progressed rapidly in most fields, despite existing laws and traditions that discriminate against them.

Szanton, M. Cristina Blanc. "Big women" and politics in a Philippine fishing town. STUDIES IN THIRD WORLD SOCIETIES (WILLIAMSBURG) June 1981, No. 16:123-41.

Tidalgo, Rosa Linda P. Integration of women in Philippine development. UNIVERSITY OF THE PHILIPPINES. SCHOOL OF ECONOMICS. DISCUSSION PAPER (QUEZON) April 1985, No. 8502:1-82.

Philippines: canvasses of women in crisis. By: Villariba, Maria C.. Series: Change International Reports: Women in Society, No. 7. (London, Change International Reports, [1982]?), 15 pp.

PHILIPPINES. BUREAU OF WOMEN AND MINORS

Philippines. Bureau of Women and Minors. Status of working women in the Philippines. (Manila, 1975), 53 pp.

PHONGPAICHIT, RASUK

Phongpaichit, Rasuk. Bangkok masseuses: origins, status and prospects. In: Women in the urban and industrial workforce; Southeast and East Asia. Edited by Gavin W. Jones. Series: Development Studies Centre. Monograph, No. 33. (Canberra, Australia, Australian National University, 1984), pp. 251-58. Series edited by Helen Hughes.

PIAMPITI, SUWANLEE

Arnold, Fred and Piampiti, Suwanlee. Female migration in Thailand. In: Women in the cities of Asia: migration and urban adaptation. Edited by James T. Fawcett, Siew-Ean Khoo and Peter C. Smith. (Boulder, CO, Westview Press, 1984), pp. 143-64.

Piampiti, Suwanlee. Female migrants in Bangkok metropolis. In: Women in the cities of Asia: migration and urban adaptation. Edited by James T. Fawcett, Siew-Ean Khoo and Peter C. Smith. (Boulder, CO, Westview Press, 1984), pp. 227-46.

PIETILA, HILKKA

Pietila, Hilkka. Women as an alternative culture here and now. DEVELOPMENT (ROME) 1984, No. 4:60-63. Asks if the female half of humanity could become the creators of an other development, which is more just and humane than the one we know today?

PIHO, VIRVE

Piho, Virve. Life and labor of the woman textile worker in Mexico City. In: Women cross-culturally: change and challenge. Edited by Ruby Rohrlich-Leavitt. (The Hague, Mouton, 1975), pp. 199-245.

PILLSBURY, BARBARA L. K.

Pillsbury, Barbara L. K.. Being female in a Muslim minority in China. In: Women in the Muslim world. Edited by Lois Beck and Nikki Keddie. (Cambridge, MA, Harvard University Press, 1978), pp. 651-73.

PIRIE, PETER

Khoo, Siew-Ean and Pirie, Peter. Female rural-to-urban migration in peninsular Malaysia. In: Women in the cities of Asia: migration and urban adaptation. Edited by James T. Fawcett, Siew-Ean Khoo and Peter C. Smith. (Boulder, CO, Westview Press, 1984), pp. 125-42.

PITTIN, RENEE

Pittin, Renee. Documentation and analysis of the invisible work of invisible women: a Nigerian case study. INTERNATIONAL LABOUR REVIEW (GENEVA) July/August 1984, 123:473-90. Discusses problems arising in the documentation and analysis of the work of secluded women. Focusing on the Muslim Hausa women of Katsina, Nigeria, the author contends that past surveys and censuses have grossly underestimated these women's economic contribution to the Nigerian economy, and that this neglect is increasing.

Une place au marche de Sopocachi; travail de femmes en Bolivie. By: Hadorn, Verena. ENTWICKLUNG, DEVELOPPEMENT (BERNE) 1985, No. 19:14-16.

La place des femmes au sein des societes et groupements cooperatifs (enquetes du BIT). By: Mavrogiannis, Dionysos. TIERS-MONDE (PARIS) April/June 1985, 26:383-92.

Le plan d'action de Lagos et les femmes. By: Savane, Marie Angelique. AFRICA DEVELOPMENT (DAKAR) January/June 1982, 7:142-48. With English summary.

Planning-centred approach to project evaluation: women in mainstream development projects. By: Staudt, Kathleen. PUBLIC ADMINISTRATION AND DEVELOPMENT (CHICHESTER) January/March 1985, 5:25-37. Describes the process and outcomes of a 'planning-centred' approach to three development projects in the Caribbean.

Plantation sector in Sri Lanka: recent changes in the welfare of children and women. By: Jayawardena, Kumari. WORLD DEVELOPMENT (OXFORD) March 1984, 12, Special issue:317-28.

Plight of Africa's women. By: Harrison, Charles. TIMES (LONDON) August 1, 1985, p. 4. Suggests that female workers' lack of status can be blamed for much of the famine crisis.

Plight of rural women: alternatives for action. By: Ahmad, Zubeida. INTERNATIONAL LABOUR REVIEW (GENEVA) July/August 1980, 119:425-38.

Poland: women's experience under socialism. By: Sokolowska, Magdalena. In: Women: roles and status in eight countries. Edited by Janet Zollinger Giele and Audrey Chapman Smock. (New York, John Wiley, 1977), pp. 349-381.

Policy strategies at the end of the decade. By: Staudt, Kathleen. AFRICA REPORT (NEW YORK) March/April 1985, 30:71-5.

Politics and female status in North Africa: a reconsideration of development theory. By: Marshall, Susan E.. ECONOMIC DEVELOPMENT AND CULTURAL CHANGE (CHICAGO) April 1984, 32:499-524. Assesses the applicability of two major theoretical perspectives for explaining national differences in female status among the five North African Muslim states of Morocco, Algeria, Tunisia, Libya, and Egypt, utilizing a composite female modernity index derived from secondary sources. The author also proposes an alternative theoretical framework to explain these divergent national patterns of female participation, highlights the central role of political elites in the late-developing states and suggests an empirical relationship between government policy toward women and female access to the modern sector in North Africa.

POLITICS AND GOVERNMENT

Brana-Shute, Rosemary. Working class Afro-Surinamese women and national politics: traditions and changes in an independent state. STUDIES IN THIRD WORLD SOCIETIES (WILLIAMSBURG) March 1981, No. 15:33-56.

Kearney, Robert N.. Women in politics in Sri Lanka. ASIAN SURVEY (BERKELEY, CALIF.) July 1981, 21:729-46.

Kitchener, Julie. Inside Libya today. NEW AFRICAN (LONDON) October 1983, No. 193:10-14. Examines the strange paradoxes that give Libya its distinctive character, including the emancipation of Libyan women.

Molyneux, Maxine. Women's emancipation under socialism: a model for the Third World? WORLD DEVELOPMENT (OXFORD) September/October 1981, 9:1019-37. Examines the policies adopted by socialist states to improve the position of women and traces some of these inequalities to the policies themselves, and to the theoretical assumptions underlying them.

Women and politics in twentieth century Latin America. STUDIES IN THIRD WORLD SOCIETIES (WILLIAMSBURG) March 1981, no. 15:1-136.

Politics of healing in Malaysia. By: Laderman, Carol. STUDIES IN THIRD WORLD SOCIETIES (WILLIAMSBURG) June 1981, No. 16:143-58. Discusses varying governmental attitudes towards midwives (bidan), who, with few exceptions, are women, and to native doctors (bomoh), who may be either male or female.

POOL, D. IAN

Pool, D. Ian. Changes in Canadian female labour force participation and some possible implications for conjugal power. In: Women in the family and the economy: an international comparative survey. Edited by George Kurian and Ratna Ghosh. (Westport, CT, Greenwood Press, 1981), pp. 245-56.

POPULATION

Berliner, Joseph S.. Education, labor-force participation, and fertility in the USSR. JOURNAL OF COMPARATIVE ECONOMICS (NEW YORK) June 1983, 7:131-57. The effect of education on Soviet fertility and female labor participation is analyzed in terms of the neoclassical theory of the household.

Chaudhury, Rafiqul Huda. Female labour force status and fertility behaviour in Bangladesh: search for policy interventions. BANGLADESH DEVELOPMENT STUDIES (DACCA) September 1983, 11:59-102.

Chen, Lincoln C.. Where have the women gone? Insights from Bangladesh on low sex ratio of India's population. ECONOMIC AND POLITICAL WEEKLY (BOMBAY) March 6, 1982, 17:364-72.

Dabat, Christine and Modak, Marianne. Femmes et controle des naissances; refus, contraintes et vecus. INSTITUT UNIVERSITAIRE D'ETUDES DU DEVELOPPEMENT. ITINERAIRES: NOTES ET TRAVAUX (GENEVA) April 1981, No. 15:1-119.

Dow, Thomas E., Jr. and Werner, Linda H.. Perceptions of family planning among rural Kenyan women. STUDIES IN FAMILY PLANNING (NEW YORK) February 1983, 14:35-43.

Farnos, Alfonso and Gonzalez, Fernando. Role of women and demographic change in Cuba. INTERNATIONAL LABOUR OFFICE. WORLD EMPLOYMENT PROGRAMME RESEARCH. POPULATION AND LABOUR POLICIES PROGRAMME. WORKING PAPER (GENEVA) August 1983, No. 138:1-52.

Helmore, Kristin. Family ties: wives and mothers. CHRISTIAN SCIENCE MONITOR (BOSTON) December 18, 1985, p. 17-19. Part 2 of 5-part series entitled: "The neglected resource; women in the developing world." Author looks at marriage and motherhood in various cultures in the less developed countries.

POPULATION

Jain, Anrudh K. and Nag, Moni. Female primary education and fertility reduction in India. POPULATION COUNCIL. CENTER FOR POLICY STUDIES. WORKING PAPERS (NEW YORK) September 1985, No. 114:1-57.

Khandker, Shahidur R. Women's role in household productive activities and fertility in Bangladesh. YALE UNIVERSITY. ECONOMIC GROWTH CENTER. DISCUSSION PAPER (NEW HAVEN, CONN.) July 1985, No. 488:1-35. Seeks to identify the factors that may affect the role of women in the rural areas of a developing country and the possible impact of these factors on fertility.

Kuniansky, Anna. Soviet fertility, labor-force participation, and marital instabililty. JOURNAL OF COMPARATIVE ECONOMICS (NEW YORK) June 1983, 7:114-30.

McCormick, John and Akello, Grace. Africa's population crisis. NEW AFRICAN (LONDON) January 1984, No. 196:21-23. Discusses the causes of Africa's runaway population growth, and asks how womeen could benefit from population control.

Newland, Kathleen. Women and population growth: choice beyond child-bearing. WORLDWATCH PAPER (WASHINGTON) December 1977, No. 16:1-32.

Numero special: radioscopie du chomage. L'ECONOMIE DE LA REUNION (STE-CLOTILDE) September/October 1986, No. 25:1-32.

Oppong, Christine and Abu, Katharine. Changing maternal role of Ghanaian women: impacts of education, migration and employment. INTERNATIONAL LABOUR OFFICE. WORLD EMPLOYMENT PROGRAMME RESEARCH. POPULATION AND LABOUR POLICIES PROGRAMME. WORKING PAPER (GENEVA) February 1984, No. 143:1-184.

Siqueira Wiarda, Ieda and Helzner, Judith Frye. Women, population, and international development in Latin America: a 1984 assessment. MANAGING INTERNATIONAL DEVELOPMENT (ARMONK, N.Y.) September/October 1984, 1:84-106.

Tienda, Marta. Community characteristics, women's education, and fertility in Peru. STUDIES IN FAMILY PLANNING (NEW YORK) July/August 1984, 15:162-69.

POPULATION

Wiarda, Ieda Siqueira and Helzner, Judith F.. Women, population and international development in Latin America: persistent legacies and new perceptions for the 1980's. UNIVERSITY OF MASSACHUSETTS AT AMHERST. PROGRAM IN LATIN AMERICAN STUDIES. OCCASIONAL PAPERS SERIES (AMHERST) April 1981, No. 13:1-40.

POPULATION CONTROL

Jain, Anrudh K. and Nag, Moni. Importance of female primary education for fertility reduction in India. ECONOMIC AND POLITICAL WEEKLY (BOMBAY) September 6, 1986, 21:1602-08.

Position of women in the labour market in Hong Kong: a content analysis of the recruitment advertisements. By: Ho, Suk-ching. LABOUR AND SOCIETY (GENEVA) September 1985, 10:333-44.

POSTEL-COSTER, ELS

Postel-Coster, Els. Misverstanden rond de kostwinner in het ontwikkelingsbeleid. INTERNATIONALE SPECTATOR (THE HAGUE) September 1983, 37:549-55.

Post-war fertility and female labour force participation rates. By: Sprague, Alison. OXFORD UNIVERSITY. INSTITUTE OF ECONOMICS AND STATISTICS. APPLIED ECONOMICS DISCUSSION PAPER (OXFORD) June 1986, No. 9:1-35.

Potential impact of changes in fertility on infant, child, and maternal mortality. By: Trussell, James and Pebley, Anne R.. Series: World Bank Staff Working Papers, No. 698; Population and Development Series, No. 23. (Washington, DC, World Bank, 1984), 44 pp.

Potraits de femmes: les intellectuelles zairoises. By: Verheust, Therese. CAHIERS DU CEDAF (BRUSSELS) October 1985, No. 6:1-148.

POVERTY

Banerjee, Nirmala. Women and poverty: report on a workshop. ECONOMIC AND POLITICAL WEEKLY (BOMBAY) October 1, 1983, 18:1693-98.

Chen, Marty. Poverty, gender, and work in Bangladesh. ECONOMIC AND POLITICAL WEEKLY (BOMBAY) February 1, 1986, 21:217-22. Redefines the three broad classes of rural households in terms of women's labour and income and describes the process of impoverishment from the perspective of women.

POVERTY

Varma, Margaret. Dual oppression: to be poor and also a woman. RUTGERS UNIVERSITY/COOK COLLEGE INTERNATIONAL AGRICULTURE AND FOOD PROGRAM. WORKING PAPER SERIES (NEW BRUNSWICK, NJ) 1985, No. 5:1-9. Deals with women and poverty, and particularly, with women in extreme povelrty and exclusion--women of the fourth world.

Poverty, gender, and work in Bangladesh. By: Chen, Marty. ECONOMIC AND POLITICAL WEEKLY (BOMBAY) February 1, 1986, 21:217-22. Redefines the three broad classes of rural households in terms of women's labour and income and describes the process of impoverishment from the perspective of women.

POWELL, DORIAN

Powell, Dorian. Role of women in the Caribbean. SOCIAL AND ECONOMIC STUDIES (MONA, JAMAICA) June 1984, 33:97-122.

PRADHAN, BINA

Pradhan, Bina. Women and development: the overlooked link. JOURNAL OF DEVELOPMENT AND ADMINISTRATIVE STUDIES (KATHMANDU) June/December 1981, 3:172-202.

PRIMARY EDUCATION

Jain, Anrudh K. and Nag, Moni. Importance of female primary education for fertility reduction in India. ECONOMIC AND POLITICAL WEEKLY (BOMBAY) September 6, 1986, 21:1602-08.

Problems concerning tubectomy operations in rural areas of Punjab. By: Pettigrew, Joyce. ECONOMIC AND POLITICAL WEEKLY (BOMBAY) June 30, 1984, 19:995-1002.

PRODUCTIVITY

Lele, Uma. Women and structural transformation. ECONOMIC DEVELOPMENT AND CULTURAL CHANGE (CHICAGO) January 1986, 34:195-221. The primary objective of this article is to explore women's distinguishing role as economic actors in traditional societies under quite different social and production-organization systems.

Progress in India - but not for women. By: Wichterich, Christa. D & C, DEVELOPMENT AND COOPERATION (BONN) March/April 1985, No. 2:18, 20. Looks at the impact of a wave of revolutions -- the "Green Revolution", which has increased rice and wheat yields, the "White Revolution", which turned traditional milk production upside down, and a "Blue" one, which modernized fish production.

PROJECT APPRAISAL

Palmer, Ingrid. Women's issues and project appraisal. IDS BULLETIN, INSTITUTE OF DEVELOPMENT STUDIES AT THE UNIVERSITY OF SUSSEX (BRIGHTON) October 1981, 12:32-39.

PROJECT EVALUATION

Staudt, Kathleen. Planning-centred approach to project evaluation: women in mainstream development projects. PUBLIC ADMINISTRATION AND DEVELOPMENT (CHICHESTER) January/March 1985, 5:25-37. Describes the process and outcomes of a 'planning-centred' approach to three development projects in the Caribbean.

Projects for women in the Third World: explaining their misbehavior. By: Buvinic, Mayra. WORLD DEVELOPMENT (OXFORD) May 1986, 14:653-64. Explains why the economic objectives of a large number of income-generation projects for poor women in the Third World have evolved into welfare action during implementation.

Promotion of credit to women entrepreneurs. By: Patel, I. G.. RESERVE BANK OF INDIA, BULLETIN (BOMBAY) December 1981, 35:1059-64. Address at the International Workshop of Women's Banking at Bhaikaka Bhavan, Ahmedabad on December 1, 1981.

PROPERTY

Jahangir, B. K. Women and property in rural Bangladesh. JOURNAL OF SOCIAL STUDIES (DHAKA) October 1986, No. 34:87-95.

Protective legislation and equal opportunity and treatment for women in Spain. By: Jimenez Butragueno, Maria de los Angeles. INTERNATIONAL LABOUR REVIEW (GENEVA) March/April 1982, 121:185-98.

Protestant women's associations in Freetown, Sierre Leone. By: Steady, Filomina Chioma. In: Women in Africa: studies in social and economic change. Edited by Nancy J. Hafkin and Edna G. Bay. (Stanford, Stanford University Press, 1976), pp. 213-37.

Providence and prostitution: image and reality for women in Buddhist Thailand. By: Thitsa, Khin. Series: Change International Reports: Women in Society, No. 2. (London, Change International Reports, 1980), 27 pp.

PUBLIC HEALTH

Buvinic, Mayra and Leslie, Joanne. Health care for women in Latin America and the Caribbean. STUDIES IN FAMILY PLANNING (NEW YORK) March 1981, 12:112-15.

Laderman, Carol. Politics of healing in Malaysia. STUDIES IN THIRD WORLD SOCIETIES (WILLIAMSBURG) June 1981, No. 16:143-58. Discusses varying governmental attitudes towards midwives (bidan), who, with few exceptions, are women, and to native doctors (bomoh), who may be either male or female.

Naisho, Joyce. Health care for women in the Sudan. WORLD HEALTH FORUM (GENEVA) 1982, 3,No.2:164-65.

Wolfe, Barbara L. and Behrman, Jere R.. Determinants of child health, mortality, and nutrition in a developing country. UNIVERSITY OF WISCONSIN-MADISON. INSTITUTE FOR RESEARCH ON POVERTY. DISCUSSION PAPERS (MADISON) January 1981, No. 643-80:1-53. The authors use data collected in a cross-sectional multipurpose survey of women of childbearing age in Nicaragua.

PULEA, MERE

Pulea, Mere. Women, employment and development. PACIFIC PERSPECTIVE (SUVA) 1983, 11, No. 2:18-28.

PURCELL, DEBORAH ROSS

Purcell, Deborah Ross. Integrating women into development; an investment in human capital. HORIZONS, U.S. AGENCY FOR INTERNATIONAL DEVELOPMENT (WASHINGTON) July/August 1983, 2:20-23. Discusses the work of AID's Office of Women in Development (WID).

PURYEAR, GWENDOLYN RANDALL

Puryear, Gwendolyn Randall. Black woman: liberated or oppressed? In: Comparative perspectives of Third World women: the impact of race, sex and class. Edited by Beverly Lindsay. (New York, Praeger, 1980), pp. 251-75.

RAASCH, SIBYLLE

Raasch, Sibylle. Mindestens die Halfte aller Arbeits- und Ausbildungsplatze fur Frauen? Zur Quotierungsforderung in dem Entwurf eines Antidiscriminierungsgesetzes der Grunen. WSI-MITTEILUNGEN (DUSSELDORF) August 1986, 39:575-82.

RAHARJO, YULFITA

Raharjo, Yulfita and Hull, Valerie. Employment patterns of educated women in Indonesian cities. In: Women in the urban and industrial workforce; Southeast and East Asia. Edited by Gavin W. Jones. Series: Development Studies Centre. Monograph, No. 33. (Canberra, Australia, Australian National University, 1984), pp. 101-28. Series edited by Helen Hughes.

RAHAT, NAVEED I.

Rahat, Naveed I.. Role of women in reciprocal relationships in a Punjab village. In: The endless day: some case material on Asian rural women. Edited by T. Scarlett Epstein and Rosemary A. Watts. Series: Women in development, Vol. 3. (Oxford, England, New York, Pergamon Press, 1981), pp. 47-81.

RAKOWSKI, CATHY A.

Saulniers, Suzanne Smith and Rakowski, Cathy A.. Women in the development process: a select bibliography on women in sub-Saharan Africa and Latin America. (Austin, Institute of Latin American Studies, University of Texas Press, 1977), 287 pp. A special publication of the Institute of Latin American Studies.

RAMACHANDRAN, P.

Ramachandran, P. and Shastri, P. P.. Intercensal urban Indian female participation rates and their variations, 1961-71: a census analysis. ECONOMIC AFFAIRS (CALCUTTA) October/December 1983, 28:816-28.

RAMAS, MARIA

Brenner, Johanna and Ramas, Maria. Rethinking women's oppression. NEW LEFT REVIEW (LONDON) March/April 1984, No. 144:33-71. The authors discuss some of the issues raised in Michele Barrett's Women's oppression today.

RAMAZANI, NESTA

Ramazani, Nesta. Arab women in the Gulf. MIDDLE EAST JOURNAL (WASHINGTON) Spring 1985, 39:258-76.

RAO, AMIYA

Rao, Amiya. Cost of development projects; women among the 'willing evacuees'. ECONOMIC AND POLITICAL WEEKLY (BOMBAY) March 22, 1986, 21:474-76. Describes the heavy price of development paid by India's women.

RASSAM, AMAL

Rassam, Amal. Introduction: Arab women; the status of research in the social science and the status of women. In: Social science research on women in the Arab world. (London, Frances Pinter; Paris, Unesco, 1984), pp. 1-13.

Raw, the cooked, and the half-baked: a note on the division of labor by sex. By: Guyer, Jane I.. BOSTON UNIVERSITY. AFRICAN STUDIES CENTER. WORKING PAPERS (BOSTON) 1981, No. 48:1-12.

RAY, A. K. AND RANGARAO, I. V

Ray, A. K. and Rangarao, I. V. Impact of technological changes on economic status of female labour. INDIAN JOURNAL OF AGRICULTURAL ECONOMICS (BOMBAY) July/September 1985, 40:244-52.

Reaching beyond university walls. By: Antrobus, Peggy. DEVELOPMENT (ROME) 1984, No. 4:45-49. Describes International Development have provided me with the encouragement to write about the work of the Women and Development (WAND) Unit of the Extra-Mural Department of the University of the West Indies (UWI): SID's Grassroots Strategies and Initiatives Programme (GRIS), and its sincere attempt to integrate a serious concern for women in development issues within the overall programme.

Rebels or status-seekers? Women as spirit mediums in East Africa. By: Berger, Iris. In: Women in Africa: studies in social and economic change. Edited by Nancy J. Hafkin and Edna G. Bay. (Stanford, Stanford University Press, 1976), pp. 157-81.

RECCHINI DE LATTES, ZULMA.

Recchini de Lattes, Zulma.. Family and female participation in the labor market in Latin America. LATIN AMERICAN RESEARCH REVIEW (ALBUQUERQUE, NM) 1982, 17, No. 1:101-04.

Recent research on women in development; review article. By: Schuster, Ilsa. JOURNAL OF DEVELOPMENT STUDIES (LONDON) July 1982, 18:511-35.

Recognizing the "invisible" woman in development: the World Bank's experience. By: World Bank. (Washington, World Bank, 1979), 33 pp.

Recommendation on women in developing countries: aspects of development cooperation. By: Nationale Advies Raad Voor Ontwikkelingssamenwerking (Netherlands). Series: Publication of the National Advisory Council for Development Corporation, No. 67. (The Hague, Ministry of Foreign Affairs, 1980), 73 pp.

REDDY, GOVIN

Reddy, Govin. Zimbabwe women: caught between the old and the new. NEW AFRICAN (LONDON) January 1985, No. 208:p. 33.

REGIONAL CONFERENCE ON THE INTEGRATION OF WOMEN IN THE ECONOMIC AND SOCIAL DEVELOPMENT OF LATIN AMERICA (1977, HAVANA, CUBA)

Regional Conference on the Integration of Women in the Economic and Social Development of Latin America (1977, Havana, Cuba). Report of the Regional Conference on the Integration of Women in the Economic and Social Development of Latin America, Havana, Cuba, 13-17 June 1977. Series: United Nations [Document], E/CEPAL/1042. (New York, United Nations, 1977), 67 pp.

REGIONAL SEMINAR FOR AFRICA ON THE INTEGRATION OF WOMEN IN DEVELOPMENT, WITH SPECIAL REFERENCE TO POPULATION FACTORS (1974, ADDIS ABABA)

Regional Seminar for Africa on the Integration of Women in Development, With Special Reference to Population Factors (1974, Addis Ababa). Report of the Regional Seminar for Africa on the Integration of Women in Development, With Special Reference to Population Factors, Addis Ababa, Ethiopia, 3 - 7 June 1974. Organized by the Centre for Social Development and Humanitarian Affairs, Department of Economic and Social Affairs, in co-operation with the Economic Commission for Africa. Series: United Nations [Document], ST/ESA/SER.B/6. (New York, United Nations, 1975), 30 pp.

REID, ELIZABETH ANNE

Reid, Elizabeth Anne. Since Mexico '75: a decade of progress? DEVELOPMENT (ROME) 1984, No. 4:76-79.

REINING, PRISCILLA [ET AL.]

Reining, Priscilla [et al.]. Village women, their changing lives and fertility: studies in Kenya, Mexico, and the Philippines. Series: AAAS publication, No. 77-6. (Washington, DC, American Association for the Advancement of Science, 1977), 273 pp.

Reinventing the past and circumscribing the future: authenticity and the negative image of women's work in Zaire. By: Wilson, Francille Rusan. In: Women and work in Africa. Edited by Edna G. Bay. (Boulder, CO, Westview Press, 1982), pp. 153-70.

REIS, JANET

Finn, Jeremy D. and Reis, Janet. Sex differences in educational attainment: the process. COMPARATIVE EDUCATION REVIEW (NEW YORK) June 1980, 24:S33-52. Examines various obstacles to women's education.

REITER, RAYNA R.

Reiter, Rayna R.. Men and women in the south of France: public and private domains. In: Toward an anthropology of women. Edited by Rayna R. Reiter. (New York, Monthly Review Press, 1975), pp. 252-82.

Relations among child quality, family structure, and the value of the mother's time in Malaysia. By: Leppel, Karen. MALAYAN ECONOMIC REVIEW (SINGAPORE) October 1982, 27:61-70.

REMY, DOROTHY

Remy, Dorothy. Underdevelopment and the experience of women: a Nigerian case study. In: Toward an anthropology of women. Edited by Rayna R. Reiter. (New York, Monthly Review Press, 1975), pp. 358-71.

Report. By: Interregional Meeting of Experts on the Integration of Women in Development, New York, 1972. Series: United Nations Publication sales no. E.73.IV.12, United Nations Document ST/SOA/120. (New York, United Nations , 1973), 77 pp. At head of title: Department of Economic and Social Affairs.

Report. By: United Nations. Commission on the Status of Women. (New York, United Nations, 1976-77, 1982), 3 vols.. Issued as supplements to the official records of the Economic and Social Council.

Report of the Regional Conference on the Integration of Women in the Economic and Social Development of Latin America, Havana, Cuba, 13-17 June 1977. By: Regional Conference on the Integration of Women in the Economic and Social Development of Latin America (1977, Havana, Cuba). Series: United Nations [Document], E/CEPAL/1042. (New York, United Nations, 1977), 67 pp.

Report of the Regional Seminar for Africa on the Integration of Women in Development, With Special Reference to Population Factors, Addis Ababa, Ethiopia, 3 - 7 June 1974. By: Regional Seminar for Africa on the Integration of Women in Development, With Special Reference to Population Factors (1974, Addis Ababa). Organized by the Centre for Social Development and Humanitarian Affairs, Department of Economic and Social Affairs, in co-operation with the Economic Commission for Africa. Series: United Nations [Document], ST/ESA/SER.B/6. (New York, United Nations, 1975), 30 pp.

Report of the world Conference of the International Women's Year, Mexico City, 19 June - 2 July 1975. By: World Conference of the International Women's Year (1975: Conference Centre of the Mexican Ministry of Foreign Affairs). Series: United Nations [Document], E/CONF.66/34. (New York, United Nations, 1976), 199 pp.

Report on Caribbean regional workshop for women in small island states: (management, communication and community mobilisation). By: Caribbean Regional Workshop for Women in Small Island States (1981: St. Georges, Grenada). (London, Commonwealth Secretariat, [1981]), 9 pp.

Report on the ILO/ECA/YWCA/SIDA workshop on participation of women in handicrafts and small industries, Kitwe, Zambia, 9-20 December, 1974. By: International Labour Office. Series: Document ILO/Tf/AFR/R.19 (Geneva, [1974]), 190 pp. At head of title: International Labour Office. Swedish International Development Authority. (Mimeographed).

Research experience with rural women. By: Acuna, Isabel Chacon. In: Latin American women: the meek speak out. Edited by June H. Turner. (Silver Spring, MD, International Educational Development, 1980), pp. 29-38. Discusses women in Costa Rica.

Research in the social sciences on North African women: problems, trends and needs. By: Baffoun, Alya. In: Social science research on women in the Arab world. (London, Frances Pinter; Paris, Unesco, 1984), pp. 41-58.

Research in the social sciences on women in Morocco. By: Belarbi, Aicha. In: Social science research on women in the Arab world. (London, Frances Pinter; Paris, Unesco, 1984), pp. 59-75.

Research of the status of women, development and population trends in Africa: an annotated bibliography. By: Kisekka, Mere. In: Bibliographic guide to studies on the status of women: development and population trends. (New York, Bowker, UNIPUB; Paris, Unesco, 1983), pp. 41-66.

Research on the status of women, development and population trends in Asia: an annotated bibliography. By: Hara, Kimi. In: Bibliographic guide to studies on the status of women: development and population trends. (New York, Bowker, UNIPUB; Paris, Unesco, 1983), [pp. 82-111].

Research on the status of women, development and population trends in Eastern Europe: an annotated bibliography. By: Tryfan, Barbara. In: Bibliographic guide to studies on the status of women: development and population trends. (New York, Bowker, UNIPUB; Paris, Unesco, 1983), pp. 113-39.

Research on the status of women, development and population trends in Latin America: an annotated bibliography. By: Feijoo, Maria del Carmen. In: Bibliographic guide to studies on the status of women: development and population trends. (New York, Bowker, UNIPUB; Paris, Unesco, 1983), pp. 141-82.

Research on the status of women, development and population trends in the Arab states: an annotated bibliography. By: Abdel Kader, Soha. In: Bibliographic guide to studies on the status of women: development and population trends. (New York, Bowker, UNIPUB; Paris, Unesco, 1983), pp. 67-81.

Research on women in Latin America: problems of networking and comparative analysis in the last decade. By: Schmidt, Steffen W.. STUDIES IN THIRD WORLD SOCIETIES (WILLIAMSBURG) March 1981, No. 15:107-33.

Resistance as protest: women in the struggle of Bolivian tin-mining communities. By: Nash, June. In: Women cross-culturally: change and challenge. Edited by Ruby Rohrlich-Leavitt. (The Hague, Mouton, 1975), pp. 261-71.

Respective roles of men and women in Indonesia. By: Subandrio, Hurustiati. In: Women in the new Asia; the changing social roles of men and women in South and South-east Asia. Edited by Barbara E. Ward. ([Paris], Unesco, 1963), pp. 230-42.

Rethinking women's oppression. By: Brenner, Johanna and Ramas, Maria. NEW LEFT REVIEW (LONDON) March/April 1984, No. 144:33-71. The authors discuss some of the issues raised in Michele Barrett's Women's oppression today.

REUNION

Numero special: radioscopie du chomage. L'ECONOMIE DE LA REUNION (STE-CLOTILDE) September/October 1986, No. 25:1-32.

Reveiw of women studies. ECONOMIC AND POLITICAL WEEKLY (BOMBAY) October 25, 1986, 21:WS 53-WS 104.

Reversible sex roles: the special case of Benares sweepers. By: Searle-Chatterjee, Mary. Series: Women in Development, Vol. 2. (Oxford, New York, Pergamon Press, 1981), 112 pp.

Review in women studies. ECONOMIC AND POLITICAL WEEKLY (BOMBAY) October 26, 1985, 20:WS-57 - WS-96.

Review of women studies. ECONOMIC AND POLITICAL WEEKLY (BOMBAY) April 27, 1985, 20:WS1-WS56. CONTENT: Ortiz, Bobbye Suckle, Changing consciousness of Central American women. -- Thorner, Alice, and Jyoti Ranadive, Household as a first stage in a study of urban working-class women. -- Levi, Luisa Accati, Wife-husband relations: differences between peasant households and modern professional-class families in North-Eastern Italy. -- Standing, Hilary, Women's employment and the household: some findings from Calcutta. -- Kelkar, Govind, Impact of household contract system on women in rural India. -- Sen, Gita and Charanjib Sen, Women's domestic work and economic activity results from national sample survey.

REY DE MARULANDA, NOHRA

Rey De Marulanda, Nohra. Las mujeres jefes de hogar. UNIVERSIDAD DE LOS ANDES. CENTRO DE ESTUDIOS SOBRE DESARROLLO ECONOMICO. DOCUMENTO (BOGOTA) September 1982, No. 68:1-66.

RICE

Badoe, Yaba Mangela. Gambia; rice and dependency. WEST AFRICA (LONDON) October 24, 1983, No. 3454:2484. Discusses the sexual politics of rice production and concludes that women are the prime losers but the cost to national food production is enormous.

RICE

Dey, Jennie. Women in African rice farming systems. FOOD AND AGRICULTURE ORGANIZATION OF THE UNITED NATIONS. INTERNATIONAL RICE COMMISSION NEWSLETTER (ROME) December 1983, 32:1-4.

Marothia, D. K. and Sharma, S. K. Female labour participation in rice farming system of Chhattisgarh region. INDIAN JOURNAL OF AGRICULTURAL ECONOMICS (BOMBAY) July/September 1985, 40:235-39.

Mencher, Joan P. and Saradamoni, K.. Muddy feet, dirty hands; rice production and female agricultural labour. ECONOMIC AND POLITICAL WEEKLY (BOMBAY) December 25, 1982, 17:A149-A167.

Sen, Gita. Paddy production, processing and women workers in India - the south versus the northeast. CENTRE FOR DEVELOPMENT STUDIES. WORKING PAPER (ULLOOR, TRIVANDRUM) December 1983, No. 186.

ROBERT, ANNETTE

Robert, Annette. Effects of the international division of labour on female workers in the textile and clothing industries. DEVELOPMENT AND CHANGE (THE HAGUE, etc.) January 1983, 14:19-37.

ROBERTS, GEORGE W.

Roberts, George W. and Sinclair, Sonja A.. Women in Jamaica: patterns of reproduction and family. (Millwood, New York, KTC Press, 1978), 346 pp.

ROBERTS, PENELOPE

Roberts, Penelope. Les femmes et les programmes de developpement rural; avec reference aux programmes-femmes finances par le Fonds Europeen de Developpement au Kenya. TIERS-MONDE (PARIS) April/June 1985, 26:299-305.

ROBERTSON, CLAIRE

Robertson, Claire. Ga women and socioeconomic change in Accra, Ghana. In: Women in Africa: studies in social and economic change. Edited by Nancy J. Hafkin and Edna G. Bay. (Stanford, Stanford University Press, 1976), pp. 111-33.

ROBERTSON, CLAIRE C.

Robertson, Claire C.. Formal or nonformal education? Entrepreneurial women in Ghana. COMPARATIVE EDUCATION REVIEW (NEW YORK) November 1984, 28:639-58.

ROBINS-MOWRY, DOROTHY

Robins-Mowry, Dorothy. Hidden sun: women of modern Japan. (Boulder, Colorado, Westview Press, 1982), 394 pp.

ROBINSON, CHRIS

Robinson, Chris and Tomes, Nigel. More on the labour supply of Canadian women. CANADIAN JOURNAL OF ECONOMICS (TORONTO) February 1985, 18:156-63.

ROBINSON, JEAN C.

Robinson, Jean C.. Of women and washing machines: employment, housework, and the reproduction of motherhood in socialist China. CHINA QUARTERLY (LONDON) March 1985, No. 101:32-57.

ROCHELEAU, DIANNE

Fortmann, Louise and Rocheleau, Dianne. Women and agroforestry: four myths and three case studies. AGROFORESTRY SYSTEMS (THE HAGUE) 1985, 2, No. 4:253-72. The involvement of women in agroforestry projects and activities is examined in case studies from the Dominican Republic, India and Kenya. Consideration for including women in agroforestry projects are discussed.

ROGERS, BARBARA

Rogers, Barbara. Domestication of women: discrimination in developing societies. (New York, St. Martin's Press, 1980), 200 pp.

ROGERS, JANET

Tessler, Mark A. and Rogers, Janet. Women's emancipation in Tunisia. In: Women in the Muslim world. Edited by Lois Beck and Nikki Keddie. (Cambridge, MA, Harvard University Press, 1978), pp. 141-58.

ROGERS, MARVIN L

Rogers, Marvin L. Changing patterns of political involvement among Malay village women. ASIAN SURVEY (BERKELEY, CALIF.) March 1986, 26:322-44.

ROGOMBE, ROSE FRANCINE

Rogombe, Rose Francine. Women; equal partners in Africa's development. AFRICA REPORT (NEW YORK) March/April 1985, 30:17-20.

ROHRLICH-LEAVITT, RUBY

Rohrlich-Leavitt, Ruby and Sykes, Barbara. Aboriginal woman: male and female anthropological perspectives. In: Toward an anthropology of women. Edited by Rayna R. Reiter. (New York, Monthly Review Press, 1975), pp. 110-26.

ROHWER, GERTRUDE

Rohwer, Gertrude. Integration durch Ausbildung; eine Strategie zur Uberwindung sozialer Disparitaten in Oman: Bemerkungen uber die Partizipationschancen von Frauen am gesellschaftlichen Entwicklungsprozess in einem islamischen Land. ORIENT (HAMBURG) September 1984, 25:391-402. With English summary, p. 458.

Role and status of women in post-harvest food conservation. By: Brandtzaeg, Brita. FOOD AND NUTRITION BULLETIN (TOKYO) January 1982, 4:33-40.

Role and status of women in the Soviet-Union: 1917 to the present. By: Rosenthal, Bernice Glatzer. In: Women cross-culturally: change and challenge. Edited by Ruby Rohrlich-Leavitt. (The Hague, Mouton, 1975), pp. 429-55.

Le role compare de la femme dans les milieux ruraux et urbains en Afrique. By: Diaroumeye, Fatoumata Agnes. MONDES EN DEVELOPPEMENT (PARIS) 1982, No. 40:481-82.

Le role de la femme dans la vie economique et sociale. By: de Senarclens, Marina. REVUE ECONOMIQUE ET SOCIALE (LAUSANNE) December 1979, 37:200-09.

Le role des services nationaux d'animation rurale et de vulgarisation agricole aupres des femmes. By: Martius von Harder, Gudrun. TIERS-MONDE (PARIS) April/June 1985, 26:317-24.

Role of farm women in agriculture: a study of Chambal command area of Madhya Pradesh. By: Sisodia, J. S. INDIAN JOURNAL OF AGRICULTURAL ECONOMICS (BOMBAY) July/September 1985, 40:223-34.

Role of rural women in community life; a case study from India. By: Jain, Devaki and Singh, Nalini. ECONOMIC BULLETIN FOR ASIA AND THE PACIFIC (BANGKOK) December 1978, 29:84-126.

Role of the Soviet woman in decision-making in trade union committees and in industry. By: Biryukova, Alexandra. LABOUR AND SOCIETY (GENEVA) September 1985, 10:307-21.

Role of women and demographic change in Cuba. By: Farnos, Alfonso and Gonzalez, Fernando. INTERNATIONAL LABOUR OFFICE. WORLD EMPLOYMENT PROGRAMME RESEARCH. POPULATION AND LABOUR POLICIES PROGRAMME. WORKING PAPER (GENEVA) August 1983, No. 138:1-52.

Role of women from fishing households: case study of a Kerala fishing village. By: Gulati, Leela. CENTRE FOR DEVELOPMENT STUDIES. WORKING PAPER (ULLOOR, TRIVANDRUM) July 1981, No. 144:1-11.

Role of women in arable cropping enterprises in farming communities of South-Eastern Nigeria: a case study. By: Okorji, Eugene C. DEVELOPMENT AND PEACE (BUDAPEST) Autumn 1985, 6:165-73.

Role of women in reciprocal relationships in a Punjab village. By: Rahat, Naveed I.. In: The endless day: some case material on Asian rural women. Edited by T. Scarlett Epstein and Rosemary A. Watts. Series: Women in development, Vol. 3. (Oxford, England, New York, Pergamon Press, 1981), pp. 47-81.

Role of women in socio-economic development: indicators as instruments of social analysis; the case of Morocco. By: El Belghiti, Malika. In: Women and development: indicators of their changing role. Series: Socio-economic studies, No. 3. (Paris, Unesco, 1981), pp. 15-32.

Role of women in socio-economic development: indicators as instruments of social analysis; the case of Nigeria and Uganda. By: Nisekka, Mere. In: Women and development: indicators of their changing role. Series: Socio-economic studies, No. 3. (Paris, Unesco, 1981), pp. 33-47.

Role of women in the Caribbean. By: Powell, Dorian. SOCIAL AND ECONOMIC STUDIES (MONA, JAMAICA) June 1984, 33:97-122.

Role of women in the development of culture in Nigeria. By: Okonjo, Kamene. In: Women cross-culturally: change and challenge. Edited by Ruby Rohrlich-Leavitt. (The Hague, Mouton, 1975), pp. 31-40.

Role of women in water supply and sanitation. By: Elmendorf, Mary L. and Isely, Raymond B.. WORLD HEALTH FORUM (GENEVA) 1982, 3, No. 2:227-30.

ROOSE, HASHIMAH

Roose, Hashimah. Changes in the position of Malay women. In: Women in the new Asia; the changing social roles of men and women in South and South-east Asia. Edited by Barbara E. Ward. ([Paris], Unesco, 1963), pp. 287-94.

ROSEN, LAWRENCE

Rosen, Lawrence. Negotiation of reality: male-female relations in Sefrou, Morocco. In: Women in the Muslim world. Edited by Lois Beck and Nikki Keddie. (Cambridge, MA, Harvard University Press, 1978), pp. 561-83.

ROSENTHAL, BERNICE GLATZER

Rosenthal, Bernice Glatzer. Role and status of women in the Soviet-Union: 1917 to the present. In: Women cross-culturally: change and challenge. Edited by Ruby Rohrlich-Leavitt. (The Hague, Mouton, 1975), pp. 429-55.

ROSS, AILEEN D.

Ross, Aileen D.. Some comments on the home roles of business women in India, Australia and Canada. In: Women in the family and the economy: an international comparative survey. Edited by George Kurian and Ratna Ghosh. (Westport, CT, Greenwood Press, 1981), pp. 317-30.

ROTHSCHILD, K. W.

Rothschild, K. W.. Note on female labour supply. KYKLOS (BASLE) 1980, 33, No. 2:246-60.

ROUSSEAU, IDA FAYE

Rousseau, Ida Faye. African women: identity crisis? Some observations on education and the changing role of women in Sierra Leone and Zaire. In: Women cross-culturally: change and challenge. Edited by Ruby Rohrlich-Leavitt. (The Hague, Mouton, 1975), pp. 41-52.

ROWE, ALAN J. AND BENNIS, WARREN

Rowe, Alan J. and Bennis, Warren. Desexing decision styles. PERSONNEL (SARANAC LAKE, N.Y.) January/February 1984, 61:43-52. The authors attempt to determine why women are thought of as being different from men in terms of their ability to perform effectively in management positions.

RUBBO, ANNA

Rubbo, Anna. Spread of capitalism in rural Colombia: effects on poor women. In: Toward an anthropology of women. Edited by Rayna R. Reiter. (New York, Monthly Review Press, 1975), pp. 333-57.

RUBIN, GAYLE

Rubin, Gayle. Traffic in women: notes on the political economy of sex. In: Toward an anthropology of women. Edited by Rayna R. Reiter. (New York, Monthly Review Press, 1975), pp. 157-210.

RUESCHEMEYER, MARILYN

Rueschemeyer, Marilyn. Demands of work and the human quality of marriage: an exploratory study of professionals in two socialist societies. In: Women in the family and the economy: an international comparative survey. Edited by George Kurian and Ratna Ghosh. (Westport, CT, Greenwood Press, 1981), pp. 331-43. Countries discussed in this chapter are the Soviet Union and East Germany.

RURAL DEVELOPMENT

Dumor, Ernest. Women in rural development in Ghana. RURAL AFRICANA (EAST LANSING) Fall 1983, No. 17:69-81.

Fatima, Burnad. Rural development and women's liberation: caste, class and gender in a grass-roots organisation in Tamil Nadu, South India. IDS BULLETIN, INSTITUTE OF DEVELOPMENT STUDIES AT THE UNIVERSITY OF SUSSEX (BRIGHTON) January 1984, 15:45-50.

Grewal, R. S. and Nandal, D. S. Impact of rural development programme on rural women in Bhiwani district of Haryana. INDIAN JOURNAL OF AGRICULTURAL ECONOMICS (BOMBAY) July/September 1985, 40:259-62.

Ming, Xiao. Women in rural economic reform. WOMEN OF CHINA (BEIJING) May 1986, No. 5:3-7.

Rural development and women in Asia: proceedings and conclusions of the ILO Tripartite Asian Regional Seminar, Mahabaleshwar, Maharashtra, India, 6-11 April 1981. By: ILO Tripartite Asian Regional Seminar (1981: Mahabaleshwar, India). Series: A WEP study. (Geneva, International Labour Office, 1982), 88 pp.

Rural development and women's liberation: caste, class and gender in a grass-roots organisation in Tamil Nadu, South India. By: Fatima, Burnad. IDS BULLETIN, INSTITUTE OF DEVELOPMENT STUDIES AT THE UNIVERSITY OF SUSSEX (BRIGHTON) January 1984, 15:45-50.

RURAL EMPLOYMENT

Acock, Alan C. and Deseran, Forrest A. Off-farm employment by women and marital instability. RURAL SOCIOLOGY (PROVO, UTAH) Fall 1986, 51:314-27. The impact of farm women's paid work experience on the quality and stability of their marriages is examined in the context of two competing frameworks - status competition and status enhancement.

Rural female labour and economic development. By: Sawant, S. D. and Dewan, Ritu. ECONOMIC AND POLITICAL WEEKLY (BOMBAY) June 30, 1979, 14:1091-99. This paper, based on a study of a sample of 150 villages in two talukas of Thane district in Maharashtra, attempts to examine the impact of economic development on rural women, particularly on their employment.

RURAL HEALTH SERVICES

Laubjerg, Kristian. Training village women as health promoters in Tanzania. WATERLINES (LONDON) January 1986, 4:29-31.

RURAL POPULATION

Ahmad, Zubeida. Plight of rural women: alternatives for action. INTERNATIONAL LABOUR REVIEW (GENEVA) July/August 1980, 119:425-38.

Erumsele, A. Akhigbe. Women's part in rural development. WEST AFRICA (LONDON) August 18, 1980, No. 3291:1539-40. Discusses some of the findings of a study on "Rural women's participation in development" just published by the United Nations Development Programme (UNDP).

Omvedt, Gail. Women and rural revolt in India. JOURNAL OF PEASANT STUDIES (LONDON) April 1978, 5:370-403. It is argued that in India, increasingly during the last decade, capitalism has developed in the countryside, and that, with the changing social relations of production, there has emerged a mass-based and militant women's movement ... This is illustrated ... especially for the state of Maharashtra.

RURAL POPULATION

Sawant, S. D. and Dewan, Ritu. Rural female labour and economic development. ECONOMIC AND POLITICAL WEEKLY (BOMBAY) June 30, 1979, 14:1091-99. This paper, based on a study of a sample of 150 villages in two talukas of Thane district in Maharashtra, attempts to examine the impact of economic development on rural women, particularly on their employment.

Women in rural development: recommendations and realities. CERES, FAO REVIEW ON AGRICULTURE AND DEVELOPMENT (ROME) May/June 1980, 75:15-42.

RURAL POVERTY

Agarwal, Bina. Women, poverty and agricultural growth in India. INSTITUTE OF ECONOMIC GROWTH. [PAPERS] (DELHI) June 1985, No. E/112/85:1-101.

Agarwal, Nina. Women, poverty and agricultural growth in India. JOURNAL OF PEASANT STUDIES (LONDON) July 1986, 13:165-220.

RURAL WATER SUPPLY

van Wijk-Sijbesma, Christine. Helping women to help themselves. WATERLINES (LONDON) April 1986, 4:29-31. Suggests that women's programmes and organizations have great potential to mobilize women to improve their own water supply and sanitation if they are not served by other programmes.

RURAL WOMEN

Acock, Alan C. and Deseran, Forrest A. Off-farm employment by women and marital instability. RURAL SOCIOLOGY (PROVO, UTAH) Fall 1986, 51:314-27. The impact of farm women's paid work experience on the quality and stability of their marriages is examined in the context of two competing frameworks - status competition and status enhancement.

Agarwal, Bina. Women and technological change in agriculture: Asian and African experience. INSTITUTE OF ECONOMIC GROWTH. [PAPERS] (DELHI) July 1984, No. E/103/84:1-55.

Agarwal, Nina. Women, poverty and agricultural growth in India. JOURNAL OF PEASANT STUDIES (LONDON) July 1986, 13:165-220.

Ahmad, Zubeida. Advancement of rural women: the emerging networks. CERES, FAO REVIEW ON AGRICULTURE AND DEVELOPMENT (ROME) March/April 1986, 19:31-35.

RURAL WOMEN

Ahmad, Zubeida and Loufti, Martha. Decently paid employment -- not more drudgery. CERES, FAO REVIEW ON AGRICULTURE AND DEVELOPMENT (ROME) July/August 1983, 16:40-46. The authors conclude that there is an urgent need for improved living and working conditions for many poor rural women.

Ahmad, Zubeida. Rural women and their work: dependence and alternatives for change. INTERNATIONAL LABOUR REVIEW (GENEVA) January/February 1984, 123:71-86.

Ahmed, Iftikhar. Rural women and technical change: theory, empirical analysis and operational projects. LABOUR AND SOCIETY (GENEVA) September 1985, 10:289-306.

Carr, Marilyn. Technology and rural women in Africa. INTERNATIONAL LABOUR OFFICE. WORLD EMPLOYMENT PROGRAMME RESEARCH. TECHNOLOGY AND EMPLOYMENT PROGRAMME. WORKING PAPERS (GENEVA) July 1980, No. 61:1-45.

Chen, Marty. Poverty, gender, and work in Bangladesh. ECONOMIC AND POLITICAL WEEKLY (BOMBAY) February 1, 1986, 21:217-22. Redefines the three broad classes of rural households in terms of women's labour and income and describes the process of impoverishment from the perspective of women.

Colfer, Carol. On circular migration -- from the distaff side: women left behind in the forests of East Kalimantan. INTERNATIONAL LABOUR OFFICE. WORLD EMPLOYMENT PROGRAMME RESEARCH. POPULATION AND LABOUR POLICIES PROGRAMME. WORKING PAPER (GENEVA) May 1983, No. 132:1-42. Focuses on male circular migration (or migration with the in;tent to return home) and its impact on the women who remain in the villages tending the farm. The area studied is East Kalimantan (Indonesian Borneo).

Dumor, Ernest. Women in rural development in Ghana. RURAL AFRICANA (EAST LANSING) Fall 1983, No. 17:69-81.

Fatima, Burnad. Rural development and women's liberation: caste, class and gender in a grass-roots organisation in Tamil Nadu, South India. IDS BULLETIN, INSTITUTE OF DEVELOPMENT STUDIES AT THE UNIVERSITY OF SUSSEX (BRIGHTON) January 1984, 15:45-50.

RURAL WOMEN

Feldman, Rayah. Women's groups and women's subordination: an analysis of policies towards rural women in Kenya. REVIEW OF AFRICAN POLITICAL ECONOMY (SHEFFIELD) 1984, No. 27/28:67-85.

Grewal, R. S. and Nandal, D. S. Impact of rural development programme on rural women in Bhiwani district of Haryana. INDIAN JOURNAL OF AGRICULTURAL ECONOMICS (BOMBAY) July/September 1985, 40:259-62.

Gupta, R. P.. Rural women and economic development. ECONOMIC AFFAIRS (CALCUTTA) July-Sept. 1983, 28:784-90.

Hurwitch-MacDonald, Jan. La incorporacion femenina a las empresas asociativas. DESARROLLO RURAL EN LAS AMERICAS (SAN JOSE) January/June 1983, 15:55-64.

Institute for Cultural Action (IDAC). Discovering self-reliance in Paraty. DEVELOPMENT (ROME) 1984, No. 4:41-44. Describes a project of women's education for self-reliance in Paraty, a rural village in Brazil.

Jahangir, B. K. Women and property in rural Bangladesh. JOURNAL OF SOCIAL STUDIES (DHAKA) October 1986, No. 34:87-95.

Jeffery, Patricia and Jeffery, Roger. Childbirth and collaboration among women in Bijnor district, Uttar Pradesh. JOURNAL OF SOCIAL STUDIES (DHAKA) July 1984, No. 25:15-33.

Khan, Zarina Rahman. Women's economic role: insights from a village in Bangladesh. JOURNAL OF SOCIAL STUDIES (DHAKA) October 1985, No. 30:13-26.

Lorfing, I. and Khalaf, M.. Economic contribution of women and its effect on the dynamics of the family in two Lebanese villages. INTERNATIONAL LABOUR OFFICE. WORLD EMPLOYMENT PROGRAMME RESEARCH. POPULATION AND LABOUR POLICIES PROGRAMME. WORKING PAPER (GENEVA) May 1985, No. 148:1-32.

Martius von Harder, Gudrun. Le role des services nationaux d'animation rurale et de vulgarisation agricole aupres des femmes. TIERS-MONDE (PARIS) April/June 1985, 26:317-24.

Michel, Andree. Dix ans d'irruption des sciences humaines dans le domaine du travail des paysannes. TIERS-MONDE (PARIS) April/June 1985, 26:261-71.

RURAL WOMEN

Michel, Andree. El trabajo invisible de las campesinas del Tercer Mundo. DESARROLLO Y SOCIEDAD (BOGOTA) January 1984, No. 13:81-97. With English summary.

Mies, Maria. Indian women in subsistence and agricultural labour. INTERNATIONAL LABOUR OFFICE. WORLD EMPLOYMENT PROGRAMME RESEARCH. RURAL EMPLOYMENT POLICY RESEARCH PROGRAMME. WORKING PAPER (GENEVA) (GENEVA) May 1984, No. 34:1-243.

Nath, Kamla. Labor-saving techniques in food processing: rural women and technological change in the Gambia. BOSTON UNIVERSITY. AFRICAN STUDIES CENTER. WORKING PAPERS (BOSTON) 1985, No. 108:1-26. Describes the methodology used in developing a project design for the introduction of sorghum and millet decorticators and flour milling units in rural areas of the Gambia in West Africa.

Nath, Kamla. Women and vegetable gardens in the Gambia: Action AID and rural development. BOSTON UNIVERSITY. AFRICAN STUDIES CENTER. WORKING PAPERS (BOSTON) 1985, No. 109:1-13. Examines Action Aid's program for improving the capacity of rural women to produce garden vegetables and to introduce marketing infrastructures.

Pettigrew, Joyce. Problems concerning tubectomy operations in rural areas of Punjab. ECONOMIC AND POLITICAL WEEKLY (BOMBAY) June 30, 1984, 19:995-1002.

Roberts, Penelope. Les femmes et les programmes de developpement rural; avec reference aux programmes-femmes finances par le Fonds Europeen de Developpement au Kenya. TIERS-MONDE (PARIS) April/June 1985, 26:299-305.

Rogers, Marvin L. Changing patterns of political involvement among Malay village women. ASIAN SURVEY (BERKELEY, CALIF.) March 1986, 26:322-44.

Sharma, Miriam. Caste, class, and gender: production and reproduction in North India. JOURNAL OF PEASANT STUDIES (LONDON) July 1985, 12:26-56.

Srivastava, J. N.. Determinants of female age at marriage in rural Uttar Pradesh. INDIAN JOURNAL OF ECONOMICS (ALLAHABAD) January 1984, 64:327-44.

Ventura-Dias, V.. Technological change, production organisation and rural women in Kenya. INTERNATIONAL LABOUR OFFICE. WORLD EMPLOYMENT PROGRAMME RESEARCH. TECHNOLOGY AND EMPLOYMENT PROGRAMME. WORKING PAPERS (GENEVA) November 1982, No. 101:1-64.

RURAL WOMEN

Willis, David K.. Meet an African farmer ... and her husband. CHRISTIAN SCIENCE MONITOR (BOSTON) July 5, 1985, p. 9-10. Discusses the role of women in producing food and the need for greater focus on rural women.

Rural women: unequal partners in development. By: Loutfi, Martha F.. Series: A WEP study. (Geneva, International Labor Office, 1980), 81 pp.

Rural women and economic development. By: Gupta, R. P.. ECONOMIC AFFAIRS (CALCUTTA) July-Sept. 1983, 28:784-90.

Rural women and state policy: the Latin American agrarian reform experience. By: Deere, Carmen Diana. WORLD DEVELOPMENT (OXFORD) September 1985, 13:1037-53.

Rural women and technical change: theory, empirical analysis and operational projects. By: Ahmed, Iftikhar. LABOUR AND SOCIETY (GENEVA) September 1985, 10:289-306.

Rural women and their work: dependence and alternatives for change. By: Ahmad, Zubeida. INTERNATIONAL LABOUR REVIEW (GENEVA) January/February 1984, 123:71-86.

Rural women at work: strategies for development in South Africa. By: Dixon, Ruth B.. (Baltimore, published for Resources for the Future by Johns Hopkins Press, 1978), 227 pp.

Rural women in Africa and technological change: some issues. By: Date-Bah, Eugenia and Stevens, Yvette. LABOUR AND SOCIETY (GENEVA) April/June 1981, 6:149-62.

RURAL-URBAN MIGRATION

Oliveira, Orlandina de. Migracion femenina, organizacion familiar y mercados laborales en Mexico. COMERCIO EXTERIOR (MEXICO, D.F.) July 1984, 34:676-87.

Yaccob, May. Ahmadiyya and urbanization: migrant women in Abidjan. BOSTON UNIVERSITY. AFRICAN STUDIES CENTER. WORKING PAPERS (BOSTON) 1983, No. 75:1-16.

Rural-to-urban migration of women in India: patterns and implications. By: Singh, Andrea Menefee. In: Women in the cities of Asia: migration and urban adaptation. Edited by James T. Fawcett, Siew-Ean Khoo and Peter C. Smith. (Boulder, CO, Westview Press, 1984), pp. 81-107.

SA'ADAWI, NAW'AL

Sa'adawi, Naw'al. Hidden face of Eve: women in the Arab world. (Boston, MA, Beacon Press, 1982), 212 pp.

SACKS, KAREN

Sacks, Karen. Engels revisited: women, the organization of production, and private property. In: Toward an anthropology of women. Edited by Rayna R. Reiter. (New York, Monthly Review Press, 1975), pp. 211-34.

SAFFIOTI, HELEIETH IARA BONGIOVANI

Saffioti, Heleieth Iara Bongiovani. Female labor and capitalism in the United States and Brazil. In: Women cross-culturally: change and challenge. Edited by Ruby Rohrlich-Leavitt. (The Hague, Mouton, 1975), pp. 60-94.

SAFILIOS-ROTHSCHILD, CONSTANTINA

Safilios-Rothschild, Constantina. Persistence of women's invisibility in agriculture: theoretical and policy lessons from Lesotho and Sierra Leone. POPULATION COUNCIL. CENTER FOR POLICY STUDIES. WORKING PAPERS (NEW YORK) September 1982, No.88:1-31.

Safilios-Rothschild, Constantina. Socioeconomic development and the status of women in the Third world. POPULATION COUNCIL. CENTER FOR POLICY STUDIES. WORKING PAPERS (NEW YORK) May 1985, No. 112:1-49. Examines the relationship between socioeconomic development and women's status in 75 developing countries.

SAFILIOS-ROTHSCHILD, CONSTATINA

Safilios-Rothschild, Constatina and Dijkers, Marcellinus. Changing sex roles in the Greek family and society. In: Changing position of women in family and society: an cross-national comparison. Edited by Eugen Lupri. (Leiden, E. J. Brill, 1983), pp. 190-97.

SAINI, AMRIK S. AND SINGH, RAJ VIR

Saini, Amrik S. and Singh, Raj Vir. Impact of diversification on income, employment and credit needs of small farmers in Punjab. INDIAN JOURNAL OF AGRICULTURAL ECONOMICS (BOMBAY) July/September 1985, 40:310-16.

SAKALA, CAROL

Sakala, Carol. Women of South Asia: a guide to resources. (Millwood, New York, Kraus International Publications, 1980), 517 pp. Foreword by Maureen L. P. Patterson.

SALAFF, JANET

Salaff, Janet and Wong, Aline. Women's work: factory, family and social class in an industrializing order. In: Women in the urban and industrial workforce; Southeast and East Asia. Edited by Gavin W. Jones. Series: Development Studies Centre. Monograph, No. 33. (Canberra, Australia, Australian National University, 1984), pp. 189-214. Series edited by Helen Hughes.

SALMONA, MICHELINE

Salmona, Micheline. L'echappee belle, ou la mobilisation generale des femmes dans l'agriculture en France. TIERS-MONDE (PARIS) April/June 1985, 26:247-60.

SALT INDUSTRY AND TRADE

Nath, Kamla. Women and technological change in The Gambia: a case study of the salt industry. BOSTON UNIVERSITY. AFRICAN STUDIES CENTER. WORKING PAPERS (BOSTON) 1985, No. 107:1-15.

SAMMAN, MOUNA LILIANE

Samman, Mouna Liliane. Activite economique des femmes du Tiers monde et perspectives de baisse de leur fecondite. TIERS-MONDE (PARIS) April/June 1983, 24:367-76.

SANCHEZ, AURELIA GUADALUPE

Sanchez, Aurelia Guadalupe and Dominguez, Ana E.. Women in Mexico. In: Women cross-culturally: change and challenge. Edited by Ruby Rohrlich-Leavitt. (The Hague, Mouton, 1975), pp. 95-110.

SANDERSON, WARREN C.

Sanderson, Warren C.. Nonutilitarian economic model of fertility and female labor force participation. REVUE ECONOMIQUE (PARIS) November 1980, 31:1045-80.

SANITATION

van Wijk-Sijbesma, Christine. Helping women to help themselves. WATERLINES (LONDON) April 1986, 4:29-31. Suggests that women's programmes and organizations have great potential to mobilize women to improve their own water supply and sanitation if they are not served by other programmes.

SAPIRO, VIRGINIA

Sapiro, Virginia. Gender basis of American social policy. POLITICAL SCIENCE QUARTERLY (NEW YORK) 1986, 101, No. 2:221-38.

SARADAMONI, K.

Mencher, Joan P. and Saradamoni, K.. Muddy feet, dirty hands; rice production and female agricultural labour. ECONOMIC AND POLITICAL WEEKLY (BOMBAY) December 25, 1982, 17:A149-A167.

Saradamoni, K.. Women's status in changing agrarian relations; a Kerala experience. ECONOMIC AND POLITICAL WEEKLY (BOMBAY) January 30, 1982, 17:155-62.

SARFATI, HEDVA

Sarfati, Hedva. Job equality for women: Progress, problems and perspectives. LABOUR AND SOCIETY (GENEVA) September 1985, 10:273-88.

SARMA, JYOTIRMOYEE

Sarma, Jyotirmoyee. Three generations in my Calcutta family. In: Women in the new Asia; the changing social roles of men and women in South and South-east Asia. Edited by Barbara E. Ward. ([Paris], Unesco, 1963), pp. 216-28. Describes differences in women's roles in each generation.

SAULNIERS, SUZANNE SMITH

Saulniers, Suzanne Smith and Rakowski, Cathy A.. Women in the development process: a select bibliography on women in sub-Saharan Africa and Latin America. (Austin, Institute of Latin American Studies, University of Texas Press, 1977), 287 pp. A special publication of the Institute of Latin American Studies.

SAVANE, MARIE ANGELIQUE

Savane, Marie Angelique. El empleo de la mujer, los cambios sociales y la liberacion femenina; el caso de Africa. COMERCIO EXTERIOR (MEXICO, D.F.) August 1980, 30:861-66. Ponencia presentada en la Mesa II, "Recursos humanos y empleo en los paises en desarrollo," del Sexto Congreso Mundial de Economistas.

Savane, Marie Angelique. Le plan d'action de Lagos et les femmes. AFRICA DEVELOPMENT (DAKAR) January/June 1982, 7:142-48. With English summary.

SAVARA, MIRA

Everett, Jana and Savara, Mira. Bank loans to lower class women in Bombay; problems and prospects. ECONOMIC AND POLITICAL WEEKLY (BOMBAY) August 25, 1984, 19:M113-M119. The authors report the results of an exploratory study of bank loans to lower caste women in Bombay. They seek to shed some light on the problems surrounding and the prospects for bank loans as an economic development strategy for poor women.

SAWANT, S. D.

Sawant, S. D. and Dewan, Ritu. Rural female labour and economic development. ECONOMIC AND POLITICAL WEEKLY (BOMBAY) June 30, 1979, 14:1091-99. This paper, based on a study of a sample of 150 villages in two talukas of Thane district in Maharashtra, attempts to examine the impact of economic development on rural women, particularly on their employment.

SCANDINAVIAN INSTITUTE OF AFRICAN STUDIES

Scandinavian Institute of African Studies. Women in Africa and development assistance, report from a seminar arranged by the Scandinavian Institute of African Studies, Uppsala, 20-21 August, 1978. (Uppsala, Sweden, Scandinavian Institute of African Studies, 1978), 55 pp.

SCHILDKROUT, ENID

Schildkrout, Enid. Dependence and autonomy: the economic activities of secluded Hausa women in Kano, Nigeria. In: Women and work in Africa. Edited by Edna G. Bay. (Boulder, CO, Westview Press, 1982), pp. 55-81.

SCHIPPERS, J. J.

Schippers, J. J. and Siegers, J. J.. Economische aspecten van een quoterings-maatregel ten behoeve van vrouwen op de arbeidsmarkt. MAANDSCHRIFT ECONOMIE (TILBURG) 1984, 48, No. 6:484-99.

SCHIPPERS, JOOP J. AND SIEGERS, JACQUES J

Schippers, Joop J. and Siegers, Jacques J. Women's relative wage rate in the Netherlands, 1950-1983: a test of alternative discrimination theories. DE ECONOMIST (LEIDEN) 1986, 134, No. 2:165-80.

SCHMIDT, STEFFEN W.

Schmidt, Steffen W.. Research on women in Latin America: problems of networking and comparative analysis in the last decade. STUDIES IN THIRD WORLD SOCIETIES (WILLIAMSBURG) March 1981, No. 15:107-33.

Schmidt, Steffen W.. Women, politics and development; a review essay. LATIN AMERICAN RESEARCH REVIEW (ALBUQUERQUE, NM) 1983, 18, No. 1:210-27.

Schooling of Vietnamese immigrants: internal colonialism and its impact on women. By: Kelly, Gail P.. In: Comparative perspectives of Third World women: the impact of race, sex and class. Edited by Beverly Lindsay. (New York, Praeger, 1980), pp. 276-96.

SCHRIJVERS, JOKE

Schrijvers, Joke. Cultuur als camouflage: Westerse weerstanden tegen vrouwen als ontwikkelingsrelevant onderwerp. INTERNATIONALE SPECTATOR (THE HAGUE) September 1983, 37:556-62.

SCHROEDER, ELAINE

Schroeder, Robert and Schroeder, Elaine. Women in Nepali agriculture: all work and no power. JOURNAL OF DEVELOPMENT AND ADMINISTRATIVE STUDIES (KATHMANDU) January 1979, 1:178-92.

SCHUL, JEAN-JACQUES

Bergmann, Hellmuth and Schul, Jean-Jacques. Liste de questions sur le role des femmes dans les projets de developpement agricole. TIERS-MONDE (PARIS) October/December 1980, 21:833-44.

SCHUSTER, ILSA

Schuster, Ilsa. Marginal lives: conflict and contradiction in the position of female traders in Lusaka, Zambia. In: Women and work in Africa. Edited by Edna G. Bay. (Boulder, CO, Westview Press, 1982), pp. 105-26.

Schuster, Ilsa. Recent research on women in development; review article. JOURNAL OF DEVELOPMENT STUDIES (LONDON) July 1982, 18:511-35.

SCHWEDER, TORE

Jensen, An-Magritt and Schweder, Tore. Engine of fertility - influenced by interbirth employment? NORWAY. STATISTISK SENTRALBYRA. DISCUSSION PAPER (OSLO) June 1986, No. 15:1-33.

Scientific and technical progress and women's work in the USSR. By: Novikova, E. E.. LABOUR AND SOCIETY (GENEVA) January/March 1982, 7:13-22.

Scientific-technological change and the role of women in development. Edited by Pamela M. D'Onofrio-Flores and Sheila M. Pfafflin. (Boulder, CO, published for the United Nations Institute for Training and Research by Westview Press, 1982), 206 pp. Includes edited papers presented at the 1979 United Nations Conference on Science and Technology for Development.

La scolarisation et la formation professionnelle des femmes en Tunisie. By: Taamallah, Lamouria. REVUE TUNISIENNE DE SCIENCES SOCIALES (TUNIS) 1982, 19, No. 68/69:107-28.

SCOTT, ALISON MACEWEN

Scott, Alison MacEwen. Desarrollo dependiente y la segregacion ocupacional por sexo. DESARROLLO Y SOCIEDAD (BOGOTA) January 1984, No. 13:99-136. With English summary.

Scott, Alison MacEwen. Women and industrialisation: examining the "female marginalisation" thesis. JOURNAL OF DEVELOPMENT STUDIES (LONDON) July 1986, 22:649-80. The article argues for attention to be paid to the micro-level processes which give rise to women's marginalisation.

SCOTT, GLORIA L.

Scott, Gloria L. and Carr, Marilyn. Women in rural Bangladesh: policies for their employment and opportunities in crop processing. Series: World Bank Staff Working Papers, No. 731. (Washington, DC, World Bank, 1985), 107 pp. (Forthcoming).

SCOTT, JOAN WALLACH

Scott, Joan Wallach. Mechanization of women's work. SCIENTIFIC AMERICAN (NEW YORK) September 1982, 247:166-87.

SCRIABINE, RAISA

Scriabine, Raisa. Self-employed women: visible and valuable. HORIZONS, U.S. AGENCY FOR INTERNATIONAL DEVELOPMENT (WASHINGTON) Summer 1985, 4:38-40. Describes the Self-Employed Women's Association (SEWA), a trade union of more than 8,000 poor women workers in Ahmedabad, India. Members include small enterpreneurs, home-based producers, and manual laborers.

SEARLE-CHATTERJEE, MARY

Searle-Chatterjee, Mary. Reversible sex roles: the special case of Benares sweepers. Series: Women in Development, Vol. 2. (Oxford, New York, Pergamon Press, 1981), 112 pp.

Selected standards and policy statements of special interest to women workers adopted under the auspices of the International Labour Office. By: International Labour Office. (Geneva, International Labour Office, 1980), 132 pp.

Selected studies on the status of women, changes and continuities in the sexual division of labour in family and society, women's education/labour force participation and demographic trends in Northern America and Western Europe from 1975: ... By: Holland, Janet. In: Bibliographic guide to studies on the status of women: development and population trends. (New York, Bowker, UNIPUB; Paris, Unesco, 1983), pp. 183-267.

Self twice-removed: Ugandan woman. By: Akello, Grace. Series: Change International Reports: Women and Society, No. 8. (London, Change International Reports, 1983?), 19 pp.

SELF-EMPLOYED

Krishnaswami, Lalita. From drudgery to dignity: the SEWA experience. LABOUR AND SOCIETY (GENEVA) September 1985, 10:323-31. Discusses the achievements of the Self-Employed Women's Association (SEWA), which is at once a union, a trust and a credit institution whose basic aim is to provide better living and working conditions for the poor, illiterate women who comprise its membership.

SELF-HELP HOUSING

Chant, Sylvia. Household labour and self-help housing in Queretaro, Mexico. BOLETIN DE ESTUDIOS LATINO-AMERICANOS Y DEL CARIBE (AMSTERDAM) December 1984, No. 37:45-68.

Isralow, Sharon. Diamond in the rough. HORIZONS, U.S. AGENCY FOR INTERNATIONAL DEVELOPMENT (WASHINGTON) Summer 1985, 4:34-37. Examines the achievements of the women and men of Sri Lanka's Kirillapone shanty town.

Self-employed women: visible and valuable. By: Scriabine, Raisa. HORIZONS, U.S. AGENCY FOR INTERNATIONAL DEVELOPMENT (WASHINGTON) Summer 1985, 4:38-40. Describes the Self-Employed Women's Association (SEWA), a trade union of more than 8,000 poor women workers in Ahmedabad, India. Members include small enterpreneurs, home-based producers, and manual laborers.

Self-images of traditional urban women in Cairo. By: El-Messiri, Sawsan. In: Women in the Muslim world. Edited by Lois Beck and Nikki Keddie. (Cambridge, MA, Harvard University Press, 1978), pp. 522-40.

SELLERS, SUZANNE

Sellers, Suzanne. Swazi women left in the lurch. NEW AFRICAN (LONDON) February 1985, No. 209:p. 45. Discusses the pressures resulting from migrant labour and discrepancies between tradition and Western practice.

SELTZER, MIRIAM, ED.

Seltzer, Miriam, ed.. Home economics and agriculture in Third World countries. (St. Paul, Center for Youth Development and Research, College of Home Economics, University of Minnesota, [1980?]), 103 pp. Seminar held in St. Paul, Minnesota on May 14, 16, 23, 1980. The seminar led to recognition that women's roles in developing areas may need to be acknowledged and dealt with directly in any attack on the food problems of the poor.

Seminar on the status of women and family planning, Istanbul, Turkey, 11 - 24 July 1972. By: Seminar on the Status of Women and Family Planning, Istanbul, 1972. Series: United Nations Document, ST/TAO/HR/46. (New York, United Nations, 1972), 40 pp. Organized by the United Nations Division of Human Rights in cooperation with the Government of Turkey.

SEN, AMARTYA

Kynch, Jocelyn and Sen, Amartya. Indian women: well-being and survival. CAMBRIDGE JOURNAL OF ECONOMICS (LONDON) September/December 1983, 7:363-80.

SEN, CHIRANJIB

Sen, Gita and Sen, Chiranjib. Women's domestic work and economic activity: results from the National Sample Survey. CENTRE FOR DEVELOPMENT STUDIES. WORKING PAPER (ULLOOR, TRIVANDRUM) August 1984, No. 197:1-37.

SEN, GITA

Sen, Gita. Paddy production, processing and women workers in India - the south versus the northeast. CENTRE FOR DEVELOPMENT STUDIES. WORKING PAPER (ULLOOR, TRIVANDRUM) December 1983, No. 186.

Sen, Gita. Women agricultural labourers -- regional variations in incidence and employment. CENTRE FOR DEVELOPMENT STUDIES. WORKING PAPER (ULLOOR, TRIVANDRUM) April 1983, No. 168:1-28.

Sen, Gita and Sen, Chiranjib. Women's domestic work and economic activity: results from the National Sample Survey. CENTRE FOR DEVELOPMENT STUDIES. WORKING PAPER (ULLOOR, TRIVANDRUM) August 1984, No. 197:1-37.

Sen, Gita. Women's work and women agricultural labourers: a study of the Indian Census. CENTRE FOR DEVELOPMENT STUDIES. WORKING PAPER (ULLOOR, TRIVANDRUM) February 1983, No. 159:1-43.

SENEGAL

Koumbidia (Senegal); developpement d'une activite maraichere villageoise. TIERS-MONDE (PARIS) April/June 1985, 26:421-28.

Venema, Bernhard. Les consequences de l'introduction d'une culture de rente et d'une culture attelee sur la position de la femme wolof a Saloum. TIERS-MONDE (PARIS) July/September 1982, 23:603-16.

Sense of their own effectiveness. CERES, FAO REVIEW ON AGRICULTURE AND DEVELOPMENT (ROME) January/February 1986, 19:44-46. An interview with Peggy Antrobus, coordinator of WAND (Women and Development Unit), a regional organization created in Barbados in 1978 as a part of the Action Plan of the United Nations Decade for Women.

Sensitivity of labor supply parameter estimates to unobserved individual effects: fixed and random effects estimates in a nonlinear model using panel data. By: Jakubson, George. PRINCETON UNIVERSITY. INDUSTRIAL RELATIONS SECTION. WORKING PAPER (PRINCETON) August 1986, No. 210:1-37; A1-A4 (various pagings).

Sex and ethnic differences in educational investment in Malaysia: the effect of reward structures. By: Wang, Bee-Lan Chan. COMPARATIVE EDUCATION REVIEW (NEW YORK) June 1980, 24:S140-59.

Sex and location differences in wages in the Australian public service. By: Chapman, Bruce J. AUSTRALIAN ECONOMIC PAPERS (ADELAIDE) December 1985, 24:296-309.

Sex differences and folk illness in an Egyptian village. By: Morsy, Soheir A.. In: Women in the Muslim world. Edited by Lois Beck and Nikki Keddie. (Cambridge, MA, Harvard University Press, 1978), pp. 599-616.

Sex differences in earnings: an analysis of Malaysian wage data. By: Chapman, Bruce J. and Harding, J. Ross. HARVARD INSTITUTE FOR INTERNATIONAL DEVELOPMENT, DEVELOPMENT DISCUSSION PAPER (CAMBRIDGE, MASS.) December 1980, No. 112:1-24.

Sex differences in earnings: an analysis of Malaysian wage data. By: Chapman, Bruce J. and Harding, J. Ross. JOURNAL OF DEVELOPMENT STUDIES (LONDON) April 1985, 21:362-76.

Sex differences in educational attainment: the process. By: Finn, Jeremy D. and Reis, Janet. COMPARATIVE EDUCATION REVIEW (NEW YORK) June 1980, 24:S33-52. Examines various obstacles to women's education.

SEX DISCRIMINATION IN EMPLOYMENT

Bielby, William T. and Baron, James N. Sex segregation within occupations. AMERICAN ECONOMIC REVIEW, PAPERS AND PROCEEDINGS (NASHVILLE) May 1986, 76:43-47.

Schippers, Joop J. and Siegers, Jacques J. Women's relative wage rate in the Netherlands, 1950-1983: a test of alternative discrimination theories. DE ECONOMIST (LEIDEN) 1986, 134, No. 2:165-80.

Zalokar, Nadja. Generational differences in female occupational attainment -- have the 1970's changed women's opportunities? AMERICAN ECONOMIC REVIEW, PAPERS AND PROCEEDINGS (NASHVILLE) May 1986, 76:378-81.

Sex inequalities in the dual system of education; the Parsis of Gujarat. By: Gould, Ketayun. ECONOMIC AND POLITICAL WEEKLY (BOMBAY) September 24, 1983, 18:1668-76.

Sex segregation within occupations. By: Bielby, William T. and Baron, James N. AMERICAN ECONOMIC REVIEW, PAPERS AND PROCEEDINGS (NASHVILLE) May 1986, 76:43-47.

Sexual barrier: legal, medical, economic and social aspects of sex discrimination. By: Hughes, Marija Matich. (Washington, Hughes Press, 1977), 843 pp. An enlarged and reissued edition of the author's original bibliography on women, entitled The Sexual barrier: legal and economic aspects of employment, published in 1970, with supplements in 1971 and 1972.

Sexual stratification: the other side of "growth with equity" in East Asia. By: Greenhalgh, Susan. POPULATION AND DEVELOPMENT REVIEW (NEW YORK) June 1985, 11:265-314. This paper explores changes in women's status on Taiwan focussing on how the traditional system of sexual stratification was perpetuated and even intensified with the rapid development of the economy.

SHAH, NASRA M.

Shah, Nasra M.. Female migrant in Pakistan. In: Women in the cities of Asia: migration and urban adaptation. Edited by James T. Fawcett, Siew-Ean Khoo and Peter C. Smith. (Boulder, CO, Westview Press, 1984), pp. 108-24.

Shah, Nasra M. and Smith, Peter C.. Migrant women at work in Asia. In: Women in the cities of Asia: migration and urban adaptation. Edited by James T. Fawcett, Siew-Ean Khoo and Peter C. Smith. (Boulder, CO, Westview Press, 1984), pp. 297-322.

SHAHANI, LETIZIA R.

Shahani, Letizia R.. On the road to Nairobi '85. DEVELOPMENT (ROME) 1984, No. 4:85-86.

SHAIB, DIANA

Azzam, Henry T. and Shaib, Diana. Women left behind: a study of the wives of Lebanese migrant workers in the oil rich countries of the region. INTERNATIONAL LABOUR OFFICE. WORLD EMPLOYMENT PROGRAMME RESEARCH. POPULATION AND LABOUR POLICIES: REGIONAL PROGRAMME FOR THE MIDDLE EAST. WORKING PAPER (BEIRUT) September 1980, No. 3:1-56.

SHAPIRA, RINA

Shapira, Rina and Etzioni-Halevy, Eva and Chopp-Tibon, Shira. Occupational choice among female academicians -- the Israeli case. In: Women in the family and the economy: an international comparative survey. Edited by George Kurian and Ratna Ghosh. (Westport, CT, Greenwood Press, 1981), pp. 345-58.

SHARMA, MIRIAM

Sharma, Miriam. Caste, class, and gender: production and reproduction in North India. JOURNAL OF PEASANT STUDIES (LONDON) July 1985, 12:26-56.

SHARMA, URSULA

Sharma, Ursula. Unmarried women and the household economy: a research note. JOURNAL OF SOCIAL STUDIES (DHAKA) October 1985, No. 30:1-12.

Sharma, Ursula. Women, work and property in North-West India. (London, New York, Tavistock, 1980), 226 pp.

SHARMA, URSULA M.

Sharma, Ursula M.. Family status production work: what does it produce? JOURNAL OF SOCIAL STUDIES (DHAKA) April 1984, No. 24:74-94. Attempts to develop some issues regarding women's work in the household, using a study of women in urban households in Simla, Himachal Pradesh.

SHASTRI, P. P.

Ramachandran, P. and Shastri, P. P.. Intercensal urban Indian female participation rates and their variations, 1961-71: a census analysis. ECONOMIC AFFAIRS (CALCUTTA) October/December 1983, 28:816-28.

SHIELDS, NWANGANGA

Shields, Nwanganga. Women in the urban labor markets of Africa: the case of Tanzania. Series: World Bank Staff Working Papers, No. 380. (Washington, DC, World Bank, 1980), 136, 2 pp.

SHINOTSUKA, EIKO

Shinotsuka, Eiko. Female workers as described in a help-wanted information magazine. JAPANESE ECONOMIC STUDIES (ARMONK, N.Y.) Spring 1984, 12:3-20.

Shinotsuka, Eiko. Women at work; equality and care of the species. FAR EASTERN ECONOMIC REVIEW (HONGKONG) Dec. 3, 1982, 118:87-90.

SHOEMAKER, SUSAN

Shoemaker, Susan. Status of women in the rural U.S.S.R. POPULATION RESEARCH AND POLICY REVIEW (AMSTERDAM) February 1983, 2:35-51.

SIDEL, RUTH

Sidel, Ruth. Women and child care in China: a firsthand report. (New York, Penguin, Revised edition, 1982), 211 pp.

SIEGERS, J. J.

Schippers, J. J. and Siegers, J. J.. Economische aspecten van een quoterings-maatregel ten behoeve van vrouwen op de arbeidsmarkt. MAANDSCHRIFT ECONOMIE (TILBURG) 1984, 48, No. 6:484-99.

SIERRA LEONE

Stevens, Yvette. Technologies for rural women's activities--problems and prospects in Sierra Leone. INTERNATIONAL LABOUR OFFICE. WORLD EMPLOYMENT PROGRAMME RESEARCH. TECHNOLOGY AND EMPLOYMENT PROGRAMME. WORKING PAPERS (GENEVA) October 1981, No. 86:1-84. Reviews available evidence from Sierra Leone on the range of technologies relevant to rural women's tasks, such as farming, water collection and food processing.

Signares of Saint-Louis and Goree: women entrepreneurs in eighteenth-century Senegal. By: Brooks, George E., Jr.. In: Women in Africa: studies in social and economic change. Edited by Nancy J. Hafkin and Edna G. Bay. (Stanford, Stanford University Press, 1976), pp. 19-44.

SILVERMAN, SYDEL F.

Silverman, Sydel F.. Life crises as a clue to social function: the case of Italy. In: Toward an anthropology of women. Edited by Rayna R. Reiter. (New York, Monthly Review Press, 1975), pp. 309-21.

SILVESTRINI-PACHECO, BLANCO

Silvestrini-Pacheco, Blanco. Women as workers: the experience of the Puerto Rican woman in the 1930's. In: Women cross-culturally: change and challenge. Edited by Ruby Rohrlich-Leavitt. (The Hague, Mouton, 1975), pp. 247-60.

SIMI, NOUMEA

Thomas, Pamela and Simi, Noumea. The new Samoan businesswoman. PACIFIC PERSPECTIVE (SUVA) 1983, 11, No. 2:5-12.

Simple technologies for rural women in Bangladesh. By: O'Kelly, Elizabeth. (Dacca, UNICEF, Women's Development Programme, 1977), 48 pp. Annexure VI to the Feasibility Survey of Productive Income Generating Activities for Women.

Since Mexico '75: a decade of progress? By: Reid, Elizabeth Anne. DEVELOPMENT (ROME) 1984, No. 4:76-79.

SINCLAIR, SONJA A.

Roberts, George W. and Sinclair, Sonja A.. Women in Jamaica: patterns of reproduction and family. (Millwood, New York, KTC Press, 1978), 346 pp.

SINGAPORE

Lim, Linda. New order with some old prejudices. FAR EASTERN ECONOMIC REVIEW (HONGKONG) January 5, 1984, 123:37-38. The position of Singapore's women throughout its brief history has been defined by traditional outlines, male dominance and female subordination.

SINGH, A. S. AND JAIN, K. K

Singh, A. S. and Jain, K. K. Diversification of Punjab agriculture: an econometric analysis. INDIAN JOURNAL OF AGRICULTURAL ECONOMICS (BOMBAY) July/September 1985, 40:298-303.

SINGH, ANDREA MENEFEE

Singh, Andrea Menefee. Rural-to-urban migration of women in India: patterns and implications. In: Women in the cities of Asia: migration and urban adaptation. Edited by James T. Fawcett, Siew-Ean Khoo and Peter C. Smith. (Boulder, CO, Westview Press, 1984), pp. 81-107.

SINGH, GEETANJALI

Singh, Geetanjali. Trying to throw off the shackles of the past. FAR EASTERN ECONOMIC REVIEW (HONGKONG) January 5, 1984, 123:29-30. Examines the situation of women in India.

SINGH, NALINI

Jain, Devaki and Singh, Nalini. Role of rural women in community life; a case study from India. ECONOMIC BULLETIN FOR ASIA AND THE PACIFIC (BANGKOK) December 1978, 29:84-126.

SINGHAL, SUSHILA

Singhal, Sushila. Development of educated women in India: reflections of a social psychologist. COMPARATIVE EDUCATION (OXFORD) October 1984, 20:355-70.

SINGHANETRA-RENARD, ANCHALEE

Singhanetra-Renard, Anchalee. Effect of female labour force participation on fertility: the case of construction workers in Chiang Mai City. In: Women in the urban and industrial workforce; Southeast and East Asia. Edited by Gavin W. Jones. Series: Development Studies Centre. Monograph, No. 33. (Canberra, Australia, Australian National University, 1984), pp. 325-38. Series edited by Helen Hughes.

SINGLE WOMEN

Sharma, Ursula. Unmarried women and the household economy: a research note. JOURNAL OF SOCIAL STUDIES (DHAKA) October 1985, No. 30:1-12.

SIPILA, HELVI LINNEA

Sipila, Helvi Linnea. Status of women and family planning: report of the special rapporteur appointed by the Economic and Social Council under Resolution 1326 (XLIV). Series: United Nations [Document], E/CN.6/575/Rev. 1. (New York, United Nations, 1975), 148 pp. United Nations publication. Sales No. E.75.IV.5.

SIQUEIRA WIARDA, IEDA

Siqueira Wiarda, Ieda and Helzner, Judith Frye. Women, population, and international development in Latin America: a 1984 assessment. MANAGING INTERNATIONAL DEVELOPMENT (ARMONK, N.Y.) September/October 1984, 1:84-106.

SIRAJ, MEHRUN

Siraj, Mehrun. Islamic attitudes to female employment in industrializing economies: some notes from Malaysia. In: Women in the urban and industrial workforce; Southeast and East Asia. Edited by Gavin W. Jones. Series: Development Studies Centre. Monograph, No. 33. (Canberra, Australia, Australian National University, 1984), pp. 163-74. Series edited by Helen Hughes.

SIRIWARDENA, B. S.

Siriwardena, B. S.. Life of Ceylon women. In: Women in the new Asia; the changing social roles of men and women in South and South-east Asia. Edited by Barbara E. Ward. ([Paris], Unesco, 1963), pp. 150-72.

SISODIA, J. S

Sisodia, J. S. Role of farm women in agriculture: a study of Chambal command area of Madhya Pradesh. INDIAN JOURNAL OF AGRICULTURAL ECONOMICS (BOMBAY) July/September 1985, 40:223-34.

Sisterhood of man. By: Newland, Kathleen. (New York, London, W. W. Norton & Company, 1979), 242 pp. A Worldwatch Institute Book.

Sisters under the sun: the story of Sudanese women. By: Hall, Marjorie J. and Ismail, Bathita Amin. (London, New York, Longman, 1981), 264 pp.

SJAFRI, AIDA

Sjafri, Aida. Socio-economic aspects of food consumption in rural Java. In: Endless day: some case material on Asian rural women. Edited by T. Scarlett Epstein and Rosemary A. Watts. Series: Women in Development, Vol. 3. (Oxford, England, New York, Pergamon Press, 1981), pp. 107-27.

SKINNER, JONATHAN

Johnson, William R. and Skinner, Jonathan. Labor supply and marital separation. AMERICAN ECONOMIC REVIEW (NASHVILLE) June 1986, 76:455-69. A simultaneous model of future divorce probability and current labor supply is estimated for married women. The results support the hypothesis that divorce probabilities increase labor supply.

SLADE, DOREN L.

Slade, Doren L.. Marital status and sexual identity; the position of women in a Mexican peasant society. In: Women cross-culturally: change and challenge. Edited by Ruby Rohrlich-Leavitt. (The Hague, Mouton, 1975), pp. 129-48.

SLOCUM, SALLY

Slocum, Sally. Woman the gatherer: male bias in anthropology. In: Toward an anthropology of women. Edited by Rayna R. Reiter. (New York, Monthly Review Press, 1975), pp. 36-50.

Slow progress on women's health. By: Davies, Wendy. NEW AFRICAN (LONDON) August 1985, No. 215:p. 42.

SMALE, MELINDA

Smale, Melinda. Women in Mauritania: the effects of drought and migration on their economic status and implications for development programs. (Washington, DC, Office of Women in Development, Agency for International Development, 1980), 163 pp. On cover: Women in Development.

SMALL FARMS

Saini, Amrik S. and Singh, Raj Vir. Impact of diversification on income, employment and credit needs of small farmers in Punjab. INDIAN JOURNAL OF AGRICULTURAL ECONOMICS (BOMBAY) July/September 1985, 40:310-16.

SMITH, MARGO L.

Smith, Margo L.. Female domestic servant and social change: Lima, Peru. In: Women cross-culturally: change and challenge. Edited by Ruby Rohrlich-Leavitt. (The Hague, Mouton, 1975), pp. 163-80.

SMITH, MICHAEL L.

Smith, Michael L.. Women of Peru's slums raise sights with communal kitchens. WASHINGTON POST (WASHINGTON) September 16, 1984, p. A13.

SMITH, PETER C.

Eviota, Elizabeth U. and Smith, Peter C.. Migration of women in the Philippines. In: Women in the cities of Asia: migration and urban adaptation. Edited by James T. Fawcett, Siew-Ean Khoo and Peter C. Smith. (Boulder, CO, Westview Press, 1984), pp. 165-90.

Fawcett, James T. and Khoo, Siew-Ean and Smith, Peter C.. Urbanization, migration, and the status of women. In: Women in the cities of Asia: migration and urban adaptation. Edited by James T. Fawcett, Siew-Ean Khoo and Peter C. Smith. (Boulder, CO, Westview Press, 1984), pp. 15-35.

Shah, Nasra M. and Smith, Peter C.. Migrant women at work in Asia. In: Women in the cities of Asia: migration and urban adaptation. Edited by James T. Fawcett, Siew-Ean Khoo and Peter C. Smith. (Boulder, CO, Westview Press, 1984), pp. 297-322.

SMITH, SHEILA

Young, Kate and Smith, Sheila. Women's disadvantage: capitalist development and socialist alternatives in Britain. DEVELOPMENT DIALOGUE (UPPSALA) 1982, No. 1/2:85-100.

SMOCK, AUDREY CHAPMAN

Smock, Audrey Chapman. Bangladesh: a struggle with tradition and poverty. In: Women: roles and status in eight countries. Edited by Janet Zollinger Giele and Audrey Chapman Smock. (New York, John Wiley, 1977), pp. 83-126.

Smock, Audrey Chapman. Determinants of women's roles and status. In: Women: roles and status in eight countries. Edited by Janet Zollinger Giele and Audrey Chapman Smock. (New York, John Wiley, 1977), pp. 385-421.

Smock, Audrey Chapman and Youssef, Nadia Haggag. Egypt: from seclusion to limited participation. In: Women: roles and status in eight countries. Edited by Janet Zollinger Giele and Audrey Chapman Smock. (New York, John Wiley, 1977), pp. 35-79.

Smock, Audrey Chapman. Ghana: from autonomy to subordination. In: Women: roles and status in eight countries. Edited by Janet Zollinger Giele and Audrey Chapman Smock. (New York, John Wiley, 1977), pp. 175-216.

So few women in engineering. By: Pearson, Richard. NATURE (LONDON) October 2, 1986, 323:p. 474.

Social and economic integration of south Asian women in Montreal, Canada. By: Ghosh, Ratna. In: Women in the family and the economy: an international comparative survey. Edited by George Kurian and Ratna Ghosh. (Westport, CT, Greenwood Press, 1981), pp. 59-80.

Social ascendancy without the fanfare. By: Ng, Margaret. FAR EASTERN ECONOMIC REVIEW (HONGKONG) January 5, 1984, 123:28-29. Discusses the status of women in Hongkong.

SOCIAL CHANGE

Kvinder, konsrelationer og social forandring. DEN NY VERDEN (COPENHAGEN) 1983, 17, No.4:1-124. Content: Wilson, Fiona, Kvinder og kommercialisering af landbruget: en diskussion af aktuelle tendenser i Mexico. - Odgaard, Rie, and Jens Dahl, Gronlandske bygdekvinder i en okonomisk forandringsproces. - Roberts, Pepe, Kvinder i landomraderne i Vestnigeria. - Thorbek, Susanne, Refleksioner fra en Bangkok slum. - Tarp, Elsebeth, Kvindekamp og kulturkamp i Mexico. - Sjorslev, Inger, Rituel magt og social undertrykkelse; kvinder i Brasilien.

Von Vietinghoff, Franciska. Women working together; spontaneous success. SUDANOW (KHARTOUM) March 1985, 10:29-30.

Social change and social control: college-educated Punjabi women 1913 to 1960. By: Maskiell, Michelle. MODERN ASIAN STUDIES (LONDON) February 1985, 19:55-83.

SOCIAL CONDITIONS

Leonard, Karen. Women in India; some recent perspectives; research note. PACIFIC AFFAIRS (VANCOUVER, B.C.) Spring 1979, 52:95-107.

Social equality: the constitutional experiment in India. By: Kumar, Manju. (New Delhi, S. Chand, 1982), 264 pp.

Social origins of the sexual division of labour. By: Mies, Maria. INSTITUTE OF SOCIAL STUDIES. OCCASIONAL PAPERS (THE HAGUE) January 1981, No. 85:1-49.

SOCIAL POLICY

Sapiro, Virginia. Gender basis of American social policy. POLITICAL SCIENCE QUARTERLY (NEW YORK) 1986, 101, No. 2:221-38.

Social policy and women in Latin America: the need for a new model. By: Flora, Cornelia Butler. STUDIES IN THIRD WORLD SOCIETIES (WILLIAMSBURG) March 1981, No. 15:91-105.

Social science research and women in the Arab world. By: Unesco. (London, Pinter, 1984), 175 pp.

SOCIAL WELFARE

Fruzzetti, Lina M. Four women's organizations of Calcutta. UNIVERSITIES FIELD STAFF INTERNATIONAL REPORTS, ASIA (HANOVER, NH) 1986, No. 4:1-5.

Socialist revolution and women's liberation in China -- a review article. By: Honig, Emily. JOURNAL OF ASIAN STUDIES (ANN ARBOR, MICH.) February 1985, 44:328-36.

Sociocultural factors mitigating role conflict of Buenos Aires professional women. By: Kinzer, Nora Scott. In: Women cross-culturally: change and challenge. Edited by Ruby Rohrlich-Leavitt. (The Hague, Mouton, 1975), pp. 181-97.

Socio-economic aspects of food consumption in rural Java. By: Sjafri, Aida. In: Endless day: some case material on Asian rural women. Edited by T. Scarlett Epstein and Rosemary A. Watts. Series: Women in Development, Vol. 3. (Oxford, England, New York, Pergamon Press, 1981), pp. 107-27.

Socioeconomic characteristics of women in a developing country and the degree of urbanization. By: Wolfe, Barbara L. and Behrman, Jere R.. UNIVERSITY OF WISCONSIN-MADISON. INSTITUTE FOR RESEARCH ON POVERTY. DISCUSSION PAPERS (MADISON) September 1980, 655-81:1-53. The study is based on a stratified random sample of over 4,000 women aged 15-45 in Nicaragua.

Socioeconomic development and the status of women in the Third world. By: Safilios-Rothschild, Constantina. POPULATION COUNCIL. CENTER FOR POLICY STUDIES. WORKING PAPERS (NEW YORK) May 1985, No. 112:1-49. Examines the relationship between socioeconomic development and women's status in 75 developing countries.

Socio-economic status of women. YUGOSLAV SURVEY (BELGRADE) November 1985, 26:3-24.

SOFER, CATHERINE

Sofer, Catherine. Emplois "feminins" et emplois "masculins": mesure de la segregation et evolution de la feminisation des emplois. INSTITUT NATIONAL DE LA STATISTIQUE ET DES ETUDES ECONOMIQUES, ANNALES (PARIS) October/December 1983, No. 52:55-85. With English summary.

SOFFAN, LINDA USRA

Soffan, Linda Usra. Women of the United Arab Emirates. (London, Croom Helm; New York, Barnes & Noble Books, 1980), 127 pp.

SOKOLOWSKA, MAGDALENA

Sokolowska, Magdalena. Poland: women's experience under socialism. In: Women: roles and status in eight countries. Edited by Janet Zollinger Giele and Audrey Chapman Smock. (New York, John Wiley, 1977), pp. 349-381.

Some aspects of unskilled labor markets for civil construction in India: observations based on field investigation. By: Bose, Swadesh R.. Series: World Bank Staff Working Papers, No. 223. (Washington, DC, World Bank, 1975), 47 pp.

Some aspirations of lower class black mothers. By: Jackson, Roberta H.. In: Women in the family and the economy: an international comparative survey. Edited by George Kurian and Ratna Ghosh. (Westport, CT, Greenwood Press, 1981), pp. 273-83.

Some comments on the home roles of business women in India, Australia and Canada. By: Ross, Aileen D.. In: Women in the family and the economy: an international comparative survey. Edited by George Kurian and Ratna Ghosh. (Westport, CT, Greenwood Press, 1981), pp. 317-30.

Some sow, others reap. By: Briceno, Maria Esperanza. In: Latin American women: the meek speak out. Edited by June H. Turner. (Silver Spring, MD, International Educational Development, 1980), pp. 137-46. The author discusses women in Colombia.

SOON, YOUNG YOON

Soon, Young Yoon. World away from women's liberation. GUARDIAN (LONDON) September 7, 1984, p. 16. Looks at why women in the Third World think their Western sisters' efforts are being misdirected.

SORENSEN, ELAINE

Sorensen, Elaine. Implementing comparable worth: a survey of recent job evaluation studies. AMERICAN ECONOMIC REVIEW, PAPERS AND PROCEEDINGS (NASHVILLE) May 1986, 76:364-72.

Sources of changes in the occupational segregation of Australian women. By: Lewis, Donald E. ECONOMIC RECORD (MELBOURNE) December 1985, 61:719-36.

SOUTH AFRICA

Thomas, Rosalind. Women; the law in Southern Africa: justice for all? AFRICA REPORT (NEW YORK) March/April 1985, 30:59-64.

Soviet fertility, labor-force participation, and marital instabililty. By: Kuniansky, Anna. JOURNAL OF COMPARATIVE ECONOMICS (NEW YORK) June 1983, 7:114-30.

Soviet women in the life of society: achievements and problems. By: Motroshilova, Nelya V.. INTERNATIONAL SOCIAL SCIENCE JOURNAL (PARIS) 1983, 35, No. 4:733-46.

SPAIN

Bollag, Daniel. Breath of feminism in macho Spain. SWISS REVIEW OF WORLD AFFAIRS (ZURICH) July 1982, 32:21-23.

Jimenez Butragueno, Maria de los Angeles. Protective legislation and equal opportunity and treatment for women in Spain. INTERNATIONAL LABOUR REVIEW (GENEVA) March/April 1982, 121:185-98.

Special issue: The political economy of women. REVIEW OF RADICAL POLITICAL ECONOMICS (NEW YORK) Spring 1984, 16:1-202.

Special report: Women in development. BANK'S WORLD (WASHINGTON) September 1985, 4:2-9. CONTENT: Messiter, Marjorie, Report from Nairobi. - Messiter, Marjorie, Q & A with Gloria Scott. - Peters, Barbara McGarry, Women in the Bank. - de Merode, Janet, A woman's memoir of Mali ... Recalls her three years as Resrep.

SPRAGUE, ALISON

Sprague, Alison. Post-war fertility and female labour force participation rates. OXFORD UNIVERSITY. INSTITUTE OF ECONOMICS AND STATISTICS. APPLIED ECONOMICS DISCUSSION PAPER (OXFORD) June 1986, No. 9:1-35.

Spread of capitalism in rural Colombia: effects on poor women. By: Rubbo, Anna. In: Toward an anthropology of women. Edited by Rayna R. Reiter. (New York, Monthly Review Press, 1975), pp. 333-57.

SPRING, ANITA

Spring, Anita. Men and women smallholder participants in a stall-feeder livestock program in Malawi. HUMAN ORGANIZATION (WASHINGTON) Summer 1986, 45:154-62.

Squatter settlement decision-making: for men only? By: Alva, Carmen Arimana. In: Latin American women: the meek speak out. Edited by June H. Turner. (Silver Spring, MD, International Educational Development, 1980), pp. 14-24. Examines the situation of women in Peru.

SRI LANKA

Isralow, Sharon. Diamond in the rough. HORIZONS, U.S. AGENCY FOR INTERNATIONAL DEVELOPMENT (WASHINGTON) Summer 1985, 4:34-37. Examines the achievements of the women and men of Sri Lanka's Kirillapone shanty town.

Jayawardena, Kumari. Plantation sector in Sri Lanka: recent changes in the welfare of children and women. WORLD DEVELOPMENT (OXFORD) March 1984, 12, Special issue:317-28.

Kearney, Robert N.. Women in politics in Sri Lanka. ASIAN SURVEY (BERKELEY, CALIF.) July 1981, 21:729-46.

SRI LANKA

Kurian, Rachel. Income distribution, poverty and employment. INSTITUTE OF SOCIAL STUDIES. OCCASIONAL PAPERS (THE HAGUE) September 1979, No. 73:1-55. Examines the marginalization of women in theory and in reality, with examples from studies carried out in Sri Lanka and Yugoslavia.

SRIVASTAVA, J. N.

Srivastava, J. N.. Determinants of female age at marriage in rural Uttar Pradesh. INDIAN JOURNAL OF ECONOMICS (ALLAHABAD) January 1984, 64:327-44.

St. Lucia's female electronics factory workers: key components in an export-oriented industrialization strategy. By: Kelly, Deirdre. WORLD DEVELOPMENT (OXFORD) July 1986, 14:823-38.

STAHN-WILLIG, BRIGITTE

Metzner, Ulrike and Stahn-Willig, Brigitte. Frauenarbeit: ein Beitrag zur gewerkschaftlichen Technikdebatte. WSI-MITTEILUNGEN (DUSSELDORF) August 1986, 39:529-36.

STANDING, GUY

Standing, Guy. Unemployment and female labour: a study of labour supply in Kingston, Jamaica. (New York, St. Martin's Press, 1981), 364 pp. Prepared for the International Labour Office within the framework of the World Employment Programme.

Status and role of women in East Africa. By: United Nations. Economic Commission for Africa. Social Development Section. Series: Social Welfare Services in Africa, No. 6. (New York, United Nations, 1967), 65 pp.

Status of the Arab woman: a select bibliography. By: Meghdessian, Samira Rafidi. Compiled by Samira Rafidi Meghdessian. (Westport, Connecticut, Greenwood Press, 1980), 176 pp. A bibliography compiled under the auspices of the Institute for Women's Studies in the Arab World, Beirut, University College, Lebanon.

Status of women. By: Ali, Ausaf. ARABIA; THE ISLAMIC WORLD REVIEW (EAST BURNHAM) October 1986, 6:56-57. Views on the place of women in Islam.

Status of women and family planning: report of the special rapporteur appointed by the Economic and Social Council under Resolution 1326 (XLIV). By: Sipila, Helvi Linnea. Series: United Nations [Document], E/CN.6/575/Rev. 1. (New York, United Nations, 1975), 148 pp. United Nations publication. Sales No. E.75.IV.5.

Status of women and property on a Baluchistan oasis in Pakistan. By: Pastner, Carroll McC.. In: Women in the Muslim world. Edited by Lois Beck and Nikki Keddie. (Cambridge, MA, Harvard University Press, 1978), pp. 434-50.

Status of women in four Middle East communities. By: Peters, Emrys L.. In: Women in the Muslim world. Edited by Lois Beck and Nikki Keddie. (Cambridge, MA, Harvard University Press, 1978), pp. 311-50. The four communities examined here include the Bedouin of Cyrenaica (Libya), a horticultural community of Shiite Muslims in south Lebanon, olive farmers, Sunni Muslims, in Tripolitania (Libya), and a Maronite Christian village in central Lebanon.

Status of women in Indonesian marriage law. By: Ghandi, Lapian. In: Women and development, perspectives from South and Southeast Asia. Edited by Rounaq Jahan and Hanna Papanek. (Dacca, Bangladesh Institute of Law and International Affairs, 1979), pp. 71-94.

Status of women in Nepal: Vol. 1, Background report. By: Acharya, Meena [et al.]. (Kathmandu, Centre for Economic Development and Administration, 1979), 4 pts in 1 vol. CONTENT: Pt. 1, Acharya, Meena, Statistical profile of Napalese women: a critical review. - Pt. 2, Bennett, Lynn, Tradition and change in the legal status of Napalese women. - Pt. 3, Pradhan, Bina, Institutions concerning women in Nepal. - Pt. 4, Shrestha, Indira, Annotated bibliography of women in Nepal.

Status of women in the eye of law in Bangladesh: proceedings of a seminar held in Dacca. December 10 - 12, 1977. Edited by Zebunnessa Rahman. (Dacca, Bangladesh Mahila Samity, [1977]?), 104 pp.

Status of women in the rural U.S.S.R. By: Shoemaker, Susan. POPULATION RESEARCH AND POLICY REVIEW (AMSTERDAM) February 1983, 2:35-51.

Status of women in Turkey: cross-cultural perspectives. By: Kagitcibasi, Cigdem. INTERNATIONAL JOURNAL OF MIDDLE EAST STUDIES (CAMBRIDGE) November 1986, 18:485-99.

Status of working women in the Philippines. By: Philippines. Bureau of Women and Minors. (Manila, 1975), 53 pp.

Le statut social de la femme; pour un nouvel ordre mondial. By: Gauffenic, Armelle. TIERS-MONDE (PARIS) April/June 1985, 26:273-81.

STAUDT, KATHLEEN

Staudt, Kathleen. Planning-centred approach to project evaluation: women in mainstream development projects. PUBLIC ADMINISTRATION AND DEVELOPMENT (CHICHESTER) January/March 1985, 5:25-37. Describes the process and outcomes of a 'planning-centred' approach to three development projects in the Caribbean.

Staudt, Kathleen. Policy strategies at the end of the decade. AFRICA REPORT (NEW YORK) March/April 1985, 30:71-5.

STAUDT, KATHLEEN A.

Staudt, Kathleen A.. Women farmers and inequities in agricultural services. In: Women and work in Africa. Edited by Edna G. Bay. (Boulder, CO, Westview Press, 1982), pp. 207-24.

Staudt, Kathleen A.. Women's politics in Africa. STUDIES IN THIRD WORLD SOCIETIES (WILLIAMSBURG) June 1981, No. 16:1-28.

STEADY, FILOMINA CHIOMA

Steady, Filomina Chioma. African women, industrialization and another development; a global perspective. DEVELOPMENT DIALOGUE (UPPSALA) 1982, No. 1/2:51-64.

Steady, Filomina Chioma. Nairobi '85:African women at the end of the decade. AFRICA REPORT (NEW YORK) March/April 1985, 30:4-8. Discusses the World Conference on the United Nations Decade for Women, to be held in Nairobi, Kenya, July 15-26, 1985.

Steady, Filomina Chioma. Protestant women's associations in Freetown, Sierre Leone. In: Women in Africa: studies in social and economic change. Edited by Nancy J. Hafkin and Edna G. Bay. (Stanford, Stanford University Press, 1976), pp. 213-37.

STEEL, WILLIAM F.

Steel, William F. and Campbell, Claudia. Women's employment and development: a conceptual framework applied to Ghana. In: Women and work in Africa. Edited by Edna G. Bay. (Boulder, CO, Westview Press, 1982), pp. 225-48.

STEINMEIER, THOMAS L

Gustman, Alan and Steinmeier, Thomas L. Wages, employment, training and job attachment in low wage labor markets for women. NATIONAL BUREAU OF ECONOMIC RESEARCH. WORKING PAPER SERIES (CAMBRIDGE, MASS.) October 1986, No. 2037:1-52. The authors analyze economic behaviour and the effects of training and income support policies in the low wage labor market for women.

STEPHEN, JUNE

Isaacman, Barbara and Stephen, June. Mozambique: women, the law and agrarian reform. Series: [African Training and Research Centre for Women] Research Series, No. 01/80. ([Addis Ababa], United Nations Economic Commission for Africa, 1980), 148 pp. "ATRCWSDD/RES01/80"

STEVENS, YVETTE

Date-Bah, Eugenia and Stevens, Yvette. Rural women in Africa and technological change: some issues. LABOUR AND SOCIETY (GENEVA) April/June 1981, 6:149-62.

Stevens, Yvette. Technologies for rural women's activities--problems and prospects in Sierra Leone. INTERNATIONAL LABOUR OFFICE. WORLD EMPLOYMENT PROGRAMME RESEARCH. TECHNOLOGY AND EMPLOYMENT PROGRAMME. WORKING PAPERS (GENEVA) October 1981, No. 86:1-84. Reviews available evidence from Sierra Leone on the range of technologies relevant to rural women's tasks, such as farming, water collection and food processing.

STEWART, MARK B.

Stewart, Mark B. and Greenhalgh, Christine A.. Work history patterns and the occupational attainment of women. ECONOMIC JOURNAL (LONDON) September 1984, 94:493-519.

STEYN, ANNA F.

Steyn, Anna F. and Uys, J. M.. Changing position of black women in South Africa. In: Changing position of women in family and society; a cross-national comparison. Edited by Eugen Lupri. Series: International studies in sociology and social anthropology, vol. 34. (Leiden, E. J. Brill, 1983), pp. 344-70.

STINEMAN, ESTHER

Stineman, Esther. Women's studies: a recommended core bibliography. (Littleton, Colorado, Libraries Unlimited, 1979), 670 pp. With the assistance of Catherine Loeb.

STOKES, RANDALL G.

Marshall, Susan E. and Stokes, Randall G.. Tradition and the veil: female status in Tunisia and Algeria. JOURNAL OF MODERN AFRICAN STUDIES (OXFORD) December 1981, 19:625-46.

STRAUCH, JUDITH

Strauch, Judith. Women in rural-urban circulation networks: implications for social structural change. In: Women in the cities of Asia: migration and urban adaptation. Edited by James T. Fawcett, Siew-Ean Khoo and Peter C. Smith. (Boulder, CO, Westview Press, 1984), pp. 60-77.

STROBEL, MARGARET

Strobel, Margaret. From Lelemama to lobbying: women's associations in Mombasa, Kenya. In: Women in Africa: studies in social and economic change. Edited by Nancy J. Hafkin and Edna G. Bay. (Stanford, Stanford University Press, 1976), pp. 183-211.

STRUCTURAL ADJUSTMENT

Conable, Barber B.. Address to the Board of Governors of the World Bank and International Finance Corporation. (Washington, World Bank, September 30, 1986), 11 pp.

Structural changes in the employment of women: 1971-1981; an analysis of the changing distribution of women's employment. QUARTERLY ECONOMIC REPORT, INDIAN INSTITUTE OF PUBLIC OPINION (NEW DELHI) May/August 1986, 30:24-33.

Struggling women and feminist struggle. By: Hurtado, Maria Elena. SOUTH; THE THIRD WORLD MAGAZINE (LONDON) October 1985, No. 60:44-45. Reports on the UN women's conference in Nairobi.

STUART, MADELEINE FISHER

Stuart, Madeleine Fisher. Developing labor resources in the Arab world: labor activity effects from school attendance and socioeconomic background among women in the East Jordan valley. (University of Southern California, 1981), 536 pp. Thesis (Ph.D.) -- University of Southern California, 1981.

Study of politics from the standpoint of women. By: Bonder, Gloria. INTERNATIONAL SOCIAL SCIENCE JOURNAL (PARIS) 1983, 35, No. 4:569-83.

SUBANDRIO, HURUSTIATI

Subandrio, Hurustiati. Respective roles of men and women in Indonesia. In: Women in the new Asia; the changing social roles of men and women in South and South-east Asia. Edited by Barbara E. Ward. ([Paris], Unesco, 1963), pp. 230-42.

Subordination right across the board. By: Abdullah, Lashidah. FAR EASTERN ECONOMIC REVIEW (HONGKONG) January 5, 1984, 123:31-32. Discusses the status of women in Malaysia.

Substitution between male and female labor in rural Indian agricultural production. By: Laufer, Leslie A.. YALE UNIVERSITY. ECONOMIC GROWTH CENTER. DISCUSSION PAPER (NEW HAVEN, CONN.) April 1985, No 472:1-24.

SUDAN

El-Bakri and Kameir, E. M.. Aspects of women's political participation in Sudan. INTERNATIONAL SOCIAL SCIENCE JOURNAL (PARIS) 1983, 35, No. 4:605-23.

Heide, Richter. Unter uns Frauen - Sudan, parteiisch gesehen. E & Z, ENTWICKLUNG UND ZUSAMMENARBEIT (BONN) March 1984, 25:11-13.

Ismail-Schmidt, Ellen. Sudan - Frauen zwischen Tradition und Moderne. E & Z, ENTWICKLUNG UND ZUSAMMENARBEIT (BONN) January 1985, 26:11-13, 20.

Naisho, Joyce. Health care for women in the Sudan. WORLD HEALTH FORUM (GENEVA) 1982, 3,No.2:164-65.

Von Vietinghoff, Franciska. Women working together; spontaneous success. SUDANOW (KHARTOUM) March 1985, 10:29-30.

Sudan - Frauen zwischen Tradition und Moderne. By: Ismail-Schmidt, Ellen. E & Z, ENTWICKLUNG UND ZUSAMMENARBEIT (BONN) January 1985, 26:11-13, 20.

SUE, MEE KWAIN

Sue, Mee Kwain. Community education training centre (CETC). PACIFIC PERSPECTIVE (SUVA) 1983, 11, No. 2:62-4. Describes a regional center established in 1963 to provide a programme of community education for women.

SUGAR INDUSTRY AND TRADE

Brockmann, C. Thomas. Women and development in northern Belize. JOURNAL OF DEVELOPING AREAS (MACOMB, ILL.) July 1985, 19:501-14.

SULLIVAN, EARL L

Lesch, Ann Mosely and Sullivan, Earl L. Women in Egypt; new roles and realities. UNIVERSITIES FIELD STAFF INTERNATIONAL REPORTS, AFRICA (HANOVER, NH) 1986, No. 22:1-9.

SUMMARY, REBECCA

Due, Jean M. and Summary, Rebecca. Constraints to women and development in Africa. JOURNAL OF MODERN AFRICAN STUDIES (OXFORD) March 1982, 20:155-66.

SUN, MARY

Sun, Mary. Traditional role rules, exceptions are striking. FAR EASTERN ECONOMIC REVIEW (HONGKONG) January 5, 1984, 123:27-28. Discusses the situation of women in China.

SUNDAR, PUSHPA

Sundar, Pushpa. Characteristics of female employment; implications of research and policy. ECONOMIC AND POLITICAL WEEKLY (BOMBAY) May 19, 1981, 16:863-71.

Sundar, Pushpa. Women's employment and organisation modes. ECONOMIC AND POLITICAL WEEKLY: REVIEW OF MANAGEMENT (BOMBAY) November 26, 1983, 18:M171-M176.

SURINAM

Brana-Shute, Rosemary. Working class Afro-Surinamese women and national politics: traditions and changes in an independent state. STUDIES IN THIRD WORLD SOCIETIES (WILLIAMSBURG) March 1981, No. 15:33-56.

Survey of research on women in the Arab Gulf region. By: Allaghi, Farida and Almana, Aisha. In: Social science research on women in the Arab world. (London, Frances Pinter; Paris, Unesco, 1984), pp. 14-40.

SURYAWANSHI, S. D. AND KAPASE, P. M

Suryawanshi, S. D. and Kapase, P. M. Impact of Ghod irrigation project on employment of female agricultural labour. INDIAN JOURNAL OF AGRICULTURAL ECONOMICS (BOMBAY) July/September 1985, 40:240-44.

SUTTON, CONSTANCE, ET AL.

Sutton, Constance, et al.. Women, knowledge, and power. In: Women cross-culturally: change and challenge. Edited by Ruby Rohrlich-Leavitt. (The Hague, Mouton, 1975), pp. 581-600. The authors describe women's relationship to knowledge and power in Morocco, among the Tlingit Indians in southwestern Alaska, and in Barbados.

Swazi women left in the lurch. By: Sellers, Suzanne. NEW AFRICAN (LONDON) February 1985, No. 209:p. 45. Discusses the pressures resulting from migrant labour and discrepancies between tradition and Western practice.

SWIFT, MICHAEL

Swift, Michael. Men and women in Malay society. In: Women in the new Asia; the changing social roles of men and women in South and South-east Asia. Edited by Barbara E. Ward. ([Paris], Unesco, 1963), pp. 268-86.

SYKES, BARBARA

Rohrlich-Leavitt, Ruby and Sykes, Barbara. Aboriginal woman: male and female anthropological perspectives. In: Toward an anthropology of women. Edited by Rayna R. Reiter. (New York, Monthly Review Press, 1975), pp. 110-26.

SZANTON, M. CRISTINA BLANC

Szanton, M. Cristina Blanc. "Big women" and politics in a Philippine fishing town. STUDIES IN THIRD WORLD SOCIETIES (WILLIAMSBURG) June 1981, No. 16:123-41.

TAAMALLAH, LAMOURIA

Taamallah, Lamouria. La scolarisation et la formation professionnelle des femmes en Tunisie. REVUE TUNISIENNE DE SCIENCES SOCIALES (TUNIS) 1982, 19, No. 68/69:107-28.

TADESSE, ZENEBWORKE

Tadesse, Zenebworke. Bringing research home. DEVELOPMENT (ROME) 1984, No. 4:50-54. Discusses on the question of research on women in Africa.

TAIWAN

Greenhalgh, Susan. Sexual stratification: the other side of "growth with equity" in East Asia. POPULATION AND DEVELOPMENT REVIEW (NEW YORK) June 1985, 11:265-314. This paper explores changes in women's status on Taiwan focussing on how the traditional system of sexual stratification was perpetuated and even intensified with the rapid development of the economy.

Li, K. T. Contributions of women in the labor force to economic development in Taiwan, the Republic of China. INDUSTRY OF FREE CHINA (TAIPEI) August 25, 1985, 64:1-8.

TALAHITE, CLAUDE

Hakiki, Fatiha and Talahite, Claude. Human sciences research on Algerian women. In: Social science research on women in the Arab world. (London, Frances Pinter; Paris, Unesco, 1984), pp. 82-89.

Talk to the men, and you get it wrong. GUARDIAN (LONDON) February 7, 1984, p. 22. Women's rights are not the issue in the Third World -- it's a question of efficiency, Gloria Scott tells Frances Cairncross.

TANZANIA

Chijumba, Beat J.. Attitudes of Tanzanian husbands toward the employment of their wives. AFRICA DEVELOPMENT (DAKAR) April/June 1983, 8:74-85.

Due, Jean M. and Anandajayasekeram, P.. Women and productivity in two contrasting farming areas of Tanzania. UNIVERSITY OF ILLINOIS. DEPT. OF AGRICULTURAL ECONOMICS. STAFF PAPER. SERIES E (URBANA) July 1982, No. 82 E-228:1-23.

Geiger, Susan. Umoja wa wanawake wa Tanzania and the needs of the rural poor. AFRICAN STUDIES REVIEW (WALTHAM, MASS.) June/September 1982, 25:45-65. Describes the national women's organization of Tanzania.

Laubjerg, Kristian. Training village women as health promoters in Tanzania. WATERLINES (LONDON) January 1986, 4:29-31.

TAPPER, NANCY

Tapper, Nancy. Women's subsociety among the Shahsevan nomads of Iran. In: Women in the Muslim world. Edited by Lois Beck and Nikki Keddie. (Cambridge, MA, Harvard University Press, 1978), pp. 374-98.

TAVAKOLIAN, BAHRAM

Tavakolian, Bahram. Women and socioeconomic change among Sheikhanzai nomads of western Afghanistan. MIDDLE EAST JOURNAL (WASHINGTON) Summer 1984, 38:433-53. Based on observations made in 1976-1977.

TAYLOR, FRANK

Taylor, Frank. Women grab management power in home of machismo. INTERNATIONAL MANAGEMENT (MAIDENHEAD) February 1984, 39:24-27. Describes how Latin American women are starting to make inroads into business.

TECHNICAL ASSISTANCE

Mack, Beverly B.. Technical assistants gain experience, improve projects. HORIZONS, U.S. AGENCY FOR INTERNATIONAL DEVELOPMENT (WASHINGTON) Summer 1985, 4:12-14. Examines the International Technical Assistance Fellowship Program funded by AID through the Center for Women in Development (SECID).

Technological change and women's work; participation and demographic behaviour: a case study of three fishing villages. By: Gulati, Leela. ECONOMIC AND POLITICAL WEEKLY (BOMBAY) December 8, 1984, 19:2089-94.

Technological change, production organisation and rural women in Kenya. By: Ventura-Dias, V.. INTERNATIONAL LABOUR OFFICE. WORLD EMPLOYMENT PROGRAMME RESEARCH. TECHNOLOGY AND EMPLOYMENT PROGRAMME. WORKING PAPERS (GENEVA) November 1982, No. 101:1-64.

TECHNOLOGICAL INNOVATIONS

Ahmed, Iftikhar. Rural women and technical change: theory, empirical analysis and operational projects. LABOUR AND SOCIETY (GENEVA) September 1985, 10:289-306.

Technologies appropriees pour les femmes africaines. By: Goncet, Odette. MONDES EN DEVELOPPEMENT (PARIS) 1985, 13, No. 49:193-99.

Technologies for rural women's activities--problems and prospects in Sierra Leone. By: Stevens, Yvette. INTERNATIONAL LABOUR OFFICE. WORLD EMPLOYMENT PROGRAMME RESEARCH. TECHNOLOGY AND EMPLOYMENT PROGRAMME. WORKING PAPERS (GENEVA) October 1981, No. 86:1-84. Reviews available evidence from Sierra Leone on the range of technologies relevant to rural women's tasks, such as farming, water collection and food processing.

TECHNOLOGY

Carr, Marilyn. Technology and rural women in Africa. INTERNATIONAL LABOUR OFFICE. WORLD EMPLOYMENT PROGRAMME RESEARCH. TECHNOLOGY AND EMPLOYMENT PROGRAMME. WORKING PAPERS (GENEVA) July 1980, No. 61:1-45.

Carr, Marilyn. Women and appropriate technology: two essays. INTERMEDIATE TECHNOLOGY DEVELOPMENT GROUP. OCCASIONAL PAPER (LONDON) 1982, No. 5:1-21. CONTENT: Appropriate technology for African women. - 2. Technologies appropriate for women: theory, practice and policy.

TECHNOLOGY

Date-Bah, Eugenia and Stevens, Yvette. Rural women in Africa and technological change: some issues. LABOUR AND SOCIETY (GENEVA) April/June 1981, 6:149-62.

Technology and rural women in Africa. By: Carr, Marilyn. INTERNATIONAL LABOUR OFFICE. WORLD EMPLOYMENT PROGRAMME RESEARCH. TECHNOLOGY AND EMPLOYMENT PROGRAMME. WORKING PAPERS (GENEVA) July 1980, No. 61:1-45.

TESSLER, MARK A.

Tessler, Mark A. and Rogers, Janet. Women's emancipation in Tunisia. In: Women in the Muslim world. Edited by Lois Beck and Nikki Keddie. (Cambridge, MA, Harvard University Press, 1978), pp. 141-58.

THADANI, VEENA N.

Thadani, Veena N. and Todaro, Michael P.. Female migration: a conceptual framework. In: Women in the cities of Asia: migration and urban adaptation. Edited by James T. Fawcett, Siew-Ean Khoo and Peter C. Smith. (Boulder, CO, Westview Press, 1984), pp. 36-59.

THAILAND

Muecke, Marjorie A.. Make money not babies; changing status markers of northern Thai women. ASIAN SURVEY (BERKELEY, CALIF.) April 1984, 24:459-70.

Theme of sexual oppression in the North African novel. By: Accad, Evelyne. In: Women in the Muslim world. Edited by Lois Beck and Nikki Keddie. (Cambridge, MA, Harvard University Press, 1978), pp. 617-28.

Third World women and development. By: McKie, David. INTERNATIONAL PERSPECTIVES (OTTAWA) July/August 1984, p. 13-16.

Third World women and social reality: a conclusion. By: Lindsay, Beverly. In: Comparative perspectives of Third World women: the impact of race, sex and class. Edited by Beverly Lindsay. (New York, Praeger, 1980), pp. 297-310.

Third world women speak out: interviews in six countries on change, development, and basic needs. By: Huston, Perdita. (New York, published in cooperation with the Overseas Development Council by Praeger, 1979), 153 pp. Countries discussed are: Tunisia, Egypt, Sudan, Kenya, Sri Lanka and Mexico.

THITSA, KHIN

Thitsa, Khin. Providence and prostitution: image and reality for women in Buddhist Thailand. Series: Change International Reports: Women in Society, No. 2. (London, Change International Reports, 1980), 27 pp.

THOMAS, PAMELA

Thomas, Pamela and Simi, Noumea. The new Samoan businesswoman. PACIFIC PERSPECTIVE (SUVA) 1983, 11, No. 2:5-12.

THOMAS, ROSALIND

Thomas, Rosalind. Women; the law in Southern Africa: justice for all? AFRICA REPORT (NEW YORK) March/April 1985, 30:59-64.

THORVE, P. V. AND GALGALIKAR, V. D

Thorve, P. V. and Galgalikar, V. D. Economics of diversification of farming with dairy enterprise. INDIAN JOURNAL OF AGRICULTURAL ECONOMICS (BOMBAY) July/September 1985, 40:317-23.

Three generations in my Calcutta family. By: Sarma, Jyotirmoyee. In: Women in the new Asia; the changing social roles of men and women in South and South-east Asia. Edited by Barbara E. Ward. ([Paris], Unesco, 1963), pp. 216-28. Describes differences in women's roles in each generation.

Three women of Kano: modern women and traditional life. By: Callaway, Barbara J. and Kleeman, Katherine E.. AFRICA REPORT (NEW YORK) March/April 1985, 30:26-29.

Tibet through our eyes (2); education: opening the door to women. By: Li, Yuan. WOMEN OF CHINA (BEIJING) August 1985, No. 8:6-7.

TIDALGO, ROSA LINDA P

Tidalgo, Rosa Linda P. Integration of women in Philippine development. UNIVERSITY OF THE PHILIPPINES. SCHOOL OF ECONOMICS. DISCUSSION PAPER (QUEZON) April 1985, No. 8502:1-82.

TIENDA, MARTA

Tienda, Marta. Community characteristics, women's education, and fertility in Peru. STUDIES IN FAMILY PLANNING (NEW YORK) July/August 1984, 15:162-69.

TILAK, JANDHYALA B. G.

Tilak, Jandhyala B. G.. Inequality by sex in human labour market discrimination and returns to education. MARGIN; QUARTERLY JOURNAL OF THE NATIONAL COUNCIL OF APPLIED ECONOMIC RESEARCH (NEW DELHI) January 1980, 12:57-80. Examines some economic aspects of discrimination against women in India.

TODARO, MICHAEL P.

Thadani, Veena N. and Todaro, Michael P.. Female migration: a conceptual framework. In: Women in the cities of Asia: migration and urban adaptation. Edited by James T. Fawcett, Siew-Ean Khoo and Peter C. Smith. (Boulder, CO, Westview Press, 1984), pp. 36-59.

TOMEH, AIDA K.

Tomeh, Aida K.. Birth order and alienation among college women in Lebanon. In: Women in the family and the economy: an international comparative survey. Edited by George Kurian and Ratna Ghosh. (Westport, CT, Greenwood Press, 1981), pp. 81-106.

TOMES, NIGEL

Robinson, Chris and Tomes, Nigel. More on the labour supply of Canadian women. CANADIAN JOURNAL OF ECONOMICS (TORONTO) February 1985, 18:156-63.

TOMODA, SHIZUE

Tomoda, Shizue. Measuring female labour activities in Asian developing countries: a time-allocation approach. INTERNATIONAL LABOUR REVIEW (GENEVA) November/December 1985, 124:661-76.

TOMSIC, VIDA

Tomsic, Vida. Women in the development of socialist self-managing Yugoslavia. ([Belgrade], Jugoslovenska stvarnost, [1980]), 211 pp. Translation of: Zena u razvoju socijalisticke samoupravne Jugoslavije.

TONGA

Faletau, Meleseini. Changing roles for Tonga's women. PACIFIC PERSPECTIVE (SUVA) 1983, 11, No. 2:45-55.

Halatuituia, Lasale and Latu, Sela N.. Women's co-operatives in Tonga. PACIFIC PERSPECTIVE (SUVA) 1983, 11, No. 2:13-17.

TONGUDAI, PAWADEE

> Tongudai, Pawadee. Women migrants in Bangkok: an economic analysis of their employment and earnings. In: Women in the urban and industrial workforce; Southeast and East Asia. Edited by Gavin W. Jones. Series: Development Studies Centre. Monograph, No. 33. (Canberra, Australia, Australian National University, 1984), pp. 305-24. Series edited by Helen Hughes.

Tough ascent for Japanese women. By: Chira, Susan. NEW YORK TIMES (NEW YORK) February 24, 1985, Section 3, p. 1-27. Equal employment opportunities for women in Japan remain scarce and male-dominated industries resist women's attempts to change traditional ways.

Toward an anthropology of women. Edited by Rayna R. Reiter. (New York, Monthly Review Press, 1975), 416 pp.

Towards a methodology of women's studies. By: Mies, Maria. INSTITUTE OF SOCIAL STUDIES. OCCASIONAL PAPERS (THE HAGUE) November 1979, No. 77:1-23. Attempts to lay down some methodological guidelines, which may be further discussed and developed into a new methodological approach which would be consistent with the social, economic and political aims of the women's movement.

Towards meeting the needs of urban female factory workers in peninsular Malaysia. By: Lean, Lim Lin. In: Women in the urban and industrial workforce; Southeast and East Asia. Edited by Gavin W. Jones. Series: Development Studies Centre. Monograph, No. 33. (Canberra, Australia, Australian National University, 1984), pp. 129-48. Series edited by Helen Hughes.

El trabajo invisible de las campesinas del Tercer Mundo. By: Michel, Andree. DESARROLLO Y SOCIEDAD (BOGOTA) January 1984, No. 13:81-97. With English summary.

Tractors against women. By: Kelkar, Govind. DEVELOPMENT (ROME) 1985, No. 3:18-21. Concludes that the Green Revolution has brought in its wake the all-India trend of pauperization and marginalization and the increased inequality between the sexes.

Tradition and the veil: female status in Tunisia and Algeria. By: Marshall, Susan E. and Stokes, Randall G.. JOURNAL OF MODERN AFRICAN STUDIES (OXFORD) December 1981, 19:625-46.

Traditional role rules, exceptions are striking. By: Sun, Mary. FAR EASTERN ECONOMIC REVIEW (HONGKONG) January 5, 1984, 123:27-28. Discusses the situation of women in China.

Traffic in women: notes on the political economy of sex. By: Rubin, Gayle. In: Toward an anthropology of women. Edited by Rayna R. Reiter. (New York, Monthly Review Press, 1975), pp. 157-210.

TRAINING OF EMPLOYEES

> Gustman, Alan and Steinmeier, Thomas L. Wages, employment, training and job attachment in low wage labor markets for women. NATIONAL BUREAU OF ECONOMIC RESEARCH. WORKING PAPER SERIES (CAMBRIDGE, MASS.) October 1986, No. 2037:1-52. The authors analyze economic behaviour and the effects of training and income support policies in the low wage labor market for women.

Training village women as health promoters in Tanzania. By: Laubjerg, Kristian. WATERLINES (LONDON) January 1986, 4:29-31.

Trappings of success, but an inner emptiness. By: Chiba, Atsuko. FAR EASTERN ECONOMIC REVIEW (HONGKONG) January 5, 1984, 123:30-31. The author discusses Japanes women.

Trends in female labour force participation and occupational shifts in urban Korea. By: Koo, Sung-Yeal. In: Women in the urban and industrial workforce; Southeast and East Asia. Edited by Gavin W. Jones. Series: Development Studies Centre. Monograph, No. 33. (Canberra, Australia, Australian National University, 1984), pp. 61-73. Series edited by Helen Hughes.

Trends in female labour force participation in Taiwan: the transition toward higher technology activities. By: Liu, Paul K. C.. In: Women in the urban and industrial workforce; Southeast and East Asia. Edited by Gavin W. Jones. Series: Development Studies Centre. Monograph, No. 33. (Canberra, Australia, Australian National University, 1984), pp. 75-100. Series edited by Helen Hughes.

Trends in women's work, education, and family building; proceedings of the Conference, Chelwood Gate, Sussex, England, May 31 - June 3, 1983. JOURNAL OF LABOR ECONOMICS (CHICAGO) January 1985, 3:S1-S396.

Triple struggle; Latin American peasant women. By: Bronstein, Audrey. (London, WOW Campaigns, 1982), 268 pp. Contains interviews with women in Ecuador, Bolivia, Peru, El Salvador and Guatemala.

TRUSSELL, JAMES

Trussell, James and Pebley, Anne R.. Potential impact of changes in fertility on infant, child, and maternal mortality. Series: World Bank Staff Working Papers, No. 698; Population and Development Series, No. 23. (Washington, DC, World Bank, 1984), 44 pp.

TRYFAN, BARBARA

Tryfan, Barbara. Research on the status of women, development and population trends in Eastern Europe: an annotated bibliography. In: Bibliographic guide to studies on the status of women: development and population trends. (New York, Bowker, UNIPUB; Paris, Unesco, 1983), pp. 113-39.

Trying to throw off the shackles of the past. By: Singh, Geetanjali. FAR EASTERN ECONOMIC REVIEW (HONGKONG) January 5, 1984, 123:29-30. Examines the situation of women in India.

TUNISIA

Beaujot, Roderic. Liberation de la femme et marche matrimonial en Tunisie. POPULATION (PARIS) July/October 1986, 41:853-59.

Ben Miled, Emna. Etude comparative du statut sexuel des femmes dans le monde mediterraneen, berbere et Africain. REVUE TUNISIENNE DE SCIENCES SOCIALES (TUNIS) 1985, 22, No. 82/83:75-110.

Marshall, Susan E. and Stokes, Randall G.. Tradition and the veil: female status in Tunisia and Algeria. JOURNAL OF MODERN AFRICAN STUDIES (OXFORD) December 1981, 19:625-46.

Taamallah, Lamouria. La scolarisation et la formation professionnelle des femmes en Tunisie. REVUE TUNISIENNE DE SCIENCES SOCIALES (TUNIS) 1982, 19, No. 68/69:107-28.

TURKEY

Kagitcibasi, Cigdem. Status of women in Turkey: cross-cultural perspectives. INTERNATIONAL JOURNAL OF MIDDLE EAST STUDIES (CAMBRIDGE) November 1986, 18:485-99.

Turkish women in the Ottoman Empire: the classical age. By: Dengler, Ian C.. In: Women in the Muslim world. Edited by Lois Beck and Nikki Keddie. (Cambridge, MA, Harvard University Press, 1978), pp. 229-44.

Twilight of a long maidenhood. By: Wittstock, Laura Waterman. In: Comparative perspectives of Third World women: the impact of race, sex and class. Edited by Beverly Lindsay. (New York, Praeger, 1980), pp. 207-28.

TZANNATOS, Z.

Tzannatos, Z. and Zabalza, A. Effect of sex antidiscriminatory legislation on the variability of female employment in Britian. APPLIED ECONOMICS (LONDON) December 1985, 17:1117-34. The authors attempt to determine whether fluctuations in aggregate employment are reflected in fluctuations in the employment of men and women, and to investigate if the sex antidiscriminatory legislation enacted in Britian during the 1970s has had any effect on the variability of female employment.

U.S.S.R.

Berliner, Joseph S.. Education, labor-force participation, and fertility in the USSR. JOURNAL OF COMPARATIVE ECONOMICS (NEW YORK) June 1983, 7:131-57. The effect of education on Soviet fertility and female labor participation is analyzed in terms of the neoclassical theory of the household.

Biryukova, Alexandra. Role of the Soviet woman in decision-making in trade union committees and in industry. LABOUR AND SOCIETY (GENEVA) September 1985, 10:307-21.

Grosheide-Van de Riet, M.F.F.. Vrouwen in de Sovjetunie. INTERNATIONALE SPECTATOR (THE HAGUE) January 1982, 37:12-20.

Kravchenko, M.. For the mother, for the family. SOVIET REVIEW, A JOURNAL OF TRANSLATIONS (ARMONK, N.Y.) Summer 1984, 25:18-24.

Kuniansky, Anna. Soviet fertility, labor-force participation, and marital instabililty. JOURNAL OF COMPARATIVE ECONOMICS (NEW YORK) June 1983, 7:114-30.

Lubin, Nancy. Women in Soviet Central Asia: progress and contradictions. SOVIET STUDIES (GLASGOW) April 1981, 33:182-203.

Motroshilova, Nelya V.. Soviet women in the life of society: achievements and problems. INTERNATIONAL SOCIAL SCIENCE JOURNAL (PARIS) 1983, 35, No. 4:733-46.

U.S.S.R.

Novikova, E. E.. Scientific and technical progress and women's work in the USSR. LABOUR AND SOCIETY (GENEVA) January/March 1982, 7:13-22.

Shoemaker, Susan. Status of women in the rural U.S.S.R. POPULATION RESEARCH AND POLICY REVIEW (AMSTERDAM) February 1983, 2:35-51.

Umoja wa wanawake wa Tanzania and the needs of the rural poor. By: Geiger, Susan. AFRICAN STUDIES REVIEW (WALTHAM, MASS.) June/September 1982, 25:45-65. Describes the national women's organization of Tanzania.

U.N. Decade for Women. By: Karaosmanoglu, Attila. BANK'S WORLD (WASHINGTON) September 1985, 4:11-12. The World Bank's statement at the world conference reviewing and appraising the achievements of the U.N. Decade for Women in Nairobi, Kenya, in July.

Underdevelopment and the experience of women: a Nigerian case study. By: Remy, Dorothy. In: Toward an anthropology of women. Edited by Rayna R. Reiter. (New York, Monthly Review Press, 1975), pp. 358-71.

UNDERGROUND ECONOMY

Berger, Brigitte and Corriher, Kurt. Underground women of the Third world. WALL STREET JOURNAL (NEW YORK) July 26, 1985, p. 20. Authors state that in addition to their role in production and marketing, women are acquiring vital leadership skills because informal institutions are springing up to accompany informal economies.

UNEMPLOYMENT

Numero special: radioscopie du chomage. L'ECONOMIE DE LA REUNION (STE-CLOTILDE) September/October 1986, No. 25:1-32.

Unemployment and female labour: a study of labour supply in Kingston, Jamaica. By: Standing, Guy. (New York, St. Martin's Press, 1981), 364 pp. Prepared for the International Labour Office within the framework of the World Employment Programme.

UNESCO

Unesco. Social science research and women in the Arab world. (London, Pinter, 1984), 175 pp.

Unfinished assignment: equal education for women. By: McGrath, Patricia L.. Series: Worldwatch Paper, 7. ([Washington], Worldwatch Institute, 1976), 47 pp.

UNITED KINGDOM

Hatton, T. J.. Female labour force participation: the enigma of the interwar period. UNIVERSITY OF ESSEX. DEPT. OF ECONOMICS. DISCUSSION PAPER SERIES (COLCHESTER) June 1986, No. 285:1-36.

Sprague, Alison. Post-war fertility and female labour force participation rates. OXFORD UNIVERSITY. INSTITUTE OF ECONOMICS AND STATISTICS. APPLIED ECONOMICS DISCUSSION PAPER (OXFORD) June 1986, No. 9:1-35.

Stewart, Mark B. and Greenhalgh, Christine A.. Work history patterns and the occupational attainment of women. ECONOMIC JOURNAL (LONDON) September 1984, 94:493-519.

Tzannatos, Z. and Zabalza, A. Effect of sex antidiscriminatory legislation on the variability of female employment in Britian. APPLIED ECONOMICS (LONDON) December 1985, 17:1117-34. The authors attempt to determine whether fluctuations in aggregate employment are reflected in fluctuations in the employment of men and women, and to investigate if the sex antidiscriminatory legislation enacted in Britian during the 1970s has had any effect on the variability of female employment.

Young, Kate and Smith, Sheila. Women's disadvantage: capitalist development and socialist alternatives in Britain. DEVELOPMENT DIALOGUE (UPPSALA) 1982, No. 1/2:85-100.

UNITED NATIONS

UN Decade for Women conference held in Nairobi. UNITED STATES. DEPARTMENT OF STATE. BULLETIN (WASHINGTON) February 1986, 86:89-92. Contains statements by Maureen Reagan, head of the U.S. delegation, in a plenary session of the conference on July 16 and in UN General Assembly Committee III on November 5.

Holford, Nicky. Easing the burden of women in a developing society: a host of good intentions. NEW AFRICAN (LONDON) December 1981, p. 39-40. Discusses the new UN Convention for the prevention of discrimination against women, which was adopted in September, and suggests that the measure should influence customs and practices all over Africa.

Perspective: United Nations Decade for Women 1976-1985; 'really only a beginning... UNITED NATIONS. UN CHRONICLE (NEW YORK) July/August 1985, 22: Special survey, p. i-xxiv.

UNITED NATIONS DEVELOPMENT PROGRAMME

United Nations Development Programme. Action oriented assessment of rural's women's participation in development. Series: Evaluation Study (United Nations Development Programme), No. 3. (New York, United Nations Development Programme, 1980), 226 pp.

UNITED NATIONS EDUCATIONAL, SCIENTIFIC AND CULTURAL ORGANIZATION

Deble, Isabelle. La deuxieme strategie de l'UNESCO a l'egard des femmes. TIERS-MONDE (PARIS) April/June 1985, 26:283-97.

UNITED NATIONS. COMMISSION ON THE STATUS OF WOMEN

United Nations. Commission on the Status of Women. Report. (New York, United Nations, 1976-77, 1982), 3 vols.. Issued as supplements to the official records of the Economic and Social Council.

UNITED NATIONS. ECONOMIC COMMISSION FOR AFRICA. SOCIAL DEVELOPMENT SECTION

United Nations. Economic Commission for Africa. Social Development Section. Status and role of women in East Africa. Series: Social Welfare Services in Africa, No. 6. (New York, United Nations, 1967), 65 pp.

UNITED NATIONS. ECONOMIC COMMISSION FOR EUROPE

United Nations. Economic Commission for Europe. Economic role of women in the ECE region. Series: United Nations [Document], E/ECE/1013. (New York, United Nations, 1980), 122 pp.

UNITED NATIONS. SECRETARY-GENERAL

United Nations. Secretary-General. Participation of women in the economic and social development of their countries. Report of the Secretary-General. (New York, United Nations, 1970), 104 pp. United Nations Publication. Sales no.: E.70.IV.4.

UNITED STATES

Acock, Alan C. and Deseran, Forrest A. Off-farm employment by women and marital instability. RURAL SOCIOLOGY (PROVO, UTAH) Fall 1986, 51:314-27. The impact of farm women's paid work experience on the quality and stability of their marriages is examined in the context of two competing frameworks - status competition and status enhancement.

UNITED STATES

Bielby, William T. and Baron, James N. Sex segregation within occupations. AMERICAN ECONOMIC REVIEW, PAPERS AND PROCEEDINGS (NASHVILLE) May 1986, 76:43-47.

Cohn, Steven and Wood, Robert. U.S. aid and Third World women: the impact of Peace Corps programs. ECONOMIC DEVELOPMENT AND CULTURAL CHANGE (CHICAGO) July 1981, 29:795-811.

Ferber, Marianne A. and Green, Carole A. Work power and earnings of women and men. AMERICAN ECONOMIC REVIEW, PAPERS AND PROCEEDINGS (NASHVILLE) May 1986, 76:53-56.

Gaston, Cheryl L. Idea whose time has not come: comparable worth and the market salary problem. POPULATION RESEARCH AND POLICY REVIEW (AMSTERDAM) 1986, 5, No. 1:15-29.

Goldin, Claudia. Maximum hours legislation and female employment in the 1920s: a reassessment. NATIONAL BUREAU OF ECONOMIC RESEARCH. WORKING PAPER SERIES (CAMBRIDGE, MASS.) June 1986, No. 1949:1-27.

Gustman, Alan and Steinmeier, Thomas L. Wages, employment, training and job attachment in low wage labor markets for women. NATIONAL BUREAU OF ECONOMIC RESEARCH. WORKING PAPER SERIES (CAMBRIDGE, MASS.) October 1986, No. 2037:1-52. The authors analyze economic behaviour and the effects of training and income support policies in the low wage labor market for women.

Hill, M. Anne. Comparison of economic models and empirical results for female labor force participation in Japan and the United State. YALE UNIVERSITY. ECONOMIC GROWTH CENTER. DISCUSSION PAPER (NEW HAVEN, CONN.) July 1982, No. 415:1-36.

Jakubson, George. Sensitivity of labor supply parameter estimates to unobserved individual effects: fixed and random effects estimates in a nonlinear model using panel data. PRINCETON UNIVERSITY. INDUSTRIAL RELATIONS SECTION. WORKING PAPER (PRINCETON) August 1986, No. 210:1-37; A1-A4 (various pagings).

Johnson, William R. and Skinner, Jonathan. Labor supply and marital separation. AMERICAN ECONOMIC REVIEW (NASHVILLE) June 1986, 76:455-69. A simultaneous model of future divorce probability and current labor supply is estimated for married women. The results support the hypothesis that divorce probabilities increase labor supply.

UNITED STATES

Maxwell, Nan L. and D'Amico, Ronald J. Employment and wage effects of involuntary job separation: male-female differences. AMERICAN ECONOMIC REVIEW, PAPERS AND PROCEEDINGS (NASHVILLE) May 1986, 76:373-77.

Medoff, Marshall H. Effect of the Equal Rights Amendment on the economic status of women. ATLANTIC ECONOMIC JOURNAL (WORDEN, IL) September 1985, 13:60-68.

Sapiro, Virginia. Gender basis of American social policy. POLITICAL SCIENCE QUARTERLY (NEW YORK) 1986, 101, No. 2:221-38.

Scott, Joan Wallach. Mechanization of women's work. SCIENTIFIC AMERICAN (NEW YORK) September 1982, 247:166-87.

Sorensen, Elaine. Implementing comparable worth: a survey of recent job evaluation studies. AMERICAN ECONOMIC REVIEW, PAPERS AND PROCEEDINGS (NASHVILLE) May 1986, 76:364-72.

Zalokar, Nadja. Generational differences in female occupational attainment -- have the 1970's changed women's opportunities? AMERICAN ECONOMIC REVIEW, PAPERS AND PROCEEDINGS (NASHVILLE) May 1986, 76:378-81.

UNITED STATES. CONGRESS. SENATE. COMMITTEE ON FOREIGN RELATIONS

United States. Congress. Senate. Committee on Foreign Relations. Women in development: looking to the future: hearing before the Committee on Foreign Relations, United States Senate, Ninety-eighth Congress, 2nd session, June 7, 1984. (Washington, DC, Government Printing Office, 1984), 245 pp.

Unmarried women and the household economy: a research note. By: Sharma, Ursula. JOURNAL OF SOCIAL STUDIES (DHAKA) October 1985, No. 30:1-12.

Unsung heroines. FAR EASTERN ECONOMIC REVIEW (HONGKONG) January 5, 1984, 123:26-40. A series of articles by women writers from a cross-section of Asian countries who survey the position of women in their own societies.

Unsung heroines: Bangladesh's unrecognized workforce gains a new self-awareness. By: Ahmad, Perveen. FAR EASTERN ECONOMIC REVIEW (HONGKONG) January 5, 1984, 123:26-27.

Unter uns Frauen - Sudan, parteiisch gesehen. By: Heide, Richter. E & Z, ENTWICKLUNG UND ZUSAMMENARBEIT (BONN) March 1984, 25:11-13.

Up from the harem? The effects of class and sex on political life in northern India. By: Devon, Tonia K.. In: Comparative perspectives of Third World women: the impact of race, sex and class. Edited by Beverly Lindsay. (New York, Praeger, 1980), pp. 123-42.

Upgrading women in Yemen: a matter of dollars and sense. By: Howe, Gary Nigel. HORIZONS, U.S. AGENCY FOR INTERNATIONAL DEVELOPMENT (WASHINGTON) Summer 1985, 4:41-42.

Urban migrant women in the Republic of Korea. By: Hong, Sawon. In: Women in the cities of Asia: migration and urban adaptation. Edited by James T. Fawcett, Siew-Ean Khoo and Peter C. Smith. (Boulder, CO, Westview Press, 1984), pp. 191-210.

URBANIZATION

Wolfe, Barbara L. and Behrman, Jere R.. Socioeconomic characteristics of women in a developing country and the degree of urbanization. UNIVERSITY OF WISCONSIN-MADISON. INSTITUTE FOR RESEARCH ON POVERTY. DISCUSSION PAPERS (MADISON) September 1980, 655-81:1-53. The study is based on a stratified random sample of over 4,000 women aged 15-45 in Nicaragua.

Urbanization, migration, and the status of women. By: Fawcett, James T. and Khoo, Siew-Ean and Smith, Peter C.. In: Women in the cities of Asia: migration and urban adaptation. Edited by James T. Fawcett, Siew-Ean Khoo and Peter C. Smith. (Boulder, CO, Westview Press, 1984), pp. 15-35.

Urbanward migration and employment of women in Southeast and East Asian cities: patterns and policy issues. By: Khoo, Siew-Ean. In: Women in the urban and industrial workforce; Southeast and East Asia. Edited by Gavin W. Jones. Series: Development Studies Centre. Monograph, No. 33. (Canberra, Australia, Australian National University, 1984), pp. 277-92. Series edited by Helen Hughes.

URDANG, STEPHANIE

Urdang, Stephanie. Last transition? Women and development in Mozambique. REVIEW OF AFRICAN POLITICAL ECONOMY (SHEFFIELD) 1984, No. 27/28:8-32.

Urdang, Stephanie. Women in Mozambique; rural transformations: women in the new society. AFRICA REPORT (NEW YORK) March/April 1985, 30:66-70.

URDANG, STEPHANIE

Urdang, Stephanie. Fighting two colonialisms. (New York, Monthly Review Press, 1979), 320 pp. The author discusses the situation of women in Guinea-Bissau.

U.S. aid and Third World women: the impact of Peace Corps programs. By: Cohn, Steven and Wood, Robert. ECONOMIC DEVELOPMENT AND CULTURAL CHANGE (CHICAGO) July 1981, 29:795-811.

USHA RAO, N. J. (NANDALIKE JAGANNATH)

Usha Rao, N. J. (Nandalike Jagannath). Women in a developing society. (New Delhi, Ashish, 1983), 180 pp.

UYS, J. M.

Steyn, Anna F. and Uys, J. M.. Changing position of black women in South Africa. In: Changing position of women in family and society; a cross-national comparison. Edited by Eugen Lupri. Series: International studies in sociology and social anthropology, vol. 34. (Leiden, E. J. Brill, 1983), pp. 344-70.

VAN ALLEN, JUDITH

Van Allen, Judith. Aba riots or Igbo 'women's war'? Ideology, stratification, and the invisibility of women. In: Women in Africa: studies in social and economic change. Edited by Nancy J. Hafkin and Edna G. Bay. (Stanford, Stanford University Press, 1976), pp. 59-85.

VAN BUREN, LINDA

van Buren, Linda. KWFT steps in to make African women bankable. AFRICAN BUSINESS (LONDON) July 1985, No. 83:10-12. Describes the Kenya Women Finance Trust.

VAN DAM, ANDRE

van Dam, Andre. Women - what role in development? D & C, DEVELOPMENT AND COOPERATION (BONN) May/June 1981, No. 3:10-13.

VAN WIJK-SIJBESMA, CHRISTINE

van Wijk-Sijbesma, Christine. Helping women to help themselves. WATERLINES (LONDON) April 1986, 4:29-31. Suggests that women's programmes and organizations have great potential to mobilize women to improve their own water supply and sanitation if they are not served by other programmes.

VANUATU

Women of Vanuatu. Integration of women in the development process. PACIFIC PERSPECTIVE (SUVA) 1983, 11, No. 2:1-4. Adapted from the paper presented by the Women of Vanuatu to the 21st South Pacific Conference, Vila.

Variabili dipendenti limitate e selezione non casuale delle osservazioni: una applicazione alla stima della funzione di salario e di offerta di lavoro delle donne sposate in Italia. By: Colombino, Ugo. GIORNALE DEGLI ECONOMISTI E ANNALI DI ECONOMIA (MILAN) May/June 1983, 42, N.S.:369-85. With English summary, p. 388.

VARMA, MARGARET

Varma, Margaret. Dual oppression: to be poor and also a woman. RUTGERS UNIVERSITY/COOK COLLEGE INTERNATIONAL AGRICULTURE AND FOOD PROGRAM. WORKING PAPER SERIES (NEW BRUNSWICK, NJ) 1985, No. 5:1-9. Deals with women and poverty, and particularly, with women in extreme povelrty and exclusion--women of the fourth world.

VEGETABLE GARDENING

Nath, Kamla. Women and vegetable gardens in the Gambia: Action AID and rural development. BOSTON UNIVERSITY. AFRICAN STUDIES CENTER. WORKING PAPERS (BOSTON) 1985, No. 109:1-13. Examines Action Aid's program for improving the capacity of rural women to produce garden vegetables and to introduce marketing infrastructures.

VELLENGA, DOROTHY DEE

Vellenga, Dorothy Dee. Women, households, and food commodity chains in southern Ghana: contradictions between the search for profit and the struggle for survival. REVIEW, FERNAND BRAUDEL CENTER (BINGHAMTON, N.Y.) Winter 1985, 8:293-318.

VENEMA, BERNHARD

Venema, Bernhard. Les consequences de l'introduction d'une culture de rente et d'une culture attelee sur la position de la femme wolof a Saloum. TIERS-MONDE (PARIS) July/September 1982, 23:603-16.

VENTURA-DIAS, V.

Ventura-Dias, V.. Technological change, production organisation and rural women in Kenya. INTERNATIONAL LABOUR OFFICE. WORLD EMPLOYMENT PROGRAMME RESEARCH. TECHNOLOGY AND EMPLOYMENT PROGRAMME. WORKING PAPERS (GENEVA) November 1982, No. 101:1-64.

VERHEUST, THERESE

Verheust, Therese. Potraits de femmes: les intellectuelles zairoises. CAHIERS DU CEDAF (BRUSSELS) October 1985, No. 6:1-148.

VIEILLE, PAUL

Vieille, Paul. Iranian women in family alliance and sexual politics. In: Women in the Muslim world. Edited by Lois Beck and Nikki Keddie. (Cambridge, MA, Harvard University Press, 1978), pp. 451-72.

VIET-NAM

Pelzer White, Christine. Collectives and the status of women: the Vietnamese experience. CERES, FAO REVIEW ON AGRICULTURE AND DEVELOPMENT (ROME) July/August 1983, 16:22-26.

Village women, their changing lives and fertility: studies in Kenya, Mexico, and the Philippines. By: Reining, Priscilla [et al.]. Series: AAAS publication, No. 77-6. (Washington, DC, American Association for the Advancement of Science, 1977), 273 pp.

VILLARIBA, MARIA C.

Villariba, Maria C.. Philippines: canvasses of women in crisis. Series: Change International Reports: Women in Society, No. 7. (London, Change International Reports, [1982]?), 15 pp.

VIVEROS-LONG, ANAMARIA

Viveros-Long, Anamaria and Krueger, Christine. Is "Women in Development" working? HORIZONS, U.S. AGENCY FOR INTERNATIONAL DEVELOPMENT (WASHINGTON) Summer 1985, 4:15-17. The authors describe how AID's Center for Development Information and Evaluation (CDIE) is making the first systematic assessment of the progress AID has made in integrating women into development activities at the project level.

Von der Bauerin zur Hilfskraft? By: Bruchhaus, Eva-Maria. E & Z, ENTWICKLUNG UND ZUSAMMENARBEIT (BONN) June 25, 1984, 25:19-21.

Von der Emanzipation des Brunnenmadchens in Heilbadern; Frauendiskriminierung, Frauenforderung durch Tarifvertrag und Tarifpolitik. By: Kurz-Scherf, Ingrid. WSI-MITTEILUNGEN (DUSSELDORF) August 1986, 39:537-49.

VON VIETINGHOFF, FRANCISKA

Von Vietinghoff, Franciska. Women working together; spontaneous success. SUDANOW (KHARTOUM) March 1985, 10:29-30.

Vrouwen in de Sovjetunie. By: Grosheide-Van de Riet, M.F.F.. INTERNATIONALE SPECTATOR (THE HAGUE) January 1982, 37:12-20.

Wage gap in Japan: changing patterns of labor force participation, schooling and tenure. By: Osawa, Machiko. ECONOMICS RESEARCH CENTER. NORC [NATIONAL OPINION RESEARCH CENTER] DISCUSSION PAPER SERIES (CHICAGO) April 1986, No. 86-1:1-29. Examines how changes in schooling and work experience over time between men and women workers have affected wage differentials observed in the post-WWII period in Japan.

WAGES

Chapman, Bruce J. and Harding, J. Ross. Sex differences in earnings: an analysis of Malaysian wage data. JOURNAL OF DEVELOPMENT STUDIES (LONDON) April 1985, 21:362-76.

Colombino, Ugo. Variabili dipendenti limitate e selezione non casuale delle osservazioni: una applicazione alla stima della funzione di salario e di offerta di lavoro delle donne sposate in Italia. GIORNALE DEGLI ECONOMISTI E ANNALI DI ECONOMIA (MILAN) May/June 1983, 42, N.S.:369-85. With English summary, p. 388.

Ferber, Marianne A. and Green, Carole A. Work power and earnings of women and men. AMERICAN ECONOMIC REVIEW, PAPERS AND PROCEEDINGS (NASHVILLE) May 1986, 76:53-56.

Kanellopoulos, Costas N.. Male-female pay differentials in Greece. GREEK ECONOMIC REVIEW (ATHENS) August 1982, 4:222-41.

Leppel, Karen. Relations among child quality, family structure, and the value of the mother's time in Malaysia. MALAYAN ECONOMIC REVIEW (SINGAPORE) October 1982, 27:61-70.

Maxwell, Nan L. and D'Amico, Ronald J. Employment and wage effects of involuntary job separation: male-female differences. AMERICAN ECONOMIC REVIEW, PAPERS AND PROCEEDINGS (NASHVILLE) May 1986, 76:373-77.

Osawa, Machiko. Wage gap in Japan: changing patterns of labor force participation, schooling and tenure. ECONOMICS RESEARCH CENTER. NORC [NATIONAL OPINION RESEARCH CENTER] DISCUSSION PAPER SERIES (CHICAGO) April 1986, No. 86-1:1-29. Examines how changes in schooling and work experience over time between men and women workers have affected wage differentials observed in the post-WWII period in Japan.

WAGES

Sorensen, Elaine. Implementing comparable worth: a survey of recent job evaluation studies. AMERICAN ECONOMIC REVIEW, PAPERS AND PROCEEDINGS (NASHVILLE) May 1986, 76:364-72.

Wages, employment, training and job attachment in low wage labor markets for women. By: Gustman, Alan and Steinmeier, Thomas L. NATIONAL BUREAU OF ECONOMIC RESEARCH. WORKING PAPER SERIES (CAMBRIDGE, MASS.) October 1986, No. 2037:1-52. The authors analyze economic behaviour and the effects of training and income support policies in the low wage labor market for women.

WANG, BEE-LAN CHAN

Wang, Bee-Lan Chan. Chinese women: the relative influences of ideological revolution, economic growth, and cultural change. In: Comparative perspectives of Third World women: the impact of race, sex and class. Edited by Beverly Lindsay. (New York, Praeger, 1980), pp. 96-122.

Wang, Bee-Lan Chan. Sex and ethnic differences in educational investment in Malaysia: the effect of reward structures. COMPARATIVE EDUCATION REVIEW (NEW YORK) June 1980, 24:S140-59.

WANGARI, ESTHER AND KOIVUKARI, MIRJAMI

Wangari, Esther and Koivukari, Mirjami. Women; the plight and the strength. DEVELOPMENT FORUM (NEW YORK) June 1986, p. 8-9. Suggests that evidence is growing that the workload of women is increasing more than ever before and that their general condition is deteriorating.

WARE, HELEN

Ware, Helen. Women, demography and development. Series: Demography Teaching notes, 0157-6232, Australian National University, Development Studies Centre, No. 3. (Canberra, Australian National University, 1981), 242 pp.

Wasting Japan's women workers. By: Woronoff, Jon. ORIENTAL ECONOMIST (TOKYO) November 1980, 48:22-24.

WATER QUALITY MANAGEMENT

Olaseha, I. O. and Namanja, Gracian Bazilious. Focusing on women for water and sanitation: the case of Mapo community in Ibadan, Nigeria. INTERNATIONAL QUARTERLY OF COMMUNITY HEALTH EDUCATION (FARMINGDALE, N.Y.) 1985/1986, 6, No. 4:335-43.

WATER SUPPLY

Bifani, Patricia. How Kenyan peasants, pastoralists and peri-urban women see water problems. WATERLINES (LONDON) January 1986, 4:16-19.

Elmendorf, Mary L. and Isely, Raymond B.. Role of women in water supply and sanitation. WORLD HEALTH FORUM (GENEVA) 1982, 3, No. 2:227-30.

WEBSTER, PAULA

Webster, Paula. Matriarchy: a vision of power. In: Toward an anthropology of women. Edited by Rayna R. Reiter. (New York, Monthly Review Press, 1975), pp. 141-56.

WEE, ANN E.

Wee, Ann E.. Chinese women of Singapore: their present status in the family and in marriage. In: Women in the new Asia; the changing social roles of men and women in South and South-east Asia. Edited by Barbara E. Ward. ([Paris], Unesco, 1963), pp. 376-409.

WEEKES-VAGLIANI, WINIFRED

Weekes-Vagliani, Winifred. Elaboration d'un cadre d'analyse pour les projets agro-alimentaires. TIERS-MONDE (PARIS) April/June 1985, 26:307-16. Etude d'un projet agro-alimentaire indonesien.

Weekes-Vagliani, Winifred and Grossat, Bernard. Women in development at the right time for the right reasons. Series: Development Centre studies. (Paris, Development Centre of the Organization for Economic Co-operation and Development, 1980), 330 pp.

WEG, MARIANNE

Weg, Marianne. Das Ende der Bescheidenheit: Probleme und Perspektiven von Frauenforderplanen. WSI-MITTEILUNGEN (DUSSELDORF) August 1986, 39:566-75.

WEHKAMP, ANDY

Wehkamp, Andy. Luchas colectivas de las obreras peruanas: los motivos de participacion y alejamiento. BOLETIN DE ESTUDIOS LATINO-AMERICANOS Y DEL CARIBE (AMSTERDAM) December 1984, No. 37:69-83.

WEISS, YORAM

Weiss, Yoram and Gronau, Reuben. Expected interruptions in labour force participation and sex-related differences in earnings growth. REVIEW OF ECONOMIC STUDIES (EDINBURGH) October 1981, 48:607-19.

WELFARE

Buvinic, Mayra. Projects for women in the Third World: explaining their misbehavior. WORLD DEVELOPMENT (OXFORD) May 1986, 14:653-64. Explains why the economic objectives of a large number of income-generation projects for poor women in the Third World have evolved into welfare action during implementation.

WERNER, LINDA H.

Dow, Thomas E., Jr. and Werner, Linda H.. Perceptions of family planning among rural Kenyan women. STUDIES IN FAMILY PLANNING (NEW YORK) February 1983, 14:35-43.

Wertewandel und Widerspruche; Erziehungsorientierungen und -probleme von Arbeiterinnen im Vergleich zweier Generationen. By: Becker-Schmidt, Regina and Knapp, Gudrun-Axeli. WSI-MITTEILUNGEN (DUSSELDORF) August 1986, 39:558-66.

WESTERN SAMOA

Thomas, Pamela and Simi, Noumea. The new Samoan businesswoman. PACIFIC PERSPECTIVE (SUVA) 1983, 11, No. 2:5-12.

Where are the women engineers? By: Florman, Samuel C.. ACROSS THE BOARD (NEW YORK) January 1982, 19:56-61. A male engineer writes: 'The ultimate feminist dream will never be realized as long as women would rather supervise the world than help build it.'

Where have the women gone? Insights from Bangladesh on low sex ratio of India's population. By: Chen, Lincoln C.. ECONOMIC AND POLITICAL WEEKLY (BOMBAY) March 6, 1982, 17:364-72.

Where to get a loan. By: Cole, Bernadette. WEST AFRICA (LONDON) November 10, 1986, No. 3610:p. 2362. Reports on Women's World Banking (WWB), an independent financial organisation set up to advance and promote entrepreneurship among women within their local economies.

Where women come last a beehive is liberation. By: Boyle, Bonnie. WASHINGTON POST (WASHINGTON) December 11, 1983, p. C1-C2.

WHITE, E. FRANCES

White, E. Frances. Women, work, and ethnicity: the Sierra Leone case. In: Women and work in Africa. Edited by Edna G. Bay. (Boulder, CO, Westview Press, 1982), pp. 19-33.

WHITE, ELIZABETH H.

White, Elizabeth H.. Legal reform as an indicator of women's status in Muslim nations. In: Women in the Muslim world. Edited by Lois Beck and Nikki Keddie. (Cambridge, MA, Harvard University Press, 1978), pp. 52-68.

Why has development neglected rural women? A review of the South Asian literature. By: Nelson, Nici. Series: Women in Development, Vol. 1. (Oxford, New York, Pergamon Press, 1979), 108 pp. Reviews the literature available on the role of women in rural development in Bangladesh, India, Pakistan and Sri Lanka.

Why women are wasted. By: Hamid, Rizu. NEW AFRICAN (LONDON) July 1983, No. 190:48. Describes some of the objectives and activities of the Commonwealth Women and Development Unit set up in the Commonwealth Secretariat in 1980.

Why women get the jobs. ECONOMIST (LONDON) August 23, 1986, 300:13-14.

WHYTE, PAULINE

Whyte, Robert Orr and Whyte, Pauline. Women of rural Asia. (Boulder, Colorado, Westview Press, 1982), 262 pp.

WIARDA, IEDA SIQUEIRA

Wiarda, Ieda Siqueira and Helzner, Judith F.. Women, population and international development in Latin America: persistent legacies and new perceptions for the 1980's. UNIVERSITY OF MASSACHUSETTS AT AMHERST. PROGRAM IN LATIN AMERICAN STUDIES. OCCASIONAL PAPERS SERIES (AMHERST) April 1981, No. 13:1-40.

WICHTERICH, CHRISTA

Wichterich, Christa. Another development with the "other" sex; a postscript on the Women's Forum in Nairobi. D & C, DEVELOPMENT AND COOPERATION (BONN) November/December 1985, No. 6:11-12.

Wichterich, Christa. Der Fortschritt drangt die Frauen ins Abseits. E & Z, ENTWICKLUNG UND ZUSAMMENARBEIT (BONN) January 1985, 26:4-5.

WICHTERICH, CHRISTA

Wichterich, Christa. Progress in India - but not for women. D & C, DEVELOPMENT AND COOPERATION (BONN) March/April 1985, No. 2:18, 20. Looks at the impact of a wave of revolutions -- the "Green Revolution", which has increased rice and wheat yields, the "White Revolution", which turned traditional milk production upside down, and a "Blue" one, which modernized fish production.

WIESE, EVA-MARIA

Wiese, Eva-Maria. Frauen tragen die Last der Entwicklung; Beispiele aus West-Afrika. E & Z, ENTWICKLUNG UND ZUSAMMENARBEIT (BONN) January 1985, 26:8-10.

Wiese, Eva-Maria. Women in rural development. D & C, DEVELOPMENT AND COOPERATION (BONN) March/April 1985, No. 2:14-17. The author suggests that, in spite of some accomplishments during the "Decade for Women", the prevailing situation of rural women indicates for Africa that for the majority of them development has so far only meant an increase of functions associated with their roles, without reaping the benefits of either a proportionately acknowledged status or any justified income benefits.

WIESER, NORA JACQUEZ

Wieser, Nora Jacquez. Ancient song, the new melody in Latin America: women and film. In: Comparative perspectives of Third World women: the impact of race, sex and class. Edited by Beverly Lindsay. (New York, Praeger, 1980), pp. 179-99.

WIESER, THEODORE

Wieser, Theodore. Italian women; between family and feminism. SWISS REVIEW OF WORLD AFFAIRS (ZURICH) May 1982, 32:12-13.

WIKAN, UNNI

Wikan, Unni. Behind the veil in Arabia: women in Oman. (Baltimore, Johns Hopkins University Press, 1982), 314 pp.

WILLIS, DAVID K.

Willis, David K.. Meet an African farmer ... and her husband. CHRISTIAN SCIENCE MONITOR (BOSTON) July 5, 1985, p. 9-10. Discusses the role of women in producing food and the need for greater focus on rural women.

WILSON, FIONA

Wilson, Fiona. Women and agricultural change in Latin America: some concepts guiding research. WORLD DEVELOPMENT (OXFORD) September 1985, 13:1017-35.

WILSON, FRANCILLE RUSAN

Wilson, Francille Rusan. Reinventing the past and circumscribing the future: authenticity and the negative image of women's work in Zaire. In: Women and work in Africa. Edited by Edna G. Bay. (Boulder, CO, Westview Press, 1982), pp. 153-70.

WITTSTOCK, LAURA WATERMAN

Wittstock, Laura Waterman. Twilight of a long maidenhood. In: Comparative perspectives of Third World women: the impact of race, sex and class. Edited by Beverly Lindsay. (New York, Praeger, 1980), pp. 207-28.

WOLF, DIANE L.

Wolf, Diane L.. Making the bread and bringing it home: female factory workers and the family economy in rural Java. In: Women in the urban and industrial workforce; Southeast and East Asia. Edited by Gavin W. Jones. Series: Development Studies Centre. Monograph, No. 33. (Canberra, Australia, Australian National University, 1984), pp. 215-35. Series edited by Helen Hughes.

WOLFE, BARBARA L.

Behrman, Jere R. and Wolfe, Barbara L.. Labor force participation and earnings determinants for women in the special conditions of developing countries. JOURNAL OF DEVELOPMENT ECONOMICS (AMSTERDAM) May/August 1984, 15:259-88. The authors focus on labor market conditions for women in Nicaragua.

Wolfe, Barbara L. and Behrman, Jere R.. Determinants of child health, mortality, and nutrition in a developing country. UNIVERSITY OF WISCONSIN-MADISON. INSTITUTE FOR RESEARCH ON POVERTY. DISCUSSION PAPERS (MADISON) January 1981, No. 643-80:1-53. The authors use data collected in a cross-sectional multipurpose survey of women of childbearing age in Nicaragua.

Wolfe, Barbara L. and Behrman, Jere R.. Impact of demographic changes on income distribution in a developing country. JOURNAL OF DEVELOPMENT ECONOMICS (AMSTERDAM) December 1982, 11:355-77. The authors use data from a stratified random sample of about 4,000 women aged 15 to 45 in Nicaragua.

WOLFE, BARBARA L.
  Wolfe, Barbara L. and Behrman, Jere R.. Socioeconomic characteristics of women in a developing country and the degree of urbanization. UNIVERSITY OF WISCONSIN-MADISON. INSTITUTE FOR RESEARCH ON POVERTY. DISCUSSION PAPERS (MADISON) September 1980, 655-81:1-53. The study is based on a stratified random sample of over 4,000 women aged 15-45 in Nicaragua.

Woman of Viet-Nam in a changing world. By: Kim, Le Kwang. In: Women in the new Asia; the changing social roles of men and women in South and South-east Asia. Edited by Barbara E. Ward. ([Paris], Unesco, 1963), pp. 462-70.

Woman the gatherer: male bias in anthropology. By: Slocum, Sally. In: Toward an anthropology of women. Edited by Rayna R. Reiter. (New York, Monthly Review Press, 1975), pp. 36-50.

Women: breaking a path; the end of the Decade for Women. WEST AFRICA (LONDON) July 22, 1985, No. 3543:1495-1500.

Women: roles and status in eight countries. Edited by Janet Zollinger Giele and Audrey Chapman Smock. (New York, John Wiley, 1977), 443 pp.

Women -- the 25 hour day, women in development. By: Kermond, Lesley. A book exhibition, 15 October - 28 November 1982. (London, Library & Resource Centre, Commonwealth Institute, 1982), 19 pp. With supplement.

Women: the missing link in development programmes. PAKISTAN & GULF ECONOMIST (KARACHI) September 29, 1984, 3:38-39. Concludes that recent studies on the role of women in agriculture all point to the same conclusion -- they contribute far more to food and agricultural production than has been generally recognized.

Women - what role in development? By: van Dam, Andre. D & C, DEVELOPMENT AND COOPERATION (BONN) May/June 1981, No. 3:10-13.

Women agricultural labourers -- regional variations in incidence and employment. By: Sen, Gita. CENTRE FOR DEVELOPMENT STUDIES. WORKING PAPER (ULLOOR, TRIVANDRUM) April 1983, No. 168:1-28.

Women among Qashqa'i nomadic pastoralists in Iran. By: Beck, Lois. In: Women in the Muslim world. Edited by Lois Beck and Nikki Keddie. (Cambridge, MA, Harvard University Press, 1978), pp. 351-73.

Women and agricultural change in Latin America: some concepts guiding research. By: Wilson, Fiona. WORLD DEVELOPMENT (OXFORD) September 1985, 13:1017-35.

Women and agricultural change in the railway region of Zambia: dispossession and counterstrategies, 1930-1970. By: Muntemba, Maud Shimwaayi. In: Women and work in Africa. Edited by Edna G. Bay. (Boulder, CO, Westview Press, 1982), pp. 83-103.

Women and agroforestry: four myths and three case studies. By: Fortmann, Louise and Rocheleau, Dianne. AGROFORESTRY SYSTEMS (THE HAGUE) 1985, 2, No. 4:253-72. The involvement of women in agroforestry projects and activities is examined in case studies from the Dominican Republic, India and Kenya. Consideration for including women in agroforestry projects are discussed.

Women and appropriate technology: two essays. By: Carr, Marilyn. INTERMEDIATE TECHNOLOGY DEVELOPMENT GROUP. OCCASIONAL PAPER (LONDON) 1982, No. 5:1-21. CONTENT: Appropriate technology for African women. - 2. Technologies appropriate for women: theory, practice and policy.

Women and child care in China: a firsthand report. By: Sidel, Ruth. (New York, Penguin, Revised edition, 1982), 211 pp.

Women and cooking energy. By: Batliwala, Srilatha. ECONOMIC AND POLITICAL WEEKLY (BOMBAY) December 24, 1983, 18:2227-30. Describes how a woman in poverty has low access to cooking fuel, spends the longest time obtaining it, and puts it to use in stoves which are not only fuel-inefficient, but which also subject her to serious or fatal disease.

Women and development. By: Brambilla, Francesco. GIORNALE DEGLI ECONOMISTI E ANNALI DI ECONOMIA (MILAN) September/December 1979, 38, N.S.:619-67. With English summary.

Women and development. By: Fleming, Victoria. WEST AFRICA (LONDON) December 7, 1981, No. 3358:2921-22. Discusses the progress and the pitfalls halfway through the International Decade for Women.

Women and development: indicators of their changing role. Series: Socio-Economic Studies, No. 3. (Paris, Unesco, 1981), 112 pp.

Women and development in Latin America and the Caribbean; lessons from the seventies and hopes for the future. By: Arizpe, Lourdes. DEVELOPMENT DIGEST (WASHINGTON) 1982, Vol. 1/2:74-84.

Women and development in Lesotho. By: Gay, Judith S.. (Washington, Lesotho, USAID, Bureau for Africa, 1982), 84 pp. (Mimeographed)

Women and development in north western Zambia: from producer to housewife. By: Crehan, Kate. REVIEW OF AFRICAN POLITICAL ECONOMY (SHEFFIELD) 1984, No. 27/28:51-66.

Women and development in northern Belize. By: Brockmann, C. Thomas. JOURNAL OF DEVELOPING AREAS (MACOMB, ILL.) July 1985, 19:501-14.

Women and development, perspectives from South and Southeast Asia. Edited by Rounaq Jahan and Hanna Papanek. (Dacca, Bangladesh Institute of Law and International Affairs, 1979), 439 pp.

Women and development: the overlooked link. By: Pradhan, Bina. JOURNAL OF DEVELOPMENT AND ADMINISTRATIVE STUDIES (KATHMANDU) June/December 1981, 3:172-202.

Women and development; the sexual division of labor in rural societies. Edited by Lourdes Beneria. (New York, Praeger, 1982), 257 pp.

Women and economic change in Africa. By: Mullings, Leith. In: Women in Africa: studies in social and economic change. Edited by Nancy J. Hafkin and Edna G. Bay. (Stanford, Stanford University Press, 1976), pp. 239-64.

Women and fieldwork. By: Bujra, Janet. In: Women cross-culturally: change and challenge. Edited by Ruby Rohrlich-Leavitt. (The Hague, Mouton, 1975), pp. 521-557.

Women and food aid; a developmental perspective. By: Katona-Apte, Judit. FOOD POLICY (GUILDFORD, ENG.) August 1986, 11:216-22.

Women and income in the Third world: implications for policy. By: Dwyser, Daisy Hilse. POPULATION COUNCIL. INTERNATIONAL PROGRAMS. WORKING PAPERS (NEW YORK) June 1983, No. 18:1-39.

Women and industralization in developing countries. Series: United Nations [Document], ID/251. (New York, United Nations, 1981), 81 pp. At head of title: United Nations Industrial Development Organization, Vienna.

Women and industrial relations: working papers of an international symposium, Vienna, September 1978. By: International Symposium on Women and Industrial Relations (1978: Vienna, Austria). 2 vols. Series: Women, Work and Society; International Institute for Labour Studies, Research Series, No. 56/57 . (Geneva, International Institute for Labour Studies, 1980), In English, French or German, with summaries in the other languages.

Women and industrialisation: examining the "female marginalisation" thesis. By: Scott, Alison MacEwen. JOURNAL OF DEVELOPMENT STUDIES (LONDON) July 1986, 22:649-80. The article argues for attention to be paid to the micro-level processes which give rise to women's marginalisation.

Women and land resettlement in Zimbabwe. By: Jacobs, Susie. REVIEW OF AFRICAN POLITICAL ECONOMY (SHEFFIELD) 1984, No. 27/28:33-50.

Women and law reform in contemporary Islam. By: Coulson, Noel and Hinchcliffe, Doreen. In: Women in the Muslim world. Edited by Lois Beck and Nikki Keddie. (Cambridge, MA, Harvard University Press, 1978), pp. 37-51.

Women and morality. SOCIAL RESEARCH (NEW YORK) Autumn 1983, 50, No. 3:487-695. Brings together various perspectives, with specific attention to the "essentially moral" character of women's "felt" experience.

Women and people's ecological movement; a case study of women's role in the Chipko movement in Uttar Pradesh. By: Jain, Shobhita. ECONOMIC AND POLITICAL WEEKLY (BOMBAY) October 13, 1984, 19:1788-93.

Women and politics in Chile. By: Kirkwood, Julieta. INTERNATIONAL SOCIAL SCIENCE JOURNAL (PARIS) 1983, 35, No. 4:625-37.

Women and politics in twentieth century Africa and Asia. STUDIES IN THIRD WORLD SOCIETIES (WILLIAMSBURG) June 1981, No. 16:1-160.

Women and politics in twentieth century Latin America. STUDIES IN THIRD WORLD SOCIETIES (WILLIAMSBURG) March 1981, no. 15:1-136.

Women and population growth: choice beyond child-bearing. By: Newland, Kathleen. WORLDWATCH PAPER (WASHINGTON) December 1977, No. 16:1-32.

Women and poverty; report on a workshop. By: Banerjee, Nirmala. ECONOMIC AND POLITICAL WEEKLY (BOMBAY) October 1, 1983, 18:1693-98.

Women and productivity in two contrasting farming areas of Tanzania. By: Due, Jean M. and Anandajayasekeram, P.. UNIVERSITY OF ILLINOIS. DEPT. OF AGRICULTURAL ECONOMICS. STAFF PAPER. SERIES E (URBANA) July 1982, No. 82 E-228:1-23.

Women and property in Morocco; their changing relation to the process of social stratification in the middle Atlas. By: Maher, Vanessa. Series: Cambridge Studies in Social Anthropology, No. 10. (London, New York, Cambridge University Press, 1974), 238 pp.

Women and property in rural Bangladesh. By: Jahangir, B. K. JOURNAL OF SOCIAL STUDIES (DHAKA) October 1986, No. 34:87-95.

Women and revolution in Iran. Edited by Guity Nashat. (Boulder, Colorado, Westview Press, 1983), 301 pp.

Women and revolution in Iran, 1905-1911. By: Bayat-Philipp, Mangol. In: Women in the Muslim world. Edited by Lois Beck and Nikki Keddie. (Cambridge, MA, Harvard University Press, 1978), pp. 295-308.

Women and rural revolt in India. By: Omvedt, Gail. JOURNAL OF PEASANT STUDIES (LONDON) April 1978, 5:370-403. It is argued that in India, increasingly during the last decade, capitalism has developed in the countryside, and that, with the changing social relations of production, there has emerged a mass-based and militant women's movement ... This is illustrated ... especially for the state of Maharashtra.

Women and schooling in the Third World: a bibliography. By: Kelly, Gail P. and Lulat, Younus. COMPARATIVE EDUCATION REVIEW (NEW YORK) June 1980, 24:S224-63.

Women and social change in Morocco. By: Maher, Vanessa. In: Women in the Muslim world. Edited by Lois Beck and Nikki Keddie. (Cambridge, MA, Harvard University Press, 1978), pp. 100-23.

Women and socioeconomic change among Sheikhanzai nomads of western Afghanistan. By: Tavakolian, Bahram. MIDDLE EAST JOURNAL (WASHINGTON) Summer 1984, 38:433-53. Based on observations made in 1976-1977.

Women and structural transformation. By: Lele, Uma. ECONOMIC DEVELOPMENT AND CULTURAL CHANGE (CHICAGO) January 1986, 34:195-221. The primary objective of this article is to explore women's distinguishing role as economic actors in traditional societies under quite different social and production-organization systems.

Women and technological change -- a case study of three fishing villages. By: Gulati, Leela. CENTRE FOR DEVELOPMENT STUDIES. WORKING PAPER (ULLOOR, TRIVANDRUM) [1982?], No. 143:1-26.

Women and technological change in agriculture: Asian and African experience. By: Agarwal, Bina. INSTITUTE OF ECONOMIC GROWTH. [PAPERS] (DELHI) July 1984, No. E/103/84:1-55.

Women and technological change in developing countries. Edited by Roslyn Dauber and Melinda L. Cain. Series: AAAS Selected Symposium, No. 53. (Boulder, CO, Westview Press for American Association for the Advancement of Science, 1981), 266 pp.

Women and technological change in The Gambia: a case study of the salt industry. By: Nath, Kamla. BOSTON UNIVERSITY. AFRICAN STUDIES CENTER. WORKING PAPERS (BOSTON) 1985, No. 107:1-15.

Women and the energy crisis in the Sahel. By: Ki-Zerbo, Jacqueline. UNASYLVA (ROME) 1981, 33, No. 133:5-10.

Women and the informal sector. IDS BULLETIN, INSTITUTE OF DEVELOPMENT STUDIES AT THE UNIVERSITY OF SUSSEX (BRIGHTON) July 1981, 12:1-62. CONTENT: Heyzer, Noeleen, Towards a framework of analysis. - Bienefeld, Manfred, The informal sector and women's oppression. - Greenstreet, Miriam, When education is unequal. - Moser, Caroline, Surviving in the suburbios. - Goddard, Victoria, The leather trade in the Bassi of Naples. - Banerjee, Nirmala, The weakest link. - Allen, Sheila, Invisible threads. - Savara, Mira, Organising the Annapurna. - Moser, Caroline, and Kate Young, Women of the working poor.

Women and the neighborhood street in Barj Hammoud, Lebanon. By: Joseph, Suad. In: Women in the Muslim world. Edited by Lois Beck and Nikki Keddie. (Cambridge, MA, Harvard University Press, 1978), pp. 541-57.

Women and the subsistence sector: economic participation and household decision making in Nepal. By: Acharya, Meena and Bennett, Lynn. Series: World Bank Staff Working Papers, No. 526. (Washington, DC, World Bank, 1983), 140 pp.

Women and the world of work. By: Nato Symposium on Women and the World of Work (1980: Lisbon, Portugal). Edited by Anne Hoiberg. Series: Nato Conference Series, III, Human Factors, Vol. 18. (New York, Published in cooperation with the Nato Scientific Affairs Division [by] Plenum Press, 1982), 390 pp. Proceedings of a NATO Symposium on Women and the World of Work held August 4-8, 1980, in Lisbon, Portugal.

Women and vegetable gardens in the Gambia: Action AID and rural development. By: Nath, Kamla. BOSTON UNIVERSITY. AFRICAN STUDIES CENTER. WORKING PAPERS (BOSTON) 1985, No. 109:1-13. Examines Action Aid's program for improving the capacity of rural women to produce garden vegetables and to introduce marketing infrastructures.

Women and water: two UN Decades share goals. By: Cotter, Jim. HORIZONS, U.S. AGENCY FOR INTERNATIONAL DEVELOPMENT (WASHINGTON) Winter 1985, 4:14-15.

Women and words in a Spanish village. By: Harding, Susan. In: Toward an anthropology of women. Edited by Rayna R. Reiter. (New York, Monthly Review Press, 1975), pp. 283-308.

Women and work in Africa. Edited by Edna G. Bay. (Boulder, CO, Westview Press, 1982), 310 pp. Based on papers presented at the 1979 annual Spring symposium of the African Studies program, held at the University of Illinois at Urbana-Champaign, entitled "Women and Work in Africa".

Women and work in West Malaysia. By: Hing, Ai Yun. JOURNAL OF CONTEMPORARY ASIA (LONDON) 1984, 14, No. 2:204-18.

Women and world development. Edited by Irene Tinker and Michele Bo Bramsen. (Washington, Overseas Development Council, 1976), 228 pp. Prepared under the auspices of the American Association for the Advancement of Science. Includes a summary of the proceedings of the AAAS seminar held in Mexico City in June 1975, and twelve papers prepared for that meeting.

Women and world development: an annotated bibliography. By: Buvinic, Mayra, et al.. (Washington, Overseas Development Council, 1976), 162 pp. Companion to: Women and world development, edited by Irene Tinker and Michele Bramsen. Product of the AAAs seminar on women in development held in Mexico City in June 1975; prepared under the auspices of the American Association for the Advancement of Science.

Women, art, and culture in the new Grenada. By: LaDuke, Betty. LATIN AMERICAN PERSPECTIVES (BEVERLY HILLS) Summer 1984, 11:37-52.

Women as an alternative culture here and now. By: Pietila, Hilkka. DEVELOPMENT (ROME) 1984, No. 4:60-63. Asks if the female half of humanity could become the creators of an other development, which is more just and humane than the one we know today?

Women as food producers and suppliers in the twentieth century; the case of Zambia. By: Muntemba, Shimwaayi. DEVELOPMENT DIALOGUE (UPPSALA) 1982, No. 1/2:29-50.

Women as workers: the experience of the Puerto Rican woman in the 1930's. By: Silvestrini-Pacheco, Blanco. In: Women cross-culturally: change and challenge. Edited by Ruby Rohrlich-Leavitt. (The Hague, Mouton, 1975), pp. 247-60.

Women at the top. By: Maher, Mary. DEVELOPMENT FORUM BUSINESS EDITION (NEW YORK) August 18, 1980, No. 60:p. 6.

Women at the University of the South Pacific. By: Crocombe, Marjorie Tuainekore. PACIFIC PERSPECTIVE (SUVA) 1983, 11, No. 2:24-8.

Women at work. By: Nishimura, Namiko. JOURNAL OF JAPANESE TRADE & INDUSTRY (TOKYO) May/June 1986, 5:46-47.

Women at work; equality and care of the species. By: Shinotsuka, Eiko. FAR EASTERN ECONOMIC REVIEW (HONGKONG) Dec. 3, 1982, 118:87-90.

Women at work in Mali: the case of the Markala cooperative. By: Caughman, Susan. BOSTON UNIVERSITY. AFRICAN STUDIES CENTER. WORKING PAPERS (BOSTON) 1981, No. 50:1-35.

WOMEN BANKERS

Carter, Mary. Women's banking expands; twenty local affiliates now active in 17 countries. DEVELOPMENT, SOCIETY FOR INTERNATIONAL DEVELOPMENT (ROME) July 31, 1984, No. 155:3. Describes the policies, procedures and design of Women's World Banking, which operates as an independent financial institution to provide loan guarantees or other security to banks and other financial institutions, and arranges technical or other advice and assistance to direct and indirect beneficiaries of guarantees.

van Buren, Linda. KWFT steps in to make African women bankable. AFRICAN BUSINESS (LONDON) July 1985, No. 83:10-12. Describes the Kenya Women Finance Trust.

Women; changing attitudes: a cooperative effort. By: Anyaoku, Emeka. AFRICA REPORT (NEW YORK) March/April 1985, 30:p. 21. The author suggests that while African governments have acknowledged the importance of strengthening women's contributions to their national economies, effective change can only come about through cooperative efforts which take into account African cultural and traditional values.

Women, class and power: examples from the Hatay, Turkey. By: Aswad, Barbara C.. In: Women in the Muslim world. Edited by Lois Beck and Nikki Keddie. (Cambridge, MA, Harvard University Press, 1978), pp. 473-81.

Women cross-culturally: change and challenge. Edited by Ruby Rohrlich-Leavitt. (The Hague, Mouton, 1975), 669 pp. Contains papers written for the session on women's movements at the 9th International Congress of Anthropological and Ethnological Sciences, held in Chicago in the late summer of 1973.

Women, demography and development. By: Ware, Helen. Series: Demography Teaching notes, 0157-6232, Australian National University, Development Studies Centre, No. 3. (Canberra, Australian National University, 1981), 242 pp.

Women; dew does well. By: Pani, Dharani K. BUSINESS INDIA (BOMBAY) January 26, 1987, No. 232:p. 34. Discusses the work of Tamilnadu Corporation for the Development of Women Ltd (DEW) in bringing economic independence to women belonging to the economically weaker sections of society.

Women, employment and development. By: Pulea, Mere. PACIFIC PERSPECTIVE (SUVA) 1983, 11, No. 2:18-28.

Women; equal partners in Africa's development. By: Rogombe, Rose Francine. AFRICA REPORT (NEW YORK) March/April 1985, 30:17-20.

WOMEN EXECUTIVES

Rowe, Alan J. and Bennis, Warren. Desexing decision styles. PERSONNEL (SARANAC LAKE, N.Y.) January/February 1984, 61:43-52. The authors attempt to determine why women are thought of as being different from men in terms of their ability to perform effectively in management positions.

Taylor, Frank. Women grab management power in home of machismo. INTERNATIONAL MANAGEMENT (MAIDENHEAD) February 1984, 39:24-27. Describes how Latin American women are starting to make inroads into business.

Women farmers and inequities in agricultural services. By: Staudt, Kathleen A.. In: Women and work in Africa. Edited by Edna G. Bay. (Boulder, CO, Westview Press, 1982), pp. 207-24.

Women, food and nutrition in Africa: perspective from Senegal. By: Basse, Marie-Therese. FOOD AND NUTRITION (ROME) 1984, 10, No. 1:65-79. Also includes: Economic change and the outlook for nutrition, prepared by the Food and Agriculture Organization of the United Nations.

Women grab management power in home of machismo. By: Taylor, Frank. INTERNATIONAL MANAGEMENT (MAIDENHEAD) February 1984, 39:24-27. Describes how Latin American women are starting to make inroads into business.

Women, health and development in the Americas; an annotated bibliography. By: Pan American Health Organization. Series: Scientific publication, No. 464. (Washington, Pan American Health Organization, Pan American Sanitary Bureau, Regional Office of the World Health Organization, 1984), 106 pp.

Women, households, and food commodity chains in southern Ghana: contradictions between the search for profit and the struggle for survival. By: Vellenga, Dorothy Dee. REVIEW, FERNAND BRAUDEL CENTER (BINGHAMTON, N.Y.) Winter 1985, 8:293-318.

Women in a developing society. By: Usha Rao, N. J. (Nandalike Jagannath). (New Delhi, Ashish, 1983), 180 pp.

Women in a Qur'anic society. By: Lamya' al-Faruqi, Lois. AL-TAWHID; A QUARTERLY JOURNAL OF ISLAMIC THOUGHT AND CULTURE (TEHRAN) July 1984, 1, No. 4:36-49.

Women in Africa and development assistance, report from a seminar arranged by the Scandinavian Institute of African Studies, Uppsala, 20-21 August, 1978. By: Scandinavian Institute of African Studies. (Uppsala, Sweden, Scandinavian Institute of African Studies, 1978), 55 pp.

Women in Africa; studies in social and economic change. Edited by Nancy J. Hafkin and Edna G. Bay. (Stanford, CA, Stanford University Press, 1976), 306 pp.

Women in African rice farming systems. By: Dey, Jennie. FOOD AND AGRICULTURE ORGANIZATION OF THE UNITED NATIONS. INTERNATIONAL RICE COMMISSION NEWSLETTER (ROME) December 1983, 32:1-4.

Women in African towns south of the Sahara: the urbanization dilemma. By: Little, Kenneth. In: Women and world development. Edited by Irene Tinker and Michele Bo Bramsen. ([Washington, DC], Overseas Development Council, 1976), pp. 78-87.

WOMEN IN AGRICULTURE

Agarwal, Bina. Women and technological change in agriculture: Asian and African experience. INSTITUTE OF ECONOMIC GROWTH. [PAPERS] (DELHI) July 1984, No. E/103/84:1-55.

Agarwal, Bina. Women, poverty and agricultural growth in India. INSTITUTE OF ECONOMIC GROWTH. [PAPERS] (DELHI) June 1985, No. E/112/85:1-101.

Arizpe, Lourdes. Les femmes paysannes et la crise agraire en Amerique latine. TIERS-MONDE (PARIS) April/June 1985, 26:325-34.

Barnes, Carolyn. Differentiation by sex among small-scale farming households in Kenya. RURAL AFRICANA (EAST LANSING) Winter/Spring 1983, No. 15/16:41-63.

Blain, Daniele. Farming system for women: the case of cassava production in Zaire. CERES, FAO REVIEW ON AGRICULTURE AND DEVELOPMENT (ROME) May/June 1985, 18:43-46.

Bruchhaus, Eva-Maria. Von der Bauerin zur Hilfskraft? E & Z, ENTWICKLUNG UND ZUSAMMENARBEIT (BONN) June 25, 1984, 25:19-21.

Chand, Ramesh and Sidhu, D. S. Impact of agricultural modernization on labour: use pattern in Punjab with special reference to women labour. INDIAN JOURNAL OF AGRICULTURAL ECONOMICS (BOMBAY) July/September 1985, 40:252-59.

Choudhury, S. and Giri, A. K. Nature and extent of female labour use in agriculture - a comparison between progressive and non-progressive area. ECONOMIC AFFAIRS (CALCUTTA) June 1986, 31:81-86.

Deere, Carmen Diana. Developpement cooperatif et participation feminine a la reforme agraire nicaraguayenne. TIERS-MONDE (PARIS) April/June 1985, 26:403-08.

Deere, Carmen Diana. Rural women and state policy: the Latin American agrarian reform experience. WORLD DEVELOPMENT (OXFORD) September 1985, 13:1037-53.

WOMEN IN AGRICULTURE

Dey, Jennie. Women in African rice farming systems. FOOD AND AGRICULTURE ORGANIZATION OF THE UNITED NATIONS. INTERNATIONAL RICE COMMISSION NEWSLETTER (ROME) December 1983, 32:1-4.

Dixon, Ruth. Land, labour, and the sex composition of the agricultural labour force: an international comparison. DEVELOPMENT AND CHANGE (THE HAGUE, etc.) July 1983, 14:347-72.

Due, Jean M. and Anandajayasekeram, P.. Women and productivity in two contrasting farming areas of Tanzania. UNIVERSITY OF ILLINOIS. DEPT. OF AGRICULTURAL ECONOMICS. STAFF PAPER. SERIES E (URBANA) July 1982, No. 82 E-228:1-23.

Helmore, Kristin. Working for survival; working for cash. CHRISTIAN SCIENCE MONITOR (BOSTON) December 19, 1985, p.18-20. Part three of a 5-part series entitled: "The neglected resource; women in the developing world," focusses on women's work in the agricultural sector as main provider of family sustenance. Also examines the deleterious effects of some development policies for women in the rural areas.

Hye, Hasnat Abdul. Mechanisation in agriculture and women in Bangladesh. JOURNAL OF SOCIAL STUDIES (DHAKA) January 1985, No. 27:78-100.

Jain, Devaki. In poor families, women's income is the lifeline. CERES, FAO REVIEW ON AGRICULTURE AND DEVELOPMENT (ROME) July/August 1984, 17:35-38. Presents an interview with the director of the Institute of Social Studies, New Delhi, describing the pressures on landless female agricultural laborers.

Kelkar, Govind. Tractors against women. DEVELOPMENT (ROME) 1985, No. 3:18-21. Concludes that the Green Revolution has brought in its wake the all-India trend of pauperization and marginalization and the increased inequality between the sexes.

Koumbidia (Senegal); developpement d'une activite maraichere villageoise. TIERS-MONDE (PARIS) April/June 1985, 26:421-28.

Kranz, Jutta and Fiege, Karin. Work never ends; problems of women in the farm economy of the Ivory Coast. D & C, DEVELOPMENT AND COOPERATION (BONN) November/December 1983, No. 6:12-13.

WOMEN IN AGRICULTURE

Laufer, Leslie A.. Substitution between male and female labor in rural Indian agricultural production. YALE UNIVERSITY. ECONOMIC GROWTH CENTER. DISCUSSION PAPER (NEW HAVEN, CONN.) April 1985, No 472:1-24.

Marothia, D. K. and Sharma, S. K. Female labour participation in rice farming system of Chhattisgarh region. INDIAN JOURNAL OF AGRICULTURAL ECONOMICS (BOMBAY) July/September 1985, 40:235-39.

Martius von Harder, Gudrun. Le role des services nationaux d'animation rurale et de vulgarisation agricole aupres des femmes. TIERS-MONDE (PARIS) April/June 1985, 26:317-24.

Mascarenhas, Ophelia. Confronting the male bias in research priorities. CERES, FAO REVIEW ON AGRICULTURE AND DEVELOPMENT (ROME) May/June 1985, 18:28-32. Suggests that agricultural research in most formerly colonial countries has two characteristics: the overemphasis of cash crops and the tendency to ignore women in the planning, development, and implementation of such research.

Mencher, Joan P. and Saradamoni, K.. Muddy feet, dirty hands; rice production and female agricultural labour. ECONOMIC AND POLITICAL WEEKLY (BOMBAY) December 25, 1982, 17:A149-A167.

Michel, Andree. Dix ans d'irruption des sciences humaines dans le domaine du travail des paysannes. TIERS-MONDE (PARIS) April/June 1985, 26:261-71.

Michel, Andree. El trabajo invisible de las campesinas del Tercer Mundo. DESARROLLO Y SOCIEDAD (BOGOTA) January 1984, No. 13:81-97. With English summary.

Mies, Maria. Indian women in subsistence and agricultural labour. INTERNATIONAL LABOUR OFFICE. WORLD EMPLOYMENT PROGRAMME RESEARCH. RURAL EMPLOYMENT POLICY RESEARCH PROGRAMME. WORKING PAPER (GENEVA) (GENEVA) May 1984, No. 34:1-243.

Muntemba, Shimwaayi. Women as food producers and suppliers in the twentieth century; the case of Zambia. DEVELOPMENT DIALOGUE (UPPSALA) 1982, No. 1/2:29-50.

WOMEN IN AGRICULTURE

Okali, C. and Cassaday, K.. Community response to a pilot farming project in Nigeria. BOSTON UNIVERSITY. AFRICAN-AMERICAN ISSUES CENTER. DISCUSSION PAPER (BOSTON) [1985], No. 10:1-28. The authors report on a preliminary study of farmers' response to alley farming, a technology designed to improve small ruminant (sheep and goat) and arable crop production in the humid zone of West Africa.

Okorji, Eugene C. Role of women in arable cropping enterprises in farming communities of South-Eastern Nigeria: a case study. DEVELOPMENT AND PEACE (BUDAPEST) Autumn 1985, 6:165-73.

Perry, Alison. Bearing the burden. WEST AFRICA (LONDON) April 22, 1985, No. 3530:785-86. Looks at the important role women playin the agricultural sector and at the severe handicpas they face, due to their double work-load and a discriminatory system.

Ray, A. K. and Rangarao, I. V. Impact of technological changes on economic status of female labour. INDIAN JOURNAL OF AGRICULTURAL ECONOMICS (BOMBAY) July/September 1985, 40:244-52.

Salmona, Micheline. L'echappee belle, ou la mobilisation generale des femmes dans l'agriculture en France. TIERS-MONDE (PARIS) April/June 1985, 26:247-60.

Sen, Gita. Paddy production, processing and women workers in India - the south versus the northeast. CENTRE FOR DEVELOPMENT STUDIES. WORKING PAPER (ULLOOR, TRIVANDRUM) December 1983, No. 186.

Sen, Gita. Women agricultural labourers -- regional variations in incidence and employment. CENTRE FOR DEVELOPMENT STUDIES. WORKING PAPER (ULLOOR, TRIVANDRUM) April 1983, No. 168:1-28.

Sen, Gita. Women's work and women agricultural labourers: a study of the Indian Census. CENTRE FOR DEVELOPMENT STUDIES. WORKING PAPER (ULLOOR, TRIVANDRUM) February 1983, No. 159:1-43.

Sharma, Miriam. Caste, class, and gender: production and reproduction in North India. JOURNAL OF PEASANT STUDIES (LONDON) July 1985, 12:26-56.

WOMEN AND DEVELOPMENT

WOMEN IN AGRICULTURE

Sisodia, J. S. Role of farm women in agriculture: a study of Chambal command area of Madhya Pradesh. INDIAN JOURNAL OF AGRICULTURAL ECONOMICS (BOMBAY) July/September 1985, 40:223-34.

Spring, Anita. Men and women smallholder participants in a stall-feeder livestock program in Malawi. HUMAN ORGANIZATION (WASHINGTON) Summer 1986, 45:154-62.

Suryawanshi, S. D. and Kapase, P. M. Impact of Ghod irrigation project on employment of female agricultural labour. INDIAN JOURNAL OF AGRICULTURAL ECONOMICS (BOMBAY) July/September 1985, 40:240-44.

Weekes-Vagliani, Winifred. Elaboration d'un cadre d'analyse pour les projets agro-alimentaires. TIERS-MONDE (PARIS) April/June 1985, 26:307-16. Etude d'un projet agro-alimentaire indonesien.

Willis, David K.. Meet an African farmer ... and her husband. CHRISTIAN SCIENCE MONITOR (BOSTON) July 5, 1985, p. 9-10. Discusses the role of women in producing food and the need for greater focus on rural women.

Wilson, Fiona. Women and agricultural change in Latin America: some concepts guiding research. WORLD DEVELOPMENT (OXFORD) September 1985, 13:1017-35.

Women: the missing link in development programmes. PAKISTAN & GULF ECONOMIST (KARACHI) September 29, 1984, 3:38-39. Concludes that recent studies on the role of women in agriculture all point to the same conclusion -- they contribute far more to food and agricultural production than has been generally recognized.

WOMEN IN AGROFORESTRY

Fortmann, Louise and Rocheleau, Dianne. Women and agroforestry: four myths and three case studies. AGROFORESTRY SYSTEMS (THE HAGUE) 1985, 2, No. 4:253-72. The involvement of women in agroforestry projects and activities is examined in case studies from the Dominican Republic, India and Kenya. Consideration for including women in agroforestry projects are discussed.

Women in Bangladesh. By: Jahan, Rounaq. In: Women cross-culturally: change and challenge. Edited by Ruby Rohrlich-Leavitt. (The Hague, Mouton, 1975), pp. 5-30.

WOMEN IN BANKING

Cole, Bernadette. Where to get a loan. WEST AFRICA (LONDON) November 10, 1986, No. 3610:p. 2362. Reports on Women's World Banking (WWB), an independent financial organisation set up to advance and promote entrepreneurship among women within their local economies.

Goodman, Matthew. Japanese women in finance. TOKYO BUSINESS TODAY (TOKYO) May 1986, p. 19-23.

WOMEN IN BUSINESS

Carter, Mary. Women's banking expands; twenty local affiliates now active in 17 countries. DEVELOPMENT, SOCIETY FOR INTERNATIONAL DEVELOPMENT (ROME) July 31, 1984, No. 155:3. Describes the policies, procedures and design of Women's World Banking, which operates as an independent financial institution to provide loan guarantees or other security to banks and other financial institutions, and arranges technical or other advice and assistance to direct and indirect beneficiaries of guarantees.

Conseil national du Ghana. Groupements a but economique de femmes solidaires; l'experience du Ghana. TIERS-MONDE (PARIS) April/June 1985, 26:451-56.

Dubow, Wendy D.. Women in business: a credit-able investment. HORIZONS, U.S. AGENCY FOR INTERNATIONAL DEVELOPMENT (WASHINGTON) Summer 1985, 4:9-11. Describes the achievements of a creative, new network of businesswomen, Women's World Banking.

Everett, Jana and Savara, Mira. Bank loans to lower class women in Bombay; problems and prospects. ECONOMIC AND POLITICAL WEEKLY (BOMBAY) August 25, 1984, 19:M113-M119. The authors report the results of an exploratory study of bank loans to lower caste women in Bombay. They seek to shed some light on the problems surrounding and the prospects for bank loans as an economic development strategy for poor women.

Mohiuddin, Yasmeen. Economic role of women: a case of occupational dependency. PAKISTAN & GULF ECONOMIST (KARACHI) February 2, 1985, 4:12-15.

Scriabine, Raisa. Self-employed women: visible and valuable. HORIZONS, U.S. AGENCY FOR INTERNATIONAL DEVELOPMENT (WASHINGTON) Summer 1985, 4:38-40. Describes the Self-Employed Women's Association (SEWA), a trade union of more than 8,000 poor women workers in Ahmedabad, India. Members include small enterpreneurs, home-based producers, and manual laborers.

WOMEN IN BUSINESS

Thomas, Pamela and Simi, Noumea. The new Samoan businesswoman. PACIFIC PERSPECTIVE (SUVA) 1983, 11, No. 2:5-12.

van Buren, Linda. KWFT steps in to make African women bankable. AFRICAN BUSINESS (LONDON) July 1985, No. 83:10-12. Describes the Kenya Women Finance Trust.

Women in business: a credit-able investment. By: Dubow, Wendy D.. HORIZONS, U.S. AGENCY FOR INTERNATIONAL DEVELOPMENT (WASHINGTON) Summer 1985, 4:9-11. Describes the achievements of a creative, new network of businesswomen, Women's World Banking.

Women in China: current directions in historical scholarship. Edited by Richard W. Guisso and Stanley Johannesen. Series: Historical Reflections: Directions, No. 3. (Youngstown, New York, Philo Press, 1981), 238 pp.

Women in contemporary Persian folktales. By: Friedl, Erika. In: Women in the Muslim world. Edited by Lois Beck and Nikki Keddie. (Cambridge, MA, Harvard University Press, 1978), pp. 629-50.

Women in Cuba: the revolution within the revolution. By: Cole, Johnnetta B.. In: Comparative perspectives of Third World women: the impact of race, sex and class. Edited by Beverly Lindsay. (New York, Praeger, 1980), pp. 162-78.

Women in development: liberalism, Marxism and Marxist-feminism. By: Bandarage, Asoka. DEVELOPMENT AND CHANGE (THE HAGUE, etc.) October 1984, 15:495-515. Discusses liberal feminism and its Marxist critique on economic modernization and Third world women.

Women in development: looking to the future: hearing before the Committee on Foreign Relations, United States Senate, Ninety-eighth Congress, 2nd session, June 7, 1984. By: United States. Congress. Senate. Committee on Foreign Relations. (Washington, DC, Government Printing Office, 1984), 245 pp.

Women in development at the right time for the right reasons. By: Weekes-Vagliani, Winifred and Grossat, Bernard. Series: Development Centre studies. (Paris, Development Centre of the Organization for Economic Co-operation and Development, 1980), 330 pp.

Women in Egypt; new roles and realities. By: Lesch, Ann Mosely and Sullivan, Earl L. UNIVERSITIES FIELD STAFF INTERNATIONAL REPORTS, AFRICA (HANOVER, NH) 1986, No. 22:1-9.

Women in fishing villages on the Kerala coast: demographic and socio-economic impacts of a fisheries development project. By: Gulati, Leela. INTERNATIONAL LABOUR OFFICE. WORLD EMPLOYMENT PROGRAMME RESEARCH. POPULATION AND LABOUR POLICIES PROGRAMME. WORKING PAPER (GENEVA) March 1983, No. 128:1-143.

Women in Hindu society: a study of tradition and transition. By: Gupta, A. R.. (New Delhi, Jyotsna Prakashan, 2nd ed., 1982), 257 pp.

Women in India; some recent perspectives; research note. By: Leonard, Karen. PACIFIC AFFAIRS (VANCOUVER, B.C.) Spring 1979, 52:95-107.

WOMEN IN INDUSTRY

Biryukova, Alexandra. Role of the Soviet woman in decision-making in trade union committees and in industry. LABOUR AND SOCIETY (GENEVA) September 1985, 10:307-21.

Kelly, Deirdre. St. Lucia's female electronics factory workers: key components in an export-oriented industrialization strategy. WORLD DEVELOPMENT (OXFORD) July 1986, 14:823-38.

Scott, Alison MacEwen. Women and industrialisation: examining the "female marginalisation" thesis. JOURNAL OF DEVELOPMENT STUDIES (LONDON) July 1986, 22:649-80. The article argues for attention to be paid to the micro-level processes which give rise to women's marginalisation.

Steady, Filomina Chioma. African women, industrialization and another development; a global perspective. DEVELOPMENT DIALOGUE (UPPSALA) 1982, No. 1/2:51-64.

Women in Islam. By: Hottinger, Arnold. SWISS REVIEW OF WORLD AFFAIRS (ZURICH) October 1980, 30:8-14.

Women in Jamaica: patterns of reproduction and family. By: Roberts, George W. and Sinclair, Sonja A.. (Millwood, New York, KTO Press, 1978), 346 pp.

Women in Kenya; revolution or evolution? By: Harris, Joan. AFRICA REPORT (NEW YORK) March/April 1985, 30:30-32.

Women in Mao's China. By: Kelkar, Govind. DEVELOPMENT (ROME) 1984, No. 4:55-58. The author recounts the history of the single most important effort to equalize women's position in society, the quest for egalitarianism in Maoist China.

Women in Mauritania: the effects of drought and migration on their economic status and implications for development programs. By: Smale, Melinda. (Washington, DC, Office of Women in Development, Agency for International Development, 1980), 163 pp. On cover: Women in Development.

Women in Mexico. By: Sanchez, Aurelia Guadalupe and Dominguez, Ana E.. In: Women cross-culturally: change and challenge. Edited by Ruby Rohrlich-Leavitt. (The Hague, Mouton, 1975), pp. 95-110.

Women in migration. INTERNATIONAL MIGRATION REVIEW (STATEN ISLAND, N.Y.) Winter 1984, 18:881-1314, special issue. PARTIAL CONTENT: Khoo, Siew-Ean, and Peter C. Smith, Migration of women to cities: the Asian situation in comparative research. - Trager, Lilian, Family strategies and the migration of women; emigrants to Dagupan City, Philippines. - Drakakis-Smith, D. W., The Changing economic role of women in the urbanization process: a preliminary report from Zimbabwe. - Pittin, Renee, Migration of women in Nigeria: the Hausa case.

Women in Mozambique; rural transformations: women in the new society. By: Urdang, Stephanie. AFRICA REPORT (NEW YORK) March/April 1985, 30:66-70.

Women in Muslim rural society: status and role in family and community. By: Ginat, Joseph. Series: The Monograph Series, Shiloah Center for Middle Eastern and African Studies, Tel Aviv University. (New Brunswick, NJ, Transaction Books, 1982), 268 pp.

Women in national development in Ghana. Prepared for USAID/Ghana by Jeanne North [and others]. (Washington, DC, Department of State, 1975), 69 pp. Issued as v.VI, Annex F of the U.S. Agency for International Development, Development Assistance Program FY1976-FY1980, Ghana.

Women in national planning: false expectations. By: Mohammadi, Pari. DEVELOPMENT (ROME) 1984, No. 4:80-81.

Women in Nepali agriculture: all work and no power. By: Schroeder, Robert and Schroeder, Elaine. JOURNAL OF DEVELOPMENT AND ADMINISTRATIVE STUDIES (KATHMANDU) January 1979, 1:178-92.

Women in Peru. By: Figueroa, Blanca and Anderson, Jeanine. Series: Change International Reports: Women in Society, No. 5. (London, Change International Reports, 1981), 16 pp.

WOMEN IN POLITICS

Bonder, Gloria. Study of politics from the standpoint of women. INTERNATIONAL SOCIAL SCIENCE JOURNAL (PARIS) 1983, 35, No. 4:569-83.

El-Bakri and Kameir, E. M.. Aspects of women's political participation in Sudan. INTERNATIONAL SOCIAL SCIENCE JOURNAL (PARIS) 1983, 35, No. 4:605-23.

Howard-Merriam, Kathleen. Women's political participation in Morocco's development: how much and for whom? MAGHREB REVIEW (LONDON) January/April 1984, 9:12-25.

Kirkwood, Julieta. Women and politics in Chile. INTERNATIONAL SOCIAL SCIENCE JOURNAL (PARIS) 1983, 35, No. 4:625-37.

Rogers, Marvin L. Changing patterns of political involvement among Malay village women. ASIAN SURVEY (BERKELEY, CALIF.) March 1986, 26:322-44.

Schmidt, Steffen W.. Women, politics and development; a review essay. LATIN AMERICAN RESEARCH REVIEW (ALBUQUERQUE, NM) 1983, 18, No. 1:210-27.

Women in power spheres. INTERNATIONAL SOCIAL SCIENCE JOURNAL (PARIS) 1983, 35, No. 4:569-756.

Women in politics in Sri Lanka. By: Kearney, Robert N.. ASIAN SURVEY (BERKELEY, CALIF.) July 1981, 21:729-46.

Women in power spheres. INTERNATIONAL SOCIAL SCIENCE JOURNAL (PARIS) 1983, 35, No. 4:569-756.

Women in rural Bangladesh: policies for their employment and opportunities in crop processing. By: Scott, Gloria L. and Carr, Marilyn. Series: World Bank Staff Working Papers, No. 731. (Washington, DC, World Bank, 1985), 107 pp. (Forthcoming).

Women in rural development. By: Wiese, Eva-Maria. D & C, DEVELOPMENT AND COOPERATION (BONN) March/April 1985, No. 2:14-17. The author suggests that, in spite of some accomplishments during the "Decade for Women", the prevailing situation of rural women indicates for Africa that for the majority of them development has so far only meant an increase of functions associated with their roles, without reaping the benefits of either a proportionately acknowledged status or any justified income benefits.

Women in rural development: recommendations and realities. CERES, FAO REVIEW ON AGRICULTURE AND DEVELOPMENT (ROME) May/June 1980, 75:15-42.

Women in rural development in Ghana. By: Dumor, Ernest. RURAL AFRICANA (EAST LANSING) Fall 1983, No. 17:69-81.

Women in rural economic reform. By: Ming, Xiao. WOMEN OF CHINA (BEIJING) May 1986, No. 5:3-7.

Women in rural-urban circulation networks: implications for social structural change. By: Strauch, Judith. In: Women in the cities of Asia: migration and urban adaptation. Edited by James T. Fawcett, Siew-Ean Khoo and Peter C. Smith. (Boulder, CO, Westview Press, 1984), pp. 60-77.

Women in southern Africa; are women integrated into development? By: Muchena, Olivia. AFRICA REPORT (NEW YORK) March/April 1983, 28:4-6.

Women in southern Africa; bibliography. AFRICA REPORT (NEW YORK) March/April 1983, 28:54-55.

Women in southern Africa; gaining political power. By: Konie, Gwendoline. AFRICA REPORT (NEW YORK) March/April 1983, 28:11-14.

Women in southern Africa; legacy of exclusion. By: Matsepe-Casaburri, Ivy. AFRICA REPORT (NEW YORK) March/April 1983, 28:7-10. Presents a brief overview of the position of women, with a focus on those belonging to disadvantaged groups.

Women in Soviet Central Asia: progress and contradictions. By: Lubin, Nancy. SOVIET STUDIES (GLASGOW) April 1981, 33:182-203.

Women in struggle. By: Davies, Miranda. THIRD WORLD QUARTERLY (LONDON) October 1983, 5:874-914. CONTENT: Davies, Miranda, An overview. - Sayigh, Rosemary, Palestine. - Unterhalter, Elaine, South Africa. - Silkin, Trish, Eritrea.

Women in Tanzania: an analytical bibliography. By: Mascarenhas, Ophelia and Mbilinyi, Marjorie J.. (Uppsala, Scandinavian Institute of African Studies; Stockholm, Swedish International Development Authority, 1983), 256 pp.

Women in the Caribbean: an annotated bibliography; a guide to material available in Barbados. By: Massiah, Joycelin. Compiled by Joycelin Massiah, with the assistance of Audine Wilkinson and Norma Shorey. Series: University of the West Indies, Cave Hill, Barbados. Institute of Social and Economic Research. Occasional bibliography series, No. 5. (Cave Hill, Barbados, Institute of Social and Economic Research (Eastern Caribbean), University of the West Indies, 1979), 133 pp.

Women in the cities of Asia: migration and urban adaptation. Edited by James T. Fawcett, Siew-Ean Khoo and Peter C. Smith. (Boulder, Colorado, Westview Press, 1984), 406 pp.

Women in the Cuban bureaucracies 1968-1974. By: Aguirre, Benigno E.. In: Women in the family and the economy: an international comparative survey. Edited by George Kurian and Ratna Ghosh. (Westport, CT, Greenwood Press, 1981), pp. 375-92.

Women in the development of socialist self-managing Yugoslavia. By: Tomsic, Vida. ([Belgrade], Jugoslovenska stvarnost, [1980]), 211 pp. Translation of: Zena u razvoju socijalisticke samoupravne Jugoslavije.

Women in the development process: a select bibliography on women in sub-Saharan Africa and Latin America. By: Saulniers, Suzanne Smith and Rakowski, Cathy A.. (Austin, Institute of Latin American Studies, University of Texas Press, 1977), 287 pp. A special publication of the Institute of Latin American Studies.

Women in the family and the economy: an international comparative survey. Edited by George Kurian and Ratna Ghosh. (Westport, Connecticut, Greenwood Press, 1981), 451 pp.

Women in the marketplace: petty commerce in Peru. By: Babb, Florence E.. REVIEW OF RADICAL POLITICAL ECONOMICS (NEW YORK) Spring 1984, 16:45-59.

Women in the media. WEST AFRICA (LONDON) March 4, 1985, No. 3523:414-15.

Women in the Muslim world. Edited by Lois Beck and Nikki Keddie. (Cambridge, MA, Harvard University Press, 1978), 698 pp.

Women in the new Asia; the changing social roles of men and women in South and South-east Asia. Edited by Barbara E. Ward. ([Paris], Unesco, 1963), 529 pp..

Women in the special economic zones and open cities (4); a visit to Zhanjiang. By: Ming, Xiao. WOMEN OF CHINA (BEIJING) January 1986, No. 1:15-18.

Women in the unorganised sector with special reference to Kerala. By: Gulati, Leela. CENTRE FOR DEVELOPMENT STUDIES. WORKING PAPER (ULLOOR, TRIVANDRUM) [July 1983]?, No. 172:1-22.

Women in the urban lajbor markets of Africa: the case of Tanzania. By: Shields, Nwanganga. Series: World Bank Staff Working Papers, No. 380. (Washington, DC, World Bank, 1980), 136, 2 pp.

Women in the workforce. WOMEN OF CHINA (BEIJING) March 1986, No. 3:13-15.

Women in Third world development. By: Charlton, Sue Ellen M.. (Boulder, Colorado, Westview Press, 1984), 240 pp.

Women in today's Cambodia. By: Boua, Chanthou. NEW LEFT REVIEW (LONDON) January/February 1982, No. 131:45-61.

Women in Turkish society. By: Cosar, Fatma Mansur. In: Women in the Muslim world. Edited by Lois Beck and Nikki Keddie. (Cambridge, MA, Harvard University Press, 1978), pp. 124-40.

Women in villages: femininity, food and freedom. By: Bolabola, Cema. PACIFIC PERSPECTIVE (SUVA) 1983, 11, No. 2:65-7.

Women in Zimbabwe: transforming the law. By: Zvobgo, Eddison. AFRICA REPORT (NEW YORK) March/April 1985, 30:p. 64-5.

Women in Zimbabwe; removing laws that oppress women. By: Zvobgo, Eddison. AFRICA REPORT (NEW YORK) March/April 1983, 28:45-47.

Women, jobs, and development. By: de Vries, Margaret G.. FINANCE AND DEVELOPMENT (WASHINGTON) December 1971, 8:4:2-9. Discusses the employment of women in developing countries in the light of recent changes in emphasis on the strategy and objectives of economic development. Also published in French, German, Portuguese, and Spanish.

Women, knowledge, and power. By: Sutton, Constance, et al.. In: Women cross-culturally: change and challenge. Edited by Ruby Rohrlich-Leavitt. (The Hague, Mouton, 1975), pp. 581-600. The authors describe women's relationship to knowledge and power in Morocco, among the Tlingit Indians in southwestern Alaska, and in Barbados.

Women, land, labour and survival: getting some basic facts straight. By: Allison, Caroline. IDS BULLETIN, INSTITUTE OF DEVELOPMENT STUDIES AT THE UNIVERSITY OF SUSSEX (BRIGHTON) July 1985, 16:24-30. This article concentrates on the questions of land access; household compositions; and the survival strategies women rely on in periods of imminent or perceived crisis.

Women left behind: a study of the wives of Lebanese migrant workers in the oil rich countries of the region. By: Azzam, Henry T. and Shaib, Diana. INTERNATIONAL LABOUR OFFICE. WORLD EMPLOYMENT PROGRAMME RESEARCH. POPULATION AND LABOUR POLICIES: REGIONAL PROGRAMME FOR THE MIDDLE EAST. WORKING PAPER (BEIRUT) September 1980, No. 3:1-56.

Women, men, and the division of labor. By: Newland, Kathleen. WORLDWATCH PAPER (WASHINGTON) 1980, No. 37:1-43.

Women, migrant labor and social change in Botswana. By: Brown, Barbara B.. BOSTON UNIVERSITY. AFRICAN STUDIES CENTER. WORKING PAPERS (BOSTON) 1980, No. 41:1-21.

Women migrants in Bangkok: an economic analysis of their employment and earnings. By: Tongudai, Pawadee. In: Women in the urban and industrial workforce; Southeast and East Asia. Edited by Gavin W. Jones. Series: Development Studies Centre. Monograph, No. 33. (Canberra, Australia, Australian National University, 1984), pp. 305-24. Series edited by Helen Hughes.

Women of Peru's slums raise sights with communal kitchens. By: Smith, Michael L.. WASHINGTON POST (WASHINGTON) September 16, 1984, p. A13.

Women of rural Asia. By: Whyte, Robert Orr and Whyte, Pauline. (Boulder, Colorado, Westview Press, 1982), 262 pp.

Women of South Asia: a guide to resources. By: Sakala, Carol. (Millwood, New York, Kraus International Publications, 1980), 517 pp. Foreword by Maureen L. P. Patterson.

Women of Southeast Asia. Edited by Penny van Esterik. Series: Monograph Series on Southeast Asia; Occasional Paper (Northern Illinois University. Center for Southeast Asian Studies), No. 9. ([De Kalb] Northern Illinois University, Center for Southeast Asian Studies, 1982), 279 pp.

Women of the United Arab Emirates. By: Soffan, Linda Usra. (London, Croom Helm; New York, Barnes & Noble Books, 1980), 127 pp.

Women of the world: Latin America and the Caribbean. By: Chaney, Elsa M.. ((Washington, DC, U.S. Dept. of Commerce, Bureau of the Census, 1984), 173 pp. Prepared under the resources support services agreement with the Office of Women in Development, Bureau for Program and Policy Coordination, U.S. Agency for International Development.

WOMEN OF VANUATU

Women of Vanuatu. Integration of women in the development process. PACIFIC PERSPECTIVE (SUVA) 1983, 11, No. 2:1-4. Adapted from the paper presented by the Women of Vanuatu to the 21st South Pacific Conference, Vila.

Women Pakistan: position, status and movement. By: Khan, Nighat S. JOURNAL OF SOCIAL STUDIES (DHAKA) October 1985, No. 30:27-40.

Women, politics and development; a review essay. By: Schmidt, Steffen W.. LATIN AMERICAN RESEARCH REVIEW (ALBUQUERQUE, NM) 1983, 18, No. 1:210-27.

Women, population, and international development in Latin America: a 1984 assessment. By: Siqueira Wiarda, Ieda and Helzner, Judith Frye. MANAGING INTERNATIONAL DEVELOPMENT (ARMONK, N.Y.) September/October 1984, 1:84-106.

Women, population and international development in Latin America: persistent legacies and new perceptions for the 1980's. By: Wiarda, Ieda Siqueira and Helzner, Judith F.. UNIVERSITY OF MASSACHUSETTS AT AMHERST. PROGRAM IN LATIN AMERICAN STUDIES. OCCASIONAL PAPERS SERIES (AMHERST) April 1981, No. 13:1-40.

Women, poverty and agricultural growth in India. By: Agarwal, Bina. INSTITUTE OF ECONOMIC GROWTH. [PAPERS] (DELHI) June 1985, No. E/112/85:1-101.

Women, poverty and agricultural growth in India. By: Agarwal, Nina. JOURNAL OF PEASANT STUDIES (LONDON) July 1986, 13:165-220.

Women; protagonists of change. DEVELOPMENT (ROME) 1984, No. 4:1-112.

Women, religion, and development in the Third World. By: Carroll, Theodora Foster. (New York, Praeger Publishers, 1983), 292 pp.

Women, remittances, and reproduction. By: Griffith, David C. AMERICAN ETHNOLOGIST (WASHINGTON) November 1985, 12:676-90. Presents and interprets data on how women in Jamaica use remittances from migrating husbands, boyfriends, sons, and so forth, and examines some of the reasons for these uses. The author concludes that seasonal-labor migration aids Jamaican peasant households in meeting the costs of reproducing themselves and their social and economic conditions.

Women, state and ideology in Iran. By: Afshar, Haleh. THIRD WORLD QUARTERLY (LONDON) April 1985, 7:256-78.

Women, Sufism, and decision-making in Moroccan Islam. By: Dwyer, Daisy Hilse. In: Women in the Muslim world. Edited by Lois Beck and Nikki Keddie. (Cambridge, MA, Harvard University Press, 1978), pp. 585-98.

Women, technology and innovation. Edited by Joan Rothschild. (Oxford, New York, Pergamon Press, 1982), pp. 289-329. Originally published as a special issue of Women's Studies International Quarterly (Oxford), Vol. 4, No. 3, 1981.

Women; the law in Southern Africa: justice for all? By: Thomas, Rosalind. AFRICA REPORT (NEW YORK) March/April 1985, 30:59-64.

Women; the plight and the strength. By: Wangari, Esther and Koivukari, Mirjami. DEVELOPMENT FORUM (NEW YORK) June 1986, p. 8-9. Suggests that evidence is growing that the workload of women is increasing more than ever before and that their general condition is deteriorating.

Women, work, and ethnicity: the Sierra Leone case. By: White, E. Frances. In: Women and work in Africa. Edited by Edna G. Bay. (Boulder, CO, Westview Press, 1982), pp. 19-33.

Women, work and property in North-West India. By: Sharma, Ursula. (London, New York, Tavistock, 1980), 226 pp.

Women, work and the family in a developing society: Taiwan. By: Lu, Yu-Hsia. In: Women in the urban and industrial workforce; Southeast and East Asia. Edited by Gavin W. Jones. Series: Development Studies Centre. Monograph, No. 33. (Canberra, Australia, Australian National University, 1984), pp. 339-68. Series edited by Helen Hughes.

Women, work, organisation and struggle. By: Gothoskar, Sujata and Banaji, Rohini. ECONOMIC AND POLITICAL WEEKLY (BOMBAY) March 5, 1983, 18:339-44. Article based on the conclusions of the authors' forthcoming book "My life is one long struggle... women, work, organisation and struggle".

Women workers in an Indian urban labour market. By: Papola, T. S.. INTERNATIONAL LABOUR OFFICE. WORLD EMPLOYMENT PROGRAMME RESEARCH. POPULATION AND LABOUR POLICIES PROGRAMME. WORKING PAPER (GENEVA) September 1983, No. 141:1-67.

Women working together; spontaneous success. By: Von Vietinghoff, Franciska. SUDANOW (KHARTOUM) March 1985, 10:29-30.

WOMEN'S EDUCATION

Bach, Rebecca and Gadalla, Saad. Mothers' influence on daughters' orientations toward education: an Egyptian case study. COMPARATIVE EDUCATION REVIEW (NEW YORK) August 1985, 29:374-84.

Hao, Keming and Zhou, Yan. Growth of women's education. WOMEN OF CHINA (BEIJING) April 1985, No. 4:2-3.

Helmore, Kristin. Family ties: wives and mothers. CHRISTIAN SCIENCE MONITOR (BOSTON) December 18, 1985, p. 17-19. Part 2 of 5-part series entitled: "The neglected resource; women in the developing world." Author looks at marriage and motherhood in various cultures in the less developed countries.

Helmore, Kristin. Learning and unlearning. CHRISTIAN SCIENCE MONITOR (BOSTON) December 20, 1985, p. 15-17. Part four of 5-part series entitled: "The neglected resource; women in the developing world." Discusses education of women in the less developed countries, particularly the contrast between opportunities for education for men and for women.

Jain, Anrudh K. and Nag, Moni. Importance of female primary education for fertility reduction in India. ECONOMIC AND POLITICAL WEEKLY (BOMBAY) September 6, 1986, 21:1602-08.

WOMEN'S EDUCATION

Robertson, Claire C.. Formal or nonformal education? Entrepreneurial women in Ghana. COMPARATIVE EDUCATION REVIEW (NEW YORK) November 1984, 28:639-58.

Wu, Wei. Going to the society. WOMEN OF CHINA (BEIJING) April 1985, No. 4:17-18.

WOMEN'S ORGANIZATIONS

Ahmad, Zubeida M.. Women's work and their struggle to organize. DEVELOPMENT (ROME) 1984, No. 4:36-40.

Helmore, Kristin. Working for survival; working for cash. CHRISTIAN SCIENCE MONITOR (BOSTON) December 19, 1985, p.18-20. Part three of a 5-part series entitled: "The neglected resource; women in the developing world," focusses on women's work in the agricultural sector as main provider of family sustenance. Also examines the deleterious effects of some development policies for women in the rural areas.

Women in power spheres. INTERNATIONAL SOCIAL SCIENCE JOURNAL (PARIS) 1983, 35, No. 4:569-756.

WOMEN'S RIGHTS

Gwaradzimba, Fadzai. Heroines find it hard; Zimbabwe, a special report. GUARDIAN (LONDON) August 23, 1985, p. 15. Author states that the assessment of the gains made by women since independence clearly indicates that emancipation does not automatically follow the establishment of a socialist society, nor does participation in the liberation struggle guarantee equality and full integration.

Hahn, Natalie D.. Losing the land. DEVELOPMENT (ROME) 1984, No. 4:26-29.

Haug, Frigga. Women's movement in West Germany. NEW LEFT REVIEW (LONDON) January/February 1986, No. 155:50-74.

WOMEN'S STUDIES

Bonder, Gloria. Los estudios de la mujer y la critica epistemologica a los paradigmas de las ciencias humanas. DESARROLLO Y SOCIEDAD (BOGOTA) January 1984, No. 13:25-38. With English summary.

Tadesse, Zenebworke. Bringing research home. DEVELOPMENT (ROME) 1984, No. 4:50-54. Discusses on the question of research on women in Africa.

WOMEN. ECONOMIC CONDITIONS

Helmore, Kristin. Awareness and action. CHRISTIAN SCIENCE MONITOR (BOSTON) December 23, 1985, p. 14-16. Part 5 of 5-part series entitled: "The neglected resource; women in the developing world." Discusses increasing awareness among women in the less developed countries of their inferior economic status and of the value of collective action.

Medoff, Marshall H. Effect of the Equal Rights Amendment on the economic status of women. ATLANTIC ECONOMIC JOURNAL (WORDEN, IL) September 1985, 13:60-68.

Mignot-Lefebvre, Yvonne. Les femmes dans l'economie, de l'invisibilite a de nouveaux modes d'organisation. TIERS-MONDE (PARIS) April/June 1985, 26:247-60.

Special issue: The political economy of women. REVIEW OF RADICAL POLITICAL ECONOMICS (NEW YORK) Spring 1984, 16:1-202.

WOMEN. EMPLOYMENT

Aguiar, Neuma. La mujer en la fuerza de trabajo en la America Latina: un resumen introductorio. DESARROLLO Y SOCIEDAD (BOGOTA) January 1984, No. 13:57-79. With English summary.

Ahmad, Zubeida and Loufti, Martha. Decently paid employment -- not more drudgery. CERES, FAO REVIEW ON AGRICULTURE AND DEVELOPMENT (ROME) July/August 1983, 16:40-46. The authors conclude that there is an urgent need for improved living and working conditions for many poor rural women.

Ahmad, Zubeida. Rural women and their work: dependence and alternatives for change. INTERNATIONAL LABOUR REVIEW (GENEVA) January/February 1984, 123:71-86.

Anker, Richard. Effect on reported levels of female labour force participation in developing countries of questionnaire design, sex of interviewer and sex/proxy status of respondent: description of a methodological field experiment. INTERNATIONAL LABOUR OFFICE. WORLD EMPLOYMENT PROGRAMME RESEARCH. POPULATION AND LABOUR POLICIES PROGRAMME. WORKING PAPER (GENEVA) July 1983, No. 137:1-76. The methods test described is conducting household surveys in India (Uttar Pradesh state) and Egypt, using different types of questionnaires; male and female interviewers; self-respondents (female only) and proxy-respondents (male and female).

WOMEN. EMPLOYMENT

Anker, Richard and Hein, Catherine. Employment of women outside agriculture in Third world countries: an overview of occupational statistics. INTERNATIONAL LABOUR OFFICE. WORLD EMPLOYMENT PROGRAMME RESEARCH. POPULATION AND LABOUR POLICIES PROGRAMME. WORKING PAPER (GENEVA) March 1985, No. 147:1-70.

Anker, Richard. Female labour force participation in developing countries: a critique of current definitions and data collection methods. INTERNATIONAL LABOUR REVIEW (GENEVA) November/December 1983, 122:709-23.

Bardhan, Kalpana. Women's work, welfare and status; forces of tradition and change in India, pt. 1. ECONOMIC AND POLITICAL WEEKLY (BOMBAY) December 14, 1985, 20:2207-20.

Bardhan, Kalpana. Women's work, welfare and status; forces of tradition and change in India, pt. 2. ECONOMIC AND POLITICAL WEEKLY (BOMBAY) December 21, 1985, 20:2262-69.

Becker-Schmidt, Regina and Knapp, Gudrun-Axeli. Wertewandel und Widerspruche; Erziehungsorientierungen und -probleme von Arbeiterinnen im Vergleich zweier Generationen. WSI-MITTEILUNGEN (DUSSELDORF) August 1986, 39:558-66.

Behrman, Jere R. and Wolfe, Barbara L.. Labor force participation and earnings determinants for women in the special conditions of developing countries. JOURNAL OF DEVELOPMENT ECONOMICS (AMSTERDAM) May/August 1984, 15:259-88. The authors focus on labor market conditions for women in Nicaragua.

Bielby, William T. and Baron, James N. Sex segregation within occupations. AMERICAN ECONOMIC REVIEW, PAPERS AND PROCEEDINGS (NASHVILLE) May 1986, 76:43-47.

Chapman, Bruce J. and Harding, J. Ross. Sex differences in earnings: an analysis of Malaysian wage data. JOURNAL OF DEVELOPMENT STUDIES (LONDON) April 1985, 21:362-76.

Chaudhury, Rafiqul Huda. Effect of mother's work on child care, dietary intake, and dietary adequacy of pre-school children. BANGLADESH DEVELOPMENT STUDIES (DACCA) December 1982, 10:33-61.

WOMEN. EMPLOYMENT

Chaudhury, Rafiqul Huda. Female labour force status and fertility behaviour in Bangladesh: search for policy interventions. BANGLADESH DEVELOPMENT STUDIES (DACCA) September 1983, 11:59-102.

Chen, Marty. Poverty, gender, and work in Bangladesh. ECONOMIC AND POLITICAL WEEKLY (BOMBAY) February 1, 1986, 21:217-22. Redefines the three broad classes of rural households in terms of women's labour and income and describes the process of impoverishment from the perspective of women.

Chijumba, Beat J.. Attitudes of Tanzanian husbands toward the employment of their wives. AFRICA DEVELOPMENT (DAKAR) April/June 1983, 8:74-85.

Cho, Uhn and Koo, Hagen. Economic development and women's work in a newly industrializing country: the case of Korea. DEVELOPMENT AND CHANGE (THE HAGUE, etc.) October 1983, 14:515-31. The authors investigate how women's economic activities have changed in relation to the pattern of economic growth in Korea in the past two decades.

Colombino, Ugo. Variabili dipendenti limitate e selezione non casuale delle osservazioni: una applicazione alla stima della funzione di salario e di offerta di lavoro delle donne sposate in Italia. GIORNALE DEGLI ECONOMISTI E ANNALI DI ECONOMIA (MILAN) May/June 1983, 42, N.S.:369-85. With English summary, p. 388.

Dalsimer, Marlyn and Nisonoff, Laurie. New economic readjustment policies: implications for Chinese urban working women. REVIEW OF RADICAL POLITICAL ECONOMICS (NEW YORK) Spring 1984, 16:17-43.

Dandekar, Hemalata C.. Impact of Bombay's textile industry on work of women from Sugao village. THIRD WORLD PLANNING REVIEW (LIVERPOOL) November 1983, 5:371-82.

Dennis, Carolyne. Capitalist development and women's work: a Nigerian case study. REVIEW OF AFRICAN POLITICAL ECONOMY (SHEFFIELD) 1984, No. 27/28:109-19.

Devi, D. Radha and Ravindran, M.. Women's work in India. INTERNATIONAL SOCIAL SCIENCE JOURNAL (PARIS) 1983, 35, No. 4:683-701.

WOMEN. EMPLOYMENT

Draper, Elaine. Women's work and development in Latin America. STUDIES IN COMPARATIVE INTERNATIONAL DEVELOPMENT (NEW BRUNSWICK, N.J.) Spring 1985, 20:3-30.

Dwyser, Daisy Hilse. Women and income in the Third world: implications for policy. POPULATION COUNCIL. INTERNATIONAL PROGRAMS. WORKING PAPERS (NEW YORK) June 1983, No. 18:1-39.

Farnos, Alfonso and Gonzalez, Fernando. Role of women and demographic change in Cuba. INTERNATIONAL LABOUR OFFICE. WORLD EMPLOYMENT PROGRAMME RESEARCH. POPULATION AND LABOUR POLICIES PROGRAMME. WORKING PAPER (GENEVA) August 1983, No. 138:1-52.

Ferber, Marianne A. and Green, Carole A. Work power and earnings of women and men. AMERICAN ECONOMIC REVIEW, PAPERS AND PROCEEDINGS (NASHVILLE) May 1986, 76:53-56.

Forray, Katalin R. Bildungswege der Frauen in Ungarn: neue Tendenzen in der Ausbildung und Beschaftigung aus soziologischer Sicht. OSTERREICHISCHE OSTHEFTE (VIENNA) 1986, 28, No. 2:107-25.

Garabaghi, Ninou K.. New approach to women's participation in the economy. INTERNATIONAL SOCIAL SCIENCE JOURNAL (PARIS) 1983, 35, No. 4:659-82.

Goldin, Claudia. Maximum hours legislation and female employment in the 1920s: a reassessment. NATIONAL BUREAU OF ECONOMIC RESEARCH. WORKING PAPER SERIES (CAMBRIDGE, MASS.) June 1986, No. 1949:1-27.

Goodman, Matthew. Japanese women in finance. TOKYO BUSINESS TODAY (TOKYO) May 1986, p. 19-23.

Gothoskar, Sujata. Free trade zones: pitting women against women. ECONOMIC AND POLITICAL WEEKLY (BOMBAY) August 23, 1986, 21:1489-92.

Gottschall, Karin. Frauen auf dem Arbeitsmarkt: Verdrangung statt Integration? WSI-MITTEILUNGEN (DUSSELDORF) August 1986, 39:514-21.

Gulati, Leela. Technological change and women's work; participation and demographic behaviour: a case study of three fishing villages. ECONOMIC AND POLITICAL WEEKLY (BOMBAY) December 8, 1984, 19:2089-94.

WOMEN. EMPLOYMENT

Gulati, Leela. Women in the unorganised sector with special reference to Kerala. CENTRE FOR DEVELOPMENT STUDIES. WORKING PAPER (ULLOOR, TRIVANDRUM) [July 1983]?, No. 172:1-22.

Gustman, Alan and Steinmeier, Thomas L. Wages, employment, training and job attachment in low wage labor markets for women. NATIONAL BUREAU OF ECONOMIC RESEARCH. WORKING PAPER SERIES (CAMBRIDGE, MASS.) October 1986, No. 2037:1-52. The authors analyze economic behaviour and the effects of training and income support policies in the low wage labor market for women.

Guzman Stein, Laura. La industria de la maquila y la explotacion de la fuerza de trabajo de la mujer: el caso de Costa Rica. DESARROLLO Y SOCIEDAD (BOGOTA) January 1984, No. 13:161-76. With English summary.

Hafner, Annemarie. Working women, their problems and trade unions in India. JOURNAL OF SOCIAL STUDIES (DHAKA) October 1985, No. 30:57-76.

Hakiki-Talahite, Fatiha. Paro e inactividad de las mujeres en Argelia: lo visible y lo invisible. DESARROLLO Y SOCIEDAD (BOGOTA) January 1984, No. 13:139-59. With English summary.

Hatton, T. J.. Female labour force participation: the enigma of the interwar period. UNIVERSITY OF ESSEX. DEPT. OF ECONOMICS. DISCUSSION PAPER SERIES (COLCHESTER) June 1986, No. 285:1-36.

Helm, Leslie and Takahashi, Kyoko. Japan's secret economic weapon: exploited women. BUSINESS WEEK (NEW YORK) March 4, 1985, No. 2883:54-55.

Hill, M. Anne. Female labor force participation in developing and developed countries -- consideration of the informal sector. REVIEW OF ECONOMICS AND STATISTICS (CAMBRIDGE, MASS.) August 1983, 65:459-68.

Hing, Ai Yun. Women and work in West Malaysia. JOURNAL OF CONTEMPORARY ASIA (LONDON) 1984, 14, No. 2:204-18.

Ho, Suk-ching. Position of women in the labour market in Hong Kong: a content analysis of the recruitment advertisements. LABOUR AND SOCIETY (GENEVA) September 1985, 10:333-44.

Honig, Emily. Contract labor system and women workers; pre-liberation cotton mills of Shanghai. MODERN CHINA (BEVERLY HILLS) October 1983, 9:421-54.

WOMEN. EMPLOYMENT

Hooper, Beverley. China's modernization; are young women going to lose out? MODERN CHINA (BEVERLY HILLS) July 1984, 10:317-43. Focuses on two areas that are prerequisites to young women having the opportunity to play an equal role in China's economic development: obtaining education, particularly higher education, and securing employment.

Humphrey, John. Growth of female employment in Brazilian manufacturing industry in the 1970s. JOURNAL OF DEVELOPMENT STUDIES (LONDON) July 1984, 20:224-47.

Jakubson, George. Sensitivity of labor supply parameter estimates to unobserved individual effects: fixed and random effects estimates in a nonlinear model using panel data. PRINCETON UNIVERSITY. INDUSTRIAL RELATIONS SECTION. WORKING PAPER (PRINCETON) August 1986, No. 210:1-37; A1-A4 (various pagings).

Jensen, An-Magritt and Schweder, Tore. Engine of fertility - influenced by interbirth employment? NORWAY. STATISTISK SENTRALBYRA. DISCUSSION PAPER (OSLO) June 1986, No. 15:1-33.

Johnson, William R. and Skinner, Jonathan. Labor supply and marital separation. AMERICAN ECONOMIC REVIEW (NASHVILLE) June 1986, 76:455-69. A simultaneous model of future divorce probability and current labor supply is estimated for married women. The results support the hypothesis that divorce probabilities increase labor supply.

Kanellopoulos, Costas N.. Male-female pay differentials in Greece. GREEK ECONOMIC REVIEW (ATHENS) August 1982, 4:222-41.

Kelkar, Govind. Tractors against women. DEVELOPMENT (ROME) 1985, No. 3:18-21. Concludes that the Green Revolution has brought in its wake the all-India trend of pauperization and marginalization and the increased inequality between the sexes.

Kelly, Deirdre. St. Lucia's female electronics factory workers: key components in an export-oriented industrialization strategy. WORLD DEVELOPMENT (OXFORD) July 1986, 14:823-38.

Khan, Zarina Rahman. Women's economic role: insights from a village in Bangladesh. JOURNAL OF SOCIAL STUDIES (DHAKA) October 1985, No. 30:13-26.

WOMEN. EMPLOYMENT

Krishnaswami, Lalita. From drudgery to dignity: the SEWA experience. LABOUR AND SOCIETY (GENEVA) September 1985, 10:323-31. Discusses the achievements of the Self-Employed Women's Association (SEWA), which is at once a union, a trust and a credit institution whose basic aim is to provide better living and working conditions for the poor, illiterate women who comprise its membership.

Lee, Bun Song and McElwain, Adrienne M. Empirical investigation of female labor-force participation, fertility, age at marriage, and wages in Korea. JOURNAL OF DEVELOPING AREAS (MACOMB, ILL.) July 1985, 19:483-500.

Leppel, Karen. Relations among child quality, family structure, and the value of the mother's time in Malaysia. MALAYAN ECONOMIC REVIEW (SINGAPORE) October 1982, 27:61-70.

Levine, Victor and Moock, Peter R.. Labor force experience and earnings: women with children. ECONOMICS OF EDUCATION REVIEW (OXFORD) 1984, 3, No. 3:183-93. Acknowledging that married women with children are observed to earn less than men, and less also than women without children, the authors examine the impact of hours worked in all past periods on the current wage rate. They find that differences in the intensity of prior work experience account for approximately half of the observed sex-related wage gap.

Lewis, Donald E. Sources of changes in the occupational segregation of Australian women. ECONOMIC RECORD (MELBOURNE) December 1985, 61:719-36.

Li, K. T. Contributions of women in the labor force to economic development in Taiwan, the Republic of China. INDUSTRY OF FREE CHINA (TAIPEI) August 25, 1985, 64:1-8.

Lorfing, I. and Khalaf, M.. Economic contribution of women and its effect on the dynamics of the family in two Lebanese villages. INTERNATIONAL LABOUR OFFICE. WORLD EMPLOYMENT PROGRAMME RESEARCH. POPULATION AND LABOUR POLICIES PROGRAMME. WORKING PAPER (GENEVA) May 1985, No. 148:1-32.

Macarthy, Peter. Notes on inequalities in male-female shares in the labour market, occupations, wages, overtime, and hours of work - Mexico, 1940-1980. PAISLEY COLLEGE OF TECHNOLOGY. DEPT. OF ECONOMICS AND MANAGEMENT. SOCIAL SCIENCE WORKING PAPER (PAISLEY) June 1984, No. 61:1-38.

WOMEN. EMPLOYMENT

Maroney, Heather Jon. Feminism at work. NEW LEFT REVIEW (LONDON) September/October 1983, No. 141:51-71.

Maxwell, Nan L. and D'Amico, Ronald J. Employment and wage effects of involuntary job separation: male-female differences. AMERICAN ECONOMIC REVIEW, PAPERS AND PROCEEDINGS (NASHVILLE) May 1986, 76:373-77.

Metzner, Ulrike and Stahn-Willig, Brigitte. Frauenarbeit: ein Beitrag zur gewerkschaftlichen Technikdebatte. WSI-MITTEILUNGEN (DUSSELDORF) August 1986, 39:529-36.

Mies, Maria. Indian women in subsistence and agricultural labour. INTERNATIONAL LABOUR OFFICE. WORLD EMPLOYMENT PROGRAMME RESEARCH. RURAL EMPLOYMENT POLICY RESEARCH PROGRAMME. WORKING PAPER (GENEVA) (GENEVA) May 1984, No. 34:1-243.

Mignot-Lefebvre, Yvonne. Les femmes dans l'economie, de l'invisibilite a de nouveaux modes d'organisation. TIERS-MONDE (PARIS) April/June 1985, 26:247-60.

Mohiuddin, Yasmeen. Female employment and social status; survey. PAKISTAN & GULF ECONOMIST (KARACHI) April 6, 1985, 4:30-33. Report based on a survey of 216 female handicraft workers located at major centres of handicraft work in north, middle and south Sind.

Nakamura, Alice and Nakamura, Masao. Dynamic models of the labor force behavior of married women which can be estimated using limited amounts of past information. JOURNAL OF ECONOMETRICS (AMSTERDAM) March 1985, 27:273-98.

Nakanishi, Tamako. Equality or protection? Protective legislation for women in Japan. INTERNATIONAL LABOUR REVIEW (GENEVA) September/October 1983, 122:609-21.

Nishimura, Namiko. Women at work. JOURNAL OF JAPANESE TRADE & INDUSTRY (TOKYO) May/June 1986, 5:46-47.

Numero special: radioscopie du chomage. L'ECONOMIE DE LA REUNION (STE-CLOTILDE) September/October 1986, No. 25:1-32.

WOMEN. EMPLOYMENT

O'Donnell, Carol. Major theories of the labour market and women's place within it. JOURNAL OF INDUSTRIAL RELATIONS (SYDNEY) June 1984, 26:147-65. Looks at theories of the labour market with reference to the situation of women workers who tend to be concentrated in particular industries and particular occupations, and whose average wage is lower than that of males.

Okojie, Christiana E. E.. Determinants of labour force participation of urban women in Nigeria: a case study of Benin City. NIGERIAN JOURNAL OF ECONOMIC AND SOCIAL STUDIES (IBADAN) March 1983, 25:39-59.

Oliveira, Orlandina de. Migracion femenina, organizacion familiar y mercados laborales en Mexico. COMERCIO EXTERIOR (MEXICO, D.F.) July 1984, 34:676-87.

Oppong, Christine and Abu, Katharine. Changing maternal role of Ghanaian women: impacts of education, migration and employment. INTERNATIONAL LABOUR OFFICE. WORLD EMPLOYMENT PROGRAMME RESEARCH. POPULATION AND LABOUR POLICIES PROGRAMME. WORKING PAPER (GENEVA) February 1984, No. 143:1-184.

Osawa, Machiko. Working mothers: changing patterns of employment and fertility in Japan. ECONOMICS RESEARCH CENTER. NORC [NATIONAL OPINION RESEARCH CENTER] DISCUSSION PAPER SERIES (CHICAGO) June 1986, No. 86-5:1-58. In this paper the differential fertility rates between paid women workers in the formal sector and family workers in the informal sector are featured to analyze the reasons why the Japanese fertility trend in the post-World War II period differs from other nations.

Papola, T. S.. Women workers in an Indian urban labour market. INTERNATIONAL LABOUR OFFICE. WORLD EMPLOYMENT PROGRAMME RESEARCH. POPULATION AND LABOUR POLICIES PROGRAMME. WORKING PAPER (GENEVA) September 1983, No. 141:1-67.

Penvenne, Jeanne. Making our own way: women working in Lourenco Marques, 1900-1933. BOSTON UNIVERSITY. AFRICAN STUDIES CENTER. WORKING PAPERS (BOSTON) 1986, No. 114:1-20.

Pittin, Renee. Documentation and analysis of the invisible work of invisible women: a Nigerian case study. INTERNATIONAL LABOUR REVIEW (GENEVA) July/August 1984, 123:473-90. Discusses problems arising in the documentation and analysis of the work of secluded women. Focusing on the Muslim Hausa women of Katsina, Nigeria, the author contends that past surveys and censuses have grossly underestimated these women's economic contribution to the Nigerian economy, and that this neglect is increasing.

Raasch, Sibylle. Mindestens die Halfte aller Arbeits- und Ausbildungsplatze fur Frauen? Zur Quotierungsforderung in dem Entwurf eines Antidiscriminierungsgesetzes der Grunen. WSI-MITTEILUNGEN (DUSSELDORF) August 1986, 39:575-82.

Ramachandran, P. and Shastri, P. P.. Intercensal urban Indian female participation rates and their variations, 1961-71: a census analysis. ECONOMIC AFFAIRS (CALCUTTA) October/December 1983, 28:816-28.

Robinson, Chris and Tomes, Nigel. More on the labour supply of Canadian women. CANADIAN JOURNAL OF ECONOMICS (TORONTO) February 1985, 18:156-63.

Robinson, Jean C.. Of women and washing machines: employment, housework, and the reproduction of motherhood in socialist China. CHINA QUARTERLY (LONDON) March 1985, No. 101:32-57.

Sarfati, Hedva. Job equality for women: Progress, problems and perspectives. LABOUR AND SOCIETY (GENEVA) September 1985, 10:273-88.

Schippers, J. J. and Siegers, J. J.. Economische aspecten van een quoterings-maatregel ten behoeve van vrouwen op de arbeidsmarkt. MAANDSCHRIFT ECONOMIE (TILBURG) 1984, 48, No. 6:484-99.

Scott, Alison MacEwen. Desarrollo dependiente y la segregacion ocupacional por sexo. DESARROLLO Y SOCIEDAD (BOGOTA) January 1984, No. 13:99-136. With English summary.

Scott, Joan Wallach. Mechanization of women's work. SCIENTIFIC AMERICAN (NEW YORK) September 1982, 247:166-87.

Sharma, Miriam. Caste, class, and gender: production and reproduction in North India. JOURNAL OF PEASANT STUDIES (LONDON) July 1985, 12:26-56.

WOMEN. EMPLOYMENT

Sharma, Ursula. Unmarried women and the household economy: a research note. JOURNAL OF SOCIAL STUDIES (DHAKA) October 1985, No. 30:1-12.

Shinotsuka, Eiko. Female workers as described in a help-wanted information magazine. JAPANESE ECONOMIC STUDIES (ARMONK, N.Y.) Spring 1984, 12:3-20.

Sofer, Catherine. Emplois "feminins" et emplois "masculins": mesure de la segregation et evolution de la feminisation des emplois. INSTITUT NATIONAL DE LA STATISTIQUE ET DES ETUDES ECONOMIQUES, ANNALES (PARIS) October/December 1983, No. 52:55-85. With English summary.

Special issue: The political economy of women. REVIEW OF RADICAL POLITICAL ECONOMICS (NEW YORK) Spring 1984, 16:1-202.

Sprague, Alison. Post-war fertility and female labour force participation rates. OXFORD UNIVERSITY. INSTITUTE OF ECONOMICS AND STATISTICS. APPLIED ECONOMICS DISCUSSION PAPER (OXFORD) June 1986, No. 9:1-35.

Stewart, Mark B. and Greenhalgh, Christine A.. Work history patterns and the occupational attainment of women. ECONOMIC JOURNAL (LONDON) September 1984, 94:493-519.

Structural changes in the employment of women: 1971-1981; an analysis of the changing distribution of women's employment. QUARTERLY ECONOMIC REPORT, INDIAN INSTITUTE OF PUBLIC OPINION (NEW DELHI) May/August 1986, 30:24-33.

Sundar, Pushpa. Women's employment and organisation modes. ECONOMIC AND POLITICAL WEEKLY: REVIEW OF MANAGEMENT (BOMBAY) November 26, 1983, 18:M171-M176.

Tomoda, Shizue. Measuring female labour activities in Asian developing countries: a time-allocation approach. INTERNATIONAL LABOUR REVIEW (GENEVA) November/December 1985, 124:661-76.

Trends in women's work, education, and family building; proceedings of the Conference, Chelwood Gate, Sussex, England, May 31 - June 3, 1983. JOURNAL OF LABOR ECONOMICS (CHICAGO) January 1985, 3:S1-S396.

WOMEN. EMPLOYMENT

Tzannatos, Z. and Zabalza, A. Effect of sex antidiscriminatory legislation on the variability of female employment in Britian. APPLIED ECONOMICS (LONDON) December 1985, 17:1117-34. The authors attempt to determine whether fluctuations in aggregate employment are reflected in fluctuations in the employment of men and women, and to investigate if the sex antidiscriminatory legislation enacted in Britian during the 1970s has had any effect on the variability of female employment.

Verheust, Therese. Potraits de femmes: les intellectuelles zairoises. CAHIERS DU CEDAF (BRUSSELS) October 1985, No. 6:1-148.

Wehkamp, Andy. Luchas colectivas de las obreras peruanas: los motivos de participacion y alejamiento. BOLETIN DE ESTUDIOS LATINO-AMERICANOS Y DEL CARIBE (AMSTERDAM) December 1984, No. 37:69-83.

Why women get the jobs. ECONOMIST (LONDON) August 23, 1986, 300:13-14.

Women in the workforce. WOMEN OF CHINA (BEIJING) March 1986, No. 3:13-15.

Women's work may help to make jobs for the girls. PACIFIC ISLANDS MONTHLY (SYDNEY) May 1986, 57:22-23.

Yamada, Tadashi and Yamada, Tetsuji. Fertility and labor force participation of married women: empirical evidence from the 1980 population census of Japan. QUARTERLY REVIEW OF ECONOMICS AND BUSINESS (URBANA, ILL.) Summer 1986, 26:35-46.

Zalokar, Nadja. Generational differences in female occupational attainment -- have the 1970's changed women's opportunities? AMERICAN ECONOMIC REVIEW, PAPERS AND PROCEEDINGS (NASHVILLE) May 1986, 76:378-81.

WOMEN. EMPLOYMENT. DISCRIMINATORY PRACTICES

Demmer, Hildegard and Kupper, Bettina. Arbeitsbelastungen von Frauen im Paketdienst. WSI-MITTEILUNGEN (DUSSELDORF) August 1986, 39:522-28.

Kurz-Scherf, Ingrid. Von der Emanzipation des Brunnenmadchens in Heilbadern; Frauendiskriminierung, Frauenforderung durch Tarifvertrag und Tarifpolitik. WSI-MITTEILUNGEN (DUSSELDORF) August 1986, 39:537-49.

WOMEN. EMPLOYMENT. DISCRIMINATORY PRACTICES

Metz-Gockel, Sigrid and Muller, Ursula. Die Partnerschaft der Manner ist (noch) nicht die Partnerschaft der Frauen; empirische Befunde zum Geschlechterverhaltnis aus der Frauenperspektive. WSI-MITTEILUNGEN (DUSSELDORF) August 1986, 39:549-58.

WOMEN. EQUAL RIGHTS

Medoff, Marshall H. Effect of the Equal Rights Amendment on the economic status of women. ATLANTIC ECONOMIC JOURNAL (WORDEN, IL) September 1985, 13:60-68.

WOMEN. SOCIAL CONDITIONS

Becker-Schmidt, Regina and Knapp, Gudrun-Axeli. Wertewandel und Widerspruche; Erziehungsorientierungen und -probleme von Arbeiterinnen im Vergleich zweier Generationen. WSI-MITTEILUNGEN (DUSSELDORF) August 1986, 39:558-66.

WOMEN. WAGES

Chapman, Bruce J. Sex and location differences in wages in the Australian public service. AUSTRALIAN ECONOMIC PAPERS (ADELAIDE) December 1985, 24:296-309.

Ferber, Marianne A. and Green, Carole A. Work power and earnings of women and men. AMERICAN ECONOMIC REVIEW, PAPERS AND PROCEEDINGS (NASHVILLE) May 1986, 76:53-56.

Gaston, Cheryl L. Idea whose time has not come: comparable worth and the market salary problem. POPULATION RESEARCH AND POLICY REVIEW (AMSTERDAM) 1986, 5, No. 1:15-29.

Gustman, Alan and Steinmeier, Thomas L. Wages, employment, training and job attachment in low wage labor markets for women. NATIONAL BUREAU OF ECONOMIC RESEARCH. WORKING PAPER SERIES (CAMBRIDGE, MASS.) October 1986, No. 2037:1-52. The authors analyze economic behaviour and the effects of training and income support policies in the low wage labor market for women.

Lee, Bun Song and McElwain, Adrienne M. Empirical investigation of female labor-force participation, fertility, age at marriage, and wages in Korea. JOURNAL OF DEVELOPING AREAS (MACOMB, ILL.) July 1985, 19:483-500.

WOMEN. WAGES

Osawa, Machiko. Wage gap in Japan: changing patterns of labor force participation, schooling and tenure. ECONOMICS RESEARCH CENTER. NORC [NATIONAL OPINION RESEARCH CENTER] DISCUSSION PAPER SERIES (CHICAGO) April 1986, No. 86-1:1-29. Examines how changes in schooling and work experience over time between men and women workers have affected wage differentials observed in the post-WWII period in Japan.

Schippers, Joop J. and Siegers, Jacques J. Women's relative wage rate in the Netherlands, 1950-1983: a test of alternative discrimination theories. DE ECONOMIST (LEIDEN) 1986, 134, No. 2:165-80.

Sorensen, Elaine. Implementing comparable worth: a survey of recent job evaluation studies. AMERICAN ECONOMIC REVIEW, PAPERS AND PROCEEDINGS (NASHVILLE) May 1986, 76:364-72.

Women's associations and rural development: Western Samoa and East New Britain. By: Meleisea, Penelope Schoeffel. PACIFIC PERSPECTIVE (SUVA) 1983, 11, No. 2:56-61.

Women's banking expands; twenty local affiliates now active in 17 countries. By: Carter, Mary. DEVELOPMENT, SOCIETY FOR INTERNATIONAL DEVELOPMENT (ROME) July 31, 1984, No. 155:3. Describes the policies, procedures and design of Women's World Banking, which operates as an independent financial institution to provide loan guarantees or other security to banks and other financial institutions, and arranges technical or other advice and assistance to direct and indirect beneficiaries of guarantees.

Women's cooperative thrift and credit societies: an element of women's programs in the Gambia. By: Ceesay-Marenah, Coumba. In: Women and work in Africa. Edited by Edna G. Bay. (Boulder, CO, Westview Press, 1982), pp. 289-95.

Women's co-operatives in Tonga. By: Halatuituia, Lasale and Latu, Sela N.. PACIFIC PERSPECTIVE (SUVA) 1983, 11, No. 2:13-17.

Women's decade; an opportunity lost. By: Obeng, Letitia. August 21, 1985, p. 17A. Author claims that the U.N. Women's Decade has failed to reach the women most in need, the absolute poor, whose voices are not heard in international fora.

Women's decade; plotting ways for women. By: Perry, Alison. WEST AFRICA (LONDON) August 5, 1985, No. 3545:p. 1596. Reports on the final document adopted at the United Nations' women's conference in Nairobi, Kenya.

UN women's decade; preparing the way. By: Cole, Bernadette. WEST AFRICA (LONDON) October 29, 1984, No. 3506:2165-66. Reports from Tanzania on the African regional preparatory meeting which will constitute the 'African position' at the UN End of Women's Decade Conference.

Women's disadvantage: capitalist development and socialist alternatives in Britain. By: Young, Kate and Smith, Sheila. DEVELOPMENT DIALOGUE (UPPSALA) 1982, No. 1/2:85-100.

Women's domestic work and economic activity: results from the National Sample Survey. By: Sen, Gita and Sen, Chiranjib. CENTRE FOR DEVELOPMENT STUDIES. WORKING PAPER (ULLOOR, TRIVANDRUM) August 1984, No. 197:1-37.

Women's economic role: insights from a village in Bangladesh. By: Khan, Zarina Rahman. JOURNAL OF SOCIAL STUDIES (DHAKA) October 1985, No. 30:13-26.

Women's emancipation in Tunisia. By: Tessler, Mark A. and Rogers, Janet. In: Women in the Muslim world. Edited by Lois Beck and Nikki Keddie. (Cambridge, MA, Harvard University Press, 1978), pp. 141-58.

Women's emancipation under socialism: a model for the Third World? By: Molyneux, Maxine. WORLD DEVELOPMENT (OXFORD) September/October 1981, 9:1019-37. Examines the policies adopted by socialist states to improve the position of women and traces some of these inequalities to the policies themselves, and to the theoretical assumptions underlying them.

Women's employment and development: a conceptual framework applied to Ghana. By: Steel, William F. and Campbell, Claudia. In: Women and work in Africa. Edited by Edna G. Bay. (Boulder, CO, Westview Press, 1982), pp. 225-48.

Women's employment and organisation modes. By: Sundar, Pushpa. ECONOMIC AND POLITICAL WEEKLY: REVIEW OF MANAGEMENT (BOMBAY) November 26, 1983, 18:M171-M176.

Women's groups and women's subordination: an analysis of policies towards rural women in Kenya. By: Feldman, Rayah. REVIEW OF AFRICAN POLITICAL ECONOMY (SHEFFIELD) 1984, No. 27/28:67-85.

Women's health: plea for a new approach. By: Gnanadason, Aruna. ECONOMIC AND POLITICAL WEEKLY (BOMBAY) September 13, 1986, 21:1630-30.

Women's involvement in high risk arable agriculture, the Botswana case. By: Fortmann, Louise. (Washington, Office of Women in Development, Agency for International Development, International Development Cooperation Agency, 1980), 27 pp. Prepared for presentation at Ford Foundation workshop on women in agriculture in Eastern and Southern Africa. Nairobi, 9-11 April, 1980.

Women's issues and project appraisal. By: Palmer, Ingrid. IDS BULLETIN, INSTITUTE OF DEVELOPMENT STUDIES AT THE UNIVERSITY OF SUSSEX (BRIGHTON) October 1981, 12:32-39.

Women's liberation in India. By: Patel, Vibhuti. NEW LEFT REVIEW (LONDON) September/October 1985, No. 153:75-86.

Women's life cycle and identity. By: Ahmad, Karuna. ECONOMIC AND POLITICAL WEEKLY (BOMBAY) January 2, 1982, 17:15-17. Discusses a seminar on women, organized by the Indian Council of Social Science Research, New Delhi, Centre for Women's Development Studies, New Delhi, Tata Institute of Social Sciences, Bombay, and Ford Foundation, New Delhi.

Women's movement in Bangladesh and the left's understanding of the woman question. By: Ahmed, Rahnuma. JOURNAL OF SOCIAL STUDIES (DHAKA) October 1985, No. 30:40-56.

Women's movement in the People's Republic of China: a study. By: Davin, Delia. In: Women cross-culturally: change and challenge. Edited by Ruby Rohrlich-Leavitt. (The Hague, Mouton, 1975), pp. 459-69.

Women's movement in West Germany. By: Haug, Frigga. NEW LEFT REVIEW (LONDON) January/February 1986, No. 155:50-74.

Women's part in rural development. By: Erumsele, A. Akhigbe. WEST AFRICA (LONDON) August 18, 1980, No. 3291:1539-40. Discusses some of the findings of a study on "Rural women's participation in development" just published by the United Nations Development Programme (UNDP).

Women's political participation in Morocco's development: how much and for whom? By: Howard-Merriam, Kathleen. MAGHREB REVIEW (LONDON) January/April 1984, 9:12-25.

Women's politics in Africa. By: Staudt, Kathleen A.. STUDIES IN THIRD WORLD SOCIETIES (WILLIAMSBURG) June 1981, No. 16:1-28.

Women's relative wage rate in the Netherlands, 1950-1983: a test of alternative discrimination theories. By: Schippers, Joop J. and Siegers, Jacques J. DE ECONOMIST (LEIDEN) 1986, 134, No. 2:165-80.

Women's role and conjugal family system in Ghana. By: Oppong, Christine. In: Changing position of women in family and society; a cross-national comparison. Edited by Eugen Lupri. Series: International studies in sociology and social anthropology, Vol. 34. (Leiden, E. J. Brill, 1983), pp. 331-43.

Women's role in economic development. By: Boserup, Ester. (New York, St. Martin's Press, [1970]), 283 pp.

Women's role in Fiji. By: Amratlal, Jyoti, [et al.]. (Suva, Fiji, South Pacific Social Sciences Association, 1975), 66 pp.

Women's role in household productive activities and fertility in Bangladesh. By: Khandker, Shahidur R. YALE UNIVERSITY. ECONOMIC GROWTH CENTER. DISCUSSION PAPER (NEW HAVEN, CONN.) July 1985, No. 488:1-35. Seeks to identify the factors that may affect the role of women in the rural areas of a developing country and the possible impact of these factors on fertility.

Women's roles and population trends in the Third World. Edited by Richard Anker, Mayra Buvinic and Nadia H. Youssef. (London, Croom Helm, 1982), 287 pp. A study prepared for the International Labour Office within the framework of the World Employment Programme ...

Women's status and fertility in developing countries: son preference and economic security. By: Cain, Mead. Series: World Bank Staff Working Papers, No. 682. (Washington, World Bank, 1984), 68 pp. Prepared as a background paper for the World Development Report 1984. Also published as No. 7 in the Population and Development Series.

Women's status in changing agrarian relations; a Kerala experience. By: Saradamoni, K.. ECONOMIC AND POLITICAL WEEKLY (BOMBAY) January 30, 1982, 17:155-62.

Women's studies: a recommended core bibliography. By: Stineman, Esther. (Littleton, Colorado, Libraries Unlimited, 1979), 670 pp. With the assistance of Catherine Loeb.

Women's studies: challenge to educational system. By: Mazumdar, Vina. ECONOMIC AND POLITICAL WEEKLY (BOMBAY) May 16, 1981, 16:890-92. Discusses some of the recommendations of the National Conference on Women's Studies, held in Bombay, April 20-24, 1981.

Women's subsociety among the Shahsevan nomads of Iran. By: Tapper, Nancy. In: Women in the Muslim world. Edited by Lois Beck and Nikki Keddie. (Cambridge, MA, Harvard University Press, 1978), pp. 374-98.

Women's work: factory, family and social class in an industrializing order. By: Salaff, Janet and Wong, Aline. In: Women in the urban and industrial workforce; Southeast and East Asia. Edited by Gavin W. Jones. Series: Development Studies Centre. Monograph, No. 33. (Canberra, Australia, Australian National University, 1984), pp. 189-214. Series edited by Helen Hughes.

"Women's work," the family and capitalism. By: Holmstrom, Nancy. SCIENCE & SOCIETY (NEW YORK) Summer 1981, 45:186-211.

Women's work and development in Latin America. By: Draper, Elaine. STUDIES IN COMPARATIVE INTERNATIONAL DEVELOPMENT (NEW BRUNSWICK, N.J.) Spring 1985, 20:3-30.

Women's work and their struggle to organize. By: Ahmad, Zubeida M.. DEVELOPMENT (ROME) 1984, No. 4:36-40.

Women's work and women agricultural labourers: a study of the Indian Census. By: Sen, Gita. CENTRE FOR DEVELOPMENT STUDIES. WORKING PAPER (ULLOOR, TRIVANDRUM) February 1983, No. 159:1-43.

Women's work and women's roles: economics and everyday life in Indonesia, Malaysia and Singapore. Edited by Lenore Manderson. Series: Monograph (Australian National University. Development Studies Centre), No. 32.. (Canberra, New York, Australian National University, 1983), 265 pp.

Women's work as viewed in present-day Algerian society. By: Khodja, Souad. INTERNATIONAL LABOUR REVIEW (GENEVA) July/August 1982, 121:481-87.

Women's work in a communal setting: the Tanzanian policy of Ujamaa. By: Fortmann, Louise. In: Women and work in Africa. Edited by Edna G. Bay. (Boulder, CO, Westview Press, 1982), pp. 191-205.

Women's work in India. By: Devi, D. Radha and Ravindran, M.. INTERNATIONAL SOCIAL SCIENCE JOURNAL (PARIS) 1983, 35, No. 4:683-701.

Women's work in the food economy of the cocoa belt: a comparison. By: Guyer, Jane I.. BOSTON UNIVERSITY. AFRICAN STUDIES CENTER. WORKING PAPERS (BOSTON) 1978, No. 7:1-35.

Women's work may help to make jobs for the girls. PACIFIC ISLANDS MONTHLY (SYDNEY) May 1986, 57:22-23.

Women's work, welfare and status; forces of tradition and change in India, pt. 1. By: Bardhan, Kalpana. ECONOMIC AND POLITICAL WEEKLY (BOMBAY) December 14, 1985, 20:2207-20.

Women's work, welfare and status; forces of tradition and change in India, pt. 2. By: Bardhan, Kalpana. ECONOMIC AND POLITICAL WEEKLY (BOMBAY) December 21, 1985, 20:2262-69.

WONG, ALINE

Salaff, Janet and Wong, Aline. Women's work: factory, family and social class in an industrializing order. In: Women in the urban and industrial workforce; Southeast and East Asia. Edited by Gavin W. Jones. Series: Development Studies Centre. Monograph, No. 33. (Canberra, Australia, Australian National University, 1984), pp. 189-214. Series edited by Helen Hughes.

WONG, ALINE K.

Wong, Aline K.. Economic development and women's place: women in Singapore. Series: Change Interantional Reports. Women in Society. No. 1. (London, Change International Reports, 1980), 20 pp.

WOOD

Ki-Zerbo, Jacqueline. Women and the energy crisis in the Sahel. UNASYLVA (ROME) 1981, 33, No. 133:5-10.

WOOD, ROBERT

Cohn, Steven and Wood, Robert. U.S. aid and Third World women: the impact of Peace Corps programs. ECONOMIC DEVELOPMENT AND CULTURAL CHANGE (CHICAGO) July 1981, 29:795-811.

Work history patterns and the occupational attainment of women. By: Stewart, Mark B. and Greenhalgh, Christine A.. ECONOMIC JOURNAL (LONDON) September 1984, 94:493-519.

Work never ends; problems of women in the farm economy of the Ivory Coast. By: Kranz, Jutta and Fiege, Karin. D & C, DEVELOPMENT AND COOPERATION (BONN) November/December 1983, No. 6:12-13.

Work power and earnings of women and men. By: Ferber, Marianne A. and Green, Carole A. AMERICAN ECONOMIC REVIEW, PAPERS AND PROCEEDINGS (NASHVILLE) May 1986, 76:53-56.

Workers and work: an activities approach. By: Horn, Robert V.. LABOUR AND SOCIETY (GENEVA) April/June 1981, 6:111-25. Concludes that the activities approach helps to give a more balanced view of women at work and of the relation between paid and unpaid work of individuals and the household.

Workers' resistance and management control: a comparative case study of male and female workers in West Malaysia. By: Halim, Fatimah. JOURNAL OF CONTEMPORARY ASIA (LONDON) 1983, 13, No. 2:131-50.

Working class Afro-Surinamese women and national politics: traditions and changes in an independent state. By: Brana-Shute, Rosemary. STUDIES IN THIRD WORLD SOCIETIES (WILLIAMSBURG) March 1981, No. 15:33-56.

Working class women and working class families in Bombay; report of a survey. ECONOMIC AND POLITICAL WEEKLY (BOMBAY) July 22, 1978, 13:1168-73.

Working for survival; working for cash. By: Helmore, Kristin. CHRISTIAN SCIENCE MONITOR (BOSTON) December 19, 1985, p.18-20. Part three of a 5-part series entitled: "The neglected resource; women in the developing world," focusses on women's work in the agricultural sector as main provider of family sustenance. Also examines the deleterious effects of some development policies for women in the rural areas.

Working mothers: changing patterns of employment and fertility in Japan. By: Osawa, Machiko. ECONOMICS RESEARCH CENTER. NORC [NATIONAL OPINION RESEARCH CENTER] DISCUSSION PAPER SERIES (CHICAGO) June 1986, No. 86-5:1-58. In this paper the differential fertility rates between paid women workers in the formal sector and family workers in the informal sector are featured to analyze the reasons why the Japanese fertility trend in the post-World War II period differs from other nations.

Working women in a Moroccan village. By: Davis, Susan Schaefer. In: Women in the Muslim world. Edited by Lois Beck and Nikki Keddie. (Cambridge, MA, Harvard University Press, 1978), pp. 416-33.

Working women, their problems and trade unions in India. By: Hafner, Annemarie. JOURNAL OF SOCIAL STUDIES (DHAKA) October 1985, No. 30:57-76.

World away from women's liberation. By: Soon, Young Yoon. GUARDIAN (LONDON) September 7, 1984, p. 16. Looks at why women in the Third World think their Western sisters' efforts are being misdirected.

WORLD BANK

Conable, Barber B.. Address to the Board of Governors of the World Bank and International Finance Corporation. (Washington, World Bank, September 30, 1986), 11 pp.

World Bank. Women in development. (Washington, DC, World Bank, 1980), 16 pp.

World Bank. Recognizing the "invisible" woman in development: the World Bank's experience. (Washington, World Bank, 1979), 33 pp.

WORLD CONFERENCE OF THE INTERNATIONAL WOMEN'S YEAR (1975: CONFERENCE CENTRE OF THE MEXICAN MINISTRY OF FOREIGN AFFAIRS)

World Conference of the International Women's Year (1975: Conference Centre of the Mexican Ministry of Foreign Affairs). Report of the world Conference of the International Women's Year, Mexico City, 19 June - 2 July 1975. Series: United Nations [Document], E/CONF.66/34. (New York, United Nations, 1976), 199 pp.

WORONOFF, JON

Woronoff, Jon. Wasting Japan's women workers. ORIENTAL ECONOMIST (TOKYO) November 1980, 48:22-24.

WRIGHT, PAUL A.

Gardner, Robert W. and Wright, Paul A.. Female Asian immigrants in Honolulu: adaptation and success. In: Women in the cities of Asia: migration and urban adaptation. Edited by James T. Fawcett, Siew-Ean Khoo and Peter C. Smith. (Boulder, CO, Westview Press, 1984), pp. 322-46.

WU, WEI

Wu, Wei. Going to the society. WOMEN OF CHINA (BEIJING) April 1985, No. 4:17-18.

YACCOB, MAY

Yaccob, May. Ahmadiyya and urbanization: migrant women in Abidjan. BOSTON UNIVERSITY. AFRICAN STUDIES CENTER. WORKING PAPERS (BOSTON) 1983, No. 75:1-16.

YAMADA, TADASHI

Yamada, Tadashi and Yamada, Tetsuji. Fertility and labor force participation of married women: empirical evidence from the 1980 population census of Japan. QUARTERLY REVIEW OF ECONOMICS AND BUSINESS (URBANA, ILL.) Summer 1986, 26:35-46.

YASHIRO, NAOHIRO

Yashiro, Naohiro. Male-female wage differentials in Japan: a rational explanation. JAPANESE ECONOMIC STUDIES (ARMONK, N.Y.) Winter 1980/1981, 9:28-61.

YATES, BARBARA A.

Yates, Barbara A.. Colonialism, education, and work: sex differentiation in colonial Zaire. In: Women and work in Africa. Edited by Edna G. Bay. (Boulder, CO, Westview Press, 1982), pp. 127-52.

YEMEN ARAB REPUBLIC

Howe, Gary Nigel. Upgrading women in Yemen: a matter of dollars and sense. HORIZONS, U.S. AGENCY FOR INTERNATIONAL DEVELOPMENT (WASHINGTON) Summer 1985, 4:41-42.

Yemenite Jewish women in Israeli rural development: female power versus male authority. By: Katzir, Yael. ECONOMIC DEVELOPMENT AND CULTURAL CHANGE (CHICAGO) October 1983, 32:45-61.

Yesterday and today in Laos: a girl's autobiographical notes. By: Levy, Banyen Phimmasone. In: Women in the new Asia; the changing social roles of men and women in South and South-east Asia. Edited by Barbara E. Ward. ([Paris], Unesco, 1963), pp. 244-65.

YOON, SOON-YOUNG

Yoon, Soon-Young. Le barrage des femmes; les femmes mossi du Burkina-Faso. TIERS-MONDE (PARIS) April/June 1985, 26:443-49.

YOUNG, KATE

Young, Kate and Smith, Sheila. Women's disadvantage: capitalist development and socialist alternatives in Britain. DEVELOPMENT DIALOGUE (UPPSALA) 1982, No. 1/2:85-100.

YOUSSEF, NADIA HAGGAG

Smock, Audrey Chapman and Youssef, Nadia Haggag. Egypt: from seclusion to limited participation. In: Women: roles and status in eight countries. Edited by Janet Zollinger Giele and Audrey Chapman Smock. (New York, John Wiley, 1977), pp. 35-79.

YOUTH. UNEMPLOYMENT

Women's work may help to make jobs for the girls. PACIFIC ISLANDS MONTHLY (SYDNEY) May 1986, 57:22-23.

YUDELMAN, SALLY W

Yudelman, Sally W. After Nairobi: A retrospective of women's development organizations in Latin America. GRASSROOTS DEVELOPMENT (ROSSLYN, VA.) 1986, 10, No. 1:20-29.

YUGOSLAVIA

Socio-economic status of women. YUGOSLAV SURVEY (BELGRADE) November 1985, 26:3-24.

ZABALZA, A

Tzannatos, Z. and Zabalza, A. Effect of sex antidiscriminatory legislation on the variability of female employment in Britian. APPLIED ECONOMICS (LONDON) December 1985, 17:1117-34. The authors attempt to determine whether fluctuations in aggregate employment are reflected in fluctuations in the employment of men and women, and to investigate if the sex antidiscriminatory legislation enacted in Britian during the 1970s has had any effect on the variability of female employment.

ZAIRE

Blain, Daniele. Farming system for women: the case of cassava production in Zaire. CERES, FAO REVIEW ON AGRICULTURE AND DEVELOPMENT (ROME) May/June 1985, 18:43-46.

Grilly, Catherine. Comite de teinturerie dans un quartier de Kinshasa (Zaire). TIERS-MONDE (PARIS) April/June 1985, 26:429-34.

Verheust, Therese. Potraits de femmes: les intellectuelles zairoises. CAHIERS DU CEDAF (BRUSSELS) October 1985, No. 6:1-148.

ZALOKAR, NADJA

Zalokar, Nadja. Generational differences in female occupational attainment -- have the 1970's changed women's opportunities? AMERICAN ECONOMIC REVIEW, PAPERS AND PROCEEDINGS (NASHVILLE) May 1986, 76:378-81.

ZAMBIA

Crehan, Kate. Women and development in north western Zambia: from producer to housewife. REVIEW OF AFRICAN POLITICAL ECONOMY (SHEFFIELD) 1984, No. 27/28:51-66.

Muntemba, Maud Shimwaayi. Dispossession and counterstrategies in Zambia 1930-1970. DEVELOPMENT (ROME) 1984, No. 4:15-17.

Muntemba, Shimwaayi. Women as food producers and suppliers in the twentieth century; the case of Zambia. DEVELOPMENT DIALOGUE (UPPSALA) 1982, No. 1/2:29-50.

Parpart, Jane L.. Class and gender on the copperbelt: women in Northern Rhodesian copper mining areas 1926-1964. BOSTON UNIVERSITY. AFRICAN STUDIES CENTER. WORKING PAPERS (BOSTON) 1983, No. 77:1-29.

ZHONG, FU

Zhong, Fu. Comrade Mao Zedong's investigations of women's conditions in the countryside. WOMEN OF CHINA (BEIJING) December 1983, No. 12:4-6.

ZHOU, YAN

Hao, Keming and Zhou, Yan. Growth of women's education. WOMEN OF CHINA (BEIJING) April 1985, No. 4:2-3.

ZIMBABWE

Gwaradzimba, Fadzai. Heroines find it hard; Zimbabwe, a special report. GUARDIAN (LONDON) August 23, 1985, p. 15. Author states that the assessment of the gains made by women since independence clearly indicates that emancipation does not automatically follow the establishment of a socialist society, nor does participation in the liberation struggle guarantee equality and full integration.

Jacobs, Susie. Women and land resettlement in Zimbabwe. REVIEW OF AFRICAN POLITICAL ECONOMY (SHEFFIELD) 1984, No. 27/28:33-50.

Reddy, Govin. Zimbabwe women: caught between the old and the new. NEW AFRICAN (LONDON) January 1985, No. 208:p. 33.

Zvobgo, Eddison. Women in Zimbabwe: transforming the law. AFRICA REPORT (NEW YORK) March/April 1985, 30:p. 64-5.

Zvobgo, Eddison. Women in Zimbabwe; removing laws that oppress women. AFRICA REPORT (NEW YORK) March/April 1983, 28:45-47.

Zimbabwe women: caught between the old and the new. By: Reddy, Govin. NEW AFRICAN (LONDON) January 1985, No. 208:p. 33.

ZOSA-FERANIL, IMELDA

Zosa-Feranil, Imelda. Female employment and the family: a case study of the Bataan export processing zone. In: Women in the urban and industrial workforce; Southeast and East Asia. Edited by Gavin W. Jones. Series: Development Studies Centre. Monograph, No. 33. (Canberra, Australia, Australian National University, 1984), pp. 387-405. Series edited by Helen Hughes.

ZURAYK, HUDA

Zurayk, Huda. Changing role of Arab women. POPULATION BULLETIN OF ECWA (BEIRUT) December 1979, No. 17:18-31.

ZVOBGO, EDDISON

Zvobgo, Eddison. Women in Zimbabwe: transforming the law. AFRICA REPORT (NEW YORK) March/April 1985, 30:p. 64-5.

Zvobgo, Eddison. Women in Zimbabwe; removing laws that oppress women. AFRICA REPORT (NEW YORK) March/April 1983, 28:45-47.

JUN 2 1 1989